KV-602-095

3035190

Restorative Justice Realities

Empirical Research in a European Context

Inge Vanfraechem
Ivo Aertsen
Jolien Willemsens
(eds.)

Eleven International Publishing
The Hague
2010

Published, sold and distributed by Eleven International Publishing
P.O. Box 85576
2508 CG The Hague
The Netherlands
Tel.: +31 70 33 070 33
Fax: +31 70 33 070 30
Website: www.elevenpub.com

Cover design: Haagsblauw, Den Haag
Layout: Textcetera, Den Haag

© 2010 I. Vanfraechem, I. Aertsen & J. Willemsens (eds.) / Eleven International Publishing, The Hague

This publication is protected by international copyright law.
All rights reserved. No part of this publication may be reproduced, stored in a retrieval system, or transmitted in any form or by any means, electronic, mechanical, photocopying, recording or otherwise, without the prior permission of the publisher.

This publication is supported by COST

© COST Office, 2010

No permission to reproduce or utilise the contents of this book by any means is necessary, other than in the case of images, diagrammes or other material from other copyright holders. In such cases, permission of the copyright holders is required. This book may be cited as: COST Action 21 *Restorative Justice Realities*.

Neither the COST Office nor any person acting on its behalf is responsible for the use which might be made of the information contained in this publication. The COST Office is not responsible for the external websites referred to in this publication.

ISBN 978-90-8974-361-9

Restorative Justice Realities

DRILL HALL LIBRARY
MEDWAY

MW
TP100 11731
KCTS

Het groene gras

Het groene gras ('the Green grass') is a book series that primarily focuses on comparative criminological work, both comparative between the Netherlands and Belgium, as well as outside. The series has a multi-disciplinary set-up, whereby the criminologists are given a prominent place in relation to other disciplines. In addition to Dutch language publications, English language works can also take their place in this series. The book series will be supervised by an editorial board comprising of Stefan Bogaerts, Willy Bruggeman, Annelies Daalder, Paul De Hert, Monica den Boer, Marleen Easton, Henk Elffers, Wim Huisman, Jeroen Maesschalck, Patrick Van Calster, René van Swaaningen, Tom Vander Beken en Paul Ponsaers. The editorial board safeguards the quality of the submitted manuscripts thanks to the peer-review procedure, and develops a proactive policy with a view to the realization of comparative studies. Furthermore, *Het groene gras* wishes to provide doctoral thesis manuscripts that complement the editorial line of the series.

The following parts appeared in this series:
- Lieven Pauwels, *Buurtinvloeden en jeugddelinquentie* (2007)
- Isabel Verwee, Paul Ponsaers & Els Enhus, *'Inbreken is mijn vak'* (2007)
- Freya Vander Laenen, *Drugpreventie bij kwetsbare groepen?* (2008)
- Marleen Easton, Lodewijk Gunther Moor, Bob Hoogenboom, Paul Ponsaers & Bas van Stokkom (eds.), *Reflections on Reassurance Policing in the Low Countries* (2008)
- Lex Cachet, Sofie De Kimpe, Paul Ponsaers & Arthur Ringeling (eds.), *Governance of Security in the Netherlands and Belgium* (2008)
- Stephan Parmentier & Paul Ponsaers (red.), *De Vlaamse advocaat: wie, wat, hoe?* (2008)
- Gudrun Vande Walle & Patrick Van Calster (red.), *De criminologische kant van het ondernemen* (2009)
- Joanna Shapland & Paul Ponsaers (eds.), *The informal economy and connections with organised crime: the impact of national social and economic policies* (2009)
- Lieven Pauwels (ed.), Wim Hardyns & Maarten Van de Velde, *Social disorganisation, offending, fear and victimisation. Findings from Belgian studies on the urban context of crime* (2010)
- Marc Cools, Sofie de Kimpe, Arne Dormaels, Marleen Easton, Els Enhus, Paul Ponsaers, Gudrun Vande Walle & Antoine Verhagen (eds.), *Police, Policing, Policy and the City in Europe* (2010)
- Stefaan Pleysier, *'Angst voor criminaliteit' onderzocht* (2010)
- Marleen Easton, Monica den Boer, Jelle Janssens, René Moelker, Tom Vander Beken (eds.) *Blurring Military and Police Roles* (2010)
- Inge Vanfraechem, Ivo Aertsen & Jolien Willemsens (eds.) *Restorative Justice Realities. Empirical Research in a European context* (2010)

Table of Contents

I **Restorative justice in Europe: introducing a research endeavour** I
  Ivo Aertsen, Inge Vanfraechem and Jolien Willemsens
1 Background 1
2 Purpose of the book 3
3 Definitions 3
4 Structure of the book 5
  References 7

2 **The evaluation of restorative justice: lessons to be learned from a**
  data collection in Europe 11
  Anne Lemonne and Ida Hydle
1 Introduction 11
2 Objectives, design and outcomes of a questionnaire aimed at
  collecting data on completed or ongoing projects in Europe 12
2.1 Objectives of the questionnaire 12
2.2 Design of the template 13
2.2.1 The status of the research projects 13
2.2.2 The scope and methodology of the research projects 14
2.3 The results of the research projects 17
2.3.1 European studies 17
2.3.2 Non-European studies 19
2.4 Critical reflections 20
3 Reflections on the potentials of the data collection 21
4 Prospects for a meta-evaluation of RJ programmes in Europe 24
5 To conclude ... 27
  References 28

3 **Out-of-court but close to justice**
  Empirical research on restorative justice in Austria 39
  Christa Pelikan
1 Introduction 39
1.1 Context: state of affairs 39
1.1.1 The scope and the importance of victim-offender mediation in
  Austria 39
1.1.2 Legal situation 40
1.2 Research: an overview 41
2 Descriptive-inventory research 42
3 Action-research 43
4 Evaluative research 47

4.1	Evaluation by the parties	47
4.2	Research on the efficacy of VOM	49
4.3	Research on recidivism	52
5	Towards a comparison and conclusion	53
	References	54

4   **Research, practice and policy partnerships**
         Empirical research on restorative justice in Belgium   **57**
         Denis Van Doosselaere and Inge Vanfraechem

1	Introduction	57
1.1	Context: state of affairs	57
1.1.1	Victim-offender mediation and conferencing in Belgium	58
1.1.2	Other types of mediation	60
1.2	Legal situation	61
1.2.1	Juveniles and young adults	61
1.2.2	Adults	61
1.3	Research: an overview	62
2	Descriptive-inventory research	63
2.1	Research on restorative justice for juveniles in Flanders	63
2.1.1	Research set-up	63
2.1.2	Organisation of the services	64
2.1.3	Mediation practice	66
2.1.4	State of affairs (2010)	67
2.2	Research on penal mediation	69
2.2.1	Research set-up	69
2.2.2	Organisation of the services	69
2.2.3	Mediation practice	70
3	Action-research	72
3.1	Experimental project on mediation for juveniles in the French Community	72
3.2	Mediation for juveniles in the French Community	74
3.3	Mediation for redress in Flanders	75
3.4	Conferencing in Flanders	78
4	Evaluative research	82
4.1	The Flemish Compensation Fund	82
4.2	Local mediation as an alternative measure for petty offences in Belgium	84
4.2.1	Research set-up	84
4.2.2	Organisation of the services	85
4.2.3	Analysis of mediation practice and recommendations	85
5	Conclusion	86
	References	88

5	Providing mediation as a nation-wide service Empirical research on restorative justice in Finland *Juhani Iivari*	95
1	Introduction	95
1.1	Context: state of affairs	95
1.1.1	Legal situation of mediation	95
1.1.2	Legal situation before the autonomous law on mediation	95
1.1.3	The Act on Mediation	96
1.2	Mediation practice	97
2	Research	99
2.1	Research carried out: a general view	99
2.2	Studies in chronological order	99
2.2.1	Studies in the 1980s: the time of action-research	99
2.2.2	A dissertation in 1991: a practical-theoretical meta-analysis	100
2.2.3	Research in the 1990s: focus on evaluation	102
2.2.4	Research in the 2000s	105
3	Follow-up of the implementation of the new Act on Mediation	117
4	Conclusions	118
	References	118

6	Depicting the development of victim-offender mediation Empirical research on restorative justice in Germany *Sönke Lenz, Elmar G.M. Weitekamp and Hans-Jürgen Kerner*	121
1	Introduction	121
1.1	Context: state of affairs	121
1.1.1	VOM in practice	121
1.1.2	The legal situation	123
1.2	Research: an overview	124
2	Descriptive-inventory research	125
2.1	The model-projects	125
2.2	Stock hold surveys	128
2.3	Data-based studies	129
3	The German VOM statistics	130
3.1	Selected results from the VOM statistics 1993-2002	132
3.1.1	Organisation does matter	132
3.1.2	Target group	132
3.1.3	Offence categories	133
3.1.4	Meeting of victims and offenders	134
3.1.5	Content of VOM agreements	134
3.2	Developments of VOM in Germany (2003 to 2005)	135
3.2.1	Structural organisation	135
3.2.2	Point of entry into the procedures	136
3.2.3	Background of offenders and victims	137
3.2.4	The offences	139
3.2.5	Consequences for the victim	140

3.2.6	Willingness to participate	141
3.2.7	Outcomes	142
4	Conclusion	145
	References	145

7	**The spontaneous bottom-up rise of mediation with youth offenders**	
	Empirical research on restorative justice in Italy	**I49**
	Anna Mestitz	
1	Introduction	149
1.1	Context: state of affairs of VOM for juveniles	149
1.1.1	Overview of the Italian juvenile criminal justice system	149
1.1.2	Implementation of RJ and VOM	151
1.1.3	Legal framework	154
1.2	Empirical research on VOM: an overview	155
2	Evaluative research	156
2.1	Research on probation, VOM and the role of social workers	156
2.2	Research on probation and RJ practices	157
2.3	Research on VOM services and practices	159
2.3.1	Discussion of the results	160
2.3.2	Organisation and distribution of the VOM services	161
2.3.3	Mediation practice	165
3	International research projects	168
4	Concluding remarks	169
	References	171

8	**Evidence based policies?**	
	Empirical research on restorative justice in the Netherlands	**I75**
	John Blad and Katrien Lauwaert	
1	Introduction	175
1.1	Context: state of affairs	175
1.2	Brief overview of mediation and conferencing in the Dutch context	178
1.3	Legislative context	180
1.4	Research	181
2	Descriptive research	181
2.1	Inventory of mediation before, during and after criminal proceedings	181
2.1.1	Set-up of the research	181
2.1.2	Research results	182
2.2	Modalities of mediation in Neighbourhood Justice Centres (NJC)	184
2.2.1	Set-up of the research	184
2.2.2	Research results	184
2.3	Exploring police mediation	185
2.3.1	Set-up of the research	185
2.3.2	Research results	186

3	Evaluative research	187
3.1	Evaluation of experiments with criminal law settlement	187
3.2	Evaluation of restorative mediation	188
3.2.1	The first evaluation in 2000	188
3.2.2	A second evaluation in 2002	189
3.2.3	Restorative mediation in practice after the evaluations	191
3.3	Evaluation of family group conferencing with juvenile offenders	192
3.3.1	The 2004 report	192
3.3.2	The 2006 report	194
3.3.3	Real Justice conferences 2000-2006	196
3.4	Victim-offender conversations	199
4	Conclusion and reflections	202
	References	204

9 | **From local trial projects to state owned services** | |
	Empirical research on restorative justice in Norway	**207**
	Ida Hydle and Siri Kemény	
1	Introduction	207
1.1	Context: state of affairs	207
1.1.1	Legal situation	207
1.1.2	Availability of VOM and FGC	208
1.2	Research: an overview	209
2	Empirical research projects	210
2.1	What has become of the mediation services?	210
2.2	Mediation in NMS – what happens? Community mediation in Norway – what is happening?	210
2.3	Evaluation of the NMS organisation	210
2.4	Close-ups of mediation at the NMS	211
2.5	Between reconciliation and prevention	211
2.6	A pilot programme of peer mediation in schools	212
2.7	Comparative analysis of the mediation services in Norway and Denmark	212
2.8	The pupil as resource	212
2.9	Immigrant women and informed mediation (conflicts in marriages)	212
2.10	'Street mediation' and conferencing	213
2.11	Mediation/conferencing as a supplement to criminal procedure; cases of serious violence	213
2.12	Conflict handling and networking in the community	214
2.13	Delegation of prosecutorial authority to refer cases for mediation to the police sergeant level	214
3	Discussion and conclusion	215
	References	215

10	The quest for sustaining research	
	Empirical research on restorative justice in Poland	219
	Beata Czarnecka-Dzialuk	
1	Introduction	219
1.1	Context: state of affairs	219
1.1.1	Victim-offender mediation in Poland	219
1.1.2	Legal framework	220
1.2	Research: an overview	222
2	Descriptive-inventory research	223
2.1	Background	223
2.2	Organisation of the services	223
2.3	Mediation practice	224
3	The first experimental programme of mediation in juvenile cases: evaluative and action-oriented research	227
3.1	Background information	227
3.2	The results of the research	228
3.2.1	Profile of the cases	228
3.2.2	Mediator's view on mediation	228
3.2.3	Participants' view	229
3.2.4	Results of the mediation process	229
4	Mediation in adult cases: evaluative research	230
4.1	Research sample	230
4.2	The mediation process	231
4.3	Mediation results	231
4.4	Judges' views	231
5	Conclusion	232
	References	233
11	Variations on a theme	
	Empirical research on restorative justice in England and Wales	235
	James Dignan	
1	Introduction: putting restorative justice research in context	235
1.1	Legislative context: stand-alone initiatives	236
1.2	Legislative context: 'mainstream' initiatives	238
2	Restorative justice research in England and Wales	241
2.1	Research focusing on 'stand-alone' restorative justice initiatives	242
2.1.1	Victim-offender mediation and reparation initiatives	242
2.1.2	Family group conferencing initiatives	246
2.1.3	Police-led conferencing	248
2.2	Research focusing on 'mainstream' restorative justice initiatives	249
2.2.1	Restorative justice interventions at the pre-prosecution stage	249
2.2.2	Restorative justice interventions at the point of first conviction	250
2.2.3	Restorative justice interventions as optional sentencing measures for 'multiply convicted' young offenders	252

2.2.4   Restorative justice initiatives for adult offenders   253
3   Concluding remarks   255
         References   257

12   **Empirical research on restorative justice in Europe: perspectives**   267
         Inge Vanfraechem and Ivo Aertsen
1   The availability of restorative practices and research throughout
         Europe   267
1.1   Restorative practices   268
1.2   Research on VOM and conferencing   268
2   Distinction between various types of research   271
3   Needs with regard to future research on restorative justice   273
         References   276

Notes on contributors   279

Information about COST   285

1 Restorative justice in Europe: introducing a research endeavour

Ivo Aertsen, Inge Vanfraechem and Jolien Willemsens

1 BACKGROUND

Since the late sixties there have been continuing theoretical and ideological debates in Europe on how the consequences of an offence can be faced and resolved more directly by those immediately involved, namely the victim and the offender, and their supporters (Christie, 1977; Wright, 1996; Walgrave, 2002; Weitekamp and Kerner, 2002; von Hirsh et al., 2003). This search was prompted by a deep dissatisfaction on the part of both victims and offenders with regard to the responses offered by the conventional criminal justice system. Many working in this field in European countries – probation workers, victim support workers, legal professionals and academics – have captured these recurrent needs and started exploring structural solutions. This unrest has also been voiced throughout the common law world where the notion of restorative justice as an alternative model first became established (Zehr, 1990; Braithwaite, 1996; Crawford and Clear, 2001; Dandurand and Griffiths, 2006; see also Dignan, this volume). In continental Europe this alternative approach predominantly takes the form of victim-offender mediation [VOM], which came into existence in the 1980s (Aertsen et al., 2004; Miers and Willemsens, 2004; Mestitz and Ghetti, 2005). At the beginning of the 21st century, European mainland countries such as Belgium, the Netherlands and Norway launched experiments with family group conferences [FGC] as well (Hokwerda, 2004; Vanfraechem, 2007; Hydle and Kémeny, this volume). The range of responses subsumed by this 'restorative justice movement' has attracted great interest not only from criminal justice practitioners and academics, but also from policymakers in charge of defining and funding criminal justice policies.

This interest is reflected, first, at a national level. An increasing number of mediation and conferencing programmes is being implemented at all levels of national criminal justice systems, with both adults and young offenders. It has been estimated that by the end of the 1990s there were more than 900 mediation programmes in operation in Europe (Lauwaert and Aertsen, 2002).[1] Mediation remains the most predominant restorative justice practice in Europe and prac-

---

[1] According to Miers (2007: 448), the number of programmes alone does not give sufficient information on the state of affairs, but at least it gives some indication.

tices vary amongst countries with regard to, for example, their scope, relation to the justice system and use of volunteers (Willemsens and Walgrave, 2007: 490). This new focus is reflected, secondly, at a pan-European level, where a number of important initiatives has been taken. In 1999, the Council of Europe agreed on *Recommendation No. R (99) 19 concerning mediation in penal matters*, which encourages Member States to provide mediation as a voluntarily accepted and confidential service (Council of Europe, 2000). In the same year, the European Commission called for research on VOM,[2] but of much greater significance was the Council of the European Union's adoption in 2001 of the *Framework Decision on the standing of victims in criminal proceedings*[3] (Van der Aa et al., 2009). Articles 10 and 17 obliged the Member States of the European Union to adapt their legislation and regulations before March 2006 in order to promote VOM. This obligation has significantly raised expectations and in particular has placed a focus on an understanding of how restorative justice in general and VOM more specifically can be implemented into law (see Willemsens, 2008).

In 2002, the COST Action A21 *Restorative Justice Developments in Europe* was approved.[4] The Action undertook a number of initiatives aimed at evaluating restorative justice policy, practice, available research results and legislation within Europe. In preparation for this COST Action, two of the editors (Aertsen and Vanfraechem) organised – with financial support from the Belgian Federal Science Policy – a seminar at the K.U.Leuven inviting experts in the field of restorative justice research from eight European countries. The experts wrote a first paper with regard to the state of the art on *empirical* research on restorative justice in their country. Under impulse of the COST Action, these papers were further extended and elaborated upon. Furthermore, a working group of the COST Action developed a template to summarise and analyse existing evaluative research on restorative justice within Europe (cf. Chapter 2). These materials, together with the discussions in the working group meetings held in the period 2002 to 2006 and subsequent updating, finally led to a comprehensive overview of empirical research on restorative justice in nine European countries.[5]

---

2   Communication on Crime Victims in the European Union: Reflections on Standards and Action. COM (1999) 349 final.
3   Council Framework Decision of 15 March 2001 on the standing of victims in criminal proceedings (20001/220/JHA).
4   COST is a European Union supported, intergovernmental framework for European Cooperation in Science and Technology, allowing the coordination of nationally funded research on a European level (http://www.cost.esf.org/). More information on COST Action A21 dealing with restorative justice research: http://www.euforumrj.org/Projects/projects.COST.htm. Aertsen was initiator of this COST Action, with the assistance of Vanfraechem and Willemsens, and chaired the COST Action during its four years of functioning (2002-2006).
5   The information in the country-based chapters of this volume has been updated until 2008, unless otherwise indicated.

2   PURPOSE OF THE BOOK

The purpose of this book is to offer an analysis of empirical research carried out within European countries with regard to restorative justice. This is not another collection of theoretical essays on restorative justice. Neither is the book dealing with international research projects (apart from the work presented in Chapter 2 and references made in the chapter on Italy), which have been implemented in Europe during the last ten years mainly with financial support from the EU. Furthermore, 'restorative justice' is investigated through its operational models; in particular the focus will be on VOM and conferencing since they are considered to be the most restorative practices (McCold and Wachtel, 2002). In the respective chapters, authors may briefly refer to other practices that are considered as restorative in their country.

The nine countries included in the book have developed research on the topic, to a varying extent. Reviewing this research and its results offers an insight on the state of affairs, not only of the research but also of the restorative practices and policies in those countries. The concluding chapter provides an overview of research results and furthermore reflects upon the difficulty of collecting comparable research materials in Europe.

Each country contributor was given a template delineating three common types of research: descriptive-inventory research, action-research and evaluative research. After a general introduction on the state of affairs with regard to the practices and legislation on VOM and FGC in their country, the authors present the different types of research conducted so far in that country in detail, including the set-up, research methodology and main results. Not all authors could strictly adhere to the scheme because of differences in restorative justice and research developments between countries, various research cultures and modes of cooperation, and combinations of the abovementioned research types. Nevertheless, the template was used as a common framework to present the available research.

3   DEFINITIONS

In collecting research results, it proved to be important to clearly set out what we would be discussing from the start. It was therefore crucial, firstly, to delimit the endeavour and, secondly, to define the concepts clearly. Our project in general aimed at collecting *empirical research* on *restorative justice* in *Europe*.

We selected those countries where research on restorative justice was already being carried out at the time of the seminar (2002). This resulted in Southern and Eastern European countries being somewhat underrepresented, even though research efforts might have evolved in the meantime (Fellegi, 2005; Casado Coronas, 2008).

We further limited our efforts to empirical research, which we subdivided in three categories: descriptive-inventory research, action-research and evaluative research. *Descriptive-inventory research* provides general information on the occurrence of restorative services and practices, and detailed information on topics such as the number of organisations, number of cases, referral agencies, funding, training and background of mediators, as well as information on concrete cases: type of cases, outcomes, participation rates, etc. In *action-research*, researchers are closely related to practice and may even be practitioners.[6] Authors were asked to provide us with the definition of action-research used in the research reports and furthermore to deal with the policy context, the partners involved in the research, and its main results. Lastly, *evaluative research* covers the evaluations by participants, the relation between restorative practices and the criminal justice system, effects on recidivism, the mediators' job perception and satisfaction, legal safeguards, and cost-effectiveness.

Restorative justice was defined as 'a process for responding to crime, based on reparation, as far as possible, of the harm caused by the crime to the victim, holding the offender accountable, and facilitating communication between them and other relevant persons involved.' For our purposes, and as already mentioned, restorative justice was further delimited to VOM and conferencing, which were defined as follows:

> 'Victim-offender mediation is mediation between victim(s) and offender(s) or "mediation in criminal matters" (or criminal cases vs. civil cases).'

> 'Mediation is a process in which victim(s) and offender(s) communicate with the help of an impartial third party, either directly (face-to-face) or indirectly via the third party, enabling victim(s) to express their needs and feelings and offender(s) to accept and act on their responsibilities.' (Mediation UK, 1994).

> 'Conferencing is a method of resolving (the effects of) a crime by bringing together a large number of stakeholders with a facilitator (see also family group conferencing). Sometimes another word is added, e.g. "community conferencing".'

> 'Family Group Conferencing is a method of resolving family difficulties by bringing together as many as possible of a young person's extended family ("welfare" FGC). When the young person has committed an offence, the victim and his or her family or supporters are also present ("youth justice" FGC, because it is usually used for juveniles; for adult offenders, see conferencing).'

The focus thus clearly lay on the one hand upon criminal cases, dealing with victims and offenders, and on the other hand upon communication processes between the parties.

---

6   For a description, see Daly and Kitcher, 1998; Aertsen and Lauwaert, 2001; Reason and Bradbury, 2001; Young, 2001.

4   STRUCTURE OF THE BOOK

After this general introduction, the following chapter outlines the results of an attempt within the COST A21 Working Group to compile information on local research programmes and to compare their results. A template was created in order for respondents to give similar country information. Attention was thereby focused on evaluations of processes and effects of restorative justice. Rather than going into too much detail about the concrete research outsets and results, Lemonne and Hydle identify opportunities and difficulties in developing such a European data collection. Differing theoretical and methodological starting points, variability in research backgrounds, and language issues (research reports often only exist in the national language, but sometimes English summaries are available, as will be shown in the country chapters) proved to be the most difficult issues.

In Austria – the first country-based chapter – VOM is applied as a diversionary measure at the prosecutor's level, both for adult and youth offenders. The practice of VOM is based on §90 of the Code of Criminal Procedure and leaves a great margin of discretion for the public prosecutor. Research started as an 'accompanying research' of two pilot-projects, which, according to the author, falls under the heading of action-research but also includes elements of evaluative research. Comparative research is available, complemented by the work done by students under the heading of descriptive-inventory research. Evaluative research has been undertaken on the topics of evaluation of the process by participants, recidivism and the efficacy of mediation in cases of partnership violence. Pelikan sees the most striking feature of research on VOM in Austria in its close connection to the criminal justice agencies, related to the interest that the relevant ministries took in getting the pilot projects established and thoroughly researched.

In Belgium, various mediation models exist for adults, at all levels of the judicial procedure. Since 2006, VOM as well as conferences have a legal basis for youth offenders. On the one hand, research is done on a variety of topics and in various fields of mediation and restorative justice, such as in prisons, schools and neighbourhoods. On the other hand, theoretical research is carried out as well. The chapter focuses on empirical research: descriptive-inventory research was done on restorative justice for juveniles, and provides an overview of the organisation of mediation services and details of mediation practice. Action-research was carried out on 'mediation for redress', mediation for youth in the French Community, and conferencing in the Flemish Community. Evaluative research covered topics such as the Compensation Fund, local mediation for petty offences, and an experimental project on mediation for juveniles in the French Community. Van Doosselaere and Vanfraechem thus conclude that empirical research is mostly limited to the field of youth offending.

Legislation on mediation exists for youth and adult offenders since 2006 in Finland. Both theoretical and empirical research have been carried out. Rather than following the template, Iivari prefers to describe the research projects in a chronological order, since it shows the evolution in research approaches. Action-research was carried out at the beginning of the mediation practice, whereby researchers were at the same time developing and evaluating the programmes. A practical-theoretical analysis and meta-analysis offered a more theoretical basis for the mediation work. In the 1990s, the focus lay on evaluating topics such as satisfaction of the parties, influences of VOM on the justice system, recidivism, job perception and satisfaction of the mediators, and cost-effectiveness. Since 2000, research has been done on the organisation of nation-wide mediation, children in mediation, social mediation with refugee communities, domestic violence, and follow-up of the new mediation law. The author concludes that various research methods have been used to study diverging topics.

Several VOM projects exist throughout Germany. VOM is based on the youth law as well as the Penal Code and Federal Code of Criminal Procedure, and is being applied as a diversionary measure for youth and adult offenders. A peculiarity with regard to research is the informal scientific cooperation network carrying out research on VOM and collecting data throughout the country. Research is therefore mostly of a descriptive-inventory nature. Lenz and colleagues differentiate between the model-projects (the first projects on VOM in Germany), stock hold surveys (a nation-wide survey on VOM) and data-based studies, which evolved to 'German VOM statistics'. The chapter focuses on the methodology and main results of the latter, which provides us with a more concrete view on the German VOM practice.

In Italy, restorative justice is, according to Mestitz, not a well-known concept and it remains mainly associated with VOM. Mediation is not legislated but can be applied as a diversionary measure by prosecutors and judges. Most initiatives are taken in the field of youth delinquency. Empirical research is mostly limited to, on the one hand, local surveys by mediation services, and, on the other hand, evaluative research on topics such as probation and VOM/restorative justice practices, as well as concrete VOM services and practices. The author presents the set-up of mediation services and mediation practice in detail. Furthermore, she presents the international research projects on VOM for juveniles and on information and data exchange. She concludes that the possibilities for carrying out independent research on VOM are rather limited in Italy.

In the Netherlands, various restorative justice practices do not fall under the heading of VOM or conferencing, such as claims settlement, HALT (a diversionary measure for juveniles) and community mediation. Besides these, other practices do fall under the heading of VOM, such as mediation by Neighbourhood Justice Centres, criminal law settlement, police mediation, restorative mediation and, possibly, victim-offender conversations. Conferencing is applied for youth offenders. According to Blad and Lauwaert, descriptive research takes stock of the modalities of mediation practices in specific contexts. Evaluative research has been carried out with regard to criminal law settlement, restorative mediation, conferencing and the relatively new victim-offender conversations. Action-research is not applied. The authors conclude that research does cover most of the practices and applies various methods. Descriptive-evaluative research is deemed to be predominant. Evaluation of the programmes is strongly related to the Ministries' decision on whether it will be continued.

In Poland, VOM can be applied for adult and youth offenders through specific articles in the Code of Criminal Law, Code of Criminal Procedure and the Law on Juvenile Responsibility, but its availability varies throughout the country. Even though the interest for mediation is growing, Czarnecka-Dzialuk concludes there is little research. Descriptive-inventory research provides a view on the organisation of services and mediation practice. The first experimental programme of VOM in juvenile cases is defined by the author as both evaluative and action-research. Evaluative research was carried out on mediation with adult offenders, studying the outcomes of mediation, recidivism rates and judges' opinions on mediation.

A vast amount of research has been carried out in the United Kingdom. Dignan focuses on the research in England and Wales and points out the importance of the changing policy context. Research focused first on the 'stand-alone' restorative justice initiatives, mostly small-scale experimental projects including VOM and reparation initiatives. This was followed by research on FGC initiatives and police-led conferencing. Several elements were introduced by youth reforms and thus become part of the mainstream approach. Research has started, but findings are still mostly tentative and inconclusive. Research projects are oriented towards restorative justice interventions at the pre-prosecution stage, at the point of first conviction and as optional sentencing for young offenders; and on interventions for adult offenders at various stages of the judicial process. The author concludes that the eclectic implementation of restorative justice initiatives impedes comparability and that research is of a variable quality.

In the concluding remarks, finally, we offer an overview of the most striking results, commonalities as well as differences between the nine countries. Furthermore, we provide some overall thoughts on the definition of research (methods); the advantages and disadvantages of comparative research in Europe; and the important influence of the legal and cultural framework in which restorative justice practices are implemented. In that way, we invite the reader to reflect upon the possibilities of national and international empirical research in Europe.

REFERENCES

Aertsen, I. and Lauwaert, K. (2001) 'Criminologie als bemiddeling', in Dupont, L. and Hutsebaut, F. (eds.) *Herstelrecht tussen toekomst en verleden. Liber Amicorum Tony Peters* (Leuven: Leuven Universitaire Pers), pp. 33-55.

Aertsen, I., Mackay, R., Pelikan, C., Willemsens, J. and Wright, M. (2004) *Rebuilding community connections – mediation and restorative justice in Europe* (Strasbourg: Council of Europe).

Braithwaite, J. (1996) 'Restorative Justice and a Better Future', *Dalhousie Law Review*, 71(1), pp. 9-32.

Casado Coronas, C. (2008) *Restorative justice: an agenda for Europe. Supporting the implementation of restorative justice in the South of Europe* (Leuven: European Forum for Restorative Justice).

Christie, N. (1977) 'Conflicts as property', *British Journal of Criminology*, 17(1), pp. 1-15.

Council of Europe (2000) *Mediation in Penal Matters: Recommendation No. R(99)19 and explanatory memorandum* (Strasbourg: Council of Europe Publishing).

Crawford, A. and Clear, R.R. (2001) 'Community Justice: Transforming Communities through Restorative Justice?', in Bazemore, G. and Schiff, M. (eds.) *Restorative Community Justice* (Cincinnati: Anderson Publishing), pp. 127-49.

Daly, K. and Kitcher, J. (1998) 'The R(evolution) of Restorative Justice through Researcher-Practitioner Partnerships', *Ethics and Justice*, (2)1, pp. 14-20.

Dandurand, Y. and Griffiths, C.T. (2006) *Handbook on Restorative justice programmes* (New York/Vienna: United Nations).

Fellegi, B. (2005) *Meeting the challenges of introducing victim-offender mediation in Central and Eastern European countries* (Leuven: European Forum for Restorative Justice).

Hokwerda, Y.M. (2004) *Herstelrecht in jeugdstrafzaken. Een evaluatieonderzoek van zeven experimenten in Nederland* (Den Haag: Boom Juridische Uitgevers).

Lauwaert, K. and Aertsen, I. (2002) 'Restorative Justice: Activities and Expectations at European Level', *ERA-Forum – Scripta iuris europaei*, 1, pp. 27-32.

McCold, P. and Wachtel, T. (2002) 'Restorative Justice Theory Validation', in Weitekamp, E. and Kerner, H.-J. (eds.) *Restorative Justice. Theoretical Foundations* (Cullompton: Willan Publishing), pp. 110-142.

Mediation UK (1994) *Victim/offender mediation: guidelines for starting a service* (Bristol: Mediation UK).

Mestitz, A. and Ghetti, S. (eds.) (2005) *Victim-Offender Mediation with Youth Offenders in Europe. An Overview and Comparison of 15 countries* (Dordrecht: Springer).

Miers, D. (2007), 'The international development of restorative justice', in Johnstone, G. and Van Ness, D.W. (eds.) *Handbook of Restorative Justice* (Cullompton: Willan Publishing), pp. 447-467.

Miers, D. and Willemsens, J. (2004) *Mapping Restorative Justice. Developments in 25 European countries* (Leuven: European Forum for Restorative Justice).

Reason, P. and Bradbury, H. (eds.) (2001) *Handbook of Action Research. Participative Inquiry and Practice* (London-Thousand Oakes-New Delhi: Sage Publications).

Van der Aa, S., Merrienboer, E., Pemberton, A., Lázaro, J., Rasquete, C., Amaral, C., Marques, F. and Pita, M. (2009) *Victims in Europe. Implementation of the EU Framework Decision on the standing of victims in criminal proceedings in the Member States of the European Union* (Lisbon: APAV).

Vanfraechem, I. (2007) *Herstelgericht groepsoverleg* (Brugge: Die Keure).

Von Hirsch, A., Roberts, J., Bottoms, A., Roach, K. and Schiff, M. (eds.) (2003) *Restorative Justice & Criminal Justice. Competing or Reconcilable Paradigms?* (Oxford-Portland: Hart Publishing).

Walgrave, L. (ed.) (2002) *Restorative Justice and the Law* (Cullompton: Willan Publishing).

Weitekamp, E. and Kerner, H.-J. (eds.) (2002) *Restorative Justice. Theoretical Foundations* (Cullompton: Willan Publishing).

Willemsens, J. (2008) *Restorative Justice: an agenda for Europe. The role of the European Union in the further development of restorative justice* (Leuven: European Forum for Restorative Justice).

Willemsens, J. and Walgrave, L. (2007) 'Section C Europe', in Johnstone, G. and Van Ness, D.W. (eds.) *Handbook of Restorative Justice* (Cullompton: Willan Publishing), pp. 488-499.

Wright, M. (1996) *Justice for victims and offenders. A restorative response to crime* (Winchester: Waterside Press).

Young, R. (2001) 'Just Cops Doing "Shameful" Business? Police-Led Restorative Justice and the Lessons of Research', in Morris, A. and Maxwell, G. (eds.) *Restorative Justice for Juveniles. Conferencing, Mediation & Circles* (Oxford-Portland: Hart Publishing), pp. 195-226.

Zehr, H. (1990) *Changing Lenses: A New Focus for Crime and Justice* (Scottdale: Herald Press).

2 The evaluation of restorative justice: lessons to be learned from a data collection in Europe

Anne Lemonne and Ida Hydle

1 INTRODUCTION

One of the most important challenges for evaluators is to specify how to produce valuable knowledge on social issues and to introduce it within institutional systems (Pondaven, 2006).

The issue of evaluation is currently of primary importance in the realm of restorative justice [RJ] in Europe. European institutions are increasingly involved in formulating recommendations regarding policies, taking into account RJ developments. Several countries have introduced RJ programmes in their legislation or practices. Various chapters of this book present national developments, encompassing aspects such as national history, the legal context, policy implementations, descriptions of RJ programmes and practices, as well as evaluation and research programmes.[1]

In contrast with most of the contributions presented in this book, this chapter does not provide an overview of particular national developments of RJ but rather aims at bringing knowledge and reflection on the issue of evaluative research in general, and meta-evaluative research in particular. More specifically, this will be performed by discussing some aspects of the work carried out in the framework of the COST Action A21 by Working Group 1 on 'Evaluative research on RJ in Europe'. For four years, this EU-funded programme has offered the opportunity for European researchers to gather empirical evaluative research on the effects of RJ and to reflect on the possibility to carry out a meta-evaluation. In this respect, debates within this Working Group can be considered as a 'case study' which sheds light on the ongoing European discourses and practices.

Thus, starting from a short description and analysis of the results of the work carried out by this Working Group, aimed at gathering existing completed or ongoing evaluative research in Europe (1), this chapter hopes to provide some reflections regarding the current limits of the data collection and its potential for interpretation in the light of the debates that have taken place during this European research programme (2). It also aims at formulating some recommendations for the future development of evaluation and meta-evaluation of RJ programmes in Europe (3).

---

1   See also European Forum for Victim-Offender Mediation and Restorative Justice (2000) and Mestitz and Ghetti (2005).

2   OBJECTIVES, DESIGN AND OUTCOMES OF A QUESTIONNAIRE AIMED AT COLLECTING DATA ON COMPLETED OR ONGOING PROJECTS IN EUROPE

2.1   Objectives of the questionnaire

According to the original version of the scientific programme of COST Action A21 (Proposal for a COST Action, 2002), one of the tasks of Working Group 1 was to deepen the knowledge on RJ in Europe by focusing, in particular, on completed or ongoing evaluative research related to victim-offender mediation [VOM] and family group conferencing [FGC] in order to better understand the process and effects of these programmes in various European countries. The study was meant to:

1) improve the knowledge of RJ research being carried out in Europe;
2) improve the understanding of the mainly qualitative methodologies being used for such research, and their respective strengths and weaknesses;
3) create an overview of the results of these evaluative research projects, from which conclusions could be drawn to support policy development in the RJ field;
4) discern gaps in the research in this field for Europe, and to set up a research agenda for the future;
5) and to achieve agreement on the methodological framework best suited to carry out specific types of research projects.

Two other, interconnected, tasks were also specified within this scientific programme: (1) to focus on organisational features, job evaluation and satisfaction of people involved in such programmes; and (2) to study national data recording systems in order to eventually set up common criteria which could stimulate all countries to collect, in the long run, information allowing for interpretation and further research in a comparable and reliable way.

Therefore, it was agreed to primarily collect available evaluative research on RJ in Europe. This was indeed considered as a first necessary step if any attempt to reach the abovementioned objectives was to be undertaken. As we will further describe, this aspect of the work was not easy to perform since lively debates rapidly took off within the group concerning the best way to design and implement this data gathering exercise and about the possibility of interpretation, at a European level, of pieces of (often national) RJ evaluative research.

The decision was however made to design and implement a template which would allow us to make an inventory of ongoing or completed evaluations in Europe. According to the initial guidelines of the scientific programme of the COST Action, the types of evaluative research that were primarily gathered were related to VOM or FGC programmes implemented at all stages of the criminal justice system. Attention was mainly focused on evaluations highlighting processes and effects of RJ. Priority was given in particular to research focusing on re-offending, participant satisfaction or outcomes of the process (such as reparation and apologies). Finally, all kinds of evaluative research projects were considered as relevant (qualitative and/or quantitative, national and/or sub-national, research on particular themes) as long as the research protocols included research questions, implied empirical data collection and/or critical evaluations of the programme.

2.2   Design of the template

The template aimed at collecting minimal information related to the framework and results of the evaluations, and at providing general references for the gathering, in the future, of additional information on these research projects, if necessary. Therefore, the template contained semi-overt questions dealing with:

1) *general descriptions*: title, contact details of the contact person for further information, existing publications and references, research status (date of completion), length of the research, type of funding, institution carrying out the research, research oversight;
2) *objectives/approach and tools*: research objectives, theoretical framework, disciplinary background, research approach and tools;
3) and the *results*: description of the main results, abstracts, summaries, etc.

Two members of the group[2] took charge of the implementation of this data collection, while the other members were invited to disseminate as extensively as possible the template in their respective countries. Forty-seven questionnaires were collected. Most of them refer to one evaluation of RJ programme in a particular country. Through a 'short-term scientific mission', financed by the COST programme, a PhD student was engaged to collect data on the impact of RJ programmes on re-offending/recidivism.[3] Once the data were gathered, they were 'coded' in a database in order to be analysed.[4]

From the analysis of these data, three criteria have been identified as delineating criteria: first, the status of the collected research; second, their applied scopes and methodologies; and third, the results of the researches. In what follows, non-exhaustive examples are used to illustrate some of these trends. This preliminary analysis provides a framework to further discuss the possibilities of developing meta-evaluative research on the effects of RJ programmes in Europe.

2.2.1   The status of the research projects[5]

Most of the research projects were carried out by academic institutions or by independent research institutes. In this context, they were usually subject to peer

---

2   Kieran O'Dwyer from Ireland and Grigor Vladimirov from Bulgaria.

3   Deidre Healy, student at the Institute of Criminology of the University College Dublin in Ireland was hosted, in January 2006, by Brian Williams, member of Working Group 1 and Professor at De Montfort University, UK. Her study-mission involved a literature review of evaluations of restorative justice programmes. This review implied a collection and detailed description of the individual studies, using the template as prepared by Working Group 1.

4   The data were coded with Nvivo 7, a programme for analysing qualitative data (creating categories, using queries, exploring and representing various dimensions of data).

5   The countries that have provided information about evaluative research projects related to the effects of RJ programmes are Austria (7), Belgium (1), England and Wales (6), Finland (8), Germany (1), Ireland (2), Spain (1), New Zealand (1), Northern Ireland (1), Norway (1), Scotland (1),

supervision. The majority of the research projects took place between 1995 and 2005 and have, as disciplinary backgrounds, criminology, sociology (including sociology of law and social policy) or law (often penal law). Only a few of them have a background in political science, psychology, anthropology or victimology. In general, the average length of the studies is quite short (from a few months to three years). Only some of them lasted for more than three years. The public sector financed most of these studies (Ministries of Justice, Interior, Social Affairs, Family Affairs, etc.). Research institutes funded approximately one fourth of the evaluative programmes. Only a few of them were initiated by NGOs, internal departments of police, justice ministries or through international public funding. Results of these projects are usually accessible *via* research reports or publications in scientific journals. A few documents or abstracts have been added to the template in order to bring additional information to the reader.

2.2.2   The scope and methodology of the research projects

The majority of the research projects concern VOM and FGC programmes, in concordance with the initial objectives as set by the scientific programme of COST Action A21. Others, however, address other kinds of restorative programmes, such as police-based cautioning, referral orders and youth offender's panels, which are expanding in countries such as Ireland and the United Kingdom (Young and Goold, 1999; O'Dwyer, 2001; O'Mahony et al., 2002; Crawford and Newburn, 2003; Wilcox et al., 2004).

Although the recorded evaluations generally focus on RJ schemes for adults, a few are also oriented towards specific groups or issues such as young offenders, violent offenders, domestic violence or immigrant populations. This narrowing down of RJ evaluation to particular issues leads to the development of specific evaluative perspectives. For example, the studies of Haidar et al. (1988) and Lins (1998) in Austria, Eskelin and Iivari (2002) in Finland, and Crawford and Newburn (2003) in the UK analysed the implementation of RJ in the youth justice system in their respective countries. Hydle and Hasund (2004) and Hydle (2006) studied, from a social anthropology and linguistics point of view, 'conflict regimes' in violent cases that occurred in Norway. In Austria, Pelikan and Hoenisch (2000) and Pelikan (2002) conducted an empirical qualitative study on the efficiency of VOM in domestic violence cases compared to the criminal procedure. Iivari and Flinck (2004) have worked on a similar subject in Finland, in the framework of a research carried out by the National Institute for Health and Welfare [STAKES].[6] Finally, the Finnish researchers Salonen and Iivari (2004) participated in the evaluation of a programme of Social Mediation for Refugee

---

Australia (9), Canada (1), United States (5). This data collection further included studies from North America, New Zealand and Australia, particularly on the subject of offending/recidivism and satisfaction of the parties. We kept these research projects in the analysis because they help to understand the particularity of the European research field. The full list of the research reports included in the database can be found in annex with this chapter.

6   Interestingly, both studies mentioned the difficulty to provide, in advance, criteria of the suitability of intimate violent cases for victim-offender mediation. These criteria cannot be based on the type of criminal offence or on the severity of the violence but would be based on benefits that can

Communities in Europe. This programme aimed at strengthening integration of refugees and to reduce racism, discrimination and social tension through social mediation practices for settling criminal cases and disputes within or between communities. In the framework of this study, commissioned by the International Organisation for Migration, Regional Office for the Baltic and Nordic States and funded by the EU (European Refugee Fund), the researchers mainly developed a process-evaluation, analysing the results of the programmes in terms of their goals.

In Europe, a few studies evaluate RJ at a trans-national level (Kilchling and Löschnig-Gspandl,[7] 1998; Miers, 2001, 2006; Miers and Willemsens, 2004; Mestitz and Ghetti, 2005). European evaluations often remain related to national programmes. A good example of this is the study of O'Dwyer (2001), which evaluated the process and impact of an Irish pilot-programme of restorative cautioning/family conferencing prior to coming into operation as a statute-based programme. The research of Dignan (1992), evaluating a specific pre-trial diversion scheme (the Kettering Adult Reparation Bureau) in the UK, is another good illustration. Evaluations are also sometimes expanded to different types of RJ programmes within the same country. For example, O'Mahony et al. (2002) studied two pilot restorative cautioning schemes for juvenile offenders carried out by the police in Northern Ireland[8] and Miers et al. (2001) analysed seven RJ schemes to identify 'best practices' according to the satisfaction rates of the parties and the reconviction rates of the offenders in the United Kingdom.[9]

Even if there have been some attempts to perform 'qualitative' meta-evaluations of RJ in Europe (Miers, 2001; Miers and Willemsens, 2004; Mestitz and Ghetti, 2005; Miers, 2006), studies based on 'quantitative' meta-evaluative methodology (where existing results from different scientific sources are quantitatively analysed and compared) remain sparse. For instance, the evaluation of the impact of the Leeds Reparation scheme on re-offending in the United Kingdom (Wynne and Brown, 1998) synthesised the results of three different studies yet concentrated on a particular scheme. The evaluation by Sherman and Strang (2007) which reviewed RJ studies in England, North America and Australia, on the effects of restorative programmes on re-offending, brought together the analysis of European and non-European studies in a large meta-evaluative context.[10] This study applied a methodological tool used extensively outside Europe, where larger scale quantitative meta-analyses have been conducted. In Canada, for example, Latimer et al. (2001) implemented a meta-evaluation of the impact of RJ schemes

---

be gained by victims and offenders as the matter proceeds. See also the chapters in this book on Austria and Finland.

7   Kilchling and Löschnig-Gspandl (1998) implemented, for example, a comparative empirical research in Germany (Baden-Württemberg) and Austria (Styria) in order to assess the differences and similarities of two VOM programmes along various features such as the type of offences referred, victim participation and victim satisfaction.

8   One pilot project operated as part of a retail theft initiative and dealt mainly with shoplifting. The other was used as an alternative for cases deemed suitable for formal caution.

9   Two of them dealt essentially with adult offenders and the other five with juveniles.

10   This study did not form part of the data collection at the time of the COST Action.

on recidivism, on the basis of 22 studies, which all had a comparison group and addressed 35 different types of interventions. Nugent et al. (2003) performed a meta-analysis of a set of studies with comparison groups to evaluate the participation in VOM and the prevalence of subsequent delinquent behaviour.

European studies often use qualitative methods based to a large extent on interviews (with professionals, offenders and victims involved in mediation or conferencing programmes) and/or on observations and/or case files/studies. When quantitative studies are performed, they are generally conducted in combination with more qualitative approaches. Researchers mostly base their work on small samples of about 100 cases or individuals.[11] Some, however, are inclined to develop more extensive quantitative studies. For example, the Austrian study of Hammerschick et al. (1994) analysed 669 victim-offender mediation files and 1,338 court files to assess the scope, the mode of case-referral and of case-handling, and the outcome of VOM files compared to court files.[12] The study of Järvinen (1992) used a sample of 350 young people in a survey focusing on mediated cases to discuss the potential of VOM as an alternative to the criminal justice system.[13] Finally, the research of O'Mahony et al. (2002) reviewed 1,861 case files (and carried out a detailed examination of 265 cases among which 70 were dealt with restoratively) during their evaluation of police-based cautioning pilots in Northern Ireland. Not surprisingly, however, the largest surveys have been developed in the UK and in non-European countries (USA, Australia) in the framework of quantitative meta-evaluation programmes. In the United Kingdom, the study of Wilcox et al. (2004) investigated, for example, the potential of restorative police cautioning in reducing the level of re-sanctioning in comparison with the traditional cautioning processes.[14] These authors based their results on a very large sample (n=29,000) containing both VOM participants and recipients of other kinds of cautions. Some non-European countries are even handling much bigger samples in the framework of evaluative researches on the effect of RJ on re-offending/recidivism or on the satisfaction of the parties (see for example Sherman et al., 2000; McGarrell, 2001; Strang, 2002; Nugent et al., 2003). They use quasi-experimental (with control groups) or experimental (with randomised control trial) approaches more frequently.

---

11   In Germany, for example, Dölling and Hartmann (2003), examining re-offending rates after participation in VOM both for juveniles and adults, used quasi-experimental, matched group design but analysed 130 VOM data files and 140 comparison group data files.

12   In addition to this survey, experts were interviewed, interviews being repeated in the course of the project.

13   This study was complemented by a number of interviews with police officers, prosecutors, judges, probation officers, other officials, mediators, victims and suspected perpetrators.

14   The authors explored the topic by comparing cautions in Thames Valley Police to cautions in other similar police forces and by comparing the different types of caution in Thames Valley. For this purpose, they performed a quantitative comparison of Thames Valley with Sussex and Warwickshire police services (two forces similar in terms of social composition and urban/rural mix plus detection and cautioning rates) and within Thames Valley, by type of caution, examined offenders cautioned between April 1998 and March 2001. Re-sanctioning was assessed over 24 months after the date of caution.

In accordance with the objectives set by the scientific programme of the COST Action A21, the compiled European evaluative research projects often measure the effects of victim-offender mediation programmes. They often also include, and sometimes only include, more descriptive aspects such as organisational features of VOM and FGC, the kind of communication used between participants and mediators, the number of agreements signed, the characteristics of the people or the cases being sent to RJ programmes, etc.[15] There is also significant interest in the evaluation of parties' satisfaction.[16] Although studies concerning the effect of RJ programmes on re-offending/recidivism do prevail in Europe, they do not seem to be at the highest level on the agenda of European research.[17] Yet, in Europe, the concept of 'effect' of a programme still seems to cover other important aspects besides those of parties' satisfaction or re-offending/recidivism rates. RJ programmes have been evaluated with regard to their effect on the criminal justice system (Haidar et al., 1988; Hammerschick et al., 1994; Crawford and Newburn, 2003) or in the light of social or theoretical issues. Projects focusing their attention on topics such as 'mediation and expression of moral emotions' (Takala, 1998a, 1998b), 'RJ theory and mediation practices' (Elonheimo, 2003, 2004), 'social mediation for refugee communities' (Salonen and Iivari, 2004) and 'the representation of mediation in newspapers' (Heikkilä, 2003) illustrate this preoccupation.

2.3   The results of the research projects

2.3.1   European studies

The European evaluations often emphasise the high rate of satisfaction of both victims and offenders that have participated in a RJ programme.[18]

The outcome of the studies focusing on re-offending and recidivism show greater variability.[19] While some studies reveal that there is no significant evidence to suggest that restorative programmes are more effective than traditional reactions to crime, others claim that reconviction rates are lower for offenders having gone through RJ programmes. Yet these studies also stress that many questions remain

---

15   See Dignan (1992), Hammerschick et al. (1994), Aertsen and Peters (1998a, 1998b), Haidar et al. (1988), O'Dwyer (2001, 2005), Järvinen (1992), Pelikan (2002) and Elonheimo (2003, 2004).

16   The studies performed by Kilchling and Löschnig-Gspandl (1998), Lins (1998), Altweger and Hitzl (2000) in Austria and Germany; Aertsen and Peters (1998a, 1998b) in Belgium; O'Dwyer (2001) in Ireland; Dignan (1992), Umbreit and Roberts (1997), Wynne and Brown (1998), Young and Goold (1999) and Miers et al. (2001) in the United Kingdom; and Warner et al. (1992) in Scotland constitute some examples that witness this interest.

17   Among the European projects focusing on this field, one can mainly mention those from Austria (Schütz, 1999), Finland (Mielityinen, 1999), Germany (Dölling and Hartman, 2003), Ireland (O'Dwyer, 2001) and the United Kingdom (Wynne and Brown, 1998; Miers et al., 2001; Wilcox et al., 2004).

18   See Dignan (1992), Warner et al. (1992), Wynne and Brown (1998), Young and Goold (1999), Kilchling and Löschnig-Gspandl (1998), Lins (1998), Altweger and Hitzl (2000), Miers et al. (2001), and O'Dwyer (2001).

19   See Wynne and Brown (1998), Schütz (1999), Mielityinen (1999), Miers (2001), O'Dwyer (2001), Dölling and Hartman (2003) and Wilcox et al. (2004).

to be elucidated to confirm this hypothesis. For example, Miers et al. (2001) compared the reconviction rates of a sample of offenders who participated in seven RJ schemes with those of a comparison group and found that there was no statistically significant difference between the groups, except for one adult scheme. Wilcox et al. (2004), in their study on the respective benefits of restorative cautioning versus traditional cautioning, also concluded that there were no statistically significant differences in terms of frequency or seriousness of subsequent offending between the groups. On the other hand, Schütz (1999) highlighted the flaws that can result in the study from the selection of the VOM cases on the basis of an empirical research comparing recidivism rates between offenders having participated in VOM and offenders having received a fine. Indeed, in the evaluated Austrian programme, state prosecutors often performed the selection of mediation cases in the light of individual (special) prevention. According to Schütz (1999) it is thus possible that only the cases with the most promising prognosis in terms of recidivism are sent to mediation.[20] Dölling and Hartman (2003) agree with this hypothesis in their study using a quasi-experimental design with matched group comparison. They showed a reduction of recidivism (33%) for people who had successfully participated in mediation but, in agreement with Schütz, suggested that positive results are more likely to be due to self-selection into the mediation process than to the efficiency of the scheme itself. Finally, Mielityinen (1999), in her study on recidivism, argued that the effect of mediation depended on the type of offence.

Finally, the evaluation of the effects of RJ programmes on the penal system reveals scattered results which depend on the scheme under examination and on the theoretical and methodological background of the researchers. For instance, the study of Haidar et al. (1988) on the Austrian pilot project 'Out-of-court conflict resolution in juvenile justice' emphasised that the introduction of VOM changed the pattern of criminal law reactions by decreasing the number of convictions of juveniles. The study of Hammerschick et al. (1994) on adult restorative programmes in the same country highlighted the difficulties for prosecutors and judges involved in 'out-of-court process' to conceive these programmes differently from the penal law orientation on punishment, that is as a mean of individual and general deterrence. This 'contamination' of RJ programmes by penal objectives has also been highlighted in others studies (see, for instance, Crawford and Newburn, 2003). Interestingly, evaluative researches on the implementation of RJ programmes in the framework of social or theoretical issues shed a new light on research avenues. For instance, the project devoted to 'mediation and expression of moral emotions' (Takala, 1998a, 1998b) investigates how moral emotions are dealt with in VOM. The project 'social mediation for refugee communities' (Salonen and Iivari, 2004) evaluated a specific programme concerning the strengthening of integration of refugees as well as the reduction of racism, discrimination

---

20   In Finland, Elonheimo (2003, 2004) through his examination of the extent to which restorative justice theory is realised within Finnish VOM, practices also concluded that cases referred to mediation mainly involved minor offences.

and social tensions. The project 'the representation of mediation in newspapers' (Heikkilä, 2003) explored what was written about mediation in cases of domestic violence in the Finnish print media.

2.3.2   Non-European studies

It is worth mentioning that studies conducted at a non-European level (for instance the studies on 'parties' satisfaction' and 're-offending/recidivism') can provide additional useful insights on the evaluation of the effects of RJ. These studies also highlight that the difficulties of establishing strong evidence and generalisations on the effects of RJ, especially with respect to recidivism, are not confined to European research. The higher satisfaction of the parties is usually confirmed by non-European studies, based on more quasi-experimental or experimental methodologies.[21]

The non-European meta-evaluations on re-offending/recidivism reveal, like in European countries, less homogeneous results. Some find no differences in re-offending/recidivism[22] while others find significant differences.[23] Finally, some provide mixed judgments and recommend further research because of the low number of studies in the meta-evaluation or the potential selection bias linked to the nature of the offence or to the offender's characteristics. The meta-evaluation by Latimer et al. (2001), for example, recommended using more randomised trials to test the impact of RJ interventions, since the selection bias, linked to the voluntary participation, could influence the lower recidivism rates of people who have participated in RJ schemes. In their meta-evaluative study of 15 programmes, Nugent et al. (2003) provided cautionary statements concerning a potential over-interpretation of the results, taking into account the small number of studies analysed. In Australia, the study of Sherman et al. (2000) on the impact of RISE on re-offending, showed that the biggest decrease in offending was recorded for

---

21 Strang's review (2002) of the RJ experiments in Canberra (known as RISE), while emphasising the victim's perspective, employed a randomised controlled design (RCT) to compare RISE participants to those undergoing normal court processing and found that FGC victims were more positive about their experience overall when compared to court-processed victims on measures of anger, sympathy, anxiety, trust and fear. Others studies, such as Hayes (2005) showed that satisfaction with the processing of their cases was high for both court and conference participants but that participants to FGC felt that the process was fairer and were more likely to have more favourable attitudes towards the victims. See also, for example, Umbreit and Coates (1992), Umbreit and Roberts (1997), Fercello and Umbreit (1999), Latimer et al. (2001), McGarrel (2001) and Strang (2002).

22 Hayes (2005) showed that among a sample of 292 first offenders, randomly assigned to FGC or youth court, recidivism was not declining for those taking part in RJ schemes. Umbreit and Coates (1999) and Griffith (1999) highlighted, on the basis of their follow-up studies on re-offending with a comparison group of offenders being proceeded traditionally, that there was no significant difference in re-offending between the two groups.

23 Maxwell and Morris (2001) found a lower rate of reconviction for FGC offenders compared to normal processing. They also mentioned that successful FGCs were related to lower reconviction rates. Daly (2001) in an extensive qualitative follow-up study confirmed that people are more inclined to commit new offences when they consider FGC as a waste of time. McGarrel (2001) and Luke and Lind (2002) also showed lower rates of re-offending for people assigned to RJ practices compared to those oriented to normal proceedings.

violent offenders (reduction of 38 crimes per 100 per year). There was only a small decrease for drunk drivers (of 6 per 100 per year) and no observed differences for juvenile shoplifters or property offenders with personal victims. Thus, the results suggested that RISE was effective with violent offenders. Yet the researchers concluded that more research would be needed to confirm these results. Finally, Hayes and Daly (2004) concluded that despite a high 'crime free' rate after FGC, its features are unrelated to these outcomes. Instead, the offenders' character-istics (including their social context) seemed to be more predictive in terms of recidivism than FGC characteristics.

2.4   Critical reflections

Despite the existence of evaluative studies on various effects of RJ in Europe, any generalisation of the abovementioned results cannot be thoroughly assessed because of the diversity of epistemological and methodological approaches, on the one hand, and the variety of programmes and their contexts, on the other hand. For instance, the RJ programmes being evaluated are often designed differently and publications often fail to specify what is really meant by concepts such as 'par-ties' satisfaction', 're-offending' or 'recidivism' and 'impact on the penal justice system'. In addition, many studies are dealing with small samples, do not always use control groups, and are certainly not always exempt from selection bias. Even when larger samples are used, authors generally advise the reader to treat results cautiously.

Some of the general trends do allow for delineating some characteristics of eval-uative researches in Europe: the majority of the researches are concerned with VOM and FGC programmes. Others, however, relate to other kinds of restorative programmes, such as police-based cautioning.
Most of the research projects were carried out by academic or independent research institutes, with the financial support of the public sector (Ministries of Justice, Interior, Social Affairs, Family Affairs, etc.). Therefore, they are often subject to peer review. In general, the average length of these studies is quite short (from a few months to three years). As expected, the objectives of the com-piled evaluative research projects often concern the effects of RJ programmes. However, they also, or sometimes only, include more descriptive aspects such as organisational features of VOM and FGC, the kind of communication used between participants and mediators, the number of agreements signed, etc. Most researches are related to a single national programme. Only a few conduct meta-evaluations.
The studies often use both quantitative and qualitative methods, small samples of around 100 to 150 cases or individuals (only a few with control groups), consist to a large extent of interviews (with professionals, offenders and victims involved in victim-offender mediation or conferencing programmes), and/or of observations and/or case studies. Some European countries seem more inclined to develop quantitative studies (Austria, Germany, Ireland and UK) than others. It is worth

mentioning that the largest surveys were carried out in the UK or in non-European countries (USA, Australia). In these studies, researchers often used quasi-experimental approaches (with control groups) or experimental approaches (with randomised control trial).

In European countries, the concept of the 'effect' of a programme embraces various meanings. Significant research efforts focus on the evaluation of parties' satisfaction. The evaluation of the influence of RJ programmes on the criminal justice system, or on the social system in general, has also been the subject of several projects. Studies concerning re-offending/recidivism do exist in Europe, but they currently do not seem to be the highest priority for European research.

Despite the existence of evaluative work in Europe, it remains difficult to draw definite conclusions concerning the effects of RJ programmes, conclusions that could support policy development in the RJ field.[24] This is due to the diversity of the topics currently under evaluation, to the variable nature of the evaluated programmes and to the multiplicity of theoretical backgrounds and methodologies used by the researchers. The method applied to gather information in our study also added an extra level of uncertainty because information on theoretical and methodological backgrounds was not always available, therefore jeopardising the possibility of establishing firm conclusions. Taking this situation into account, it seems valuable to adopt a more reflective position with regard to the work accomplished. In order to do this, we will present the debates having taken place during the COST Action A21, around the design of this questionnaire in particular, and around the topic of the evaluation of RJ programmes in general. Both will help to discern some of the reasons for limits to data gathering and to reflect on the potential methodologies allowing for future evaluation and meta-evaluation of RJ programmes in Europe.

3   REFLECTIONS ON THE POTENTIALS OF THE DATA COLLECTION

The objectives of a better understanding of the (mainly qualitative) methodologies used in the RJ research field in Europe, and of identifying the gaps in this domain, could partly be reached by collecting and analysing ongoing or completed evaluations in various European countries. Thus, our gathering of evaluative research in the field of RJ helped to improve knowledge of research being undertaken and to give an overview of the kind of research developed in Europe. This work led also to the realisation that the evaluation of RJ could be looked upon from various starting points, from different theoretical and methodological options. In short, it provided an opportunity to better understand how researchers raised questions and envisioned problems. It provides an interesting resource when a researcher decides to start with or to accomplish the evaluation of RJ in

---

24   This is especially the case for the re-offending/recidivism studies that lack homogeneous conclusions.

Europe. It is worth mentioning, however, that for the representative nature of the completed and ongoing evaluative research projects in Europe, the database could still be improved, both at the quantitative and qualitative level.[25] The trends mentioned above are thus only valid at a certain moment in time since research is always evolving.

Nevertheless, as mentioned above, the initial aim of creating an 'objective overview' of the results of the evaluative research projects, from which conclusions could be drawn to support policy development in the RJ field, can hardly be considered as having been achieved in the framework of this research.

Some of the reasons for this shortcoming were probably the challenging working conditions and organisation of the COST Action programmes (which only fund researchers' travelling and meetings),[26] but also the variability of scientific and cultural backgrounds[27] of the members of the Working Group. Although the conditions provided by the COST programme were highly valuable in allowing researchers to meet face-to-face in order to deeply reflect on the perspective of meta-evaluation of RJ programmes in Europe, they also explain why the project has still to be considered as a 'work-in-progress'. And although the multi-disciplinary and multi-cultural background of the researchers were positive sources of thought and inspiration for debates, it at the same time increased the difficulties for the members to agree on the objectives and methodologies considered as valuable in the implementation of a meta-analysis of RJ programmes in Europe and to properly analyse the data gathered in this framework.

Epistemological and methodological questions have been the subject of many discussions within the Working Group from the start. For some participants, for example, the objective of a meta-evaluation essentially had to consist of sharing 'good practices' in terms of evaluation. For others, it had to 'look critically at the principles of evaluation' of RJ and 'to reflect on new models of evaluation'. For others still, it had to produce tangible 'proof' with respect to the effectiveness of RJ. Therefore, with such variable objectives, it is not surprising that difficulties arose rapidly in the design of a common questionnaire. Particularly for those aiming at critically studying the principles of evaluation and reflecting on evaluation mod-

---

25   Information from the research projects gathered may not be representative of all research carried out in Europe. This is firstly because these evaluative research projects focus mainly on particular effects of restorative justice, and, secondly, because only evaluative research from nine European countries has been collected. In addition, not all evaluations could be registered for 'western countries' that have extensive experience in the field of restorative justice. Furthermore, even though little evaluative research experience exists in Eastern European countries, this situation could change in the near future. Both elements imply a need for actualisation of the database.

26   Thus, funding of the 'research' in itself and the time really needed to perform proper and innovative work is not provided for within the COST programme; it is supposed to be funded at national level.

27   Our disciplinary backgrounds were law, criminology, sociology of law, policing, social anthropology and political sciences; and participants were French, German, Portuguese, Dutch, Italian, Norwegian, Bulgarian and Irish, although our common language, written and oral, is English. Research publications are however not always available in English, which caused difficulties when wanting to go in-depth into the analysis of theoretical and methodological positions, as well as in the secondary analysis of the results.

els, the criterion of selection of the researches to be gathered, were considered to be too restrictive. Indeed, according to them, the data collection only focused on 'some' effects of RJ programmes. These effects were mainly understood to be effects on re-offending and on parties' satisfaction.[28] However, to them, the effects of RJ programmes could not only be considered from the perspective of instrumental effects on people directly involved in RJ events. The understanding of symbolic effects at an institutional level, for example, should also deserve attention in the analysis of the acceptance of RJ programmes in various countries. In conclusion, to them, the data collection hindered the possibility of evaluating 'unintended effects' or 'effects not yet studied' but nevertheless deserves at least as much attention in the field of evaluative research. Many times, the objective of the questionnaire in itself has thus been questioned during the discussions of the Working Group.

In addition to the challenges related to the objectives of the data collection, the choice of the 'tool' to perform it was also the subject of many discussions. Some participants considered that the gathering of data and the potential for meta-analysis of RJ evaluations was too 'mechanistic' if it was only carried out through a questionnaire. For example, it is clear that when collecting completed or ongoing evaluations of RJ programmes in Europe, various people from several countries helped to gather these data. They often had to fit it into the pre-existing template of the questionnaire, diminishing therefore the richness of the answers and the possibility for accurate comparison.[29] The coding process showed indeed that it was sometimes difficult to compare various evaluative programmes only on the basis of the answers to the questionnaire since, often, it remained really unclear whether a recorded category covered another one sufficiently (cf. infra). Even if this problem is encountered by many sociological studies (also at a national level), it is obviously increased in studies at an international level, taking into account the multi-cultural, multi-lingual and multi-disciplinary background of the researchers and the variety of evaluative national contexts upon which they rest. Thus, because of a lack of accurate information on their theoretical and methodological backgrounds, it was difficult, without further information, to interpret with 'certainty' the data they had collected. Thus, if a meta-evaluation is carried out, access to the original reports is essential and authors should be contacted, if necessary, in order to correctly interpret the data (cf. infra). The challenging working conditions provided by the COST Action programme certainly restricted the possibilities for succeeding in such a large and extensive comparative study in the field of RJ in Europe.

---

28 In the initial scientific programme of the COST Action, these effects were identified as pertinent to analyse.

29 Some members of Working Group 1 summarised the main information and results of the evaluative research, often on the basis of information provided by authors of these studies or even by contact-persons gathering information in these countries. When no documents were available in English, these filters impeded a deeper understanding of the studies.

Thus, although it may seem as though this section focuses excessively on the specific conditions of working with a COST Action, important lessons can be learned from it for future RJ meta-evaluation programmes. Time and funding would certainly constitute the first essential working condition. While data gathering, analysis and comparative work have to be organised around methodological considerations, they also entail minimal material conditions. Both aspects are thus important issues at stake when thinking about developing meta-evaluative research in Europe.

4   PROSPECTS FOR A META-EVALUATION OF RJ PROGRAMMES IN EUROPE

Despite the problems regarding data collection not reaching the initial objectives, particularly its failure to provide results about the overall effects of RJ programmes that could be used for policy recommendations, the work was nevertheless worthwhile. Indeed, as mentioned, the data collection provided a good opportunity to get informed about some kinds of evaluative research developed in Europe and to identify gaps in the scientific European justice field, as well as to clarify potential models or strategies which could be investigated further if evaluative research were to be conducted in Europe. In this respect, it is worth emphasising that at least two different models of evaluation can be identified. Each model encompasses to some extent a particular objective, research strategy and methodology.[30]

In the first model, meta-evaluation of RJ programmes aims mainly to demonstrate its effectiveness (in particular in terms of re-offending/recidivism or in terms of the parties' satisfaction). The discourse associated with this model emphasises that evaluations of RJ are numerous but often insufficiently detailed and that researchers within RJ have a tendency to overestimate beneficial effects of mediation programmes.[31] According to this discourse, if a programme objectively demonstrates its merits using sound empirical measures, it has potential. Confidence in a kind of model or practice of RJ can then also only be justified after 'positive results have been replicated in a number of similar programmes'. This model thus implies a research strategy consisting of the identification of 'a core set of evaluation criteria' allowing for a systematic evaluation of RJ programmes: outcomes from specific intervention models must be tested on differ-

---

30   In another collective contribution, these various voices have also been expressed. See articles presented in the framework of the COST Action by Working Group 1 members and published in the *British Journal of Community Justice* (Dale & Hylde, 2008; Faget, 2008; Hartmann, 2008; Lazaro & Marques, 2008; Lemonne, 2008; Pemberton & Winkel, 2008; Williams, 2008). The publications illustrate quite well the different positions taken by the different members of this Working Group regarding evaluation. The term 'model' in this chapter implies rationalities held by the various actors.

31   It is often argued by the proponents of this model that claims about success stories of restorative justice are based on research protocols with inherent weaknesses or design flaws that limit the conclusions that can be validly drawn from a given set of outcome results (e.g. Latimer et al., 2001).

ent types of cases. Moreover, specific restorative interventions are believed to lead directly to certain effects.

This kind of approach has already been largely developed in the framework of the Campbell Collaboration in general and of the Campbell and Justice group in particular. This body implements meta-evaluative research on various themes in the field of crime and justice, i.e. compiling systematic reviews of various initiatives by synthesising the quantitative results from a large number of individual evaluations, collected from around the world (Weisburd et al., 2001). The difficulty with such a strategy of meta-evaluation is that individual evaluations are often of different programme types and on very different kinds of RJ cases. Therefore, the methodology used in the framework of such meta-evaluative research projects has to be quite specific. Research groups have to follow a particular protocol: a Scientific Maryland Scale (SMS) has been created to discriminate between studies on the basis of their methodological soundness. According to this scale, at least, an evaluation should employ experimental (randomly based trial) or at least quasi-experimental design (where the progress of one group of participants is measured against that of a matched comparison group) (Shadish et al., 2002).

This type of meta-evaluative research thus implies a focus on the effectiveness of only theoretically and methodologically comparable programmes, and therefore restricts the analysis of other available knowledge in other types of research. In the long run, it could unfortunately also normalise and standardise the evolution of evaluation models (and maybe of the RJ programmes themselves) for the purpose of further meta-evaluation. This is, for example, a risk incurred when suggestions are made in the European field to use protocols aiming at standardising measures of RJ programmes with the aim of meta-evaluating programmes on a European scale.

This methodology is also based on the idea that only the characteristics of the RJ programmes determine their impact, omitting to consider other potential factors such as, for example, the combined effects of restorative and other penal or social programmes. This model is based on the philosophy that the evaluation of RJ programmes can only be drawn from the commonalities they share, the assumption being that, at a certain level, 'evaluation' but also 'RJ' are universal concepts taking place in a 'universal penal and social system'. Therefore, it risks setting aside necessary, interesting and ontological questions about the evaluation of RJ at a European level.

In the debates of the Working Group, the discourse related to this 'positivist' model was developed in parallel with another discourse that can be associated to a 'relativist' (relational or dialogical) conception of meta-evaluation (Nelken, 1994).

The 'relativist' discourse questions whether favoured themes regarding the evaluation of the effects of RJ programmes have to be the satisfaction of the participants in mediation and the recidivism rates of offenders. This discourse highlights that this kind of research is now, and will in the future, inevitably be subject to methodological bias of greater or lesser importance.[32] Indeed, for both kinds of research, it is difficult to control bias due to the consensual nature of RJ programmes. In terms of satisfaction of the parties, for example, those who are most disappointed, or the most reluctant to take part in mediation, refuse to take part. The same is true for those who have decided to 'move on' and who do not wish to discuss the conflict any further. In terms of recidivism, the existence of 'dark numbers' prevents us from having any certitude about statistical results produced by individual studies. Recidivism only means that people have been caught once again committing an act that is illegal. In addition, the use of control groups to compare performance of the traditional system with restorative processes is not an easy task: the adoption of randomly based trial often collides with criminal legal procedural and ethical principles. This discourse also emphasises the inappropriateness of trying to analyse inputs and outputs of RJ without looking at the system in which it takes place.

According to the relativist (or relational or dialogical) model, RJ programmes as well as their evaluations should thus of necessity be recast in the largest analysis of the political, economical and social context in which specific scientific knowledge is produced. As Passeron (1991) argues, the explanation in social sciences is always historically and socially oriented and the specificity of any sociological reasoning is to come and go between historical (and social) contexts and experimental reasoning. This model also argues that, in order to perform valuable analysis of RJ programmes, it is simply necessary to go beyond the simple logic of 'proof' (to prove that RJ produces good results for an institution or for individuals) and to place ourselves in a logic of 'discovery': in identifying the 'unexpected' or 'perverse' consequences of VOM or conferencing, in envisioning new themes of research, in discovering new ways to perform evaluations. In such a model, the motivation to carry out meta-evaluations of RJ at a European level should not only be to 'prove' the instrumental effectiveness of mediation or of conferencing in order to gain the support of the political and judicial decision makers or of the public,[33] it should also consist of considering their unintended and symbolic effects.

This model of meta-evaluative research is thus based on the idea that the terms 'evaluation' or 'RJ' are not 'universalised' or 'standardised'. A meta-evaluation should thus allow for the discovery of the reasons for *discrepancy* between conceptions, to learn from the *diversity* of approaches. The real added value of a data collection and analysis of RJ evaluations performed at a European level would thus help researchers to think about theory and practices and to question their relationships with their own subjects of research in illuminating 'dissimilarities'

---

32   This discourse also emphasises that research on RJ programmes in Europe is more descriptive than evaluative and unequally developed in European countries. A significant number of so-called evaluative research projects are indeed influenced by organisational features of victim-offender mediation and conferencing, by the kind of communication used between participants and mediators and by the number of agreements signed without always making them problematical.

33   No scientist has ever been able to prove the effectiveness of prison in preventing recidivism, yet imprisonment has universally been adopted as a reaction to illegal acts.

and sharpening 'contrasts'. It should allow for apprehending the complexity of the issues at stake and the various grounds on which RJ programmes and evaluations are built in Europe. At a European level, meta-evaluations in the field of RJ, from a relativist perspective, could thus help to perform a critical analysis of the concept of RJ itself, reflecting on its various (and sometimes unintended) effects, studying further potential offender or victim issues, etc. Such a strategy could, according to its proponents, better highlight the political decisions regarding RJ than the ambition to only statistically 'measure' the instrumental effects of VOM and FGC programmes.

5   To conclude …

This chapter described the design and implementation of a questionnaire which was used as a tool aimed at gathering an integrated overview of completed or ongoing research on RJ programmes in Europe. Several results from extra-European researches were also included for the sake of comparison.

After describing the results and limits inherent to the analysis of the database, this chapter addressed the potential of meta-evaluation in the field of European RJ research. Two important reasons were identified which prevented a thorough analysis of the results gathered in the database, especially with regard to the effects of RJ programmes: first, the particular working conditions of the COST Action, and second, the various epistemological and methodological approaches of the Working Group 1 members, especially when dealing with the objectives and methodologies required to assess the meta-evaluation.

In this respect, it is worth mentioning that two different models of evaluation were debated within the Working Group: a 'positivist' and a 'relativist' or relational (dialogical) model. The first model envisions evaluation of some specific instrumental effects, mainly through experimental and quasi-experimental methods and quantitative analysis. The second model puts the main emphasis on the fact that RJ policies and programmes are often a compromise between conflicting values and, therefore, that decisions on which they rest in fact hide a variety of unanswered questions which have a profound impact on their implementation. As a result, the relativist model is more suitable to deconstruct the references, norms and issues at stake that led to the political representation and implementation of RJ in a specific country.

Both models also refer to a particular vision of the relationship between 'science' and 'politics'. In the positivist model, the 'scientific character' of the model supports the ideal of political neutrality of evaluation. In contrast, the relativist model does not envision the evaluation of RJ univocally. Such an evaluative process can, in that view, only be implemented in reference to a given social and political context, in which actors debate various interests, express preferences and define aims with regard to costs and effects of a particular policy. According to this model, meta-evaluation of RJ programmes puts a heavy emphasis on the complexity of phenomena, both in terms of characteristics and effects.

Since these models imply different objectives, research strategies and methodologies, a challenge for future research devoted to meta-evaluation in Europe is to define their goals and limits (see for comparative work, Nelken, 1994). A fundamental exercise to be carried out when performing empirical work should be to evaluate similarities and/or differences between both approaches and to assess to what extent they can be combined within a unique strategy.

REFERENCES

Aertsen, I. and Peters, T. (1998a) 'Mediation and RJ in Belgium', *European Journal on Criminal Policy and Research*, 6(4), pp.507-525.

Aertsen, I. and Peters, T. (1998b) 'Mediation for reparation: The victim's perspective', in Fattah, E. and Peters, T. (eds.), *Support for crime victims in a comparative perspective* (Leuven: Leuven University Press), pp. 229-251.

Crawford, A. and Newburn, T. (2003) *Youth Offending and Restorative Justice* (Cullompton: Willan Publishing).

Dale, G. and Hydle, I. (2008) 'Challenging the Evaluation of Norwegian Restorative Justice Experiences', *British Journal of Community Justice*, 6(2), pp. 69-76.

Daly, K. (2001) 'Conferencing in Australia and New Zealand. Variations, Research Findings and Prospects', in Morris, A. and Maxwell, G. (eds.) *Restorative justice for Juveniles. Conferencing, Mediation & Circles* (Portland: Hart Publishing), pp. 59-84. Available at: www.aic.gov.au/rjustice/sajj

Dignan, J. (1992) 'Repairing the damage: Can Reparation be Made to Work in the Service of Diversion', *The British Journal of Criminology*, 32(4), pp. 453-472.

Dölling, D. and Hartmann, A, (2003) 'Reoffending after victim-offender mediation in juvenile court proceedings', in Weitekamp, E. and Kerner, H.-J. (eds.) *Restorative justice in context. International practice and directions* (Cullompton: Willan Publishing), pp. 208-228.

Elonheimo, H. (2004) 'Restoratiivinen oikeus ja suomalainen sovittelu', *Oikeus*, 2/2004, pp. 179-199 [Journal "Justice"].

Elonheimo, H. (2003) *Restorative Justice Theory and Finnish Mediation Practices*, paper presented to the 3rd Annual Conference of the European Society of Criminology, NSfK's 45th Research Seminar, 27-30 August 2003, Scandinavian Research Council for Criminology, pp. 72-77 (Helsinki).

Eskelin, O. and Iivari, J. (2002) 'Victim-Offender Mediation with juvenile offenders in Europe: The case of Finland', in *Victim-Offender Mediation: Organization and Practice in the Juvenile Justice Systems*, Bologna, Italy: Research Institute on Judicial Systems, National Research Council (IRSIG – CNR). Available at www.irsig.cnr.it/reports/testi_reports

European Forum for Victim-Offender Mediation and Restorative Justice (ed.) (2000) *Victim-offender Mediation in Europe. Making Restorative Justice Work* (Leuven: Leuven University Press).

Faget, J. (2008) 'Epistemological Reflections on the Evaluation of Restorative Justice Practices', *British Journal of Community Justice*, 6(2), pp. 77-83.

Fercello, C., and Umbreit, M. (1999) *Client Evaluation of Family Group Conferencing* (St. Paul: Centre for Restorative Justice and Mediation, University of Minnesota).

Griffith, M. (1999) *The Implementation of Group Conferencing in Juvenile Justice in Victoria, Restoration for Victims of Crime Conference* (Australia, Australian Institute of Criminology). Available at: www.aic.gov.au/conferences

Haidar, A., Leirer, H., Pelikan, C. and Pilgram, A. (eds.) (1988), *Konflikte regeln statt strafen! Über einen Modellversuch in der österreichischen Jugendgerichtsbarkeit* (Wien: Verlag für Gesellschaftskritik).

Hammerschick, W., Pelikan, C. and Pilgram, A. (1994) 'Soziale Konflikte vor Gericht und im Außergerichtlichen Tatausgleich – eine Gegenüberstellung', in Hammerschick, W., Pelikan, C. and Pilgram, A. (eds.), *Ausweg aus dem Strafrecht – Der außergerichtliche Tatausgleich*, Jahrbuch für Rechts- und Kriminalsoziologie '94 (Baden-Baden: Nomos), pp. 95-129.

Hartmann, A. (2008) 'Federal Statistics of Victim-Offender Mediation in Germany', *British Journal of Community Justice*, 6(2), pp. 55-68.

Hayes, H. (2005) 'Assessing Reoffending in Restorative Justice Conferences', *The Australian and New Zealand Journal of Criminology*, 38(1), pp. 77-101. Available at: http://www.aic.gov.au/rjustice/docs/2005-06-hayes.pdf

Hayes H. and Daly, K. (2004) 'Conferencing and Re-offending in Queensland, Australia', *The Australian and New Zealand Journal of Criminology*, 37(2), pp. 167-199. Available at: http://www.aic.gov.au/rjustice/docs/2004-08-hayes.pdf

Hydle, I. and Hasund, I.K. (2004) 'Evaluating a Norwegian RJ project: mediation as supplement to punishment in cases of serious violence', *Newsletter of the European Forum for Victim-Offender Mediation and Restorative Justice*, 5(2), pp. 1-3.

Hydle, I. (2006) 'An Anthropological contribution to peace and conflict resolution studies', *Journal of Contemporary Justice Review*, 9(3), pp. 257-267.

Iivari, J. and Flinck, A. (2004) The evaluation report has been published in *Fin-Soc Evaluation Reports*, 5/2004 (Helsinki). See also www.stakes.fi/finsoc (with English abstract).

Järvinen, S. (1992) *Rikkosten Sovitellu Suomessa* English summary in Publication Number 15, National Research Institute of Legal Policy.

Kilchling, M. and Löschnig-Gspandl, M. (1998) 'Vergleichende Perspektiven zum Täter-Opfer-Ausgleich in Baden-Württemberg und der Steiermark – Ausblick auf ein vergleichendes empirisches Forschungsprojekt', in Friedrich-Ebert-Stiftung (ed.) *Der Täter-Opfer-Ausgleich (TOA): Moderner Beitrag zur Konfliktregulierung und zur Sicherung des sozialen Friedens* (Potsdam: Eigenverlag). Available at: www.gpk-ev.de/toa.htm

Latimer, J., Dowden, C. and Muise, D. (2001) *The Effectiveness of Restorative Justice Processes: A Meta-Analysis* (Canada, Department of Justice).

Lazaro, J. and Marques F. (2008) 'What to do with these Victims?', *British Journal of Community Justice*, 6(2), pp. 93-97.

Lemonne, A. (2008) 'Comparing the Implementation of Restorative Justice in Various Countries: Purpose, Potential and Caveats', *British Journal of Community Justice*, 6(2), pp. 43-53.

Lins, J. (1998) *Der Außergerichtliche Tatausgleich bei Jugendlichen* (Linz: University of Linz).

Luke, G. and Lind, B. (2002) 'Reducing Juvenile Crime: Conferencing versus Court', *Crime and Justice Bulletin: Contemporary Issues in Crime and Justice*, 69, pp. 1-20. Available at: http://www.lawlink.nsw.gov.au/lawlink/bocsar/ll_bocsar.nsf/pages/bocsar_pub_cjb

Maxwell, G. and Morris, A. (2001) 'Putting Restorative Justice into Practice for Adult Offenders', *The Howard Journal of Criminal Justice*, 40(1), pp. 55-69.

McCold, P. (2008) 'Protocols for Evaluating Restorative Justice Programmes', *British Journal of Community Justice*, 6(2), pp. 9-28.

McGarrell, E. (2001) *Restorative Justice Conferences as an early response to Young Offenders*, Juvenile Justice Bulletin, Washington DC, Office of Juvenile Justice and Delinquency Prevention, US Department of Justice. Available at: http://www.ncjrs.gov/pdffiles1/ojjdp/187769.pdf

Mestitz A. (2008) 'Organisational Features of Victim-Offender Mediation with Youth Offenders in Europe', *British Journal of Community Justice*, 6(2), pp. 29-42.

Mestitz, A. and Ghetti, S. (eds.) (2005) *Victim-Offender Mediation with Youth Offenders in Europe* (Dordrecht: Kluwer International).

Mielityinen, I. (1999) *Rikos ja sovittelu. Valikoituminen, merkitys ja uusintarikollisuus [Crime and mediation. Selection of Cases, the Significance and Meaning of Mediation to the Participants, and Reoffending]*, National Research Institute of Legal Policy, Publications No. 167 (Helsinki). Available at: www.om.fi/optula/24878.htm

Miers, D. (ed.) (2001) *An International Review of RJ* (London: Home Office).

Miers, D. (2006) 'La justice réparatrice en Europe : état des développements et de la recherche', *Les Cahiers de la Justice* (Paris: Dalloz), pp. 94-110.

Miers, D. and Willemsens, J. (2004) *Mapping Restorative Justice: Developments in 25 European Countries* (Leuven: European Forum for Restorative Justice).

Miers, D., Maguire, M., Goldie, S., Sharpe, K., Hale, C., Netten, A., Uglow, S., Doolin, K., Hallam, A., Enterkin, J. and Newburn, T. (2001) *An Exploratory Evaluation of RJ Schemes*, Crime Reduction Research Series, Paper 9, Available at: www.homeoffice.gov.uk/rds

Nelken, D. (1994) 'Whom can we trust? The Future of Comparative Criminology', in Nelken, D. (ed.) *The Future of Criminology* (London: Sage Publications), pp. 220-243.

Nugent, W., Williams, M. and Umbreit, M. (2003) 'Participation in VOM and the Prevalence and Severity of Subsequent Delinquent Behaviour: A Meta-Analysis', *Utah Law Review*, p.137 – Available at: http://www.law.utah.edu/_webfiles/academic/journals/utahlawreview/2003_1/06Nugent.pdf

O'Dwyer, K. (2001) *Restorative Justice Initiatives in the Garda Síochána – Evaluation of the Pilot Programme*, Garda Research Unit Report 4/01.

O'Dwyer, K. (2005) *Evaluation of the police restorative cautioning programme in Ireland*, Report in progress.

O'Mahony, D., Chapman, T. and Doak, J. (2002) *Restorative cautioning: a study of police-based cautioning pilots in Northern Ireland*, Northern Ireland Office Research and Statistical Series: Report No. 4. Available at: www.nio.gov.uk

Passeron, J.-C. (1991) *Le raisonnement sociologique. L'espace non poppérien du raisonnement naturel* (Paris: Nathan).

Pelikan, C. (2002) 'Victim-Offender-Mediation in Domestic Violence Cases – A Comparison of the Effects of Criminal Law Intervention: the Penal Process and Mediation. Doing Qualitative Research', *Forum Qualitative Sozialforschung / Forum: Qualitative Social Research* [On-line Journal], 3(1). Available at: http://www.qualitative-research.net/fqs-texte/a2324/1-02pelikan-e.htm

Pelikan, C. and Hoenisch, B. (2000) *Die Wirkungsweise strafrechtlicher Interventionen bei Gewaltstraftaten in Paarbeziehungen*. Research Report (Vienna: Institute for the Sociology of Law and Criminology).

Pemberton, A., Winkel, F.-W. and Groenhuijsen, M.S. (2008) 'Evaluating victim experiences in restorative justice', *British Journal of Community Justice*, 6(2), pp. 99-119.

Pondaven, M. (2006) 'Pourquoi inscrire l'évaluation des activités et de la qualité des prestations dans les principes de l'évaluation des politiques publiques', *Journal du droit des jeunes*, 258, pp. 40-46.

Proposal for a COST Action (2002) *Restorative justice developments in Europe* (Leuven/Brussels).

Salonen, J. and Iivari, J. (2004) *Evaluation of the 'Let's Talk – Social Mediation for Refugee Communities in Europe' Project*, IOM. Available at: www.iom.fi/letstalk/doc/LetsTalk_Evaluation.pdf

Shadish, W, Cook, T. and Campbell, D. (2002) *Experimental and Quasi-experimental Designs for Generalised Causal Inference* (Boston: Houghton Mifflin).

Sherman, L. and Strang, H. (2007) *Restorative justice: the evidence* (London: The Smith Institute).

Schütz, H. (1999) 'Die Rückfallshäufigkeit nach einem Außergerichtlichen Tatausgleich bei Erwachsenen', *Österreichische Richterzeitung*, 77, pp. 161-166.

Strang, H. (2002) *Repair or Revenge: Victims and Restorative Justice* (Oxford: Oxford University Press).

Takala, J.-P. (1998a) *Mediation and expression of moral emotions*, Finland, Publications No. 151 (Helsinki).

Takala, J.-P. (1998b) *Moraalitunteet rikosten sovittelussa*. Oikeuspoliittisen tutkimuslaitoksen julkaisuja 151, (Helsinki). Available at: www.om.fi/optula/24881.htm. English summary Available at: www.om.fi/optula/4878.htm.

Umbreit, M. and Coates, R. (1999) 'Victim-Offender Mediation Empirical Studies Analysis', *Research and Resources Review*, 1(1) (St. Paul: Centre for RJ and Peacemaking, University of Minnesota). Available at: http://2ssw.che.umm.edu/rjp

Warner, S., Netten, A. and Knapp, M. (1992) Making Amends: Justice for Victims and Offenders: An Evaluation of the SACRO Reparation and Mediation Project (Hampshire: Ashgate Publishing).

Weisburd, D., Lum, C. and Petrosino, A. (2001) 'Does research design affect study outcomes in criminal justice?', *Annals of the American Academy of Political and Social Sciences*, 578, pp. 50-100.

Williams, B. (2008) 'European Perspectives on the Evaluation of Restorative Justice: Empathy, Offending and Attitudes, A Promising New Avenue for Research?', *British Journal of Community Justice*, 6(2), pp. 85-92.

Wilcox, A., Young, R., and Hoyle, C. (2004) *Two-Year resanctioning study: a comparison of restorative and traditional cautions*, online report No. 57/04. Available at: www.homeoffice.gov.uk/rds/

Wynne, J. and Brown, I. (1998) 'Can Mediation Cut Reoffending?', *Probation Journal*, 45, pp. 21-26.

Young, R. and Goold, B. (1999) 'Restorative police cautioning in Aylesbury- from degrading to reintegrative shaming ceremonies', *Criminal Law Review*, pp. 126-138.

ANNEX

References of the research reports included in the database

European research

1. Accompanying research of a pilot project: 'Out-of-court conflict resolution in juvenile justice', Austria
   Haidar, A., Leirer, H., Pelikan, C. and Pilgram, A. (eds.) (1988), *Konflikte regeln statt strafen! Über einen Modellversuch in der österreichischen Jugendgerichtsbarkeit* (Wien: Verlag für Gesellschaftskritik).

2. 'Out-of-court-conflict resolution in general criminal law', Austria
   Hammerschick, W., Pelikan, C. and Pilgram, A. (1994) 'Soziale Konflikte vor Gericht und im Außergerichtlichen Tatausgleich – eine Gegenüberstellung', in Hammerschick, W., Pelikan, C. and Pilgram, A. (eds.), *Ausweg aus dem Strafrecht – Der außergerichtliche Tatausgleich*, Jahrbuch für Rechts- und Kriminalsoziologie '94 (Baden-Baden: Nomos), pp. 95-129.

3. Empirical qualitative study of the efficacy of VOM in domestic violence cases as compared to the criminal procedure, Austria
   Pelikan, C. (2002) 'Victim-Offender-Mediation in Domestic Violence Cases – A Comparison of the Effects of Criminal Law Intervention: the Penal Process and Mediation. Doing Qualitative Research', *Forum Qualitative Sozialforschung / Forum: Qualitative Social Research* [On-line Journal], 3(1). Available at: http://www.qualitative-research.net/fqs-texte/a2324/1-02pelikan-e.htm
   Pelikan, C. and Hoenisch, B. (2000) *Die Wirkungsweise strafrechtlicher Interventionen bei Gewaltstraftaten in Paarbeziehungen. Research Report* (Vienna: Institute for the Sociology of Law and Criminology).

4. Comparative empirical research in Germany (Baden-Württemberg) and Austria (Styria)

Kilchling, M. and Löschnig-Gspandl, M. (1998) 'Vergleichende Perspektiven zum Täter-Opfer-Ausgleich in Baden-Württemberg und der Steiermark – Ausblick auf ein vergleichendes empirisches Forschungsprojekt', in Friedrich-Ebert-Stiftung (ed.) *Der Täter-Opfer-Ausgleich (TOA): Moderner Beitrag zur Konfliktregulierung und zur Sicherung des sozialen Friedens* (Potsdam: Eigenverlag). Available at: www.gpk-ev.de/toa.htm

5. Empirical research on the satisfaction of victims concerning the VOM procedure and its outcome, Austria
   Altweger, A. and Hitzl, E. (2000) *Kundenzufriedenheit der Geschädigten im ATA Innsbruck'* (Innsbruck: Akademie für Sozialarbeit).

6. Empirical research on victim and offender satisfaction with VOM procedure and the sustainability of the outcome in the field of juvenile justice, Austria
   Lins, J. (1998) *Der Außergerichtliche Tatausgleich bei Jugendlichen* (Linz: University of Linz).

7. Empirical research comparing recidivism rates of offenders having participated in VOM and of offenders having received a fine, Austria
   Schütz, H. (1999) 'Die Rückfallshäufigkeit nach einem Außergerichtlichen Tatausgleich bei Erwachsenen', *Österreichische Richterzeitung*, 77, pp. 161-166.

8. VOM with adult offenders in Belgium
   Aertsen, I. and Peters, T. (1998a) 'Mediation and RJ in Belgium', *European Journal on Criminal Policy and Research*, 6(4), pp.507-525.
   Aertsen, I. and Peters, T. (1998b) 'Mediation for reparation: The victim's perspective', in Fattah, E. and Peters, T. (eds.), *Support for crime victims in a comparative perspective* (Leuven: Leuven University Press), pp. 229-251.

9. RJ Theory and Mediation Practices in Finland
   Elonheimo, H. (2004) 'Restoratiivinen oikeus ja suomalainen sovittelu', *Oikeus*, 2/2004, pp. 179-199 [Journal "Justice"].
   Shorter English version: Henrik Elonheimo (2003) *Restorative Justice Theory and Finnish Mediation Practices*, paper presented to the 3rd Annual Conference of the European Society of Criminology, NSfK's 45th Research Seminar, 27-30 August 2003, Scandinavian Research Council for Criminology, pp. 72-77 (Helsinki).

10. Mediation in practice in Finland and assessment of mediation as alternative to the criminal justice system
    Järvinen, S. (1992) *Rikkosten Sovitellu Suomessa* English summary in Publication Number 15, National Research Institute of Legal Policy.

11. Victim-offender mediation in cases of intimate partner violence, Finland
    Iivari, J. and Flinck, A. (2004) The evaluation report has been published in *FinSoc Evaluation Reports*, 5/2004 (Helsinki). See also www.stakes.fi/finsoc (with English abstract).

12. Social Mediation for Refugee Communities in Europe, Finland
    Salonen, J. and Iivari, J. (2004) *Evaluation of the 'Let's Talk – Social Mediation for Refugee Communities in Europe' Project*, IOM. Available at: www.iom.fi/letstalk/doc/LetsTalk_Evaluation.pdf

13. Children in VOM in Finland
    Eskelin, O. and Iivari, J. (2002) 'Victim-Offender Mediation with juvenile offenders in Europe: The case of Finland', in *Victim-Offender Mediation: Organization and Practice in the Juvenile Justice Systems*, Bologna, Italy: Research Institute on Judicial Systems, National Research Council (IRSIG – CNR). Available at www.irsig.cnr.it/reports/testi_reports
14. The Presentation of Domestic Violence Mediation in Finnish Newspapers
    Heikkilä, H-K (2003) *The Presentation of Domestic Violence Mediation in Finnish Newspapers*. Stakes, Aiheita 10/2003 (Helsinki).
15. Mediation and expression of moral emotions, Finland
    Takala, J.-P. (1998a) *Mediation and expression of moral emotions*, Finland, Publications No. 151 (Helsinki).
    Takala, J.-P. (1998b) *Moraalitunteet rikosten sovittelussa*. Oikeuspoliittisen tutkimuslaitoksen julkaisuja 151, (Helsinki). Available at: www.om.fi/optula/24881.htm. English summary Available at: www.om.fi/optula/4878.htm.
16. Crime and mediation: selection of cases, the significance and meaning of mediation to the participants, and re-offending (Finland)
    Mielityinen, I. (1999) *Rikos ja sovittelu. Valikoituminen, merkitys ja uusintarikollisuus [Crime and mediation. Selection of Cases, the Significance and Meaning of Mediation to the Participants, and Reoffending]*, National Research Institute of Legal Policy, Publications No. 167 (Helsinki). Available at: www.om.fi/optula/24878.htm
17. Examination of re-offending rates after participation in victim offender mediation, Germany
    Dölling, D. and Hartmann, A, (2003) 'Reoffending after victim-offender mediation in juvenile court proceedings', in Weitekamp, E. and Kerner, H.-J. (eds.) *Restorative justice in context. International practice and directions* (Cullompton: Willan Publishing), pp. 208-228.
18. Victim-offender mediation in serious violence cases, Norway
    Hydle, I. and Hasund, I.K. (2004) 'Evaluating a Norwegian RJ project: mediation as supplement to punishment in cases of serious violence', *Newsletter of the European Forum for Victim-Offender Mediation and RJ*, 5(2), pp. 1-3.
    Hydle, I. (2006) 'An Anthropological contribution to peace and conflict resolution studies', *Journal of Contemporary Justice Review*, 9(3), pp. 257-267.
19. Evaluation of Restorative Justice pilot programme of the police in Ireland
    O'Dwyer, K. (2001) *RJ Initiatives in the Garda Síochána – Evaluation of the Pilot Programme*, Garda Research Unit Report 4/01.
20. Evaluation of the police restorative cautioning programme in Ireland
    O'Dwyer, K. (2005) *Evaluation of the police restorative cautioning programme in Ireland*, Report in progress.
21. Restorative cautioning: a study of police-based cautioning pilots in Northern Ireland
    O'Mahony, D., Chapman, T. and Doak, J. (2002) *Restorative cautioning: a study of police-based cautioning pilots in Northern Ireland*, Northern Ireland Office Research and Statistical Series: Report No. 4. Available at: www.nio.gov.uk

22. Evaluation of mediation and reparation schemes in Scotland
Warner, S., Netten, A. and Knapp, M. (1992) *Making Amends: Justice for Victims and Offenders: An Evaluation of the SACRO Reparation and Mediation Project* (Hampshire: Ashgate Publishing).

23. An exploratory evaluation of seven RJ schemes in UK
Miers, D., Maguire, M., Goldie, S., Sharpe, K., Hale, C., Netten, A., Uglow, S., Doolin, K., Hallam, A., Enterkin, J. and Newburn, T. (2001) *An Exploratory Evaluation of RJ Schemes*, Crime Reduction Research Series, Paper 9, Available at: www.homeoffice.gov.uk/rds

24. Evaluation of pilot programme for referral orders and youth offender panels, UK
Crawford, A. and Newburn, T. (2003) *Youth Offending and Restorative Justice* (Cullompton: Willan Publishing).

25. Evaluation of Kettering Adult Reparation Bureau – a pre-trial diversion scheme, UK
Dignan, J. (1992) 'Repairing the damage: Can Reparation be Made to Work in the Service of Diversion', *The British Journal of Criminology*, 32(4), pp. 453-472.

26. Impact of Restorative cautioning: findings from a reconviction study, UK
Wilcox, A., Young, R., and Hoyle, C. (2004) *Two-Year resanctioning study: a comparison of restorative and traditional cautions*, online report No. 57/04. Available at: www.homeoffice.gov.uk/rds/

27. Evaluation of the impact of the Leeds Reparation scheme on re-offending, UK
Wynne, J. and Brown, I. (1998) 'Can Mediation Cut Reoffending?', *Probation Journal*, 45, pp. 21-26.

28. Small scale study of police cautioning in Aylesbury, UK
Young, R. and Goold, B. (1999) 'Restorative police cautioning in Aylesbury - from degrading to reintegrative shaming ceremonies', *Criminal Law Review*, pp. 126-138.

29. Evaluation of criminal conflict schemes in Leeds and Coventry, UK
Umbreit, M. and Roberts, A. (1997) 'VOM in England: An assessment of two programs', in Pisapia, G. and Antonucci, D. (eds), *The Promise of Mediation* (Milan: CEDAM), pp. 63-83.

Non-European research
30. Evaluation of RJ conferencing in Australia
Daly, K. (2001) 'Conferencing in Australia and New Zealand. Variations, Research Findings and Prospects', in Morris, A. and Maxwell, G. (eds) *Restorative justice for Juveniles. Conferencing, Mediation & Circles* (Portland: Hart Publishing), pp. 59-84. Available at: www.aic.gov.au/rjustice/sajj

31. Assessing re-offending in RJ cautions – a re-analysis of McCold and Wachtel's data
Hayes, H. (2005) 'Assessing Reoffending in Restorative Justice Conferences', *The Australian and New Zealand Journal of Criminology*, 38(1), pp. 77-101. Available at: http://www.aic.gov.au/rjustice/docs/2005-06-hayes.pdf

32. Assessment of re-offending rates in two schemes in Australia
Maxwell, G. and Morris, A. (2001) 'Putting Restorative Justice into Practice for Adult Offenders', *The Howard Journal of Criminal Justice*, 40(1), pp. 55-69.

33. Review of RJ experiments in Canberra with emphasis on the victim's perspective, Australia
Strang, H. (2002) *Repair or Revenge: Victims and Restorative Justice* (Oxford: Oxford University Press).

34. Evaluation of the impact of RISE on re-offending, Australia
Sherman, L, Strang, H. and Woods, D. (2000) *Recidivism Patterns in Canberra Reintegrative Shaming Experiment (Rise)* (Canberra: Centre for RJ, Research School of Social Sciences, Australian National University). Available at: www. aic.gov.au

35. Findings of three studies examining the implementation of group conferencing in the juvenile justice system in Victoria, Australia
Griffith, M. (1999) *The Implementation of Group Conferencing in Juvenile Justice in Victoria, Restoration for Victims of Crime Conference* (Australia, Australian Institute of Criminology). Available at: www.aic.gov.au/conferences

36. A comparison of conferencing vs. court as a means of reducing juvenile crime in New South Wales, Australia
Luke, G. and Lind, B. (2002) 'Reducing Juvenile Crime: Conferencing versus Court', *Crime and Justice Bulletin: Contemporary Issues in Crime and Justice*, 69, pp. 1-20. Available at: http://www.lawlink.nsw.gov.au/lawlink/bocsar/ll_bocsar.nsf/pages/bocsar_pub_cjb

37. Evaluation of the impact of conferencing on re-offending in Queensland, Australia
Hayes H. and Daly, K. (2004) 'Conferencing and Re-offending in Queensland, Australia', *The Australian and New Zealand Journal of Criminology*, 37(2), pp. 167-199. Available at: http://www.aic.gov.au/rjustice/docs/2004-08-hayes.pdf

38. Client evaluation of family group conferencing at 12 sites in Minnesota, USA
Fercello, C., and Umbreit, M. (1999) *Client Evaluation of Family Group Conferencing* (St. Paul: Centre for Restorative Justice and Mediation, University of Minnesota).

39. Analysis of VOM in four sites, USA
Umbreit, M. and Coates, R. (1999) 'Victim-Offender Mediation Empirical Studies Analysis', *Research and Resources Review*, 1(1) (St. Paul: Centre for RJ and Peacemaking, University of Minnesota). Available at: http://2ssw.che.umm.edu/rjp

40. Examining the processes and outcomes of RJ conferences as an early response to young offenders, USA
McGarrell, E. (2001) *RJ Conferences as an early response to Young Offenders*, Juvenile Justice Bulletin, Washington DC, Office of Juvenile Justice and Delinquency Prevention, US Department of Justice. Available at: http://www.ncjrs.gov/pdffiles1/ojjdp/187769.pdf

41. A meta-analysis of the impact of Restorative Justice schemes on recidivism
Latimer, J., Dowden, C. and Muise, D. (2001) *The Effectiveness of Restorative Justice Processes: A Meta-Analysis* (Canada, Department of Justice).
42. Participation in VOM and the prevalence of subsequent delinquent behaviour: A meta-analysis
Nugent, W., Williams, M. and Umbreit, M. (2003) 'Participation in VOM and the Prevalence and Severity of Subsequent Delinquent Behaviour: A Meta-Analysis', *Utah Law Review*, p.137 – Available at: http://www.law.utah.edu/_webfiles/academic/journals/utahlawreview/2003_1/06Nugent.pdf

3 Out-of-court but close to justice

Empirical research on restorative justice in Austria

Christa Pelikan

1   INTRODUCTION

1.1   *Context: state of affairs*[1]

1.1.1   The scope and the importance of victim-offender mediation in Austria
In Austria, victim-offender mediation [VOM] is a part of the criminal procedure and it is applied nationwide for juvenile and adult offenders that have been
brought to the notice of the state prosecutors. It is a diversionary practice, with
the state prosecutors acting as the gatekeepers and them exercising discretion as
to whether to refer a case to the VOM service. The VOM services are a branch of
the association *Neustart. Neustart* – the former Association for Probation Assistance and Social Work – is the agency entrusted with the task of organising and
conducting VOM. It does so in cooperation with the state prosecutors' office, but
according to its own internal professional rules with regard to mediation. Recruitment, training and professional guidance rest exclusively with the association.
What follows are a few figures demonstrating the importance of VOM in relation
to other measures meted out by the criminal procedure. The total number of
suspected persons referred to the bureaus of the 'ATA' (*Auszergerichtlicher Tatausgleich* – the Austrian version of VOM) in the year 2001 was almost 9,000, and
about 8,800 in 2002 according to ATA documentation. In a study based on court
and state prosecutors' registers by Arno Pilgram (2001) there were 7,837 cases in
the year 2000. A little more than a quarter concerned juvenile cases. The VOM
cases amounted to a little less than one-fifth of all the cases that were diverted
under the new 'Diversion Package', diversion making up 26% of all responses to
crime at state prosecutor and court level.[2] All kinds of measures/sanctions taken
together, the percentage of VOM (4.7%) was higher than that of unconditional
prison sentences (2.8%).
Since 1997 there has been a marked reduction in referrals to VOM for young
persons. This trend became even more pronounced in 2002 and continued
in the year 2003. The number of referrals of adult suspects increased steadily
between 2001 and 2005 and has now – after a slight decrease in 2006 – reached

---

1   We include figures up to the year 2006.
2   The diversion package consists of (1) a fine, (2) probation with or without probation assistance, (3)
     community service, and (4) ATA.

a total number of 7,028 cases. Altogether 8,502 cases were referred in 2006, with VOM now accounting for about 18% of all diversionary measures taken in 2006. Another indicator of the role and importance of ATA is the fact that, in the field of juvenile justice, there were 270 unconditional prison sentences compared to 1,591 juveniles referred to VOM. In the year 2006, the majority of conflicts dealt with were 'situational conflicts', i.e. offences that stem from a one-off confrontation, typically quarrels, brawls, or assaults in public spaces that result in minor, or even more severe physical injury (almost 60% of juvenile and about 43% of the adult cases). For adults, this category is followed by partnership violence cases (24%). An additional 9% of cases concern disputes between family members and relatives, and another 16% are conflicts within social circles, meaning between friends and acquaintances. Neighbourhood conflicts account for only 7% of all cases. For juveniles, about 14% of the cases originated in conflicts in schools; conflicts within social circles, mostly with friends, amount to 16% (figures calculated on the basis of the Annual Activity Report of Neustart of 2006, Proyer and Wurmbrand, 2006).

1.1.2   Legal situation

On 1 January 2000 the amendment to the Code of Criminal Procedure – mainly consisting of a 'diversion package' – came into force. The practice of VOM in Austria is now based on §90 *Strafprozessordnung* (StPO)[3] that permits the state prosecutor to drop a charge[4] when the offender takes responsibility for the act, shows readiness to confront its causes, and makes an effort to compensate the victim in any way that seems appropriate, and/or undertakes to refrain from behaviour that led to the offence. The injured party should participate in the mediation procedure, insofar that he/she is willing to do so. In any case, the injured party has to agree to compensation.

The distinction that still exists between the practice concerning young offenders (age 14 to 18) and adult offenders pertains to the scope of offenders included. As with juveniles in general, penalties are half that for adults and therefore the offences that can be referred to VOM – and have in fact to be considered for referral by the state prosecutors – are all those up to a penalty of 10 years for young persons and 5 years for adults. In the case of juveniles, this includes the vast majority of offences. For both groups, offences that result in the victim's death are excluded. Thus the practice can be described as 'diversionary in nature and discretionary in application' (Miers, 2001: 7), leaving the state prosecutor a rather wide margin for discretion. There are nevertheless two legal restrictions to the referral of cases to VOM: firstly, the requirement of no severe guilt being related to the offence[5] and, secondly, the requirement to take care of individual and general deterrence, i.e. to

---

3   Code of Criminal Procedure.
4   Literally, step back from the prosecution of an offence.
5   The assessment of the severity of guilt is a matter of the prosecutor's (or the judge's) discretion. He is guided in his judgement by considerations of penal law dogmatics and by the prevailing sentencing practice.

make sure that punishment is not called for to prevent the offender from future offending and (this relates to adults only) to deter the general public.[6]

Apart from the prosecutor's initial diversionary decision, there is the subsidiary discretion of the judge to refer cases to mediation if the state prosecutors have abstained from doing so. It is used very rarely though.

The Austrian Association *Neustart* that provides VOM services throughout Austria and is active in the whole field of criminal law related services, is a fully autonomous organisation, a *Verein* as concerns its legal status, although one has to take into account the fact that the whole private organisation is 'on the payroll' of the Ministry of Justice and thus publicly funded. Its legal status has a bearing on the position the *Verein* has vis-a-vis the State. Nevertheless, it has always acted as an independent pressure group in the field of criminal justice and this has been of special importance in the course of instigating and shaping the pilot projects 'Out-of-court conflict resolution in juvenile justice' and 'Out-of-court conflict resolution in general (adult) criminal law'.

We would like to conclude by way of a general observation concerning the perception of the amendment to the Code of Criminal Procedure, and the 'diversion package'. The decision of the lawmakers to make VOM one of the instruments within a wide array of diversionary measures was – without success – opposed by the Institute for the Sociology of Law and Criminology and – albeit half-heartedly – by the protagonists of the ATA. As a consequence of this decision, VOM has indeed become 'swallowed' by the diversionary tide. It has been pushed to the fringes and has become one of a range of diversionary instruments: one that is used only for very specific crimes, predominantly those where a more permanent relationship is at stake. The percentage of domestic violence cases has accordingly increased considerably. On the other hand, ironically, public perception is that diversion *is* the ATA, and whenever diversion is mentioned in Austria, people think of it in terms of VOM.

1.2   Research: an overview

Research in Austria in the field of VOM and RJ started as 'accompanying research' carried out by the Institute for the Sociology of Law and Criminology. We will deal with this in more detail under the subheading 'action-research'.

As soon as VOM was established within the Juvenile Justice Act and the pilot project for the application of VOM in adult law had further broadened its scope, a considerable number of small and middle-sized studies started to surface – the majority done by students of psychology or law writing theses, or by students of the Academy of Social Work who chose VOM as subject for the written work they have to present for their final exams (*Diplomarbeit*). These studies deal with client (victim and/or offender) satisfaction, with different types of cases and methods of handling them, or an attempt at comparison of the legal basis of VOM in different

---

6   With regard to this condition that relates to all of the diversionary measures, one speaks about the 'clause of individual and general deterrence'.

countries. Since some of these studies contain valuable information concerning client satisfaction or the efficiency of VOM, we will later report on a selected few of them.

Marianne Löschnig-Gspandl and Michael Kilchling have done a piece of comparative research, looking at the practice of VOM in the Austrian province of Styria on the one hand and at the TOA practice (*Täter-Opfer Ausgleich*, i.e. mediation) in Baden-Württemberg in Germany on the other hand (Kilchling and Löschnig-Gspandl, 1998).

One of the more ambitious projects was carried out by Hannes Schütz who was a volunteer at the Vienna ATA-bureau and later became a researcher at the Institute for Criminal Law and Criminology at the University of Vienna. This was to become the most extensive recidivism study so far, and it will be presented in the section 'evaluative research'.

Another more elaborated 'evaluation research' was done by ourselves. To be more precise, this was a study on the efficiency of criminal law intervention in domestic violence cases. The interventions compared are VOM on the one hand and the conventional criminal procedure on the other hand. This was predominantly qualitative research with only a small 'framing' quantitative assessment carried out by Bernhard Hoenisch, a law graduate and social worker who had done more extensive quantitative research on the use of the ATA in domestic violence cases in the context of his paper for his social work diploma.

The most striking feature of research on VOM in Austria is its close connection to the criminal justice agencies, stemming from the interest the relevant ministries – the Ministry of Justice and the Ministry of Family and Youth Affairs – took in getting the pilot projects established and – from the very beginning – thoroughly researched. In the case of the accompanying research on the first pilot project, the outcome of this research, and even more so the procedure of accompanying the efforts of the professions involved in the pilot project, and of social science becoming part of the discourse, has influenced the lawmaking process and the concrete shape of the Juvenile Justice Act 1988.

2   DESCRIPTIVE-INVENTORY RESEARCH

The accompanying research fulfilled the function of inventory research in the pilot stage. Later on, the ATA bureau in Vienna took on the task of assembling statistical data and assembling an annual report containing information on the development of cases and different types of cases, on the socio-demographic characteristics of victims and offenders, as well as on their relation vis-a-vis the criminal justice system (first or repeat offenders), the mode of handling the case at the ATA and the type of outcome, as well as the type of reaction of the state prosecutors' office. This cannot be regarded as proper research though, but instead it is documentation that can provide the researcher with important 'basic' material.

This is also the place to mention in more detail the research done by Marianne Löschnig-Gspandl and Michael Kilchling, comparing VOM with adults in Styria on the one hand and in Baden-Württemberg on the other hand. This research was conducted as part of the research programme of the Max Planck Institute for Foreign and International Criminal Law in Freiburg/Breisgau. The researchers analysed 575 TOA cases and 1,110 ATA cases. The collection of data happened between March 1996 and February 1998 in Styria, while the Baden-Württemberg data pertain to the period December 1994 to May 1996.

Although the two programmes do have a lot of similarities as far as their history and the practice of mediation is concerned, they also have remarkable differences. There is a difference regarding the type of offences referred to the respective VOM agencies, with the majority of offences being offences leading to physical injury and property offences in Austria, and offences against personal honour[7] in Baden-Württemberg. In addition, offences in Styria were more likely to have been committed by more than one offender and against more than one victim – they are more likely to have a group-character or 'collective' character. Finally, offences in Styria that came to the ATA were predominantly those where there was a close relationship (small relational distance): family and partnership incidents. In Baden-Württemberg neighbourhood and workplace conflicts are more likely to be referred.

Mediators in Styria were less restricted by directives of the prosecutors concerning time and expected content of the endeavour, as was the case in Baden-Württemberg. But the most relevant findings pertain to the readiness of victims and offenders to cooperate, to the mode of the mediation procedure and to victim satisfaction. Seventy-two percent of the alleged offenders and 74% of the victims that were referred in Germany, compared to 93% of the offenders and 92% of the victims that were referred in Austria, were prepared to cooperate. In Styria direct mediation was the predominant mode (73%); in Baden-Württemberg direct mediation occurred in only 36% of the cases. In Styria an agreement was reached in 85% of cases; this was 75% in Baden-Württemberg. 87% of the victims in Styria were satisfied, while this was 65.5% in Baden-Württemberg.

3   ACTION-RESEARCH

The following is a detailed account of the research efforts that were going on within the accompanying research of the two Austrian pilot projects (within juvenile justice and within general criminal law) which we have characterised as a mixture or fusion of action-research and evaluation research.

The first pilot project took place in the period October 1984 to March 1986 and the results were presented in a special volume of the *Kriminalsoziologische Bibli-*

---

7   These are defined as *Privatanklagedelikte* (prosecution only on the request of the victim) in Austria and are therefore not suited for referral.

ografie[8] titled: '*Konflikte regeln statt Strafen! Über einen Modellversuch in der öster-reichischen Jugendgerichtsbarkeit*' (Haidar et al., 1988). The pilot project in general criminal law started in the beginning of the year 1992 and lasted throughout that year. This time a volume of the *Jahrbuch für Rechts- und Kriminalsoziologie* was dedicated to the presentation of the results of the project (Hammerschick et al., 1994). As already stated, this research should be seen in the context of criminal law reform: the reform of the Juvenile Justice Act in the first case and the 'diversion package' in the second case. The research commissioned by the Austrian Ministry of Justice and the Ministry of Family and Youth Affairs, the latter mainly responsible for the financial side, was supposed to provide information for the 'design' of these reform efforts. It was intended to supply policy makers with scientifically grounded arguments. One can say that the accompanying research projects are the manifestation of a conscientious effort to ground criminal law reform in empirical data and scientifically guided reflection. Accordingly, the commissioning agencies were the Ministry of Justice and the Ministry of Family and Youth Affairs for the pilot project on juvenile offenders, and the Ministry of Justice alone for the second pilot project concerning adult offenders. Funding came from the Ministry of Family and Youth Affairs for research on the first pilot project, and from the Austrian Fund for Scientific Research for the second research project on VOM in adult cases. Staffing was – as usual – a tight affair: there were two full time researchers, Christa Pelikan and a colleague (Gertraud Baumgartner for the first project and Walter Hammerschick for the second one). Arno Pilgram, another senior researcher, was in a supervisory position.

The research design assembled and combined different methodological approaches. They corresponded to the different questions to be answered by this research, namely:

– What is the potential spectrum or the 'reservoir' of cases with regard to the number and the type of cases that could have been referred to VOM?
– What do the cases that have actually been referred to VOM look like? What consideration prevailed with state prosecutors when referring a case?
– How were these cases regarded and handled by the VOM services?
– How did the state prosecutors react to the outcome of mediation?
– In which way were professional 'structures of relevance' (the modes of perception, of cognition and of motivation) affected by working within the pilot project? Did the perception and the attitude of state prosecutors, of probation workers and of administrators change in the course of the pilot project?

The research activities undertaken were:

1) An analysis of a sample of files from the state prosecutors' office and the courts. Sampling took place at those courts where the pilot project was located and it included files from the two years prior to the start of the pilot project. The following type of information was derived from the files: characteristics

---

8   A scientific journal published on a quarterly basis between 1973 and 1992 by members of the Institute for the Sociology of Law and Criminology.

of the case as defined in terms of the criminal code, personal characteristics of offenders and victims and their relationship, more specifically their 'relational distance', the 'justification' the offender offered for the act and the reaction by the state prosecutor and the judge. Data processing produced a large number of tables showing these items and the combination thereof that marked cases suited for a referral to VOM.

2) An analysis of the files of all cases that had in fact been referred to VOM, from the start of the pilot project, following the same lines as applied to the sample from all criminal cases.

3) Documentation by the ATA workers following a scheme developed by the researchers. This was case-specific documentation, focusing on the way the VOM procedure advanced, and an assessment of the outcome by the mediators.

4) A series of interviews with the social workers/mediators based on this documentation to supplement the information on cases and on case processing, i.e. on the concrete steps taken and their evaluation of its effect on victims and offenders.

5) Case-specific interviews with the state prosecutors and/or judges responsible for the ATA cases documented.

Steps 2 to 5 were intended to bring together views and perceptions of the different professions dealing with a specific case. Through this method, differences in professional outlook came into focus, as well as differences between mediation services and between individual mediators.

6) The interviews were repeated in the course of the pilot project. The diachronic perspective[9] that this allowed enabled the researchers to learn about processes of change that took place 'in the heads' of the actors and of the way practical work and continuous communication contributed to this process.

7) An attempt was made in the pilot project on juveniles to find a group of voluntary participants in the project – victims as well as offenders – that were prepared to talk with the researcher about their experience. Due to the complicated procedure of gaining access to these people, it was only possible to carry out very few interviews, but they served as a useful complement to the results of the interviews with legal professionals and with mediators.

The researchers became part of the process and this is what we have called the 'action-research part' of the whole research endeavour (Pelikan, 2002). They served as go-betweens between the different professions and the different project sites, stimulating comparison and reflection on the work and the perception of the professions involved. They introduced some theoretical concepts to advance

---

9   The diachronic perspective looks at sequences of events and developments, while the synchronic perspective focuses on the interplay of different factors of influence at one point in time.

and to direct this reflection on the practical work and they became interpreters of the different professional outlooks and the respective professional rationale/logic. Looking back at this experience after several years, and reflecting on what made it special and altogether fruitful, we arrive at the following conclusion:

> 'In this research we had loops of feedback established between researchers and other professionals, especially the social workers, that became an integral part of the research project. (...) at that time we succeeded in starting and in keeping up an intensive and fruitful exchange (...) with the accompanying researcher functioning as an instigator for systematic scientifically guided ongoing reflection. In retrospective, two factors can be discerned that were influential in establishing a positive exchange: 1) this was an innovative, even an avant-garde project (almost everything was new and the actors saw themselves as avant-garde); 2) a hierarchy of knowledge and competence was not (yet) existent because everything was new to everybody. Researchers were co-actors and the VOM workers were co-researchers. One remains doubtful whether this constellation or any functional equivalent can ever be reproduced to realise the ideal of research that takes part in criminal policy efforts' (Pelikan, 2002: 55).

The results of the accompanying research first of all point to an overwhelming success, especially with regard to offender and victim participation and to the rate of agreements/settlements achieved, resulting in the cases being discharged by the state prosecutors. These results became apparent both on the level of quantitative and qualitative data. Within the pilot project with juvenile offenders, the participation rate of the young offenders was about 90% and the (voluntary) participation of victims was even higher with only 4% of those contacted not willing to cooperate. One important result was that the probability of having the conflict resolved and an agreement reached was considerably higher when a direct contact between victim and offender was established. The overall rate of successfully resolved conflicts, i.e. cases that had resulted in an agreement and its fulfilment, was about 75% of all cases referred to the ATA. It amounts to about 90% of the cases where the ATA bureau had succeeded in establishing contact with the offender.

The picture was, as we had expected, somewhat different with regard to adults. Here we found about 85% of the alleged offenders and the same percentage of victims prepared to participate in VOM, resulting in 72% of the cases referred to the ATA (VOM) being carried by the will of both parties to join in the mediation effort. Of these, as many as 86% ended up with some kind of agreement. The interest in achieving symbolic reparation and restoring the balance was more pronounced than the desire to achieve material compensation, both for victims and offenders. This, of course, stems from the fact that the majority of cases were located in the immediate close social environment and concerned petty and minor physical damages and threats. Also with adults, although face-to-face encounters in mediation were never forced upon the parties, those cases where direct mediation did take place showed a rate of compliance that was considerably higher than for cases where there was only indirect mediation (Hammerschick et al., 1994: 139).

In deciding whether to drop the charges, the gatekeepers largely considered a successfully concluded ATA as sufficient basis. But they also did so quite often (in about 35% of those cases) where the outcome of the mediation procedure was reported as unsuccessful, i.e. where no agreement was reached.

The qualitative analysis had pointed to the process of changing public prosecutors' and judges' thinking in the course of working with the new instrument of conflict resolution. It showed the difficulties of getting closer to an understanding of the out-of-court endeavour as something different from the penal law orientation on punishment as a means of – individual and general – deterrence. It was not so easy to convey the peace-making quality of mediation as an instrument of restorative justice carrying value in its own right (Pelikan, 2000a: 148).

4   EVALUATIVE RESEARCH

In this section we report on a few remarkable studies out of the large number of small research projects mentioned above.

4.1   Evaluation by the parties

The majority of the projects concentrate on the experience and the evaluation of the VOM procedure and its outcome by offenders and/or victims.

Josef Lins' study of 'Out-of-Court Offence Compensation with Juvenile Offenders' aimed at assessing client satisfaction of victims and offenders who had experienced VOM, as well as the viability of the VOM outcome for these clients (Lins, 1998). It was part of a practical work assigned for a course in sociology at the University of Linz, Upper Austria; the work was done by students under the supervision of Josef Lins as the director of studies and it was published as a report of the University of Linz. The research included only juveniles and it was carried out by way of a questionnaire sent out to the clients of the ATA in the region of Linz during the year 1996. The data analysis consisted of linear computation of the answers and a few simple correlations. The questions focused on the emotions experienced during the individual talks and during the mediation session, on the quality and comprehensibility of the information provided by the mediator, and the space and time victims and offenders felt was given for expressing their needs, their options and ideas. In a more general way, the space and the opportunity given for participation was looked into and, finally, satisfaction with the outcome was assessed. The results highlighted the importance of the experience of 'procedural justice' and less so of 'material justice', i.e. the content of the outcome. They point to a high overall satisfaction, as expressed by the statement that one would commend this procedure to other persons (78% for men, 63% for women). On the other hand, there is – in our opinion – some ground for concern, e.g. regarding the highest percentage of respondents attributing the greatest influence on the outcome to the mediator. Also, 16% agreed with the statement that they had no opportunity at all to contribute to the outcome. It was especially women in the role of the victim who experienced this lack of active participation. Another interesting result in that respect pertains to the way the influence of the other party is perceived. While offenders felt that the influence exerted by the victim was great, this was much less so for the victim who regarded the influence exerted by the perpetrator to be average or non-existent.

There is a more recent study on client satisfaction by Andrea Altweger and Evelyn Hitzl, 'Consumer Satisfaction of Injured Parties in VOM in Innsbruck' (Altweger and Hitzl, 2001). This research was also done in the course of university studies during the period from October 2000 to May 2001. The research design corresponds to that of the Linz study: a questionnaire was sent out and subjected to simple quantitative data analysis. Apart from general satisfaction, which again proved to be very high (83% of both victims and offenders indicated a 'high or very high' satisfaction), the questionnaire included questions concerning perceptions of the mediator's impartiality; his/her ability to give legal advice in the course of the procedure; on feelings and emotions in the course of the mediation session; on perceptions of the perpetrator's readiness to accept responsibility; and on the outcome of the process, i.e. on restoration, reconciliation and reparation (*bereinigen und wiedergutmachen*). Finally, it also included questions on 'behavioural' learning effects achieved by the VOM procedure. Contrary to the study of Josef Lins, the Innsbruck study showed a higher degree of satisfaction among women, especially in cases involving domestic violence, but also in the context of conflicts with other family members and relatives, and with conflicts that had occurred at the workplace or at school and had been reported to the police. Another result that became evident pertains to the effects of indirect versus direct mediation. The percentage of direct mediation is rather low in the Innsbruck region. Thus it is even more important to point to the fact that the perception of the perpetrator as having taken responsibility was considerably more often (74%) visible and 'felt' by the victims when involved in direct mediation, as against only 45% of victims in general. In that respect, it is equally important to realise that quite a high percentage of victims, especially women, felt uneasy in the course of the confrontation. Seven percent even experienced feelings of fear and anxiety. The former head of the ATA team in Innsbruck emphasised the importance of these results. He believes that the work of the mediators ought to be improved. The role of the victim has to be considered very carefully. A balance has to be struck between caring for her safety and giving reassurance on the one hand, and shaping opportunities for fruitful confrontation, a kind of confrontation that encourages the perpetrator to take responsibility and allows for a convincing expression of this endeavour vis-a-vis the victim, on the other hand.

Once again we would like to point to the results of the comparison done by Marianne Löschnig-Gspandl and Michael Kilchling, which shows rather high rates of victim satisfaction as well as a high proportion of direct mediation in Austria's province of Styria (see above).

4.2   Research on the efficacy of VOM

The most important studies that exist so far deal with the effect of VOM in cases of domestic violence. Significantly detailed research of this kind was done at the Institute for the Sociology of Law and Criminology; it resulted in a two-volume research report (Pelikan and Hoenisch, 2000).[10] As was the case with the accompanying research of the initial pilot project, this project was placed within a legal policy context and was associated with the effort to introduce the 'diversion package' as part of a reformed criminal procedural law. More specifically, it was to provide information on the effects of VOM in domestic violence cases.[11] At that time a considerable percentage (about 25%) of VOM consisted of this type of case and this fact met with the critique of the protagonists of the women's movement. They wanted the introduction of a clause as part of this diversion package that would rule VOM non-applicable to these cases. The project's specific aim was to produce a list of criteria that would guide case selection and placement, i.e. assist state prosecutors in their decision-making with regard to these cases.

The research design consisted of three steps: (1) observation of procedures, (2) interviews with clients and follow-up interviews after several months, and (3) interviews with the professionals handling the case. The qualitative data collection was supplemented by a 'framing' collection of data from files of the ATA bureau in Vienna. These files contained information about all the cases pertaining to violence in partner relationships that had been referred to the ATA by the Vienna state prosecutors' office during a four-month period of time (1.1.1998 to 30.4.1998). The information regarding the type of the case, the personal characteristics of the alleged offender as well as the victim, and the way the case was handled and settled by the mediators and lastly by the state prosecutors, was derived from these files by using a short assessment instrument. The observation of both court procedures and VOM procedures that constituted the first step of assembling qualitative data, had a double purpose: to provide access to the partners and ex-partners where an incident of violence had come to the notice of the police and consequently the state prosecutor, and to supply the researchers with an additional set of data, i.e. offer an opportunity to hear and to see how the parties interact with each other and how they interact with criminal law agencies, including the set-up of VOM. We concentrated on observing the actual sessions in the course of the VOM procedure, involving the partners and the social workers/mediators at the ATA bureau in Vienna and in Salzburg. One has to know that the mediation sessions – in both Vienna and Salzburg – follow a rather sophisticated and elaborate professional design that aims at bringing into effect the two main working principles of mediation: recognition and empowerment (Pelikan, 2002: 21-22).

---

10   An English version is published on the website http://www.restorativejustice.org (Pelikan, 2000b).
11   It was commissioned by the Ministry of Justice and funded in cooperation with the Ministry of the Interior and the Ministry of Family and Youth Affairs.

Observation of the relevant procedures, the 'single talks' with only one partner and the mediation session involving both partners, meant sitting in the background and listening while the sessions took place. We applied the same instrument of observation to court trials dealing with cases of domestic violence. These procedures are open to the public and therefore the presence of the researcher posed no problem. In this way we assembled 36 written observation records of court procedures and 25 records from VOM, comprising both individual talks and mediation talks. They follow as closely as possible the course of the procedures. In addition, we attempted to characterise the setting and the performance, i.e. participant behaviour.

Concerning the second task of observation – the recruitment of clients for the intensive interviews planned – we faced considerable difficulties with regard to establishing contact with the men that had to show up in court. Very few were prepared to make arrangements for an interview. This was, of course, easier to achieve after having observed a mediation session. But we succeeded in conducting 76 intensive interviews altogether with clients comprising both first and follow-up talks. The follow-up interviews took place after four to six months. We asked permission to contact the clients again at the end of the first interview, which was usually readily granted. For this second step of data collection we used a kind of checklist, even though the interviews were conducted in an open and associative way, following the flow of conversation as closely as possible. The courtroom or VOM experience constituted the starting point for talking about the relevant events. From there the client's conversation covered both the past and the future.

Finally, as a third step we conducted two kinds of experts' interviews. Firstly, a case-related interview was done with the mediator, immediately or shortly after they had finished the mediation we observed. We had very few of these case-related interviews with the trial judges or the state prosecutors due to organisational obstacles; usually it was difficult to pin them down while they were trying to rush off to their next trial. These case-related interviews are an important contribution to the 'triangulation of perspectives' we were trying to achieve. We had already applied this methodological device in a more limited version with the accompanying research described above. This method of bringing together various points of observation is intended to achieve greater variety and greater density of description and, starting from that, a higher degree of complexity in grasping and understanding the relevant phenomena – in this case: the efficacy of criminal law interventions.

The case-related interviews added a professional perspective to the perspective of offenders and victims and to the researcher's perspective as they emerged from the observations. Since the mediation and the court procedure as an intervening process were at the core of our research interest, the way the professionals saw themselves and their actions, and the significance they attach to their role, constitute an indispensable part of the whole picture (Pelikan, 2002: 34). Secondly, we conducted a series of more lengthy interviews with judges and with state prosecutors – experts' interviews in a more narrow sense – about the problem of criminal law intervention in domestic violence cases in general, focusing on exercising dis-cretion regarding referral to VOM and the criteria guiding these referrals. These interviews also produced important statements that complemented the framing quantitative research and the analysis of the VOM cases. The statements made by prosecutors and judges related to the modes of cooperation between the courts and the VOM agency. One of the pivotal conclusions to be drawn from these interviews concerns the need to provide extensive and intensive information to judges and state prosecutors with regard to the function, the potential effects and the potential values of VOM (Pelikan, 2002: 36).

The qualitative analysis, or scientifically guided re-interpretation of the different data assembled and brought together ('triangulated'), was done with the help of a model or flow chart depicting the diachronic course of events and the various forces of influence that came to bear upon the use, or the mobilisation of the criminal law agencies and of VOM procedures, and on their preventive and 'peace-making' effects. These forces, or the variables taken into consideration, were: the nature, the type of the incidence of violence; the constellation, the balance/imbal-ance of power in the relationship of the partners; their individual socio-economic and personal resources (qualifications, communication skills); the dispositions, attitudes and coping strategies acquired in the course of their life (the socialisa-tion process), and especially the attitudes towards state agencies and authorities. Within the diachronic model, three sets of variables were represented: (1) constel-lations of conditions (as listed above), (2) sequences (courses) of events, and (3) interventions and effects/outcomes. Analysis started with looking at individual cases, followed by comparing cases and by contrasting cases alongside the differ-ent aspects or variables. Within each of the three sets of variables, we introduced relevant differences ('differences that make a difference') and from there – by establishing correlations between the differences of conditions, of sequence and of effect – we attempted to develop typologies. We arrived at a 'typology of the restorative process that describes the efficacy of the VOM procedure according to different constellations of cases and the power relation that marked them'. Thus we found:

1) VOM as a reinforcement of change. Two subtypes exist:
    a. VOM reinforcing change as a mutual effort, initiated by both partners;
    b. VOM as a reinforcement of change, enforced by the woman who gets con-firmation of her claim to freedom from violence in the private sphere in the course of the VOM procedure;
2) VOM as the beginning of reformation (the individual prevention effect – a rather rare constellation);
3) VOM supporting separation; and finally
4) VOM at its limits, i.e. cases where VOM's effort proved futile and where vio-lence occurred again.

Taking into consideration the criminal law intervention investigated – the crim-inal court procedure as well as the VOM procedure – we came to realise that these procedures are effective mainly as reinforcement of dynamics already set in

motion, i.e. of change and of efforts that were brought about either by both partners, or by the woman alone as a consequence of the occurrence of violence that
was made public by calling in the police. This is more pronounced with the out-of-
court procedure of mediation, a procedure that is apt to address deeper relational
power structures, to make them visible and to reinforce their transformation.
Only very rarely does something new start, and a conversion or a reformation of
the alleged perpetrator takes place; this holds true for both the criminal procedure and for VOM.
Where we find an instrumental use of the criminal law interventions, i.e. where
the appeal to the agencies of criminal law is intended to signal a warning to the
partner that has acted violently, both the formal and the informal procedure are
quite well suited to fulfil the function of 'drawing a line'. In other words, the
function of an affirmation of the norm can be achieved quite well by the court
procedure, but also by the VOM procedure.

There is another small study concentrating on cases of violence in partnerships
by Alexandra Lechner (1988): 'Partner violence. VOM as a mode of intervention.
An investigation into the situation of injured parties'. This student of the Academy for Social Work in Innsbruck has made an attempt at finding out about the
long-term effects of VOM on perpetrators and on victims who had been through
this procedure two to three years previously. She was given access to the addresses
of clients through the ATA service in Innsbruck and tried to establish contact by
mail or telephone. Of the 15 cases selected, she finally conducted 10 interviews,
predominantly with the victim, though in one case she was also able to talk to
the male offender. The interview directive was developed in cooperation with the
female mediator who did most of these cases in Innsbruck. The outcome of the
research is a collection of case stories that served to derive some conclusions concerning mediation work with this type of offence. The reactions and experiences
of the female victims cover a broad range: from the complete lack of any positive
change ('he only takes more care now not to leave any visible marks when he
starts beating me') to a complete change of the attitude of the man ('it's 100:1')
who had heard from a competent person that his actions are not to be tolerated
by herself and by the society. In between, there were cases where violence has
stopped, but a complete estrangement of the partners has occurred, and a case
where the woman stated that she had experienced a process of empowerment
though the attitude of her partner had not changed at all, but he is with a new
family and she was therefore not exposed to further violence from him.

4.3   Research on recidivism

There is a well-designed piece of quantitative research dedicated to the issue of
recidivism (Schütz, 1999). Its qualities are derived from the fact that a control
group was established and from the length of the period of time observed and

controlled, namely three years. Hannes Schütz[12] who presented this study as his doctoral thesis succeeded in getting the support of the Ministry of Justice and eventually the courts in Vienna and Salzburg to gain access to their records. As to the profile of the cases included, the researcher restricted his scrutiny to cases of minor assault (*Leichte Körperverletzung*) and – as concerns the reaction of the court – to the sentence of a fine. There were altogether 361 ATA cases and 7,952 court cases.

The comparison of all cases points to a recidivism rate of 14% for the VOM cases and 33% for cases that had resulted in a fine. When looking at perpetrators with a previous conviction, the difference became less pronounced: 30% for the VOM cases versus 47% for the court cases (10% for those without a previous conviction who had been at the ATA and 22% for those who received a fine).

Hannes Schütz explicitly points to a potential flaw in these results, namely that of a selection effect for the VOM cases. One has to consider the possibility that state prosecutors select cases for referral to VOM on the basis of their prognosis with regard to individual (special) prevention. Thus the court cases might from the outset represent those with a less favourable prognosis. This selection effect is indeed one of the most frequently mentioned flaws of recidivism studies of 'alternative measures' in general.[13]

5   TOWARDS A COMPARISON AND CONCLUSION

What strikes the observer when looking at the Austrian scene with regard to research is the close relationship between the practice of the ATA service and the multitude of research done in this field. It started, of course, with the way the accompanying research was designed and the kind of mutual feedback that was established at the time when VOM appeared in the field of legal and criminal policy. But the ATA workers were obviously always very willing to help students with their research and are also ready to profit from the research done and the results produced.

Criminal policy considerations have accounted for research initiatives that investigate the efficacy of VOM practices and their application to cases of partnership violence. In general, one can say that for this type of qualitative research and its results to become useful and influential it needs the cooperation of VOM agencies, of policy makers and researchers. Quite often this research is discarded as producing only anecdotal evidence that is difficult to use in public debate.

Recidivism studies are still perceived as indispensable for public debate. Recidivism is *the* measure that decides whether a new programme, or an alternative strategy 'works', despite a considerable amount of research that has shown that recidivism, or rather non-recidivism (*Legalbewährung*), depends on factors or influences that lie outside the criminal justice system. A further step in this

---

12   With the assistance of the Vienna ATA-service.
13   See the meta-analysis done for the Canadian Department of Justice (Latimer et al., 2001).

development is cost-benefit analysis as a tool that provides policy makers with powerful arguments. The problem with RJ practices and research that focus predominantly or exclusively on recidivism and on cost-benefit analysis is that it has to leave out the most potent quality of this approach to justice, namely the sense of justice and of active participation (which are closely related) experienced by people involved in these practices and 'doing justice in this way'. It is the eternal problem of restorative justice and its place within or outside the criminal justice system. And, research will have to live up to this challenge.

REFERENCES

Altweger, A. and Hitzl, E. (2001) *Kundenzufriedenheit der Geschädigten im ATA Innsbruck'* (Innsbruck: Akademie für Sozialarbeit).

Haidar, A., Leirer, H., Pelikan, C. and Pilgram, A. (eds.) (1988) *Konflikte regeln statt strafen! Über einen Modellversuch in der österreichischen Jugendgerichtsbarkeit* (Wien: Verlag für Gesellschaftskritik).

Hammerschick, W., Pelikan, C. and Pilgram, A. (1994) 'Soziale Konflikte vor Gericht und im Außergerichtlichen Tatausgleich – eine Gegenüberstellung', in Hammerschick, W., Pelikan, C. and Pilgram, A. (eds.), *Ausweg aus dem Strafrecht – Der außergerichtliche Tatausgleich*, Jahrbuch für Rechts- und Kriminalsoziologie '94, (Baden-Baden: Nomos), pp. 95-129.

Kilchling, M. and Löschnig-Gspandl, M. (1998) 'Vergleichende Perspektiven zum Täter-Opfer-Ausgleich in Baden-Württemberg und der Steiermark – Ausblick auf ein vergleichendes empirisches Forschungsprojekt', in Friedrich-Ebert-Stiftung (ed.), *Der Täter-Opfer-Ausgleich (TOA): Moderner Beitrag zur Konfliktregulierung und zur Sicherung des sozialen Friedens* (Potsdam: Eigenverlag), pp. 45-59.

Latimer, J., Dowden, C. and Muise, D. (2001) *The Effectiveness of Restorative Justice Practices: A Meta-Analysis* (Canada: Research and Statistics Division, Department of Justice).

Lechner, A. (1998) *Gewalt in Paarbeziehungen. Der Außergerichtliche Tatausgleich als mögliche Interventionsform. Eine Nachuntersuchung des Jahres 1995 bei Betroffenen* (Innsbruck: Akademie für Sozialarbeit der Caritas).

Lins, J. (1998) *Der Außergerichtliche Tatausgleich bei Jugendlichen* (Linz: University of Linz).

Miers, D. (2001) *An International Review of Restorative Justice*, Crime Reduction Research Series Paper 10 (London: Home Office).

Neustart (ed.) (2002) *Daten zum ATA 2001*, unpublished internal report (Wien).

Pelikan, C. (2000a) 'Victim-Offender Mediation in Austria', in The European Forum for Victim-Offender Mediation and Restorative Justice (ed.), *Victim-Offender Mediation in Europe. Making Restorative Justice Work* (Leuven: Leuven University Press), pp. 125-153.

Pelikan, C. (2000b) *VOM in Domestic Violence Cases. A Research Report*. Available at: http://www.restorativejustice.org.

Pelikan, C. (2002) 'Victim-Offender-Mediation in Domestic Violence Cases – A Comparison of the Effects of Criminal Law Intervention: the Penal Process and Mediation. Doing Qualitative Research', *Forum Qualitative Sozialforschung/Forum: Qualitative Social Research* [On-line Journal], 3(1). Available at: http://www.qualitative-research.net/fqs-texte/a2324/1-02pelikan-e.htm.

Pelikan, C. and Hoenisch, B. (2000) *Die Wirkungsweise strafrechtlicher Interventionen bei Gewaltstraftaten in Paarbeziehungen. Research Report* (Vienna: Institute for the Sociology of Law and Criminology).

Pilgram, A. (2001) 'Die Strafprozessnovelle 1999 und ihre Auswirkungen auf Diversion und Strafverfolgung', in Bundesministerium für Inneres (ed.), *Sicherheitsbericht 2001. Kriminalität 200. Bericht über die Innere Sicherheit in Österreich* (Wien: BMI), pp. 451-470.

Proyer, D. and Wurmbrand, D. (2006) *Bericht des Vereins NeuSTART über das Jahr 2006*, unpublished report (Wien).

Schütz, H. (1999) 'Die Rückfallshäufigkeit nach einem Außergerichtlichen Tatausgleich bei Erwachsenen', *Österreichische Richterzeitung*, 77, pp. 166-169.

4 Research, practice and policy partnerships

Empirical research on restorative justice in Belgium

Denis Van Doosselaere and Inge Vanfraechem

1 INTRODUCTION

In this chapter we present the empirical research carried out in Belgium with regard to mediation and conferencing. The first paragraph points out that Belgium is a complex country, where competences are spread out over various authorities. This may lead to, for example, different names for similar practices such as 'local mediation' and 'mediation at the police level', or to a different degree of implementation of restorative practices. Nevertheless, one can conclude that mediation is available at every stage for adult offenders and at public prosecutor and juvenile courts level for young offenders. Conferencing is only available at the level of the juvenile courts. Various types of research have been carried out on different practices. Research includes studying the possibilities of implementing practices (3.1 and 3.2); description of organisations and practices (2.1 and 2.2); action-research whereby a new practice is evaluated and at the same time adapted according to the research results; and evaluation of mediation practices (4.1 and 4.2). We conclude that practices have developed rather extensively over recent years and that although research is still lacking in certain areas, various topics have been studied. Research does remain focused on the field of youth justice.

1.1 Context: state of affairs

In this paragraph, we first (1.1.1) describe the state of affairs with regard to victim-offender mediation [VOM] and family group conferencing [FGC] in Belgium.[1] In a second sub-section (1.1.2), we briefly point out some other restorative practices, which will not be further discussed in this chapter either because they do not strictly fall under the terms VOM and FGC or because they do not deal with criminal matters.

---

[1] The practice of FGC as it exists in Belgium for youth delinquents fits within the definition used for this book since it is based on the New Zealand model (Vanfraechem, 2005), but because the model was adapted to fit the Belgian situation and legal context, we prefer to use the term conferencing.

1.1.1   Victim-offender mediation and conferencing in Belgium

Belgium is a federal state: besides the federal institutions, there are three communities (the Flemish, the French and the German) as well as three regions (the
Flemish, the Walloon and the Region of Brussels as Capital). On the one hand,
the Communities and Regions have legal competency over 'person-related matters'. Therefore, they are responsible for the overall implementation of measures
regarding youth delinquency and for some of the person-oriented programmes
in the field of adult criminal law. On the other hand, the federal parliament provides for the main legislation regarding youth justice, criminal law and criminal
procedure. The federal government funds some programmes, also with respect
to restorative justice [RJ], whereas other VOM and FGC programmes are mostly
financed by the Communities or Regions. The federal structure of the Belgian
state partially explains why practices may vary in the different parts of the country (Aertsen, 2000; Lemonne and Vanfraechem, 2005), for instance 'local mediation' (French Community) is called 'mediation at the level of the police stage' in
the Flemish Community.

Juveniles and young adults[2]

Since the reformed Youth Justice Act,[3] mediation and conferencing may be proposed by the public prosecutor (mediation) or the judge (mediation and conferencing). Since it is considered as an offer to the parties, they can voluntarily choose
whether or not to take part in the communication process.

For youth offenders, VOM is available in every judicial district (Aertsen, 2000;
Spiesschaert et al., 2001; Balcaen, 2006; Berbuto and Van Doosselaere, 2007).
Conferencing has also been available in all judicial districts since the implementation of the Youth Justice Act (2007). The mediation and conferencing work is
carried out by NGOs in the sector of youth assistance. Many NGOs in the French
Community have built a service exclusively for mediation (Van Doosselaere,
2003, 2005). The aim is to separate the mainly offender-oriented activities of
community service from mediation practices.[4] This distinction is meant to strive
for a RJ-oriented mediation model with a balance between attention for the victim

---

2   The age of criminal responsibility is 18 (but may be lowered to 16 for exceptional cases).

3   Wet 15 mei 2006 tot wijziging van de wet van 8 april 1965 betreffende de jeugdbescherming, het
     Wetboek van strafvordering, het Strafwetboek, het Burgerlijk Wetboek, de nieuwe gemeentewet
     en de wet van 24 april 2003 tot hervorming van de adoptie [Law of 15 May 2006 to modify the law
     of 8 April 1965 on youth protection, Code of Criminal Procedure, Code of Criminal Law, Code of
     Civil Law, new Municipality Law and Law of 24 April 2003 to modify adoption – *our translation*]
     B.S., 2 June 2006 (second edition) and Wet 13 juni 2006 tot wijziging van de wetgeving betreffende
     de jeugdbescherming en het ten laste nemen van minderjarigen die een als misdrijf omschreven
     feit hebben gepleegd [Law of 13 June 2006, to change the legislation on youth protection and tak-
     ing on cases of youngsters who committed an act described as a crime – *our translation*], *B.S.*, 19
     July 2006 (second edition).

4   As shown by the names chosen for these specific activities: '*Espace-Médiation*' (Mediation-Space)
     or '*Ouverture-Médiation*' (Mediation-Prelude), for example. Research was carried out on deter-
     mining the preferred place to situate mediation at (cf. infra, 3.1 Experimental project on mediation
     for juveniles in the French Community and 3.2 Mediation for juveniles in the French Community
     of Belgium).

and for the offender (Van Doosselaere and Gailly, 2002). In the Flemish Community, services may also offer community service and training projects (these are so-called 'constructive settlements' – cf. infra 2.1.4).

Professionals guide the mediation and conferencing processes: there is only one experimental programme working with volunteers (juvenile mediation, Leuven). No financial contribution is asked from offenders and victims. The 'Support Service Special Youth Care' [OSBJ][5] worked out a standard registration scheme that enhanced the comparability of data.

A so-called Compensation Fund is available in every Flemish province (Swinnen, 2007).[6] This fund is made available to juveniles who have no financial means to compensate the victims for damages. The offender is allowed to undertake voluntary work for a limited number of hours, for which he is reimbursed by the fund. These earnings go directly to the victim.

Conferencing for youth delinquents was piloted in Flanders during the period of November 2000 to November 2003, and later on included in the Youth Justice Act, which led to its national implementation (Vanfraechem 2003a, 2005, 2007a; Seykens and Van Doosselaere, 2007; Vandebroek and Vanfraechem, 2007).

In the French Community, short training sessions on mediation and conferencing are organised on an ad hoc basis. A federation to which most of the French speaking NGOs are affiliated[7] organises monthly meetings during which topics such as case studies and policy problems are discussed. Training sessions regarding mediation and conferencing were organised regularly by OSBJ in the Flemish Community.

Adults

Various projects coexist in the context of adult criminal law: local mediation (French Community) or mediation at the level of the police (Flemish Community); penal mediation (at the level of the prosecutor); and pre- and post-sentence mediation (French Community) or mediation for redress (Flemish Community).[8] So-called 'local mediation' (mediation at the police level) has been developed in a limited number of cities for minor offences. Different types of local mediation exist (Lemonne and Aertsen, 2003). The mediation services vary in their degree of cooperation with the police and the public prosecutor's office and are funded by various public authorities.[9]

---

5   'Ondersteuningsstructuur Bijzondere Jeugdzorg' [OSBJ] is a non-governmental organisation that was partly set up to coordinate restorative and 'constructive' practices – namely mediation, community service and educational projects – in Flanders. The service is subsidised by the Flemish Community, Ministry of Welfare. More information can be found at www.osbj.be

6   Cf. infra, 4.1. Evaluation of the functioning of the Flemish Compensation Fund.

7   FEMMO, Fédération des équipes Mandatées en Milieu Ouvert.

8   The use of different terms in the French and Flemish Community shows the different implementation in various parts of the country, cf. 3.3. Mediation for redress and 4.2. Local mediation as an alternative measure for petty offences in Belgium. The term 'local mediation' appears to be confusing, especially in an international context, but it is the term used in practice in the French-speaking part of Belgium thus we will refer to it as such throughout the chapter.

9   Cf. infra, 4.2. Local mediation as an alternative measure for petty offences in Belgium.

Penal mediation is available within the public prosecutor's office in every judicial district and is carried out by civil servants (so-called justice assistants) in a diversion scheme (Lemonne, 1999).[10]

Mediation for redress or 'pre- and post-sentence mediation' is offered by two independent NGOs – one in Flanders and one in the French-speaking part of the country – that have local services in every judicial district.[11] Both non-profit organisations provide figures on their work in their annual reports.[12] Moreover, Buonatesta (2004) presents figures on the practice of mediation in prisons and discusses different issues related to it, especially the link between mediation and release on parole.[13]

Furthermore, 'RJ advisers' were available in every prison until 2008.[14] Their task was not to work individually with inmates and victims, but to re-orient the prison culture towards a culture of RJ. As agents of change, they built projects in order for offenders to develop useful skills and to work out appropriate prison structures which take into account victims' viewpoints.[15] The reasons why the function of RJ adviser was abolished, after 8 years of practice and a lot of international attention, are not clear. The decision was made rather unexpectedly at central level at the Ministry of Justice. The function of RJ adviser was transformed into a more general one to assist the prison governor in general management tasks.

1.1.2   Other types of mediation

Mediation has spread gradually to many areas of social life. It is not the purpose of this chapter to enumerate all the fields or institutions which mediators have entered.[16] It is nevertheless worth noting that in February 2005,[17] mediation was introduced in the Code of Civil Procedure, as a third way of resolving conflicts, alongside judicial procedure and arbitration. Furthermore, conferencing has been implemented in schools (Burssens and Vettenburg, 2006) and programmes of peer mediation exist in schools as well.

---

10   Beyens (2000) compared figures of four years of penal mediation. See also Vanneste (1997) and Hanozin et al. (1997).

11   *Suggnomè* in the Flemish Community and *Médiante* in the French Community work as 'national' organisations on RJ and are recognised and subsidised by the federal Ministry of Justice for offering pre-sentence mediation. For offering post-sentence mediation (in prisons), Suggnomè further receives subsidies from the Flemish Community.

12   www.suggnome.be and www.mediante.be.

13   See also *Slachtoffer in Beeld* – Suggnomè (2002).

14   They were civil servants working in the Ministry of Justice (not private consultants).

15   Cf. infra, 1.3. Research: an overview on the project 'Restorative prisons'.

16   For example in hospitals (Law of 22 April 2002 with regard to patients' rights) or family mediation (Law of 19 February 2001).

17   Loi du 21 février 2005 modifiant le Code judiciaire en ce qui concerne la médiation [Law changing the Code of Civil Procedure with regard to mediation – *our translation*], M.B., 22.03.05.

1.2   Legal situation

1.2.1   Juveniles and young adults

The 1965 Youth Justice Act indirectly allowed for the practice of mediation (under the heading of 'a philanthropic or educational service'). Since the beginning of the 1990s, the Belgian federal government has discussed the modification of the Act and has asked a working group to draw up a proposal. Finally, in 2006, the Youth Justice Act was adapted: it still adheres to a youth protection philosophy but also clearly includes elements of RJ, most concretely in the practices of mediation and conferencing. Moreover, judges have to give preference to these 'restorative offers' (art. 37 §1) while the possibility of mediation has to be considered by the public prosecutor before the case is sent to the judge (art. 45 quater §1).[18]

1.2.2   Adults

Local mediation is regulated in Brussels by a circular letter of the public prosecutor's office (January 1998). In other parts of the country, local cooperation agreements are established. Penal mediation is regulated by the law of 10 February 1994 and the Royal Decree of 24 October 1994.[19] In not too serious cases, the law offers the public prosecutor the possibility of proposing, among other things, mediation in exchange for the dismissal of the formal procedure (Aertsen, 2000: 158).

Pre- and post-sentence mediation (also called mediation for redress) is regulated by the law of 22 June 2005 and the Royal Decrees of 26 January 2006 (Eyckmans, 2006; Lemonne, 2007).[20] It is available at all stages of the criminal procedure and for all types of offences. The decision to participate in mediation is taken by persons 'with a direct interest' in the criminal procedure and not by judicial authorities whose task is limited to inform potential parties about the availability of the process.

---

18 For a discussion on the position of RJ in the youth law, see Vanfraechem (2007b, 2007a) and Vandebroek and Vanfraechem (2007). For a description of procedures and juridical questions see Berbuto and Van Doosselaere (2007). For a more general overview of the Youth Justice Act, see Put and Walgrave (2006) and Put (2007).

19 Cf. infra, 2.2.2. Organisation of the services.

20 Loi du 22 juin 2005 introduisant des dispositions relatives à la médiation dans le Titre préliminaire du Code de procédure pénale et dans le Code d'instruction criminelle [Law of 22 June 2005, introducing dispositions with regard to mediation in the Introductory title of the Code of Criminal Procedure and in the Code of Criminal Procedure – our translation], M.B., 27.07.06; Arrêté royal du 26 janvier 2006 fixant les critères d'agrément des services de médiation visés à l'art. 554, § 1er du code d'instruction criminelle et Arrêté royal du 26 janvier 2006 réglant la composition et le fonctionnement de la Commission Déontologique Médiation visée à l'art. 554, § 1er du code d'instruction criminelle [Royal Decree of 26 January 2006, stipulating the conditions for agreement of mediation services with regard to art. 554§1 of the Code of Criminal Procedure and the Royal Decree of 26 January 2006, regulating the composition and functioning of the Deontological Mediation Commission with regard to art. 554§1 of the Code of Criminal Procedure – our translation], M.B., 01.02.2006.

1.3   *Research: an overview*

Different research projects about VOM and FGC, such as mediation for redress and conferencing for youth delinquency, have been established in Belgium (see also Aertsen 2000: 184-186) and will be discussed more in depth in this chapter. Other RJ-related research will not be discussed, since it does not concern empirical research on mediation and conferences; we briefly outline the main projects of this other RJ-related research in this paragraph.

Within the prison setting, a project was started to make the prison more 'restorative'. The set-up of the project took place in the aftermath of particular events and policy developments in Belgian society (the Dutroux-case, resulting in more attention for victims), as well as in the context of research findings (prisons being overcrowded and not leading to positive results, victims' questions and needs towards prisons and prisoners). In 1997, a research project called 'Building stones for a coherent restorative and victim-oriented criminal justice policy' was initiated. 'Restorative detention' arose from this as a sub-project and became an independent pilot project in January 1998. Action-research was set up in six prisons by the universities of Liège and Leuven. In 2000, the Ministry of Justice decided to recruit 'RJ advisers' for each prison throughout the country, thus generalising the project and moving some of the action-researchers into service and support functions. Different reports have been written in Dutch and French over the years.[21] No empirical research has been carried out to date.[22]

An action-research was set up on conferencing in schools in Flanders. The first part of the report presents an inventory of reactions towards disciplinary problems in schools, with special emphasis on restorative reactions. The second part focuses on scientific guidance and evaluation of an experiment 'conferencing in schools', which used action-research and ran from December 2001 to April 2004 (Burssens and Vettenburg, 2006). Teachers and school counsellors were trained to facilitate the conferences. The project continues in the context of 'time-out' programmes, whereby a youngster can be temporarily taken out of school in order to calm the situation and to search for a constructive solution.[23]

Different reports are written on alternative measures and sanctions in general, but they do not really include empirical research.[24] Theoretical research has also

---

21   See, for instance, Brouckmans et al., 1998; Vandeurzen et al., 1999; Christiaensen et al., 2000; Demet et al., 2000; Aertsen et al., 2001; Hodiaumont and Malempré, 2001; Van Camp, 2001a, 2001b; Hodiaumont et al., 2004; Van Camp et al., 2004; and Aertsen, 2005.

22   PhD research on RJ and detention is being carried out at the University of Liège (Dubois, 2009) and at the Free University of Brussels (Claes, personal communication, January 2008; not yet published).

23   Since the conflicts do not usually entail criminal offences in a strict sense, we will not further describe the research results.

24   See, for instance, Mary and De Fraene, 1996; De Ruyver et al., 1997; Martin and Meyvis, 1997; Meyvis and Martin, 1997.

been developed on various topics, e.g. on the concept of RJ, the idea of 'reintegrative shaming' and the notion of 'linkedness'. [25]

As mentioned, we will further limit ourselves to specific empirical research projects on VOM and conferencing in Belgium. We will discuss three different types of research: descriptive-inventory research, action-research and evaluative research.

2   DESCRIPTIVE-INVENTORY RESEARCH

2.1   *Research on restorative justice for juveniles in Flanders*[26]

The aim of this research was two-fold. On the one hand, the practice of three specific 'measures'[27] to act on youth delinquency was studied to understand whether and to what extent these measures may be considered as restorative. On the other hand, a theoretical concept of RJ was developed, on the basis of which the three practices were evaluated. Although this research was mainly descriptive in character, it also included theoretical reflections.

2.1.1   *Research set-up*

The research was carried out in the period December 2000 to December 2002. It was funded by the Department of Special Youth Assistance of the Flemish Community, and carried out by three universities: Ghent University, the Free University of Brussels and the Catholic University of Leuven. Three full-time researchers worked on the project and various reports were written in Dutch.

The objective during the first year of the project was to present an overview of three practices in Flanders:[28] VOM, community service and educational projects. Since an overall view on the practices was not available, explorative and descriptive research was the first step to be undertaken. To collect data on practices, the yearly reports (of services providing those three measures) and other relevant

---

25   See, for instance, Walgrave and Aertsen, 1996; Aertsen, 2001; Walgrave, 2000, 2002; Deklerck and Depuydt, 2004; Claes et al., 2005; Aertsen et al., 2006; and Deklerck, 2007.

26   Several unpublished research reports are available in Dutch: Nuytiens et al. (2000), Spiesschaert et al. (2001), Van Dijk et al. (2002a, 2002b). Some reflections are published in English in Claes et al. (2003). We discuss the results as they are presented in the reports, therefore it is the opinions of the actors in the field interviewed that are put forward. In the last sub-section, we present some more recent figures (2007) to add on to this descriptive research which presents the state of affairs in 2001.

27   In the Belgian youth protection system (which is, as explained above, still mostly adhered to in the Youth Justice Act of 2006), a youngster is considered to be in need of protection when something goes wrong. When he commits 'a fact described as a crime', 'measures' are taken by the youth judge in order to ensure the juvenile's protection. The young offender is considered not to be responsible for what he does, thus cannot commit 'crimes' nor receive 'punishment' according to the philosophy of the law.

28   The research was funded by the Flemish Community. The Flemish Ministry of Welfare aimed at developing a restorative practice linked to youth care. Therefore, this research was only carried out in Flanders.

documents (internal notes, working instruments) were studied. These written documents were analysed on the basis of topic lists which were also sent to the practitioners and used as a basis for semi-structured interviews (Van Dijk et al., 2002a: 6-11). Problems and points for attention were outlined through a literature review and interviews with practitioners, which served as a basis to develop a more evaluative research during the second year (Nuytiens et al., 2002: 3 and following).

The objective during the second year was threefold: to give a quantitative overview of the practices (looking at the dossiers of the services, the dossiers in the judicial system and the organisation of the services); to elaborate on the concept of RJ; and to use this concept to formulate advice, suggestions and possible alternatives for the restorative-oriented practices. The figures were captured by the yearly reports of 2001 of the various services (Nuytiens et al., 2002: 8). The total number of mediation cases was looked at, as well as the relative proportion compared to the total number of cases dealt with by the prosecutor or the juvenile judge.[29] On the basis of the total number of cases, the workload for the personnel was studied, taking into account that they also do more general work (e.g. training, administrative work) and that different types of cases can lead to a different workload (e.g. very complicated cases).[30]

An analysis was further carried out with regard to the theoretical concept of RJ, based on discussions between researchers and professors of the three universities. International researchers were invited to take part in the discussions. Different working-texts were written and discussed. Topics of agreement and consensus were looked for and led to the further development of the concept. The elaborated concept was then used to compare it to the actual practices, with the aim of giving them a deeper theoretical basis.

2.1.2   Organisation of the services

The authors collected information on the organisation of the mediation services.[31] Eleven mediation services for juveniles were available in Flanders in 2002 (Nuytiens et al., 2002: 29). Some of these services provided community service and educational projects besides mediation. The services worked with youth offenders and received referrals from public prosecutors as well as from juvenile judges.

---

29 A form was sent to the different judicial actors in order to receive some basic information on the decisions taken in 2000 and 2001. A form was also sent to the different mediation services to get an idea about the funding as well as available personnel.

30 Several methodological problems were encountered. The figures in the annual reports were not registered in a systematic manner. The figures from the judicial actors only represented cases in which an actual judicial decision was taken. Dismissals of charges were not taken into account and of course non-registered cases were not captured by this method. Thirdly, not all judicial actors reported back: a complete set of data was gathered for only three judicial districts. Finally, except for one, all mediation projects were covered. Internal validity is – according to the authors – rather high, since the practitioners are free to speak, the anonymity being guaranteed (Van Dijk et al., 2002a: 11-12).

31 Since practice changed over the years, we add a paragraph on the state of affairs in 2007 (2.1.4).

Regarding the organisation of the services (Van Dijk et al., 2002b: 84), the researchers distinguished various models. Several services have taken the initiative to set up a mediation project: services of special youth care; cooperative initiatives by public services, welfare services, special youth care services and judicial institutes; and services set up specifically to start alternative measures for juveniles. Different types of employers were identified: services of special youth care, public services (Community or Federal Ministry of Justice) and autonomous organisations with the aim of 'guidance of performances of an educational or philanthropic nature'. Mediation services can be located in different types of settings: within a service of special youth care, autonomous housing, together with other mediation services, or together with other alternative measures for juveniles (and possibly mediation services for adults). Towards the outside world, the mediation service could either profile itself as an autonomous service or as part of several alternative services.[32]

The public prosecutor as well as the juvenile judge could refer cases to mediation. According to the services studied, everybody should have the option to participate in mediation, no matter what level of the judicial procedure the case is at, or how serious the case is. The prosecutor referred most of the cases. Mediation services thought this was the best scenario, since mediation is then extra-judicial and the voluntariness of the parties to participate is guaranteed, which would not really be the case if a judge refers a case. All services worked under the mandate of a judicial authority, but referrals from other agencies or people are possible as well. The mediator asked a mandate from a judicial authority when the referral was received from outside the justice system. Mediation services were organised according to judicial districts, which enhanced the cooperation with the judicial authorities (Van Dijk et al., 2002a: 104-106).

With regard to good practices, no strict internal rules were available because of the voluntariness of the communication process, but mediation services did point out certain rules.[33] When a meeting was set, participants were expected to be at the meeting or at least to give notice of non-attendance in good time. The parties in general supported the rules, since it is a voluntary procedure. When the rules were not followed, it could be a reason to stop the mediation process. Certain rules could be put forward with regard to the actual meeting, so people would be treated with respect. A leaflet was made available to the participants so they knew what mediation is, what it stands for and what the main characteristics are (Van Dijk et al., 2002b: 172-173). A signed agreement was expected to be put into practice. Besides these informal rules, the mediation services put forward some methodological working principles, for example neutrality, voluntariness, confi-

---

32 As mentioned before, mediation can be offered either by a mediation service or by a service offering other (restorative or 'alternative') practices as well.

33 The mediator should give the parties the chance to read the report to be handed over to the prosecutor. Parties can adapt that report on their account. If youngsters do not want to participate in the mediation, this decision should be respected. If youngsters use violence, this will be reported.

dentiality and a basic attitude of the mediator including empathy and sincerity (Van Dijk et al., 2002b: 173-174).

Concerning training, mediation services referred to different moments and structures of consultation: concrete cases could be discussed in team meetings. Steering committees offered a forum for consultation with the judicial authorities and other services involved (e.g. victim assistance, lawyers, prosecutors and judges). Monthly meetings and seminars with regard to different topics were organised (Van Dijk et al., 2002b: 134).

2.1.3   Mediation practice[34]

Coincidental fluctuations at the local level could – according to the mediators – lead to a variation in the referrals. The numbers did not give a view on the qualitative aspects of the cases and there was no uniformity with regard to the way dossiers were compiled: registration differed in every service, which impeded comparability (Van Dijk et al., 2002a: 115-116). The registration depended on what could be considered a case (crime or offender) and on whether cases were started in a certain year or were still continuing from the year before (Van Dijk et al., 2002b: 136). In 2001, 1,293 youngsters were referred to mediation (Nuytiens et al., 2002: 30). On average, mediation processes took about three months. The time between the crime and the start of mediation varied; the aim was to have the start of mediation closely related to the facts since parties are then more likely to be willing to participate (Van Dijk et al. 2002a: 98). In general, in 2001 dossiers were handled within 11 to 22 weeks after the referral (Nuytiens et al., 2002: 49).

For three judicial districts (Ieper, Leuven and Tongeren), enough information was available to have a look at the proportion of mediation cases compared to the total amount of cases dealt with by the public prosecutor's office or the court during that year. The researchers referred to concrete figures in various judicial districts, showing that enormous differences existed.[35]

Most of the services were oriented towards youth between 12 and 18 years old, but were open to working with youth younger than 12. Mediators stated that the young person should recognise his own responsibility and that mediation is especially effective for first offenders, but should not be limited to those offenders (Van Dijk et al., 2002b: 137).

Different selection criteria were put forward by the services concerning the type of offences dealt with. Firstly, there had to be a victim that suffered identifiable damage. The crime had to be reported and the police investigation had to be com-

---

34   Note that, again, this information comes from the services themselves, since the information is gathered from their yearly reports or by the interviews.

35   In 2000 and 2001, no cases were referred to mediation in Ieper. In Leuven, the prosecutors referred 13.2% of the cases in 2000; in 2001, prosecutors referred to mediation in 12% of the cases, the youth court in 1.9% of the cases, taking into account this was the first year that mediation was available at the level of the youth court. In Tongeren, prosecutors referred 1.8% of the cases in 2000 and 1.5% in 2001 (Nuytiens et al., 2002: 53-64). In Leuven, around four-fifths of the (partially) completed mediations at the level of the prosecutor were dismissed (Nuytiens et al., 2002: 71).

pleted. Serious crimes could be dealt with, as long as the mediator worked carefully with the case. Judicial institutions still did not use mediation often enough, according to the mediators. With regard to the seriousness of the offence, the consequences of the crime had to be taken into consideration, not the objective facts as such: the crime may in fact be qualified as not serious, but participants may regard the consequences as serious, and vice versa. A condition to start the mediation was that offenders had a certain notion of responsibility so they realised that they had done something wrong (Van Dijk et al., 2002a: 98).

The figures of 2001, although incomplete, showed that 74.5% of the cases were property offences and 23% were crimes against persons. A minority of cases concerned indecent assault, traffic offences and others. In about 6% of the cases, adult co-offenders were involved (Nuytiens et al., 2002: 29-48).

With regard to the division between direct and indirect mediations, the services noted that there were not enough direct mediation cases (Van Dijk et al., 2002a: 97). Practice learned that direct mediation led to more intensive positive feelings about the process. Not participating in direct mediation was linked to different reasons (Van Dijk et al., 2002b: 193): fear of meeting the other party, not wishing to meet the other party, fear of not being able to cope with meeting the other party and not wishing to be reminded of the facts.[36]

The outcomes included different forms of restoration (Van Dijk et al., 2002b: 163). To provide for financial compensation, the youngster could find work, pay out of his own pocket or use the Compensation Fund.[37] Parents could pay, as well as their insurance company. Symbolic reparation or community service was possible, as well as moral restoration, for instance writing a letter of apology.

The judicial authorities could take several decisions after the mediation. The prosecutor often dismissed the case when a positive result was achieved.[38] If the case was prosecuted, the judge took the result of mediation into account. For mediation services, not reaching an agreement was not necessarily a negative result: further considerations needed to be taken into account, for instance whether the parties were satisfied (Van Dijk et al., 2002b: 188).

2.1.4   State of affairs (2010)

After the completion of the research project and the report, practice has further developed with regard to mediation in Flanders.[39] Firstly, the Flemish Community has decided to provide for services on 'Restorative and Constructive Settlements' (RCS) in every judicial district.[40] After the entry into force of the adapted

---

36   The report does not offer further explanation on these categories. One can wonder for instance what the difference between the first and third reason could entail. Further research with regard to non-participating parties would be interesting (Pemberton et al., 2006).

37   Cf. supra, 1.1.1. Mediation and conferencing in Belgium.

38   No concrete figures are presented.

39   We provide an update based on yearly reports since no research has been carried out since 2002. Since the research was limited to Flanders, we limit the update to Flanders as well.

40   In Dutch called 'Herstelgerichte en Constructieve Afhandelingen', or 'HCA'. Not all services provide for all the measures, cf. http://data.osbj.be/db/organisatie_overzicht.php (download 14.06.2007).

Youth Justice Act in 2006, these services do not only implement mediation and conferencing ('restorative settlements'), but also community service and educational projects ('constructive settlements') as well as the newly introduced measure 'parental training'.[41]

Organisation of the services
With the new Youth Justice Act, the Flemish Government had a legal basis to uniformly implement RCS-services throughout Flanders. Furthermore, the law explicitly formulates the possible referral procedures from the prosecutor and judge to the services. Reports by the services to the judicial authorities are to be strictly limited (because of confidentiality) and are subject to the parties' approval (art. 45 quater §4 and art. 37 quater §2).
The OSBJ had the task of coordinating the services, providing juridical and scientific information on youth delinquency and training on various topics. The OSBJ gave their input to the local steering groups and tried to come to a uniform implementation of RCS throughout Flanders.[42] It has, together with Suggnomè, developed a deontological code, which is being used informally.

Mediation in practice
The Youth Justice Act formulates clear conditions in order for mediation and conferencing to be offered to the parties: a victim has to have been identified, and parties have to take part on a voluntary basis and they should consent during the whole communication process (art. 45 quater and art. 37bis §1).
In 2001, a uniform registration scheme was developed by the OSBJ and it is being used by the RCS services since 2003. Figures are available for 2009 (Balcaen, 2010): 4,050 youngsters were referred to mediation, which entails 2,639 files (co-offenders are integrated into one file) and 3,832 victims. The cases dealt with were property crimes (69%) and crimes against persons (28%). Ninety-eight percent of the young offenders were male and the public prosecutor refers most cases. In a good third of the cases (37%), the whole communication process was completed.[43] In cases where parties went through the whole process, they usually came to an agreement. In cases where mediation was not carried out, the victim did not want to take part in the mediation process (31%) or did not have a further question (25%). About 14% of the young offenders did not want to take part. When an agreement was reached, it was most often complied with in practice (96%). Most mediation processes were indirect (81%).

---

41 In 'parental training', parents that are clearly indifferent towards their child's offending behaviour may be ordered to follow a course (art. 29bis and 45bis, Youth Justice Act; see also Berghmans, 2007).
42 www.osbj.be: the tasks with regard to restorative measures have been limited in the mean time.
43 In previous years (2005 to 2006), this was about half of the cases (44-46%).

2.2   Research on penal mediation

The general research question formulated by Raes (2006: 22) in her PhD research was whether *'penal transaction[44] and penal mediation as forms of justice with par-ticipatory, consensual and negotiated aspects at the level of the public prosecutor in practice lead to a communicative and participatory/horizontal justice or whether they remain more close to vertical justice?'* To reach a conclusion, the author studied the aim of implementing penal transaction and penal mediation, how they are put into practice, and whether they lead to a more horizontal justice. For our chapter, we limit ourselves to the results with regard to the practice of penal mediation and more specifically regarding the measure of repairing the damages (Raes, 2006: 303-377).

2.2.1   Research set-up
This PhD dissertation was written in the context of a research project called *'Con-temporary punishment'*, carried out by two research departments of the Free University of Brussels (Criminology and Metajuridica). Three promoters and four researchers were involved in the research, which took place from 2000 to 2005. Raes carried out theoretical research, as well as *'exploratory qualitative field research'*, which she considered to be *'penological empirical research'* (Raes, 2006: 23). She used a triangulation of methods, namely participative observations, analysis of documents and open interviews. The research started in December 2001 and the report was finished in 2006. The empirical research about penal mediation took place in the period from July to November 2002 and covered the judicial district of Brussels.[45]

2.2.2   Organisation of the services
Penal mediation is regulated by the Code of Criminal Procedure (art. 216ter). The public prosecutor may propose four measures to the suspect, which can be combined: reimbursing or repairing the damages towards the victim; medical treatment or therapy; training programme (maximum 120 hours); and community service (maximum 120 hours). Penal mediation can be offered in cases where the public prosecutor would not demand more than two years of imprisonment.[46] Although 'penal mediation' covers the four measures, in practice mediation is only applied to repair the damages vis-a-vis the victim.
'Justice assistants'[47] carry out the mediation work: they lead the preliminary nego-tiations with the parties. When an agreement is reached, the prosecutor must

---

44 In Dutch called *'minnelijke schikking'*, in which the public prosecutor invites the offender to repair damages to the victim and to pay a sum of money to the State.

45 For a period of 17 days, 31 encounters (of the justice assistant with the parties: 20 with offenders, 8 with victims and 3 between victim and offender) as well as twelve formal mediation sessions were observed. In nine cases the parties did not show up but the dossiers were analysed.

46 See also Lemonne (1999) and Aertsen (2000).

47 Justice assistants are mostly *'social workers and their general duty is to assist the public prosecutor in carrying out penal mediation'* (Lemonne, 1999: 137).

agree with its content. The procedure is concluded with a formal mediation session, which is led by the magistrate. It is considered to be a confirmation of the agreement between the victim and the offender. The justice assistant is responsible for following up the implementation of the agreement.

A uniform procedure was developed in Flanders through the '*Draaiboek bemiddeling in strafzaken*' (handbook penal mediation), which is used by all justice assistants. In practice, variations and differences still existed, according to Raes' research. A Circular (1999) determined that penal mediation should be oriented towards restoration and thus preferably be implemented in cases with an identifiable victim. In Brussels, a handbook was created for the public prosecutor (Brussels Vademecum).[48]

Yearly reports by the Houses of Justice,[49] indicate the total number of mediation cases in Belgium. Because Raes carried out her research in 2002 in Brussels, she referred to the national data of 2002 (Raes, 2006: 318-320): 6,084 dossiers were selected for penal mediation, of which 1,219 dossiers in Brussels. This represented 0.2% (for Belgium) or 0.08% (Brussels) of the total amount of cases that were dealt with at the prosecutor's level. Most cases at the prosecutor's level were dismissed (78.23%).

Raes (2006: 326-328) referred to two other forms of mediation, which were according to the justice assistants closely linked to penal mediation since they would cover similar crimes, namely 'pre-sentence and post-sentence mediation' on the one hand and 'local mediation' on the other hand.[50]

2.2.3 Mediation practice

As mentioned above, Raes limited her research to the judicial district of Brussels. Most cases dealt with property crimes (49%) and crimes against persons (34%). Cases were of a less serious nature and therefore the risk of net-widening was real, according to the justice assistants. They stated that sometimes cases would be better dealt with through local mediation, because it works on 'a deeper level' and it is less directly related to the judicial system.

Of the 1,219 dossiers selected in 2002 in Brussels, VOM was applied in 58% of the cases. It was mostly combined with another measure, which may be explained by prosecutors first considering the effect on the offender rather than the impact on the victim. In what follows, we only discuss the practice and results of VOM

---

48 According to a justice assistant who was interviewed (Raes, 2006: 323), all justice assistants use the same procedure in Brussels.

49 The House of Justice is an official institution in each judicial district. It is, among other things, the place of work of justice assistants who are involved in the implementation of numerous existing measures and sentences for adults (Dantinne, 1999) as well as the support of victims in the judicial proceedings.

50 Because Raes studied the practice of Brussels, these terms are used (and not the Flemish terms 'mediation for redress' and 'mediation at the level of the police').

(Measure 1: repairing the damages).[51] The mediation procedure as described in the research is as follows.

Justice assistants send a letter to the parties (victim and offender) in which they invite them to participate. The offender knows that the prosecutor will be informed about the offender's decision to participate or not.

When victims decide not to participate, the justice assistant sends them a form asking for their reasons not to participate. In Brussels, more offenders decided not to respond than victims (113 offenders compared to 19 victims). The number of offenders and victims who did not want to participate was almost identical (38 offenders, 39 victims).

According to the research observations, the first encounter usually took place in the office of the justice assistant, an environment considered more conducive to communication than the imposing settings of the court. However, since the office was located in the court buildings, the judicial framework was still present. The justice assistant met the offender first, then the victim. A lawyer or trusted person was welcome to be present, but seldom was. The aim of the first encounter was to motivate the parties to participate. The parties were free to decide whether or not to participate, but since they knew that judicial action might follow if they refused, it may have been – according to the author – more appropriate to speak about 'informed consent' rather than 'true voluntariness'. Although finding out the truth was not the aim of mediation, the crime and the suspect's involvement in it should have been made clear. The purpose of the mediation process was to reach an agreement.

According to justice assistants and as observed by Raes, offenders took part in mediation to avoid appearance in court and to accept their responsibility. Victims participated because of reparation; they were satisfied that something was being done with their case; and they were concerned with the future and the possible re-offending by the suspect. Again according to justice assistants, it was important for the victim to know what had happened, why the offender had committed the offence and whether he had taken responsibility for it.

Most of the mediations were indirect: this process was called 'shuttle diplomacy' (Raes, 2006: 350).[52] The agreement most often covered paying the damages (32%), but also in some cases involved explanations and excuses (25%), written apologies to the victim (18%), a promise by the offender not to re-offend (13%), oral apologies (3%) and reparation *in natura* (2%). Justice assistants indicated that the prosecutor confirmed almost all agreements. When no agreement could be reached, the prosecutor was informed. The justice assistants regretted that the prosecutor seldom informed them of the final decision in the case.

---

51 It is important to mention that with regard to the other three measures (therapy, training and community service), justice assistants are considered as mediators between the offender and the public prosecutor.

52 Raes (2006: 356) indicates she has no figures regarding to the proportion of direct/indirect mediations.

After the mediation process, a formal mediation session followed and formalised the agreement, and any other measures taken, between victim and offender. Raes referred to the yearly report of the Houses of Justice, according to which 43% of the cases in Brussels led to a formal mediation session, which took place in the office of the prosecutor. There were no formal guidelines as to how to conduct such a session. The victim was seldom present. According to Raes (2006: 368-369), the tone of these sessions was rather moralising and disapproving towards the offence and the suspect, which could be related to the fact that prosecutors were (in 2002) not so familiar with mediation.

Justice assistants were responsible for following up the implementation of the agreement and for reporting to the prosecutor on this matter. Raes (2006: 373) stated that according to the yearly report of the Houses of Justice, only 4% of the offenders 'failed' to implement the agreement after a formal mediation session took place. She further referred to the yearly statistics of the public prosecutors' offices, which revealed that penal mediation in Brussels took on average 651 days, which includes the judicial procedure or the time an offender needs to collect the money. She questions whether one year and a half (or even more) can still be considered a 'quick response', which was the intention of policy makers when preparing the law with regard to penal mediation.

3   ACTION-RESEARCH

The following four researches were labelled 'action-research'. The first two are, according to us, rather 'accompanying researches', in the sense that an assessment was made on possible future implementation in practice. The last two researches, on mediation for redress and conferencing, are action-research in a more strict sense since an actual practice was started up and evaluated.

3.1   *Experimental project on mediation for juveniles in the French Community*[53]

This research tried to assess the possibility of entrusting community service organisations[54] of the French Community with carrying out victim-juvenile offender mediation. It can be considered as an 'accompanying action-research', in which the study focused on whether a certain practice could be implemented. The French Community funded the research (1989 to 1991). The first phase (nine months) involved sensitising the social partners concerned (magistrates and com-

---

53   A report was written in French (Scieur et al., 1991). Even though this research is rather old, we think it is important to give the reader an idea about what issues were involved in practice, when it was first developed. This will help to understand the context and development of the practice of mediation in Belgium: VOM for juveniles has developed within a youth care context, which leads to certain characteristics typical to the Belgian situation and might lead to the practice being offender-oriented (Lemonne and Vanfraechem, 2005).

54   These are organisations that provide for community service for youth delinquents.

munity service organisations); informing the public at large through the organisation of a conference; experimenting with the practice of mediation in one judicial district; and developing tools of evaluation.

The objectives of the second phase (six months) were to extend the project to other judicial districts that might be interested; to develop groups of exchange and reflection with community services organisations and juvenile judges; to make systematic use of the data collected by the community service organisations; and to study the possibility of extending the projects to the sector of specialised care. Semi-structured questionnaires were developed and sent to community service organisations to enable them to answer the questions on all their files. A sample of 214 records for 124 youngsters was used.

The first part of the report evaluated the meetings between the magistrates and the services carrying out mediation (Scieur et al., 1991: 4-28). The concept was delineated: the aim of mediation was not to reach an agreement on financial aspects as such, but to sensitise the parties involved. The roles of the youngster, the victim and the judge were described. The essential objectives of mediation were for youngsters to realise the consequences of their offence and to put the victim at ease. The necessity of the agreement depended on the objective of the mediation: if the objective was to bring the parties together to meet and talk, that might be enough. But the aim could also be to achieve an agreement on the reparation. The proportionality of the agreement was an issue, as well as the method of repairing the harm: direct reparation of victim's damages and restitution were possible.

The first section of the report went on to discuss the link to judicial decisions. Mediation was encompassed by Article 37, §2, 2b of the Youth Justice Act (1965) and was thus considered to be a pedagogical measure, extending the concept of reparation in the law. Conditions for mediation between the youngster and the victim were described.

Next, the reactions of the magistrates were set out: all magistrates interviewed were in favour of mediation, but they had different opinions on how to implement it. Some questions arose: does mediation as such suffice as a reaction, or should it be combined with other measures? On what basis can one say that mediation is 'successful'? What about the victims?

The first section also presented the reactions of the community service organisations: is the point of view of the offender respected? Is it legitimate for us to take care of the victim? Is talking about the victim not enough? Are we able to undertake mediation and especially to undertake a meeting between offender and victim?

A second part of the report described the analysis of the data. Some data were quantitative (profiles of offenders and victims, type of decisions), while other data were qualitative (perception of the offender about the offence and the victim). The researchers concluded that the youngsters sent to the service had a profile which would suit mediation. The youngsters were old enough to accept their responsibility and were willing to do so. They were not really aware of the victim dimension and a meeting could help in that respect (Scieur et al., 1991: 59). The community service organisations could include mediation in the guidance mission as mandated by magistrates.

The third part of the report is the synthesis of the context in which mediation emerged in various countries and a presentation of the Belgian context. The last part looked at the possibility of extending the project towards the sector of specialised care.

3.2   Mediation for juveniles in the French Community[55]

In their 1999 report, Billen and Poulet called their research about 'Mediation in the Community Service Organisations' (*La médiation dans les services de prestations éducatives et philantropiques*) an 'accompanying action-research'. The research, which they presented as exploratory, is – according to us – more descriptive and evaluative.

During a period of just over a year, two people took part in this research. They analysed the mediation cases of three community service organisations in the period from September 1997 to December 1998. Initially, three NGOs (*Arpège, Gacep* and *Radian*), officially mandated by the French Community to organise community service, wanted this 'new' part of their job, i.e. the organisation of mediation, to be assessed. The French Community, the King Baudouin Foundation (*Fondation Roi Baudouin*) and the Belgian Lottery granted a small amount of money to fund this assessment.

The policy context of research is never neutral, and this was especially so in this case. Over the last few years, different government departments had been working, as mentioned, on the reform of the 1965 Youth Justice Act. Every proposal included mediation, but the traditional Belgian conflicts of competencies between the Communities and the federal level did not enhance the discussions on the reform. This research was meant to open the dialogue: who does (or should do) what and how should it be done?

The three NGOs mentioned above worked with a committee involving various representatives of those who might be 'interested' in mediation (whether in favour or not): judges, lawyers, representatives of victim associations and academics. The sponsors were also involved in the partnership.

---

55   We know of a French publication of the final report (Billen and Poulet, 1999). An extensive summary of the final report can be found in *Mille Lieux Ouverts*, Actes de la journée d'étude du 1/12/99, 'La médiation auteur-victime dans la justice des mineurs. Réflexions à partir de trois expériences en communauté française', 24 April 2000.

One of the main goals of the research was opening the discussion about media-tion and its use.[56] The authors wanted to explore the general objectives of media-tion; to analyse the local juvenile assistance policies and their link with mediation practice; to check if the mediation methods were appropriate; and to assess the satisfaction level of the different parties involved.

Collective and individual discussions with the professionals provided data on the practices, the framework and the methods used by the professionals. A stand-ardised form was elaborated to ensure that the services gathered the same kind of information. Various elements were analysed concerning the collection and analysis of process and output-data about mediation practices, such as types of referrals, characteristics of victims and offenders, completion rates and so on. The results were discussed with the professionals and the steering group. Semi-structured interviews with target groups of magistrates (two per judicial district), as well as with victims and offenders (15 files) were organised.

The results were set out as conclusions and recommendations. Mediation was – according to the authors – considered to be an interesting measure, as long as the programme was developed and implemented in a restorative network. Mediation within the judicial system is quite different from other types of mediation. Refer-rals should not only come from the public prosecutor's office, but also from the juvenile judge. The NGOs appointed by the French Community to organise com-munity service are 'not the worst place to carry out mediation' (p.102), because their settings allow for mediation to take place in a restorative-oriented context.[57] Finally, the authors provided some ideas on how to ensure that the restorative philosophy remains the basis of 'judicial mediation': frequent public speeches about restorative and relational mediation; good financing of the mediation serv-ices to maintain their high quality; regular evaluation of their work by independ-ent researchers; development of a restorative-oriented organisation of the judicial system; a list of mediation exclusion criteria instead of a list of appropriateness criteria; and recognising that mediation has its limits.

3.3   Mediation for redress in Flanders[58]

In this report, action-research was defined as a combination of an experiment and research. In the field of practice, a process of planned change was set up, in this particular case by introducing a new modality of dealing with the problem of crime. Parallel to this 'action', research was developed on how the process of change evolved (what are hindering and enhancing factors) and what the effects

56   The context of the research is important in that sense: mediation would be implemented in serv-ices that mainly deal with youngsters carrying out community service. Services were therefore not used to taking the victims' view into account (see also Lemonne and Vanfraechem, 2005).

57   This is formulated rather negatively. Internationally, discussion arises as to the degree of 'restor-ativeness' of community service and educational projects (e.g. Bazemore and Walgrave, 1999; McCold and Wachtel, 2002).

58   The aim of this project was to start mediation for more serious crimes, those which the prosecutor had already decided to prosecute (Peters and Aertsen, 1995; Aertsen, 1999; Aertsen, 2000: 159).

were. Finally, the report tried to formulate conclusions aimed at achieving generalisations of the practice.

The action-research took place in the period January 1993 to December 1995. The King Baudouin Foundation (Aertsen et al., 1994: 7) financed the project during the first period, while the Ministry of Justice financed the second phase (November 1994 to December 1995) (Aertsen and Van Garsse, 1996: 2 and 18). It was carried out by the research group Penology and Victimology at the Catholic University of Leuven.

The mediation for redress project started in a policy context in which the role of punishment and its societal function were reflected upon (Aertsen et al., 1994: 2-4). Negative evaluations of punishment and imprisonment, as well as attention for the needs of the victim, the restoration of societal order and reintegration of the offender, have led to the search for a more adequate solution. This research project was developed more out of a research interest than as the result of a concrete policy making decision.

It consisted of a cooperation project between three partners (Aertsen et al., 1994: 7-9): the research group Penology and Victimology of the Catholic University of Leuven; the public prosecutor's office in Leuven; and a non-profit organisation for judicial welfare work. Besides these three partners, a steering committee followed up the actual practice of mediation.[59]

The general aim of the research project (Aertsen et al., 1994: 6) was to develop a new societal form of reaction within the context of criminal justice, whereby restoration by the offender towards the victim is essential. It implied a systemic research into the method of mediation, as well as the judicial decision-making in the dossiers that were mediated. On the basis of concrete mediation cases, one could evaluate whether, and to what extent, this restorative approach is realisable, and its significance within the criminal justice context.

The concrete aim (Aertsen et al., 1994: 6) was linked to the actual practice of mediation: offender and victim were assisted in their communication process by a neutral third person. Mediation has several aims: to offer the victim a possibility to achieve restoration of the material and immaterial damage; to offer the offender the possibility to make up for the crime towards the victim; to offer the criminal justice system the possibility to take the mediated agreement into account in the further proceedings; and to achieve these three aims by means of a voluntary agreement between victim and offender.

Different methods were used to evaluate the aims (Aertsen et al., 1994: 10-11). Dossiers were compiled for each case based on the mediators' diaries in which they noted all the steps taken in the case, as well as letters sent out and personal notes.

---

59   One part-time researcher was involved in the project during the whole period, as well as a part-time mediator who was linked to the university. Two part-time co-workers were involved in the summer of 1994, for three months, to interview victims and offenders. A student at the university did most of the research in 1994 with regard to the attitudes of professionals towards the mediation project (Aertsen and Van Garsse, 1996: 1 and 19).

The practice of mediation was assessed through these diaries. Besides this evaluation, an end-evaluation was carried out by interviewing offenders and victims, once their dossier had been closed and provided they were willing to participate. Two temporary co-workers interviewed the participants. Judicial dossiers were studied to gain an idea about the judicial decision-making. Finally, a survey was done with various groups of professionals in order to discover attitudes and opinions of police, caregivers and lawyers on the design and possibilities of mediation.

The first report (Aertsen et al., 1994) included an overview of certain data: selection of the cases, overview of the cases, profile of victims and offenders, quantitative data on the dossiers, process and content of mediation, motivation of parties involved and evolution of their attitude, and the working principles.

Secondly, an evaluation of the different aims and methods was presented. The methods used in mediation entailed positive elements as well as obstacles. Interviews with the parties gave an idea about the effect on victim and offender; their opinion on the process of mediation and the mediator; their experience with direct mediation; the relation between mediation and the justice system; and their general experience with mediation. In general, the results were quite positive.[60] Victims said they experienced positive effects with regard to dealing with their emotions. Offenders were more positive than victims about the effect the mediation may have on preventing recidivism. Victims and offenders were generally satisfied with the timing and location of the mediation, but about half of the victims felt that mediation should have taken place earlier. Most of the victims and offenders thought the mediator was neutral and that he should be connected to the justice system somehow.

The judicial dossiers were studied to get an idea about the influence of the mediation on further judicial decision-making. This included the decision of the prosecutor to prosecute after mediation and the effect on the punishment ordered by the judge.

Professionals were interviewed in order to get an idea about whether or not the project could be generalised. Three groups of professionals received a written questionnaire: police, lawyers and care providers. Statements were included on the following topics: the desirability of mediation; its feasibility; the effects on the offender, victim and the judicial system; and the acceptance of the design of mediation by their own profession as well as by other professions. A second part of the questionnaire included seven hypothetical cases covering various levels of seriousness of crimes and consequences for the victim. The respondents were asked how they would like to see the case being dealt with. In general, professionals had a (very) positive attitude towards the idea of mediation, especially when it came to first offenders. Even when it was proposed as an alternative to prison, they did not disapprove of it, although the police did voice some concerns. The

---

60 But only 20 victims and 17 offenders were interviewed, so the results should be interpreted with caution.

facts influenced the way the professionals dealt with a case: the more serious the cases, the less appropriate they found mediation.

In concluding remarks, the practice of mediation was described and recommendations were made to enhance the design of the project and the actual practice.

In the second report, the first chapter described the further development of the project: the concept of mediation, the continuation of the project, and conclusions and perspectives. The second chapter linked mediation and restoration to the criminal justice system. More concretely, the position of the victims was studied: how can they be included in the justice system in a way that enhances the possibility of restoration towards them as well as towards society? Conditions in order to achieve restoration within the criminal justice system were studied. According to the authors, the practice of penal mediation, established by law in February 1994, offered a possibility to include the victim's interests within the criminal justice system. Community service offered a possibility to include restoration towards society. It could be carried out on the basis of the law on penal mediation, as well as the law on probation. The concluding remarks further noted that restoration and mediation would be achievable in the existing criminal justice system, but various elements ought to be taken into account such as ensuring that mediation is not 'recuperated' by the criminal justice system; broadening the idea of mediation through its implementation in various settings; and constant follow-up of its implementation (Aertsen and Van Garsse, 1996: 134-136).

3.4   Conferencing in Flanders[61]

In this project, action-research was described as a field of tension between research and practice, whereby the researcher has regular contact with the practitioners. On the one hand, theoretical elements can be integrated into practice and there is feedback from the researcher towards practice. On the other hand, practitioners inspire the research and ask questions and point out problems. Through this kind of research, the researcher is in the middle of the practice, but a certain level of objectiveness can still be maintained (Vanfraechem, 2001: 39). As a researcher, there is therefore a continual tension between involvement and keeping a distance regarding the practice. The research instruments (questionnaires, observation scheme) offer a filter for the subjective practice and its observation (Vanfraechem, 2002: 37-44).

The pilot project was set up in Flanders with regard to conferencing for serious juvenile delinquency during the period November 2000 to October 2003. Some mediation services continued to implement conferencing afterwards.[62]

---

61 Reports were written in Dutch, but articles in English are available as well (Vanfraechem, 2001, 2002, 2003a, 2003b, 2003c, 2005, 2007a; Vanfraechem and Walgrave, 2001, 2004a, 2004b, 2005, 2006).

62 The practice was further followed up in the framework of the researcher's PhD thesis in 2003-2005 (Vanfraechem, 2007a).

The project was situated at the level of the juvenile court: juvenile judges referred cases. Since it was a pilot-project, there was neither a legal basis nor an obligation to refer cases (Vanfraechem, 2001: 25-37), which resulted in not so many cases being referred. The research was funded by the Flemish Community, Ministry of Welfare, and carried out by the Research Group on Youth Criminology of the Catholic University of Leuven. The initiative for the project was taken when the Minister of Welfare of the Flemish Community wrote an open letter[63] inviting agencies to develop new initiatives and projects. The pilot project on conferencing was approved and was situated in the context of RJ, which the Minister considered to be one of three priorities for policy making (next to handling 'difficult' youngsters and thematic support and innovative projects). Thus, there was a clear policy-making context. The final report was handed over to the Ministry in November 2003. Because of its promising results, the Federal Ministry of Justice took an interest in it and implemented it in the reformed Youth Justice Act. Therefore, conferencing can be implemented throughout Belgium since April 2nd, 2007.[64]

Various partners were involved in this research project. The Research Group on Youth Criminology carried out the research. Mediators received training in conferencing methods and facilitated the communication processes between parties. A general Steering Committee was set up to oversee the pilot project in which different professionals were represented: juvenile judges, lawyers, social services, victim assistance, mediation services and others. A methodology group followed up and developed the actual practice; the mediators and the researcher were involved in this.

One full-time researcher carried out the work during a three-year period. During the first year, a full-time postdoctoral researcher[65] was also involved in helping to develop the research instruments. External financing funded his position. Students also observed some conferences and did interviews.

The general aim of the research (Vanfraechem, 2001: 39-40) was to find out whether or not conferences would be applicable in Flanders, and if so for whom. Six research questions were outlined:

1) Can conferencing be applied within the Belgian youth system, and if so how?
2) Are the legal safeguards guaranteed for the parties?
3) Are the participants satisfied with the process of conferencing?
4) Are the supporters of the young person strengthened in their educational role?

---

63   Letter by the then Minister of Welfare Mieke Vogels, dd 21 December 2000.
64   This did not influence the number of referrals too much: 114 youngsters were referred to conferencing in 2009 throughout Flanders, involving 81 files and 166 victims. In 24 dossiers, a conference was held including 33 youngsters and 41 victims. This means that only about 30% of the young offenders and 25% of the victims referred actually took part in a conference (Balcaen, 2010: 29-30). Where conferences did not take place, this was mostly because the victim did not want to participate (71%).
65   Dr. Nathan Harris, who worked at the Australian National University. He was involved in the RISE project in Canberra, Australia.

5) Can recidivism be reduced?
6) What is the relation between conferencing and closed institutions?[66]

Different research methods were used to evaluate the aims (Vanfraechem, 2001: 40-51). Through the study of the judicial dossier, certain items were recorded, for instance demographic elements and previous crimes. The facilitators filled out a questionnaire with regard to the preparation of the conference. An observation scheme presented a systematic overview of the conference. A semi-structured questionnaire was used to interview victims, offenders and offenders' parents in person. Ideally, victims were contacted about two weeks after the conference. The questionnaire was partly based on questionnaires used in RISE (Canberra, research by Sherman, Strang and others), New Zealand (the research by Maxwell and Morris) and some other areas in Australia (the research by Daly).[67] An overview of literature that constituted the theoretical part of the report was presented. It gave the researcher the opportunity to answer questions from the practitioners on certain topics.

The practice of conferencing is described in the research report (Vanfraechem, 2003a: 21-119): 54 conferences took place for 58 youngsters during the pilot project (a conference could be organised for the co-offenders together). Afterwards, another 51 young offenders participated in 39 conferences (2004 to 2005). In about half of the conferences (2000 to 2003), the victim was present. In a fifth, their partner or a family member represented them. The number of conferences with at least one victim present later increased to 32 out of 39 and in two other conferences the victim was represented (2004 to 2005). It therefore seems as though the experience of the facilitator may have an influence in motivating the victim to attend (Vanfraechem, 2007a).

The conferences took on average about two hours and fifteen minutes. They took place at a mediation centre or a local cultural centre, usually at night or during the weekend to accommodate working participants. An agreement was reached in all conferences and the juvenile judges accepted all agreements. Lawyers were almost always present for the young offender.[68] A police officer was present to read out the facts and point out the seriousness of the crime. In a few cases, the social worker of the youth court was present to support the youngsters. Just a few victims were aware of the existence of victim assistance, even though the conferences dealt with rather serious offences, for which referral to victim assistance by the police is obligatory in Belgium (De Fraene et al., 2005).

---

66 This research question was added during the last year of the project (Vanfraechem, 2003a: 16).

67 See, for instance, Sherman et al. (1997), Maxwell and Morris (1996) and Daly (2001).

68 In the Belgian legal system, the youngster has the right to have a lawyer present at all stages of the judicial procedure. The newly reformed Youth Justice Act seems to exclude lawyers from the communication process, which leads to heated debates (Vandebroek and Vanfraechem, 2007).

Since cases were referred at a rather slow rate, not too many conferences were held (105 conferences during five years, in five judicial districts). This limited the possibility to generalise the results. Nevertheless, some promising results were achieved (Vanfraechem, 2003a: 120-214, 2004). A referral procedure was worked out so that conferencing could be included in the existing legal provisions. Since no legislation was at hand,[69] some judicial problems still stood, such as the judicial position of the police and the availability of legal advice for the victim. The lawyers involved in the conferences did safeguard procedural guarantees. The juvenile judge kept an overview of the proceedings and checked judicial issues as well as the proportionality of the agreements.

The participants felt that their rights were protected. In general, participants were satisfied with various aspects of the conference, although some points of attention still remained, such as ensuring that all participants could have their say. Some youngsters brought along several support people, others only their parents and a lawyer. Facilitators thought that the involvement of an extended network led to better results. Victims could bring support persons as well. Although they brought fewer support persons, they felt well supported.

Recidivism was hard to measure, especially since no control group could be used. Through the study of the judicial dossiers, it was found that for 22% of the youngsters who participated in a conference new crimes were recorded 6 to 18 months after the conference. For 58% of youngsters that were referred to a conference, but did not attend, new crimes were recorded.[70] Recidivism did not impede the implementation of the conference agreement (i.e. almost all agreements were correctly implemented) and the new crimes appeared to be of a less serious nature than the ones committed before the conference.

Conferencing could influence the decision to place a youngster in a juvenile secure unit, as well as the decision to remove them from the centre.[71] Where conferences were used as an alternative to confinement, the youngster would attend the conference instead of being sent to an institution. Youngsters who were already in an institution could leave the institution to attend a conference or to implement the agreement reached. That way, the needs of the victim would be taken into account and the youngster's return to his home would be facilitated.

Besides these research questions, further issues arose when studying the developing practice: safeguarding the confidentiality of the meeting; presence or absence of victims at the conference; role of the police, lawyer and social service; defining

---

69 At the time of research (2000 to 2005). The new Youth Justice Act did not solve the problems mentioned (Vandebroek and Vanfraechem, 2007).

70 The fact that they chose not to participate (or that there was another reason why they could not participate) may have influenced the recidivism rate (Vanfraechem, 2005: 290). Since these percentages are based on a small number of dossiers, they should be treated carefully.

71 Since this research question was only added during the last year, it was only studied in a hypothetical manner, namely by asking judges and personnel of the closed institutions what they considered the possible relation between confinement in an institution and conferencing could entail (Vanfraechem, 2003a).

the damages; the relation of the underlying problems of the juvenile and restoration of the damages.

4   EVALUATIVE RESEARCH

4.1   The Flemish Compensation Fund[72]

This research entailed three elements: a study of the institutional position of the Compensation Fund;[73] observation and description of the functioning of the fund; and an inquiry on the satisfaction and general experience of victims, offenders and relevant third persons. We mainly focus on the third part, since it described the mediation aspects.[74] The first element of the research (locating the Compensation Fund at the level of the province) was carried out on the basis of a literature study and interviews with professionals of administrative and constitutional law. For the second topic (description of the functioning of the fund), the researcher observed and studied the practice of the fund. The research was considered as an evaluation and action-research, whereby the researcher observes the practice, but also participates in it (Stassart, 1999: 10-13). It is not clear from the report, though, to what extent the 'action' part was really put into practice, therefore we would rather catalogue it as an evaluative research.

The project was funded by the province Vlaams-Brabant and the Flemish Community Commission. A researcher at the Research Group on Penology and Victimology, Catholic University of Leuven, was employed for a period of ten months and two weeks full-time from 1998 to 1999.

Methodologically, a registration form was made in order to register the necessary data on the file (Stassart, 1999: 98-102). People were either interviewed in person or over the phone, reaching a response rate of 50%. A standardised scheme was used for the interviews, with closed and open questions. Twenty-one offenders, 29 victims, 18 significant persons for the offender and 3 significant persons for the victim were interviewed. The personal interviews took place at the university, which is a neutral venue. Two students were paid to interview the participants.

The evaluation of the project by the parties was positive. Victims and offenders showed a positive attitude towards the fund. Although the offer to participate was unexpected, they did not hesitate in taking it up. Different motives were put forward as reasons to participate (Stassart, 1999: 104-107).

Offenders saw it as a chance to make up to the victim. Most respondents thought that it was not a good idea to have parents pay for the damage and they explicitly

---

72   A report was written in Dutch (Stassart, 1999). See also Van Dijk et al. (2002b: 91).

73   Cf. supra 1.1.Victim-offender mediation and conferencing in Belgium.

74   If a young offender wishes to compensate the damages for the victim through a mediation process, but does not have the resources to do so, he can apply for the fund to pay for his 'volunteer work' so that the damages can be paid directly to the victim.

wanted the offender to take an active role. Most offenders felt that the offer to participate in mediation should be made to all offenders, while four out of ten victims disagreed and did not think the offer should be made to all offenders (Stassart, 1999: 110-111).

Almost all victims and offenders were satisfied: 51.9% of the victims were very satisfied and 89.7% would participate again. Forty percent of the offenders were very satisfied and 76.2% would participate again. Two thirds of the offenders found the victim's demands reasonable. Almost all victims thought mediation was a better solution than the judicial procedure, since the latter is too complex, too time-consuming and not oriented towards victims. Of the offenders, 61.9% and 46.4% of the victims thought the offer to participate should be made sooner after the crime.

Participants did not get a broader view on facts, persons and feelings, which could – according to the author – be linked to the fact that a lot of mediations happened indirectly, i.e. the mediator conveyed the feelings and expectations without victim and offender meeting face-to-face. On the one hand, 57.1% of the offenders stated that their participation did not have an added value for the victim or that they did not know of such a value. This could again be linked to the indirect communication process. On the other hand, 68.9% of the victims thought their participation had an effect on at least one offender (co-offenders could be involved). Victims felt it was important for the offender to see what he did to the victim and that he could take responsibility. Possibly reducing recidivism is also important for the victims. Forty-five percent felt it helped them as a victim to deal with what had happened. Offenders felt that it was important for them to take responsibility, and that the mediation led to a change within themselves and their family. Almost all parties were satisfied with the mediator. Most people felt recognised and free in taking decisions; offenders felt this even more than victims.

Direct mediation took place in half of the cases. In those direct mediations, 20% of the victims and 54.5% of the offenders were at first scared of the idea of meeting the other party in person. In the end, almost all were happy to have met the other party. Half of the offenders and 4 out of 10 victims did not want to meet the other party face-to-face for different reasons. If the direct meeting had been a necessary condition for mediation, most of them would still have participated.

Some other elements were discussed in the report, for instance the source of money for the Compensation Fund: offenders thought taxpayers or sponsors should pay for the fund; victims agreed with some reservations. What was the significance of the fund for victims? Most of them thought it was important to 're-educate' the offender. They saw it as a reassurance to themselves or as a unique happening. Offenders thought the mediation was more personal, more pleasant, less severe and yet more effective than the traditional system.

Victims and offenders were asked about their satisfaction with the further handling of the case on different levels: information received, opportunity for further judicial reaction and their opinion on taking into account the results of the mediation by the prosecutor. One third of the offenders did not really know what action the prosecutor took in their case. Only 20.7% of the victims were aware of further action. Of the respondents, 54.2% of them did not expect to be informed, but would have liked to be informed. Furthermore, 96.6% of the victims thought the offender did enough to make up for the crime and 89.7% thought that no further reaction was needed. All offenders felt that they did enough and 85.7% felt that no further reaction was needed. Finally, 76.2% of the offenders and 65.5% of the victims thought the prosecutor should take the result of the mediation into account in all cases.

4.2   Local mediation as an alternative measure for petty offences in Belgium[75]

4.2.1   Research set-up

The research was carried out from January to September 2003 and funded by the Minister of Economy and Scientific Research, in charge of Urban Policy. The Criminological Research Group of the Free University of Brussels (ULB) and the Penology and Victimology Research Group of the Catholic University of Leuven collaborated in the research. Two part-time researchers were involved. The study scrutinises services in Brussels and in Flanders.

'Local mediation' (or mediation at the level of the police) was defined as an alternative measure for minor offences. It was initiated at the moment of the registration of a complaint towards adult offenders. Police forces referred the complainant to the closest mediation service. The offences included contraventions and minor misdemeanours such as conflicts related to limited material harm, or involving persons who know each other or who see each other on a regular basis. On the basis of these definitions, eleven mediation services were selected for the research.

Three main objectives were assigned to the research. The first objective entailed clarifying the aims, the institutional link and the organisational framework of local mediation and more specifically in relation with penal mediation.[76] The second aim entailed analysing practices developed by the different projects towards their target audiences (types of demand, types of resolutions, partnerships etc.). A third goal included realising an exploratory study related to the satisfaction of the parties, the way local mediation is perceived by the public and the follow-up of the offenders. But due to a lack of time and means, this part of the research simply defined the relevant themes, which would merit their own research.

Different methods were used to achieve the two goals. Firstly, an important documentary research entailed a literature review on mediation in general but also an analysis of the circular letters, the activity reports of the services, internal notes, working instruments and websites. Secondly, semi-structured and unstructured interviews were conducted with local mediators. The semi-structured interviews clarified the status, working place, administrative authority, privileged mediation techniques etc. of the mediators. The unstructured interviews were conducted

---

75   A report is available in both Dutch and French (Aertsen and Lemonne, 2003a, 2003b).
76   Cf. supra, 1.1.1. Victim-offender mediation and conferencing in Belgium.

around case files in order to clarify the practices. Thirty files were analysed. Lastly, a focus group was held. The main methodological problems mentioned were that quantitative data presented by the services were not uniform and were related to different periods of time, which impeded the presentation of generalised data.

4.2.2   Organisation of the services

The researchers accurately described the organisation of the services. Local specificities were numerous and cannot be summarised here. Nevertheless we would like to mention some important characteristics.

Various public authorities funded the selected services: the Ministry of Interior Affairs, the local authority or the police zone. The nature of the funding could limit the geographical area covered by the service and permanent funding was not guaranteed. Most of the services were institutionally attached to a municipality. Some of them depended directly on the police forces.

The main common aim was to relieve police and prosecutors from an overload of work. A greater attention to victims was present in every project but RJ aims seemed to be more explicit in the Flemish projects.

A common regulation existed in Brussels (a circular letter issued by the prosecutor) but not in Flanders where steering groups, at the level of a judicial district, tried to coordinate and sustain the projects. Eighteen mediators (part- or full-time) worked in the eleven services, but not all of them were trained in mediation techniques.

Most of the files in Brussels dealt with people who did indeed know each other or who would see each other again, which was not the case in Flanders. Generally, files were selected by police forces but in some areas the public prosecutor selected cases as well. The main crime in Brussels was assault, while in Flanders the emphasis lay on minor property offences.

Direct mediation was, in principle, privileged but practice showed that indirect mediation was used much more frequently. Criteria used for the success or failure of mediation varied. Collaboration with police forces and prosecutors was described as of good quality in Flanders. Collaboration with other types of mediation services was more systematic in Brussels.

4.2.3   Analysis of mediation practice and recommendations

In Flanders as well as in Brussels, the research showed how 'local mediation' could comprise a variety of practices. The researchers have tried to define a typology of local mediation services by distinguishing three types of rationality.

The first one was called 'authoritarian local mediation'. This kind of mediation was more or less similar to the formal judiciary reaction. Mediation focused on the offender and aimed less at communication between stakeholders than at restitution. In this model, mediation was firstly considered as a management tool for the problems encountered by criminal justice.

The second type was called 'insular mediation', where mediation functioned as a small island inside a judicial procedure. Here, mediators were more neutral and better trained. They considered the judicial institution as a partner with which they had to collaborate. The process focused on negotiation-restitution as well as on interpersonal relations.

The last type was 'local community mediation'. Mediation was considered as an alternative dispute resolution and as a service to the citizens. Interpersonal mediation was privileged. Mediation but also social or therapeutic techniques were used. Mediators did not feel obliged to work with police forces and the criminal justice system that were perceived as partners, just like other partners.

The researchers insisted that, above all, these types must be considered as ideal forms against which practices could be positioned. Each type had advantages but also potential risks and limitations, which were further analysed by the researchers.

Questions about the link between the judicial and mediation rationale were raised. As a consequence, the researchers recommended to clarify the aims of local mediation and to define a more uniform approach. This uniformity should not be imposed but should be the result of a discussion with all partners involved. The researchers suggested that local mediation should be applied as soon as possible as a diversion method, and, if possible, before the complaint has been registered by the police. Police forces should inform those involved in the conflict about the advantages and disadvantages of the different ways of resolving their conflict without having to make a report. The local mediator should keep a specific role in comparison with the social mediator: his action, focused on the complaint, should be relayed to other mediators, if an underlying problem appears and if both parties ask for it. Collaboration with other mediators could be easier if local mediators were integrated in a 'House of Mediation'.

Programmes of local mediation should be extended to the whole population but not without guarantees. Mediators should for instance be well trained and have the opportunity to discuss cases; legal consequences and relations with the public prosecutor have to be clarified; and mid- or long-term financing should be found. Reform of local mediation is complex and should – again according to the authors – be associated with a global idea about the role and place of our criminal justice system in our society.

5   CONCLUSION

The questions raised by Aertsen (2000: 190), can be answered tentatively.

> 'Will a consistent vision be elaborated and will a coherent and advanced policy on restorative justice and victim-offender mediation be carried out? Will restorative justice be high enough on the political agenda to start a coordinated approach between the federal government, the College of Prosecutors-General and the Communities?'

In recent years, we have witnessed a positive evolution since legislation has been implemented for juveniles as well as for adults. Suggnomè and OSBJ in Flanders and Médiante in the French Community are organisations that strive for a standardised implementation in the two Communities. Mediation is available for adults at every stage of the legal procedure. Mediation and conferencing are available for young offenders throughout the country. A Compensation Fund continues to be available in Flanders. However, the future will show to what extent organisations offering mediation services can guarantee their independence from the judicial actors since legislative documents clearly make the link between them.

Extensive research has been done, but more empirical research is needed, for instance to collate a systematic overview of the mediation practice for adults in Flanders and for adults and juveniles in the French Community. Quantitative data are needed in order to guide policy decisions and form a basic starting point for further research. More training and development of good practice are also required. Research is needed on the relation between practices of RJ and the justice system, as well as on the ability of legislation to enhance the use of mediation and conferencing. Limited research is available on recidivism,[77] cost-effectiveness and the perception of the mediator. No research has used control and experimental groups, which impedes generalisation of the data. Research on legal safeguards has begun,[78] but no general comparison to the criminal justice system is available.

Notwithstanding these limitations, we note that information is available on the practice of mediation with juveniles in Flanders, as well as in the French Community (albeit to a smaller extent). Mediation for redress, penal mediation and local mediation for adults have been researched, as has the use of the Compensation Fund for youngsters in Flanders. The action-research on conferencing gives an idea about the actual practice, as well as some methodological issues that arise when implementing such a practice.

We can end on a positive note by stating that efforts have been made in Belgium to empirically research mediation and conferencing in criminal cases. Furthermore, action-research has proven to be effective in implementing new practices and influencing policy making. In that respect, the difference with the Netherlands (as described in this volume) is striking. In the Netherlands, practices seem to be strictly evaluated (often according to 'criminal' justice criteria, rather than RJ criteria) and abandoned when they do not fulfil the obligations. In Belgium, policy-making has been increasingly directed towards RJ (see for instance the implementation of mediation at all levels for adult offenders after the 2005 law and the inclusion of conferencing in the Youth Justice Act of 2006) even though

---

77   Through the study of judicial dossiers, a first attempt has been undertaken in the action-research on conferencing for juveniles in Flanders (Vanfraechem, 2007a).
78   Some issues in this regard are addressed by the research on conferencing for juveniles (Vanfraechem, 2003a). The principal discussion has been covered by e.g. Eliaerts and Dumortier (2002). See also Moreau (2004) and Lauwaert (2008).

research is not so extensive (see also Vanfraechem, 2009). We can conclude that in Belgium, practice, theory (research) and policy do seem to go hand-in-hand on the road to restorative justice, mutually enforcing each other's strengths and challenging their self-evident decisions and ideas.

References

Aertsen, I. (1999) 'Mediation bei schweren Straftaten – auf dem Weg zu einer neuen Rechtskultur?' in Pelikan, C. (ed.) *Mediationsverfahren: Horizonte, Grenzen, Innensichten (Jahrbuch für Rechts- und Kriminalsoziologie)* (Baden-Baden: Nomos Verl.-Ges.), pp. 115-138.

Aertsen, I. (2000) 'Victim-Offender Mediation in Belgium', in European Forum for Victim-Offender Mediation and Restorative Justice (ed.) *Victim-Offender Mediation in Europe. Making Restorative Justice Work* (Leuven: Leuven University Press), pp. 153-192.

Aertsen, I. (2001) 'Herstelrecht in Europees perspectief', *Panopticon*, 22(5), pp. 409-422.

Aertsen, I. (2005) 'Restorative Prisons: A Contradiction in Terms?', in Emsley, C. (ed.) *The Persistent Prison. Problems, Images and Alternatives* (London: Francis Boutle Publishers), pp. 196-213.

Aertsen, I., Christiaensen, S., Daeninck, Ph., Van Camp, T. and Van Win, T. (2001) *Wetenschappelijke ondersteuning van het project herstelgerichte detentie* (Leuven: K.U. Leuven).

Aertsen, I., Daems, T. and Robert, L. (eds.) (2006) *Institutionalizing Restorative Justice* (Cullompton: Willan Publishing).

Aertsen, I. and Lemonne, A. (2003a) *La médiation locale comme 'mesure alternative pour les délits de faible importance en Belgique'.* Available at: http://solvay.edu/FR/Programmes/Desmap/seminaires/documents/mediationlocalerapport2003.doc (download 14.06.2007).

Aertsen, I. and Lemonne, A. (2003b) *Lokale bemiddeling of schadebemiddeling als 'alternatieve maatregel voor lichte misdrijven in België'.* Available at: http://www.politiquedesgrandesvilles.be/content/themes/safety-security/lokale_bemiddeling.pdf (download 14.06.2007).

Aertsen, I., Van Garsse, L. and Peters, T. (1994) *Herstelbemiddeling. Onderzoeksrapport periode 1/1/1993-31/10/1994* (Leuven: K.U. Leuven), published in Lampaert, F. (ed.) *Gevangenis en Samenleving II* (Brussel: Koning Boudewijnstichting), pp. 165-222.

Aertsen, I. and Van Garsse, L. (1996) *Tussen dader en slachtoffer: bemiddeling in de praktijk. Onderzoeksrapport herstelbemiddeling periode 1/11/1994-31/12/1995, unpublished report* (Leuven: K.U. Leuven).

Balcaen, L. (2006) *De belangrijkste cijfers herstelbemiddeling, gemeenschapsdienst en leerprojecten voor minderjarigen 2004.* Available online at www.osbj.be/publicaties/cijfersHCA2004.pdf

Balcaen, L. (2010) *HCA Cijfernota 2009*. Available at: www.osbj.be – jaarverslagen en rapporten.

Bazemore, G. and Walgrave, L. (eds.) (1999) *Restorative Juvenile Justice – Repairing the Harm of Youth Crime* (Monsey: Willow Tree Press).

Berbuto, S. and Van Doosselaere, D. (2007) 'Les offres restauratrices; approche pratique et questions juridiques', in Moreau, T. and Berbuto, S. (eds.) *Réforme du droit de la jeunesse. Questions spéciales* (Liège: Antemis), 97, pp. 53-111.

Beyens, K. (2000) 'Strafuitvoering en justitiële hulpverlening. Vier jaar bemiddeling in strafzaken: 1995-1998', *Panopticon*, pp. 260-270.

Berghmans, M. (2007) 'Positie van de ouders', in Put, J. and Rom, M. (eds.) *Het Nieuwe Jeugdrecht* (Gent: Larcier), pp. 215-234.

Billen, D. and Poulet, I. (1999) *La médiation dans les services de prestations éducatives et philanthropiques. Évaluation de trois projets pilotes, rapport final* (Bruxelles: Synergie).

Brouckmans, P., De Jaegher, K., Vandeurzen, I., Verhoeven, H. and Verstraete, A. (1998) *Vrijheidstraf en herstelrecht: kan dat?* (Leuven: K.U. Leuven).

Buonatesta, A. (2004) 'La médiation entre auteur et victime dans le cadre de l'exécution de la peine', *Revue de Droit Pénal et de Criminologie*, 2, pp. 242-257.

Burssens, D. and Vettenburg, N. (2006) 'Herstelgericht groepsoverleg op school. Een constructief antwoord op ernstige incidenten op school', in Walgrave, L. and Vettenburg, N. (eds.) *Herstelgericht groepsoverleg. Nieuwe wegen in de aanpak van jeugddelinquentie en tuchtproblemen* (Leuven: LannooCampus), pp. 71-99.

Christiaensen, S., Vandeurzen, I., Verhoeven, H., Bastiaensen, R. and Van de Ven, K. (2000) *Herstelgerichte detentie. Van actie-onderzoek naar beleidsvoering* (Leuven: K.U. Leuven).

Claes, M., Spiesschaert, F., Van Dijk, C., Vanfraechem, I. and Van Grunderbeeck, S. (2003) 'Alternative practices for juvenile justice in Flanders (Belgium): the case for mediation', in Walgrave, L. (ed.) *Repositioning Restorative Justice. Restorative Justice, Criminal Justice and Social Context* (Cullompton: Willan Publishing), pp. 255-270.

Claes, E., Foqué, R. and Peters, T. (eds.) (2005) *Punishment, Restorative Justice and the Morality of Law* (Antwerpen: Intersentia).

Daly, K. (2001) *South Australia Juvenile Justice (SAJJ) Research on Conferencing, Technical Report No.2: Research Instruments in Year 2 (1999) and Background Notes* (Brisbane: School of Criminology and Criminal Justice, Griffith University). Available at: http://www.aic.gov.au/rjustice/sajj/tech-report-2.pdf.

Dantinne, M., (1999) 'Maisons de justice', *Journal des tribunaux*, 5947, pp. 773-781.

De Fraene, D., Lemonne, A. and Nagels, C. (2005) 'Débats autour de la victime: entre science et politique', *Revue de droit de l'ULB*, 31(1), pp. 55-92.

Deklerck, J. (2007) 'Re-link-ing de-linq-uency : why the mediation process works', in Mackay, R., Bosnjak, M., Deklerck, J., Pelikan, C., van Stokkom and Wright, M. (eds.) *Images of restorative justice theory* (Frankfurt am Main: Verlag für Polizeiwissenschaft), pp. 185-204.

Deklerck, J. and Depuydt, A. (2004) 'Straf, herstel en verbondenheid. Van indi-vidualiserende naar personerende verantwoordelijkheid', in van Stokkom, B. (ed.) *Straf en herstel. Ethische reflecties over sanctiedoeleinden* (Den Haag: Boom Juridische Uitgevers), pp. 211-228.

Demet, S., Jacqmain, C. and Parello, E. (2000) *Le développement d'un concept de justice restaurative dans le cadre carcéral. Recherche-action au sein des établisse-ments pénitentiaires d'Andenne, Tournai et Jamioulx* (Liège: Université de Liège).

De Ruyver, B., Vander Beken, T. and Van Daele, L. (1997) *Toepassing van de alter-natieve afdoening. Een oriënterende studie* (Brussel: Koning Boudewijnstich-ting).

Dubois, C. (2009) *La justice réparatrice en milieu carcéral: plasticité d'une fonction et malléabilité d'un concept criminologique.* Thèse de doctorat (Liège: Université de Liège).

Eliaerts, C. and Dumortier, E. (2002) 'Restorative justice for juveniles: in need of procedural safeguards and standards', in Weitekamp, E. and Kerner, H.-J. (eds.) *Restorative Justice in Context: International Practice and Directions* (Cul-lompton: Willan Publishing), pp. 204-223.

Eyckmans, D. (2006) *Mediation in Belgium: law of 22 June 2005 Implementing Mediation in the Code of Criminal Procedure.* Available at: http://www.restora-tivejustice.org/articlesdb/articles/7250

Hanozin, C., Piers, A., Van Boven, B., Vanempten, N. and Vanneste, C. (1997) 'La loi du 10 février 1994 organisant une procédure de médiation pénale en Belgique. Evaluation de sa mise en application', *Revue de Droit Pénal et de Criminologie*, 6, pp. 589-635.

Hodiaumont, F. and Malempré, H. (2001) *Orienter l'exécution des peines vers la réparation, Rapport de recherche final* (Liège: Université de Liège).

Hodiaumont, F., Malempré, H., Aertsen, I., Daeninck, Ph., Van Camp, T. and Van Win, T. (2004) *Vade-mecum justice réparatrice en prison* (Gent: Academia Press).

Lauwaert, K. (2008) *Herstelrecht en procedurele rechtswaarborgen* (Antwerpen: Maklu).

Lemonne, A. (1999) 'The development of Restorative Justice – the case of penal mediation in Belgium', *Kriminalistik Arbog*, Kriminalistik Skriftserie nr.7 (Copenhagen: Copenhagen University), pp. 131-147.

Lemonne, A. and Aertsen, I. (2003) *La médiation locale comme 'mesure alterna-tive pour les délits de faible importance en Belgique. Rapport final*, unpublished (Brussels: U.L.B., Centre de recherches criminologiques).

Lemonne, A. and Vanfraechem, I. (2005) 'Victim-Offender Mediation for Juve-niles in Belgium', in Mestitz, A. and Ghetti, S. (eds.) *Victim-Offender Media-tion with Youth Offenders in Europe* (Dordrecht: Springer), pp. 181-208.

Lemonne, A., (2007) 'Chronique de criminologie – evolution récente dans le champ de la médiation en matière pénale: entre idéalisme et pragmatisme', *Revue de Droit Pénal et de Criminologie*, 3, pp. 156-166.

Martin, D. and Meyvis, W. (1997) *Mesures et peines alternatives – Vademecum pénologique* (Kortrijk-Heule and Brussels: UGA).

Mary, Ph. and De Fraene, D. (1996) *Sanctions et mesures dans la communauté. état de la question en Belgique* (Brussels: Fondation Roi Baudouin).

Maxwell, G. and Morris, A. (1996) 'Research on Family Group Conferences with Young Offenders in New Zealand', in Hudson, J., Morris, A., Maxwell, G. and Galaway, B. (eds.) *Family Group Conferences: Perspectives on Policy and Practice* (Monsey: The Federation Press-Criminal Justice Press), pp. 88-110.

McCold, P. and Wachtel, T. (2002) 'Restorative Justice Theory Validation', in Weitekamp, E. and Kerner, H.-J. (eds.) *Restorative Justice. Theoretical Foundations* (Cullompton: Willan Publishing), pp. 110-142.

Meyvis, W. and Martin, D. (1997) *Alternatieve maatregelen en straffen*, Vol.1 and 2 (Kortrijk-Heule and Brussels: UGA).

Moreau, T. (2004) 'Quelques questions juridiques à propos des mesures de diversion et de la médiation dans le champ de la protection de la jeunesse', in Bosly, H.-D., Born, M., Broly, C. et al. (eds.) *La réaction sociale à la délinquance juvénile. Questions critiques et enjeux d'une réforme* (Brussels: Dossier de la Revue de Droit Pénal et de la Criminologie, La Charte), pp. 69-98.

Nuytiens, A., Van Grunderbeeck, S., Spiesschaert, F. and Vanthuyne, T. (2002) *Herstelgerichte afhandelingen van delicten gepleegd door minderjarigen: Leerprojecten – Gemeenschapsdiensten – Herstelbemiddeling. Eindrapport,* unpublished (Belgium: VUB, UGent and K.U. Leuven).

Pemberton, A., Winkel, F.W. and Groenhuijsen, M.S. (2006) 'Op weg naar slachtoffergerichte theorievorming in het herstelrecht', *Tijdschrift voor Herstelrecht,* 6(1), pp. 48-64.

Peters, T. and Aertsen, I. (1995) 'Restorative justice: In search of new avenues in judicial dealings with crime. The presentation of a project of mediation for reparation' in Fijnaut, C., Goethals, J., Peters, T. and Walgrave, L. (eds.) *Changes in society, crime and criminal justice in Europe,* vol.1 (Antwerp: Kluwer Rechtswetenschappen België), pp. 311-342.

Put, J. (2007) 'The Juvenile Justice System in Belgium' in Giostra, G. (coord.) and Patanè, V. (ed.) *European Juvenile Justice Systems*, vol. I (Milano: Giuffrè Editore), pp. 3-37.

Put, J. and Walgrave, L. (2006) 'Belgium: From Protection Towards Accountability?' in Muncie, J. and Goldson, B. (eds.) *Comparative Youth Justice* (London–Thousand Oaks–New Delhi: SAGE Publications), pp. 111-126.

Raes, A. (2006) *Een communicatieve en participatieve justitie? Een onderzoek bij het openbaar ministerie als hedendaagse bestraffer,* unpublished Phd dissertation (Brussels: Vrije Universiteit Brussel).

Scieur, Y., Van Duüren, F. and Van Duüren, N. (1991) *Bilan de la seconde phase du projet expérimental de résolution de conflit en matière de protection de la jeunesse. La médiation victime – jeune contrevenant,* unpublished (Louvain-La-Neuve).

Seykens, V. and Van Doosselaere, D. (2007) 'La Concertation Restauratrice en Groupe: une offre, une proposition, mais encore', *Mille Lieux Ouverts,* 37, pp. 41-50.

Sherman, L., Braithwaite, J., Strang, H., Barnes, G.C., Christie-Johnston, J., Smith, S. and Inkpen, N. (1997) *Experiments in Restorative Policing. Reintegra-*

tive Shaming of Violence, Drink Driving and Property Crime: A Randomised Controlled Trial. Available at: http://www.aic.gov.au/rjustice/rise/progress/1997.pdf

Slachtoffer in Beeld – Suggnomè (2002) *De uitbouw van een herstelgericht aanbod aan gedetineerden vanuit de Vlaamse Gemeenschap,* unpublished report (Leuven: Suggnomè).

Spiesschaert, F., Van Dijk, C., Vanfraechem, I. and Van Grunderbeeck, S. (2001) *Fact Sheet. Restorative Justice. An overview and the historical background of alternative and restorative practices in the field of juvenile justice within the Flemish community in Belgium,* unpublished paper (Leuven: K.U. Leuven).

Stassart, E. (1999) *Wetenschappelijke ondersteuning bij de implementatie en ontwikkeling van het provinciaal vereffeningsfonds. Onderzoek naar de optimale werking ervan en grondige evaluatie,* unpublished report (Leuven: K.U. Leuven).

Swinnen, M. (2007) *Inleiding,* paper presented at the conference 'Vijf kleine fietsjes met een grote bel ... over het provinciaal Vereffeningsfonds', November 23 (Leuven).

Van Camp, T. (2001a) *Beleving van de gedetineerde en houding ten aanzien van het slachtoffer en herstel. Een literatuurstudie. Rapport 1,* unpublished report (Leuven: K.U. Leuven).

Van Camp, T. (2001b) *Herstelgerichte detentie: aandachtspunten en accenten voor een gedifferentieerde invulling. Rapport 2. Een literatuurstudie naar de beleving van detentie en de mogelijk gedifferentieerde houding ten aanzien van herstel en slachtoffers bij verschillende groepen gedetineerden,* unpublished report (Leuven: K.U. Leuven).

Van Camp, T., Van Win, T., Aertsen, I., Daeninck, Ph., Hodiaumont, F. and Malempré H. (2004) *Vademecum herstelrecht en gevangenis* (Gent: Academia Press).

Vandebroek, M. and Vanfraechem, I. (2007) 'Bemiddeling en hergo', in Put, J. and Rom, M. (eds.) *Het Nieuwe Jeugdrecht* (Gent: Larcier), pp. 147-182.

Vandeurzen, I., Verhoeven, H., Verstraete, A., and Willemsens, J. (1999) *Slachtoffer- en herstelgerichte detentie. Visie- en activiteitenverslag,* unpublished report (Leuven: K.U. Leuven).

Van Dijk, C., Van Grunderbeeck, S., Spiessachaert, F. and Vanthuyne, T. (2002a) *Herstelgerichte afhandelingen van delicten gepleegd door minderjarigen: Leerprojecten – Gemeenschapsdiensten – Herstelbemiddeling, Tussentijds Rapport,* unpublished report (Belgium: VUB, UGent and K.U. Leuven).

Van Dijk, C., Van Grunderbeeck, S., Spiessachaert, F. and Vanthuyne, T. (2002b) *Herstelgerichte afhandelingen van delicten gepleegd door minderjarigen: Leerprojecten – Gemeenschapsdiensten – Herstelbemiddeling, Appendix: sociaal descriptief luik,* unpublished report (Belgium: VUB, UGent and K.U. Leuven).

Van Doosselaere, D. (2003) 'De bemiddeling dader-slachtoffer in de Franse Gemeenschap', *Nieuwsbrief Suggnomè,* 4(4), pp. 3-7.

Van Doosselaere, D. (2005) 'La médiation auteur mineur-victime: forme et conditions de la réforme', in Christiaens, J., De Fraene, D. and Delens-Ravier, I. (eds.) *Protection de la jeunesse Formes et réforme. Jeugdbescherming Vormen en hervormingen* (Brussels: Bruylant), pp. 207-218.

Van Doosselaere, D. and Gailly, P. (2002) 'La médiation auteur mineur d'âge-victime: le point de vue des praticiens', *Droit de la Jeunesse, CUP* (Liège: Université de Liège), pp. 105-129.

Vanfraechem, I. (2001) *Een wetenschappelijk onderzoek over de toepassing van Family Group Conferences (Herstelgericht groepsoverleg) in Vlaanderen. Tussentijds Rapport Eerste Onderzoeksjaar*, unpublished report (Leuven: K.U. Leuven).

Vanfraechem, I. (2002) *Een wetenschappelijk onderzoek over de toepassing van Family Group Conferences (Herstelgericht groepsoverleg) in Vlaanderen. Eindrapport*, unpublished report (Leuven: K.U. Leuven).

Vanfraechem, I. (2003a) *Herstelgericht groepsoverleg in Vlaanderen. Verslag van een wetenschappelijk begeleid pilootproject*, unpublished report (Leuven: K.U. Leuven).

Vanfraechem, I. (2003b) 'Implementing Family Group Conferences in a Legalistic System. The example of Belgium', in Walgrave, L. (ed.) *Repositioning Restorative Justice. Restorative Justice, Criminal Justice and Social Context* (Cullompton: Willan Publishing), pp. 313-327.

Vanfraechem, I. (2003c) 'Family group conferences in Vlaanderen: herstelgericht groepsoverleg (Hergo)', *Tijdschrift voor Jeugdrecht en Kinderrechten*, 4(3), pp. 142-148.

Vanfraechem, I. (2005) 'Evaluating conferencing for serious juvenile delinquency', in Elliott, E. and Gordon, R. (eds.) *Restorative Justice: emerging issues in practice and evaluation* (Cullompton: Willan Publishing), pp. 278-295.

Vanfraechem, I. (2007a) *Herstelgericht groepsoverleg: een constructief antwoord voor ernstige jeugddelinquentie* (Brugge: Die Keure).

Vanfraechem, I. (2007b) 'New youth law in Belgium incorporates restorative justice', *Newsletter of the European Forum for Restorative Justice*, 8(1), pp. 5-6.

Vanfraechem, I. (2007c) 'Herstel en de Belgische jeugdwet', *Tijdschrift voor herstelrecht*, 7(3), pp. 7-18.

Vanfraechem, I. (2009) 'Een constructief antwoord op (jeugd)delinquentie: recidive verminderen? Reflecties over 'managerialism' in België en Nederland', *Tijdschrift voor herstelrecht*, 9(3), pp. 8-18.

Vanfraechem, I. and Walgrave, L. (2001) 'Een wetenschappelijk experiment met Herstelgericht Groepsoverleg', *Panopticon*, 22(5), pp. 479-493.

Vanfraechem, I. and Walgrave, L. (2004a) 'Herstelgericht groepsoverleg voor jonge delinquenten in Vlaanderen. Verslag van een actie onderzoek', *Panopticon*, 25(6), pp. 27-46.

Vanfraechem, I. and Walgrave, L. (2004b) 'Restorative conferencing in Belgium. A way to decrease confinement of youth offenders?', *Corrections Today*, pp.72-75.

Vanfraechem, I. and Walgrave, L. (2005) *Conferencing Serious Juvenile Delinquents in Belgium*. Available at: http://www.restorativejustice.org/rj3/Feature/2005/March/belgium.htm

Vanfraechem, I. and Walgrave, L. (2006) 'Les conférences de groupe familial (Family Group Conferences)', *Les cahiers de la justice* (Paris: Editions Dalloz), pp. 153-174.

Vanneste, C. (1997) 'Pratique de la médiation pénale au parquet de Bruxelles', *Travail d'intérêt général et médiation pénale – Socialisation du pénal ou pénalisation du social*, Actes du Colloque international à l'occasion du 60ème anniversaire de l'Ecole des Sciences Criminologiques Léon Cornil U.L.B., 3 au 5 avril 1996, Ph. Mary (ed.) (Brussels : Bruylant), collection des travaux de l'Ecole des Sciences Criminologiques Léon Cornil, pp. 111-122.

Walgrave, L. (2000) *Met het oog op herstel* (Leuven: Leuven University Press).

Walgrave, L. (ed.) (2002) *Restorative Justice and the Law* (Cullompton: Willan Publishing).

Walgrave, L. and Aertsen, I. (1996) 'Reintegrative shaming and restorative justice. Interchangeable, complementary or different?', *European Journal on Criminal Policy and Research*, 4(4), pp. 57-75.

5 Providing mediation as a nation-wide service

Empirical research on restorative justice in Finland

Juhani Iivari

1 INTRODUCTION

1.1 Context: state of affairs

1.1.1 Legal situation of mediation
Until the year 2006, mediation in criminal cases was not regulated by a separate law in Finland. This gave rise to certain problems, e.g. citizens in different parts of Finland did not have equal access to mediation services. However, since 1966, it has been possible to take mediation into account in criminal law, e.g. in cases where prosecution of criminal actions was waived. Mediation was introduced in criminal law in 1997 and could lead to non-prosecution or the waiving of penal sanctions. Efforts for clearer legislation and clear government guidelines on the mediation procedure started in the 1990s.

1.1.2 Legal situation before the autonomous law on mediation
Before a separate law was passed, criminal law recognised the value of mediation in Section 15a of the Decree on the Enforcement of the Penal Code. Since no special procedure had been institutionalised within the realm of prosecutorial functions, the question of how such mediation should be furthered was raised. The process of organising mediation was left to institutions outside the criminal justice system. The role of criminal justice officials, especially the public prosecutor, was limited to referring cases deemed suitable for mediation to the proper institutions.

Secondly, no formal conditions for non-prosecution had been laid down as regards the results of the mediation process. Mediation itself could well serve as a reason for non-prosecution. The process could also fail if the victim was unwilling to participate even if the offender wanted to participate in mediation. In addition, the prosecutor could take into account sincere attempts to start a mediation process. Formally, a failed mediation was not described as 'mediation between the offender and the victim' but as 'the action taken by the offender to prevent or remove the effects of his/her offence'. In principle, the courts could similarly take into account mediation or the action taken by the offender to participate in mediation when considering the waiving of the sentence or in the severity of the sentence.[1]

---

[1] For example, in determining the amount of the fine or the length of the prison sentence, both unconditional and conditional.

In the beginning of September 2001, the Ministry of Social Affairs and Health set up a broadly based taskforce for preparation of a law on the organisation of victim-offender mediation [VOM] services on a nation-wide basis in Finland. The taskforce submitted its final proposal in April 2002. The proposal was based on the report drawn up by a special reporter (see Iivari, 2001b). According to the proposed bill, the management, guidance and control of mediation activities would be given to the Ministry of Social Affairs and Health.[2] Provincial State Offices would be responsible for ensuring the availability of mediation services in each province. They would have the responsibility for providing mediation services in cooperation with municipalities. In order for mediation services to be provided, each municipality should enter into an agreement referred to in Section 2, Subsection 2 of the Municipality Act (365/1995) with the respective Provincial State Office.

1.1.3   The Act on Mediation

The Act on Mediation in Criminal and Certain Civil Cases (9.12.2005/1015) entered into force on the 1st of January 2006. The goal of the act was to extend mediation in criminal cases to the whole country. Because of the act, mediation has been available throughout the country since June 2006, and all citizens have equal access and equal right to good quality mediation, regardless of their place of residence.[3]

The goal of the law was to ensure sufficient government funding for mediation services, to organise the national management, supervision and monitoring of mediation services, and to create conditions for long-term monitoring and development. The act also aims to make the mediation procedure more uniform, and to provide sufficient attention to the legal protection of parties in the mediation process. It contains provisions on the administrative organisation of mediation services, government compensation for operating expenses and the procedure for carrying out mediation. In addition to the law, further provisions on the duties and the composition of the national Advisory Board on mediation in criminal cases and certain civil cases are laid down by Government Decree (12.04 2006/267).

From the start, mediation has had a close relationship to social work, prevention of exclusion and, in particular, child welfare. The main responsibility for the nationwide development of mediation services and the general supervision, management and monitoring of mediation services, falls within the sphere of competence of the Ministry of Social Affairs and Health.

Each State Provincial Office (5 in total) is responsible for arranging mediation services and for ensuring that they are available throughout the province. The services are primarily provided on the basis of 'commission agreements'. A State Provincial Office makes an agreement with a municipality or some other public

---

2   The administration of the nationwide mediation service moved to STAKES (National Research and Development Centre for Welfare and Health – now National Institute for Health and Welfare) on 1 January 2008.

3   For an English version of the Act: http://info.stakes.fi/sovittelu/EN/legislation/index.htm

or private service provider. If under exceptional circumstances a commission agreement cannot be made in some area, the State Provincial Office will provide the necessary services in that area through hired personnel or in some other manner it deems suitable.

Expenses incurred in the provision of mediation services are compensated from government funds (€6.3 million per year in 2008). The amount of government funding is confirmed annually based on estimates of the average expenses related to maintaining mediation offices, appropriate service provision and training for people involved in providing mediation services. The amount of funding for service providers is calculated on the basis of following criteria: the number of inhabitants, the surface area and the crime situation in the area covered. At the moment there are 26 regional offices for mediation in Finland.

The government appoints an Advisory Board for Victim-Offender Mediation for a period of three years at a time. It acts under the auspices of STAKES, which is responsible for national supervision, monitoring and development of mediation services.

In principle any type of crime can be dealt with through mediation regardless of the category of the crime. Crimes are dealt with using mediation if they are deemed eligible for this approach, taking into account the nature and method of the offence, the relationship between the suspect and the victim, and other issues related to the crime as a whole. A crime cannot be referred to mediation, however, if the victim is under age and has a special need for protection on account of the nature of the crime or his/her age. For instance, sexual offences against children are not eligible for mediation. Also assaults where the victim is very young should not be referred. Cases involving domestic violence are not eligible if the violence in the relationship is recurring or if the parties have already been to mediation for their domestic violence situation. Domestic violence cases are also not eligible if the offender's attitude to the offence or the relationship between the offender and the victim otherwise indicates that the offender regards the use of violence as an acceptable way of dealing with problems in the relationship. In domestic violence, mediation is only possible if the case is referred by the police or the public prosecutor.

1.2   *Mediation practice*

Mediation may be proposed by the suspect, the victim, the police or prosecuting authority or some other authority. If the suspect or the victim is under age, his/her custodian or other legal representative has the right to propose mediation. In cases involving a legally incompetent adult, the person supervising his/her interests may also propose mediation. However, only the police or prosecuting authority has the right to propose mediation if the crime involves violence that has been directed at the suspect's spouse, child, parent or other comparably close relative (Chapter 3, Section 13 of the Act).

When the police or prosecuting authorities consider a case to be eligible for mediation as mentioned above (and laid down in section 3(1) of the Act), they must inform the suspect and the victim of the possibility of going to mediation, unless otherwise provided in subsection 2 (violence against close relative) of this section. If the suspect or the victim is under age, the information on the possibility to mediate must also be given to his/her custodian or other legal representative. In cases involving a legally incompetent adult, the information must always be given to both the person him/herself and the person looking after his/her interests (Chapter 3, Section 13 of the Act).

Before deciding to start mediation, the mediation office must ensure that the conditions for mediation laid down in section 2 are fulfilled (including personal and voluntary acceptance of mediation by the parties, capacity to understand the meaning of mediation and its solutions, information on parties' rights and position in mediation). It must also assess the eligibility of the case for mediation. If it is a civil case, the mediation office must also assess whether it is expedient to resort to mediation. The person in charge of the mediation office decides on whether to accept a case for mediation or not (Chapter 3 Section 15 of the Act).

When a mediation office accepts a case for mediation, it must:
1) appoint a conciliator to the case who is suitable for the task on the basis of his/her experience and personal characteristics, and who is not disqualified in the way referred to in the Administrative Procedure Act (434/2003);
2) obtain documents necessary for mediation from the police, prosecuting authority, courts or other parties, and this with the consent of the parties;
3) ensure the availability of an interpreter or translator if one of the parties needs this in order to understand the discussions held in mediation or to be understood in it (because he/she does not have a command of the language in which the mediation process will be held, because of a sensory or speech defect, or some other reason);
4) and, after mediation, inform the police or prosecuting authority of the mediation process and its outcome, notwithstanding the provisions on secrecy (Chapter 3, Section 16 of the Act).

The duties of the mediator are to:
1) arrange mediation meetings between the parties;
2) conduct the mediation process without bias and with respect for all parties;
3) help the parties to find a mutually satisfactory solution in order to redress the mental and material harm the victim has suffered because of the crime;
4) give the parties information on legal assistance and other services available;
5) draw up a written document reflecting the agreement reached between the parties in the mediation process which should be signed by the parties;
6) and, after mediation, submit a report on the mediation process to the mediation office.

2   RESEARCH

2.1   Research carried out: a general view

In Finland different types of research on VOM, both theoretical and empirical, have been carried out. Recent research on mediation has concerned the implementation of the national organisation of mediation, especially the administrative structures and financing of mediation. Both academics and students have carried out these studies. The researchers concerned have worked at universities and at the research institutes STAKES and the National Research Institute of Legal Policy.[4]

The research topics have been the following: evaluation of the implementation of the VOM programme (programme evaluation, participatory action-research), evaluation of the process and impact of VOM (process and impact evaluation), mediation in the context of reflexive justice (theoretical and comparative research on national and international models of different kinds of mediation), victims' and offenders' experiences of mediation (empirical observations and interviews in the frame of process and impact evaluation), the cost-effectiveness of mediation versus court proceedings (empirical comparative research), moral emotions in VOM (observation research under process and impact evaluation), national availability and practical organisation of mediation services (national survey).

Methods such as interviews, observation, participatory action-research, surveys, statistical multivariable analysis and literature analysis have been used. The emphasis has been on different kinds of evaluation methodologies. In the following, the research carried out is presented in a chronological way since this clearly shows an evolution in research approaches.

2.2   Studies in chronological order

2.2.1   Studies in the 1980s: the time of action-research

VOM started in Finland as an experimental two-year project in 1983. From the very beginning it was clear for the organisers that evaluation research was needed in order for the outcomes and significance of the project to be discussed impartially with the officials of the criminal justice system and other stakeholders (politicians). This is why it was important to develop the project according to the method of process evaluation (action-research in the frame of process evaluation). The aim of the research was to evaluate both the practical implementation and the goal achievement of the project and the resulting organisational models. Thus the process evaluation mainly focused on the assessment of the project management and the project development, and on whether or not the programme and the intervention responded to the objectives of the relevant plans of action. The study

---

4   The National Research Institute of Legal Policy is affiliated with the Ministry of Justice. Both of them are leading national research actors in their fields receiving financing from the State budget.

covered the experimental years of the project, 1984 and 1985, and it was financed by the Academy of Finland.[5]

The results of the study were quite positive as regards the participation of the parties (victims and offenders), the fulfilment of agreements, and the work of lay mediators. Less positive results were related to the participation by officials (especially the police) and their cooperation with the project, and to the inadequate funding (Iivari, 1985, 1988). Moreover, during the implementation of the programme, the research group split up into two conflicting parties. One group of researchers criticised the programme for having excessively keen contacts with the officials and for being dependent on the police and the prosecutors to such an extent that the project was in danger of loosing its original aim of offering a real alternative to the criminal justice system (Grönfors, 1992).[6]

To put it briefly, the project achieved its main aims to such a degree that the city of Vantaa decided to implement this new paradigm as an additional method in the field of child welfare activities. Also, the officials of the criminal justice system felt that mediation of crimes and disputes was useful for them as a complementary system. Accordingly, there was a clear policy context for the research: the decision-makers and officials in the police, in the prosecution office and in the court decided to recommend that the municipality of Vantaa should continue the programme.

With regard to methodology, this study was action-research, concentrating on programme implementation in the framework of process evaluation. Action-research refers to participatory research conducted by a project coordinator. In more detail, in this case participatory research encompasses the fact that the project coordinator was – together with two other researchers – at the same time developing and evaluating the programme implementation and its outcomes. Consequently, it was participatory research about the process and results of setting up and implementing a process, but also evaluative research on the mediation process and outcome at the individual level. The methods included participatory observation, interviews, data collection by questionnaires and multivariable data analysis (see Iivari, 1988).

2.2.2 A dissertation in 1991: a practical-theoretical meta-analysis

A practical-theoretical research on international models of mediation in the context of reflexive justice took place at the end of the 1980s and at the beginning of the 1990s. It was commissioned and funded by the Academy of Finland (Iivari, 1991).

The basis for this study was the increasing theoretical discussion on the effectiveness of the legal and administrative systems of the State and the various arrange-

---

5   The Academy of Finland provides funding for high-quality scientific research, serves as an expert organisation in science and science policy, and strengthens the position of science and research.

6   The second group was the so-called university group who was responsible for theoretical questions of mediation. Researcher Juhani Iivari led the practical field research.

ments that arise from among the general public, from the 'community' and the everyday life of citizens, and the relations between these two 'system' levels.

From the point of view of this problem, Teubner's (1988a, 1998b) interpretation of the evolution of law is very important. In his theory of reflexive law, the justification of situation-linked solutions in a certain stage of self-government becomes important. The view that law develops towards diverging and increasingly independent partial systems and subsystems is an interesting point of departure for the development of mediation.

In the study, the concept of reflexive law has been analysed and operationalised as an ideal form of law in three definitions:

(i)   Reflexive law in its ideal form emphasises partial systems that are increasingly independent and self-regulating.
(ii) Reflexive law in its ideal form shall be assumed to be in dynamic interaction with its functional environment, and to influence this environment.
(iii) Reflexive law in its ideal form emphasises the realisation of law so that the objects of law become the subjects of law, with the right to express their needs through the methods of free discourse, and so that the expression of these needs is also guaranteed.

The multi-level dependence of the different types of VOM on the official criminal justice system shows that VOM, as an institution, does not involve any independent partial or subsystem of law, as part of the set of concepts of reflexive law. It is more a question of a system that is subordinate to law. This conclusion means that the question of the institutionalisation of mediation is important. The different ways of proceeding with cases in mediation and the autonomous nature of the method of mediation, however, give clear indications that the conditions for the development of mediation as a self-regulating legal system do exist. The procedural nature of mediation raises such hopes.

On the basis of the evaluations that have been made of the initial results of mediation, only modest success has been achieved in reaching the goals of the different types of mediation (the political significance of mediation in its functional environment). So far, those types of mediation that cooperate with the official criminal justice system have had only a limited effect on practices in this system. However, certain features in the development, such as legislative reforms, clearly create a favourable environment for achieving the goals of the different types of mediation, for example the strengthening of diversion.

Finally, the study tentatively analyses the theoretical confrontation between the mediation approach and the punishment approach. The components of special prevention and general prevention are imbued with new meaning in mediation: from the point of view of mediation, an important indicator of special prevention is the individual treatment of offenders, treatment which minimises the experience of punishment, and where the individual needs of the offender and the victim are taken into consideration. Mediation as a preventive approach is carried out as an interactive solution to a conflict where the offender compensates the damage to the victim. From the point of view of general prevention, mediation should be able to help in fostering and strengthening the idea in the mind of the public that mediation is a way of restoring social peace and the value of the norms that have been violated. It is unclear to what extent the experiences that have been gained so far with the different types of mediation achieve the goals described here. Ultimately, the solution to this question is connected with the publicity that the entire system of mediation receives, and with the degree to which the public at large accepts it. The question can be answered more fully when mediation is developed and a separate study has been carried out on this.

2.2.3 Research in the 1990s: focus on evaluation

2.2.3.1 General remarks
It can well be argued that evaluative research started in Finland on a more general level in the beginning of the 1990s just because of the increasing use of mediation in some big cities in the country. There was a need to better understand the strengths and weaknesses of mediation from different starting points, firstly in order to define its position in relation to the criminal law (including criminal procedural law) and, secondly, to define its applicability as a nation-wide system, either in social care or in criminal justice proceedings.

The evaluation studies of that time utilised both quantitative and qualitative research methods. Such studies were done from 1993 to 2000. The research projects were commissioned by the Ministry of Social Affairs and Health and the Ministry of Justice, and conducted by STAKES and the National Research Institute of Legal Policy. The reports have been published in Finnish, most of them include English summaries (Järvinen, 1993; Aaltonen, 1998; Takala, 1998; Mielityinen, 1999; Iivari, 2001a). Altogether, five researchers have been involved in these studies, one for each study.[7]

2.2.3.2 Main results

Satisfaction
Many of the studies mentioned here (Iivari, 1988; Takala, 1998; Mielityinen, 1999) have investigated the experiences and attitudes of the parties regarding mediation by interview, observation and survey methods. The studies consistently found that a big majority of both victims and offenders were satisfied with the mediation process, the mediators and the compensation for the damage. Moreover, reports on many different mediation cases show that the feelings of hostility and suspicion between the parties dissolved, sometimes even during the mediation session. The victims were able to explain the difficulties, damages and injuries caused by the offence openly and face-to-face with the offender. The offenders, for their part, reported that mediation showed them the consequences in concrete terms and increased their willingness to provide for reparation. Most

---

7   The numerous theses written by students are not mentioned here.

offenders also stated that mediation has discouraged them, or at least postponed them, from committing new offences.

In addition, mediation processes had been organised correctly; a great majority of the parties (70 to 80%) was satisfied (feelings of fairness) with the mediation process and outcomes. Voluntary participation was high because about 75% of the referred criminal cases had led to mediation sessions, and of these about 80% had led to an agreement. About 80% of the agreements had been fulfilled as well. However, there is one important point that should be remembered: cases referred to mediation had been carefully chosen from the category of suitable cases, i.e. prosecutors and police generally had chosen minor crimes for referral.

Comparative research using observation and interview methods and a control group showed that the parties were more satisfied with the process and outcome of mediation than with the process and the outcome of the normal court procedure (Takala, 1998).

Influences on the criminal justice system
Mediation had most influenced prosecutors' decision-making: diversion occurred in more than half of the cases, very often also in non-complainant crimes.[8] The attitudes of the criminal justice officials have also generally changed: the longer mediation had been utilised, the more content the officials were (Mielityinen, 1999). However, among the criminal justice officials there is some suspicion about the ability and competence of lay mediators and there has been a conflict of opinions between the state prosecutor and the coordinators concerning the scope of mediation: the state prosecutor wanted to confine mediation to petty crimes, while the coordinators wanted to increasingly widen its scope into the areas of serious violent crimes. One big black hole in the research into the impact of mediation on the criminal justice system is the lack of research on the effect of mediation on determining the sentence (measuring punishment), i.e. we do not know if and to what extent mediation is affecting sentencing, e.g. leniency of punishment.

Recidivism
In research carried out by Mielityinen (1999), recidivism has been defined on the basis of the police recording new crimes according to the data set by Statistics Finland.[9] The data included comparative statistical analysis on recidivism concerning 1,004 mediated offenders and 17,632 non-mediated offenders.[10] These

---

8   In Finland crimes are divided into two categories: complainant and non-complainant crimes. In complainant crimes (minor), the victim can decide independently to prosecute or not to prosecute the case in court. Non-complainant crimes are more serious crimes where the onus for laying the charge lies with the public prosecutor.

9   Statistics Finland operates administratively under the Ministry of Finance, but is fully and independently responsible for its activities, services and statistics. Statistics Finland has about 1,100 people working for it, 200 of whom are employed as statistical interviewers.

10   Weighting coefficients were used, i.e. size was taken into account in statistical significance tests and standardising methods were used.

two groups were standardised with regard to earlier criminal offending, age, sex and crime.

There was some criticism on the methodology used in this comparative study, namely on the forming of the control group. The main problem was that the variables were not adequate for a comprehensive study. The constellation of the four variables mentioned above did not allow for a reliable and valid comparison. For example, it was not possible to standardise variables like family background (social status), housing and success in school. Anyway, the study showed that recidivism was a little lower in mediation cases than in cases that were not mediated. The study also suggested that the younger the offender was during mediation, the less likely he/she was to re-offend compared to the control group.

Job perception and satisfaction

Job perception and satisfaction of mediators have been evaluated in many studies in Finland. The same result was obtained in all of them: astonishingly positive outcomes. But there are problems as well. If the mediators do not have enough cases, they become frustrated and leave. There has also been discussion among the coordinators about the heterogeneity of mediators and the ways in which mediators could be bound more intensively and for a longer period to the mediation task. Coordinators are also concerned about whether the training and competence of mediators are adequate (Mielityinen, 1999).

Cost-effectiveness

Mediation has also been studied in Finland from the perspective of cost-effectiveness, comparing the benefits and savings gained by mediation with the costs of criminal justice proceedings from the viewpoint of the local state authorities, offenders and crime victims (Aaltonen, 1998). An assessment has been carried out into whether mediation is economically beneficial and if so, to what extent. The aim had thus been to determine how efficient society's resources are being used and how the cost effects of mediation are distributed between the parties concerned. While concentrating on the direct monetary costs and benefits, this type of research also makes allowance for other financial advantages. Combining the financial advantage perspective with mediation significantly improves the potential for making the present system of compensation for the consequences of and damage caused by crimes more economical.

The research indicated that mediation is beneficial to society. Resources are used more efficiently, thereby producing greater welfare in society. The advantage of mediation from the victim's point of view lies primarily in various forms of compensation and the availability of compensation in general. The financial burden on the offender is not as high in mediation as it is in criminal proceedings. The biggest savings arise from the absence of court proceedings and the consideration of charges. The local authorities provide the facilities for mediation and this raises their costs. On the other hand, mediation may in the long term prove more economical to the local authorities if more and more young offenders stop their criminal behaviour.

The empirical material for the study consisted of criminal cases (n=18/13)[11] in which a mediation process had been carried out. Due to the limited amount of material, the results cannot be generalised to apply to all conciliation cases (3,050 in 1995), but some conclusions may be drawn. All in all, mediation could, with the 3,050 cases, save society €2.15 million per year. Taken into account that the average cost of a criminal case handled in the court is €1,000, and that the average price of a mediated case is €250, the savings for the criminal justice system are significant.[12]

2.2.4 Research in the 2000s

2.2.4.1 How to organise, administer and finance nation-wide mediation

In Finland, VOM proliferated spontaneously up to 2006 without special legislation or financing by the State, based on the voluntary activity of municipalities. As a consequence, only the biggest municipalities organised mediation: they clearly had more resources and a greater need to utilise VOM, especially in crimes committed by children and juvenile delinquents. At the end of the 1990s, this way of organising mediation came to an end. The widening of mediation on a voluntary basis stopped and people in small municipalities still did not have the mediation facilities – about 30% of the population did not have access to mediation.

The state of affairs was widely experienced as a problem of equality. Notwithstanding the place of residence, every citizen should have the right and access to mediation in crimes where it was possible and where they voluntarily wanted to take part. Also, the heterogeneous financing, use and position of mediation gave cause for concern. Still another phenomenon that was emphasised entailed the discovery that cases referred to mediation were more serious than before: at the end of the 1990s, for instance, prosecutors began to refer more and more cases of domestic violence to mediation. It was heavily criticised that lay mediators were working with such serious crimes and it was argued that this was bound to cause problems of legal protection and to jeopardise the rights of women. This is why, for example, the need for extra training for mediators was strongly emphasised.

As a result, the Ministry of Social Affairs and Health and the Ministry of Justice started negotiations on how to organise nationwide mediation services. It was also argued that the problems related to legal protection and cooperation between officials and lay mediators and the need for training should be resolved in a new and better way. Juhani Iivari from STAKES was appointed as a reporter with the task of drafting a report for the government (see Iivari, 2001b).

In addition to this research, the Ministry of Social Affairs and Health and STAKES decided to carry out follow-up research in 2003 in order to understand the direction that mediation was taking (Salonen, 2004).

---

11 The original sample consisted of 18 cases, but only 13 of them were eligible for all aspects of the research analyses. The remaining five cases were utilised partly.
12 In the calculation it must be taken into account that some cases go to court in spite of mediation having taken place.

Table 1   Organisation of VOM in Finnish municipalities in 1999 and 2003

How VOM is organised	1999			2003*		
	Number of munici-palities	% of munici-palities	% of cases	Number of munici-palities	% of munici-palities	% of cases
Own office	34	7.5	72.0	27	6.1	70.0
Outsourcing to another municipality or NGO	74	16.4	21.0	84	18.9	5.0
Officials (additional post)	83	18.4	2.4	74	16.7	6.0
Other way	64	14.2	4.6	40	9.2	19.0
No possibility to mediate	157	34.7		66	14.9	
No answers	40	8.8		153	34.5	
Total	452	100	100	444	100	100

* The number of municipalities decreased from 452 in 1999 to 444 in 2004.

Source: Salonen, 2004, p.31.

In the year 1999, the national comparison showed that the way mediation was organised affected its efficiency in terms of the total volume of cases. Municipalities with their own mediation offices applied mediation most extensively, representing an overwhelming majority of all cases (72%). For municipalities that were purchasing mediation services from organisations, the corresponding figure was 21%, i.e. the second highest. In the overall analysis, the alternative 'some other way of organising mediation' processed only 4.6% of cases. As stated above, the most common way of organising mediation was to include it in the duties of a municipal employee. This arrangement, however, resulted in the lowest number of mediation cases in the whole country (2.4%).

When comparing VOM practice in the years 1999 and 2003, we can see a clear regression. In 1999, VOM services were offered in 56.5% of the municipalities, but only in 50.9% of the municipalities in 2003. The number of mediation offices decreased as well, from 34 in 1999 to 27 in 2003. An even clearer change can be found when comparing caseloads: in 1999 altogether 4,573 cases were referred to mediation; this amounted to only 3,046 cases in 2003. It is unquestionable that there is a need for mediation. The majority of the municipalities that claimed not to have a mediation service also said that there was a clear need for it, but that no monetary resources were available. In addition, the VOM services are concentrated in the South of Finland and especially in the capital area (Helsinki and Vantaa) where more than 35% of the whole national caseload of mediation was carried out. Small municipalities were suffering from a lack of resources and due to this outsourcing the mediation service decreased from 21% to 5% in 2003.

In order to rectify this situation, some municipalities tried to provide VOM services using volunteers and without having any special organisation, and with the help of social workers in police stations. In Table 1 'other way' means that volunteers and social workers in police stations handled 19% of all VOM cases in 2003, compared to only 4.6% in 1999. This is explained by the fact that the number of social workers in police stations increased and by the fact that they began to work actively in mediation. To summarise, one could say that the scarce municipal resources, especially in small municipalities, cut down the number of municipal mediation offices and the frequency of outsourcing mediation services, while increasing weakly resourced voluntary activities.

The situation of the VOM services was very alarming and demonstrated the need for legislation on mediation. A boost for this was given by research results: mediation was started in 93% of the cases referred. In 96% of these cases, an agreement was reached. And, at least 81% of the agreements were fulfilled completely or partly.

2.2.4.2 Mediation statistics under the new law on mediation

In 2006, the Act on Mediation came into force and 25 mediation offices were founded so that the opportunity to take part in mediation is available for everybody in the country. Among other things, this resulted in a very rapid increase of mediation cases (Iivari et al., 2008). A total of 11,120 criminal and civil cases were referred to mediation in Finland in 2008. This represented a 13.9% increase compared to the previous year. Based on data collected from mediation offices by the National Institute for Health and Welfare [THL], the total number of mediated cases included 10,876 criminal cases and 244 civil cases. Of all penal code offences in 2008, 2.02% were referred to mediation. In 2007, the rate was 1.9%. The percentage is relatively small for a variety of reasons. For instance, very few serious crimes are in fact referred to mediation.

The data for 2008 show that violent crimes (incl. interpersonal violence) accounted for 48% of all criminal cases referred to mediation. Aggravated assaults (i.e. grievous bodily harm), in turn, accounted for 0.5%. Criminal damage followed violent crime in terms of frequency of referral with a share of 19%. Interpersonal violence accounted for 8.7% of all crimes. These percentages do not include civil cases.

The 2008 figures on criminal cases referred to mediation are approximately the same as in the previous year. The percentage of violent crimes (incl. interpersonal violence) of all criminal cases referred to mediation in 2008 grew by 2.7% compared with 2007, when they accounted for 45.3%[13] of the cases. The share accounted for by menace increased by 1.2% compared to 2007 (4.2%). By contrast, the shares accounted for by theft, criminal damage and invasion of domestic premises decreased by approximately 1%.

---

13   Menace was included into violent crimes in 2007, when the share was 49%. In 2008, the corresponding share would have been 52%. As regards violent crimes, the 2008 statistics do not include menace. This is based on the concept of interpersonal violence, specifying that the violence is physical violence causing danger to life or health (Penal Code, Chapters 20 and 21). Defamation, invasion of domestic premises and menace are divided into separate categories based on the Penal Code (Chapters 24 and 25). In the 2007 statistics, these were included as cases of interpersonal violence, if the parties were regarded as being in a close relationship.

Figure 1   Criminal and civil cases referred to mediation, 1 June to 31 Dec 2006, 2007 and 2008 in % *).

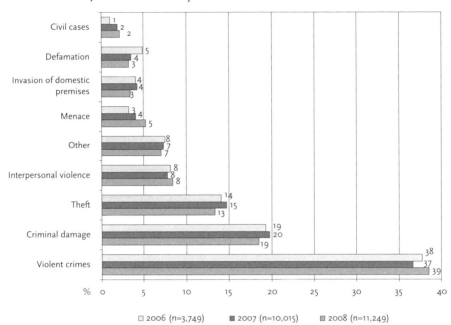

*)   The national statistics start from 1 June 2006, when the Act on Mediation in Criminal and Certain Civil Cases entered into force.

The total number of criminal cases referred to mediation in 2008 increased some 14% compared to 2007. The total number of violent crimes (incl. interpersonal violence) was 5,277, which meant an increase of about 19% on 2007. Of all violent crimes, petty assaults increased the most, that is, by 28%. In turn, interpersonal violence increased by 21% and assault by 17%. The number of cases of menace (n=594) referred to mediation nearly doubled in 2008.

These increases are explained by the fact that, although very few serious and complex crimes are referred to mediation, there has been a clear increase in the collaboration and mutual trust between authorities and mediation offices as operations have gradually progressed. As the amount of training provided to mediators has increased, so too has authorities' confidence in the knowledge and know-how of the mediators. This has in turn encouraged authorities to refer cases to mediation. In addition, the positive results of mediation have further bolstered authorities' confidence in the process of mediation.[14]

---

14   Preliminary data from an interview survey by police and prosecuting authorities, with permission from Research Director Juhani Iivari.

Before mediation offices undertake mediation, they have to determine whether the criminal case is suitable for mediation. In 2008, mediation was undertaken in 70.6% of all criminal cases (incl. interpersonal violence) referred to mediation. The mediation process was interrupted in 9.6% of all criminal cases. More accurate percentages on the share of criminal cases in mediation in 2008 are not available, since, in some cases, the mediation decisions were not made until 2009.

Referring cases to mediation
The vast majority (i.e. 74%) of criminal cases referred to mediation are submitted by the police. Public prosecutors submit 22% of the criminal cases to be mediated and parents only 0.2%. In 2008, of all criminal cases referred to mediation, 56% were offences under public prosecution and 44% were complainant offences. The number of civil cases submitted to mediation was 244, which represents some 2% of all mediated cases. The cases referred to mediation during the year involved a total of 21,205 people: 12,282 suspected offenders and 8,923 complainants. Men accounted for 82% and women for 18% of the suspected offenders. As for the complainants, 63% were men and 37% women. The mediation cases involved a total of 1,653 legal persons[15] as complainants.

Figure 2   Interpersonal violence cases as a percentage of criminal cases referred to mediation in 2008, by province. *)

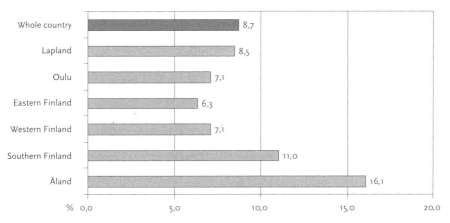

*)   Civil cases have not been taken into account in the calculation (cf. Figure 1).

---

15   Typically, legal persons in mediation cases include housing co-operatives, insurance companies etc.

Mediation in cases of interpersonal violence

In 2008, the number of mediated cases of interpersonal violence increased some 20% compared to the previous year. In fact, the increase is likely to have been even greater, seeing as defamation, invasion of domestic premises and menace are no longer recorded as interpersonal violence. The vast majority (85%) of cases of interpersonal violence referred to mediation are assault cases. In all, offences under public prosecution accounted for 83.2% of interpersonal violence cases and complainant offences for 16.8%.

Of the cases of interpersonal violence, 77% were referred to mediation by the police and 23% by public prosecutors. Cases of interpersonal violence still seem to create a division between practices, which is evident from the differences in referral to mediation across provinces, for instance.

Different age groups in mediation

The age distribution of suspected offenders in 2008 is consistent with figures from the previous year: 47% of the suspects were under the age of 21. In turn, suspected offenders under the age of 15 accounted for a 14% share. This percentage remained at the same level as in 2007. Of the complainants, 28% were under the age of 21. The data clearly indicate that mediated offences are directed at the adult population.

Figure 3   Age distribution of suspected offenders in mediated criminal and civil cases, 1 June to 31 Dec 2006, 2007 and 2008, in %

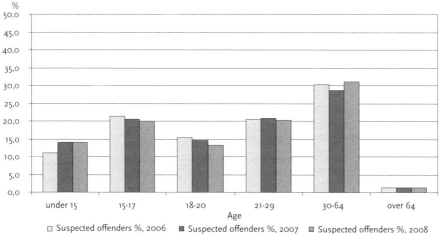

□ Suspected offenders %, 2006   ■ Suspected offenders %, 2007   ▨ Suspected offenders %, 2008

Figure 4   Age distribution of complainants in mediated criminal and civil cases, 1 June 31 Dec 2006, 2007 and 2008, in %

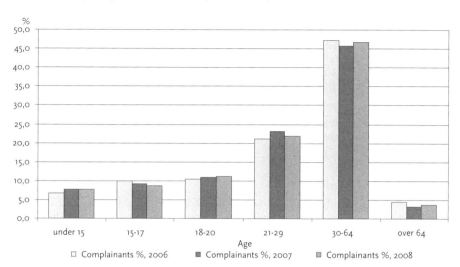

Mediation agreements
The 2008 statistics show that 70% of all mediated criminal cases (incl. interpersonal violence) resulted in agreements or resolutions. The share accounted for by interpersonal violence was 6.6%. Accurate percentages at the calendar year level are not available, since, in some cases, the mediation process was still ongoing at the turn of the year. The mediation cases undertaken during the year resulted in a total of 9,737[16] *separate compensation settlements*. Monetary compensations accounted for 44.4% and work compensations for 4.6% of the different types of compensation. The combined value of the monetary and work compensations was €1,930,192. The combined value of the compensations increased 15.2% compared to the previous year. However, their proportion decreased in relative terms by some 4%. Compared with the same period, the proportion accounted for by work compensation remained at about 5%. Altogether 51% of the mediation agreements were so-called intangible settlements: apologies (34%), waivers of claims (12%), acceptable behaviour contracts (4.5%) and return of property (0.6%). The types of agreements in 2008 largely follow the same distribution as in 2007. As a whole, so-called intangible settlements seem to be on the rise: their share increased slightly compared to 2007 (47%).

---

16   These separate compensation settlements cannot be directly related to mediation agreements reached during the year, since a single agreement may include several types of compensations in one and the same criminal liability.

Table 2   Monetary value of compensations in mediated criminal and civil cases, by province in 2007 and 2008, in €

	Combined value of monetary compensations		Monetary value of work compensations, €		Total, €	
	2008	2007	2008	2007	2008	2007
Southern Finland	690 461	631 355	31 647	22 691	722 108	654 046
Western Finland	524 956	403 960	36 385	33 778	561 341	437 738
Eastern Finland	286 687	293 986	7 748	23 135	294 435	317 121
Oulu	194 438	122 962	10 559	16 742	204 997	139 704
Lapland	120 765	116 112	8 855	6 046	129 619	122 158
Åland	14 691	4 723	3 000	440	17 691	5 163
Whole country	1 831 998	1 573 098	98 194	102 832	1 930 192	1 675 930

2.2.4.3 Children in victim-offender mediation (2001-2002)
The Ministry of Social Affairs and Health financed a two-year research project 'Children in victim-offender mediation in Finland', conducted by Dr. Ossi Eskelinen and researcher Terhi Raitanen in Tampere. The aim of the research project was to evaluate the impact and experiences of mediation in cases involving children under the age of criminal responsibility (15 year). The project took place in six cities: Helsinki, Tampere, Nokia, Joensuu, Vaasa and Oulu. A wide array of research data – qualitative and quantitative – had been collected and analysed. Complainants' experiences were included as well. The research report was published in 2005 (Eskelinen, 2005) and an article in English was published in 2005 (Eskelinen and Iivari, 2005).

This study produced practical information on different aspects of mediation in cases where the offender is under the age of 15. There is no doubt that mediation is needed in these cases – even in the opinion of the offenders themselves. The data sets of different types suggest that re-offending can be prevented by rapid intervention at an early stage. However, a precondition for this is that the child him/herself plays an active role in the efforts to institute change, in addition to which his/her life situation and environment should support the efforts made. Approximately 50-60% of the offenders under 15 years stop offending immediately or with a small delay after a single offence. The problem lies with children who have committed a large number of offences and for various reasons experience difficulties in life management. It is the same group that both engages in offending and has problems. A survey questionnaire to the child welfare authorities indicated that many of these children have problems. School problems (truancy, bullying and learning difficulties) were very common. Mental problems had been reported as well. Problems generally accumulate among those children who have committed a large number of offences. In addition to children under the age of 15, accumulation of crimes thus also seems to affect older children. In the police records the most problematic group of children have dozens of offences – at worst nearly one hundred. But even if they had committed prior offences, these children have participated in mediation at least once.

It is very likely that at least in some cases it would have been possible to prevent re-offending through rapid intervention and mediation. Therefore children should be referred to mediation immediately after they have committed an offence. A small minority of children have participated in mediation several times; some of them have stopped offending only after several mediation processes. Repeated mediation alone is not necessarily an effective way of stopping the child from committing offending behaviour. It can be asked whether mediation alone is helpful in the case of children who commit repeated offences or whether it can be seen as an intervention that will result in a wide variety of other support measures. Some children need more efficient measures. One possible alternative is to make mediation an indispensable part of child welfare work. The demanding nature of mediating with children should also be reflected in the training of mediators. The mediation system for children under the age of 15 still needs to be developed further in many respects.

2.2.4.4 'Let's Talk' – Social mediation for refugee communities in Europe in 2003

The project was coordinated by the IOM (International Organisation of Migration) Regional Office for the Baltic and Nordic States in the year 2003 and participants were VOM offices of Helsinki and Vantaa from Finland and NECASS (North-East Consortium for Asylum Support Services), Newcastle and North-West and West Midland from the UK. The project lasted only one year.

The project was aimed at empowering refugees, refugee communities and organisations working with refugees in social mediation activities, with a view to facilitating the integration of refugees into the host societies, building their capacities in intercommunication skills, mediating in criminal cases and disputes, and preventing multi-ethnic crime and racism. In addition, this initiative aimed at lowering the threshold for contacts between refugees and the local population through the enhancement of the understanding of mutual cultural patterns, traditions, behaviour, values/attitudes and social rules/norms. The project also aimed at creating structures through which multi-ethnic conflicts could be processed. This was done through training programmes and seminars for persons with a refugee background as well as for existing victim-offender mediators in Finland and the UK. EU-wide networking of actors implementing social mediation has been carried out through the organisation of a European seminar and an exchange-training programme. Information dissemination has been guaranteed through the production of training material and the establishment of a website as a forum for cooperation and information sharing.

The project has been evaluated through a comprehensive process evaluation study (Salonen and Iivari, 2004). The objective of the evaluation was to analyse both the effectiveness and relevance of the practical implementation of the project and the models the project has produced. Moreover, in the evaluation, focus has been on assessing the project development/planning, selecting the trainers and trainees, networking between officials/stakeholders as well as starting up and implementing the project. The social mediation training model was assessed in terms of its relevance in view of the future wider implementation methods in the area of social mediation.

The indicators were set up by expressing the targets of the evaluation in a semi-structured questionnaire aiming at establishing a so-called SWOT analysis (Strengths, Weaknesses, Opportunities and Threats). The project Steering Committee has also evaluated and monitored the activities and the whole process from the viewpoint of each partner, national authority and the IOM Commission. The evaluation process and its results have been included in the final project report (Salonen and Iivari, 2004). To summarise the results of the project, one can say that:

- The project suffered somewhat from a lack of proper planning and background research in the UK. This was highlighted by the fact that difficulties in crossing over original areas of expertise were not taken into account;
- The training programmes have succeeded relatively well in both project areas. Also the cooperation between the partners has been successful;
- The information activities, as well as the networking activities, are very difficult to evaluate in this phase of the project. Actual results will become visible only later;
- A remarkable amount of things were achieved in a very short time.

The 'Let's Talk' project has given sufficient impulse to develop social mediation in refugee issues. To ensure that this valuable work will continue, researchers recommend that:

- a new experimental project for social mediation be developed;
- the project should last at least two years and involve one or two new countries/ partners in addition to the existing project areas;
- enough time be devoted to careful planning and research prior to planning;
- and the project should also involve evaluation properly phased with the project activities.

After the end of the project, VOM-cases of refugees have increased dramatically in the Vantaa mediation office. In a short time, more than 20 criminal cases were referred and mediated successfully.

2.2.4.5 Meeting domestic violence in mediation (2001-2004)

With the support of the Ministry of Social Affairs and Health, the Ministry of Justice and the Slot Machine Association, a development and research programme was started in the summer of 2001 by the Association of Mother Shelter Homes, the Crisis Centre for Raped Women (Tukinainen), the Finnish Association of Mediators and STAKES, in order to clarify the possibilities and limitations of mediation in cases of domestic violence.

In the follow-up study, the programme was evaluated in the framework of realistic evaluation (Pawson and Tilley, 1997) as shown in Figure 5.

Figure 5   The framework of realistic evaluation of the project 'Meeting domestic violence'

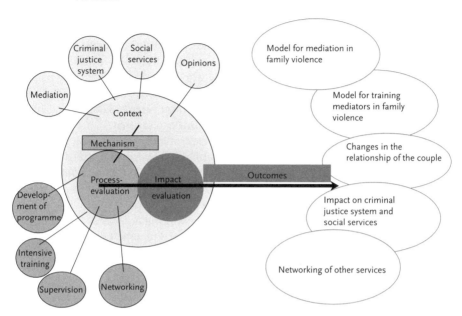

In the realistic evaluation, the central concepts are CMO (Context – Mechanism – Outcomes), i.e. the programme has been researched in the real context of the society. The programme – meeting domestic violence in mediation – in itself is a mechanism and outcomes are the intended aims of the programme. To research the context means to take seriously the conditions set by the surrounding society, culture, values and attitudes of stakeholders (e.g. of the criminal justice system), the climate of opinions (the press), the social services available, the social situation of clients, etc.

The mechanism of mediation in cases of domestic violence underwent special development. The programme specifically aimed at enhancing efforts to tackle domestic violence by providing intensive training for mediators specialising in the topic. There was a consensus opinion that such intensive training should be systematic, broad and provided through a development project concentrating on the task. The aim was to spread skills and experience and to disseminate information about expertise among other relevant parties. In the mechanism, special attention was also paid to the resources the mediation offered to victims and offenders and to their experiences of resolving domestic violence through mediation.

The parties were interviewed using a panel method,[17] the first time immediately after the final mediation session and the second time one year later. Mediators and coordinators were interviewed twice as well, once in the beginning and once at the end of the project. In addition to this, the members of the court (judges and lay-judges) were interviewed in eleven cases (six that were not mediated, and five that were mediated) of domestic violence, each time immediately after the court handled the case.

Quantitative data, consisting of documents of domestic violence cases (altogether 416), were collected in experimental areas (Helsinki, Vantaa, Tampere and Kokkola) from prosecutors and courts. Of all cases (416), 204 were referred to mediation and in 134 cases the mediation led to an agreement. Quantitative data were analysed in a multi-variable way answering for example the questions 'how often', 'what kind of cases' and 'why' prosecutors referred them to mediation and 'how' the courts treated them.

In realistic evaluation, the methods of process and impact evaluation are combined. The objective of the evaluation was to (i) analyse both the effectiveness and the relevance of the practical implementation of the programme, and (ii) to analyse the model of mediation that the programme had produced. The first objective focuses on assessing the programme development and planning, training, networking between the officials and stakeholders, the starting up and implementation of the programme, as well as the experiences of parties. Here, the evaluation assesses, amongst other things, whether the programme was implemented the way it was planned and if it contributed to the desired outcomes and what kind of unexpected or undesired processes the action had started. The second objective assesses whether the mediation training model and the programme implementation are relevant in view of the future, wider, implementation methods in the area of mediation in domestic violence.

The development of the programme ended on 31 January 2004, having lasted two and a half years in four localities selected for the intensive training (Helsinki, Vantaa, Tampere and Kokkola). STAKES implemented a follow-up study on the programme. The first version of the follow-up study (by Aune Flinck and Juhani Iivari, 2004) was evaluated by referees in the summer of 2004. After the experimental phase, the impact of the programme was evaluated more extensively in a national conference in autumn 2004 where outside experts and officials appraised the results and their significance to society.

According to the results, the criteria for VOM in domestic violence cases cannot be set in advance on the basis of the type of criminal offence or the severity of violence. Suitability for VOM and the benefit that may be gained from it should be evaluated on a case-by-case basis, on the basis of the evaluation criteria linked with the complainant, the person suspected of committing the offence, and the

---

17   The panel method involves measuring the research object at least two times, with a certain interval in between, in order to have information about the impact of intervening variables, in this case the impact of mediation.

circumstances.[18] Mediation should be voluntary and confidential. Special attention must be paid to legal protection, the complainant's resources,[19] the offender's motives, and the parties' willingness to face each other, to negotiate and to seek mutually beneficial solutions. The mediator's role and expertise are extremely important.

From the statistical material it became clear that prosecutors referred cases of domestic violence to VOM on various grounds. In some of the municipalities studied, the Prosecutor-General's instructions – stating that mainly complainant offences and milder offences were suitable for mediation – were followed strictly. Serious offences involving domestic violence were referred to mediation extremely rarely. The study also showed that, when cases went to mediation, in half of the cases the court did not take mediation into account at all. In half of the cases, mediation was mentioned in the court decision as a ground for alleviating the sentence or for waiving the sentence altogether.

On the basis of the research findings it can be said that mediation in domestic violence cases has the potential to provide a starting point for the parties to solve their violence-related problems and can provide support for coping.[20] In these cases, mediation requires development and special skill. That is, training has to be developed for mediators and the way they should conduct mediation needs to be explored further. The report makes some recommendations for the training of mediators in domestic violence cases and for the development of the mediation service system. On the basis of the research results and the experiences obtained during the project, a best practice model for VOM in cases of domestic violence was presented separately as an appendix.

3   FOLLOW-UP OF THE IMPLEMENTATION OF THE NEW ACT ON MEDIATION

When Parliament adopted the Act on Mediation, the Parliamentary Legal Committee decided that the implementation of the law had to be followed up by researchers in order to identify possible areas for improvement of the law. STAKES' research director Juhani Iivari was nominated as the researcher in charge. The research consists of both quantitative and qualitative evaluation research concerning the cases, the referrals, the handling of cases by the prosecutors and by the court, the

---

18 The suitability of the case for mediation in domestic violence depends on the nature of the case, on the nature of the violence, on the mental and social ability of couples, on circumstances, and on the relationship between the parties (married, engaged, open marriage, children in the family, etc.).

19 These include the following: do they have the mental and social power to participate in mediation as an equal party or not, do they for example have support persons to help them to participate in mediation etc.

20 By 'support for coping' we mean the mental support given to parties in the mediation session. Research has shown that many of the parties (especially women) said afterwards that the supporting and encouraging attitude of the mediator was very important, even decisive, in their decision to start seeking help.

impact on waiving sentences, the agreements and their fulfilment, and – finally – on the experiences of victims and offenders with mediation. The study took place in 2007 and 2008; it has been finalised and published (Iivari, 2010).

4   Conclusions

The most important results of the research described above generally indicate that the parties, the mediators and the various officials are satisfied with mediation in Finland. However, referral behaviour has varied greatly among prosecutors and police, and there has not been any common system for the referral of cases or for the significance given by officials to mediation in the criminal procedure. That is why a lot is expected of the new law on mediation.

Methodologically, we utilised the available repertoire of research methodologies very extensively, but the reliability and coverage sometimes posed problems. We have had a wide range of research activities in Finland in the field of mediation, but the development, process and outcome of mediation have not been followed up systematically. For instance, there is no systematic data collection on a national level. Now – thanks to the new law – this situation is changing.

Future areas for research are the follow-up of the implementation of the law and a nationwide data collection system. It is also important to start a study on the impact of mediation at the prosecution stage, especially during court proceedings.

References

Aaltonen, A. (1998) *Sovittu juttu – sopuhinta. Rikossovittelun kustan-nusvaikutukset oikeuskäsittelyyn verrattuna*, Raportteja 230 (Helsinki: STAKES).

Eskelinen, O. (2005) *Hermot vapautu ja tuli puhdas olo. Alle 15-vuotiaiden rikosten sovittelun käytännöt ja vaikutukset. Lapset riksoten sovittelussa -tutkimusprojektin raportti*, Julkaisuja 2005:3 (Helsinki: Sosiaali- ja tervesyminsiteriö).

Eskelinen, O. and Iivari, J. (2005) 'Victim-Offender Mediation with juvenile offenders in Finland', in Mestitz, A. and Ghetti, S. (eds.) *Victim-Offender Mediation with Youth Offenders in Europe. An overview and comparison of 15 countries* (Dordrecht: Springer), pp. 115-136.

Flinck, A. and Iivari, J. (2004) *Lähisuhdeväkivalta sovittelussa. Tutkimus- ja kehittämishankkeen realistinen arviointi*, arviointiraportteja 5/2004 (Helsinki: FinSoc).

Grönfors, M. (1992) 'Mediation – a Romantic Ideal or Workable Alternative', in Messmer, H. and Otto, U. (eds.) *Restorative Justice on Trial* (Netherlands: Kluwer Academic Publishers), pp. 419-429.

Iivari, J. (1985) *Sovittelu rikosten ja riitojen vaihtoehtoisena ratkaisuna. Kokemuksia Vantaan Sovitaan-projektin käynnistämisestä vuosilta 1983-1984*, 2/1985 (Helsinki: Oikeusministeri-ön vankeinhoito-osaston julkaisuja).

Iivari, J. (1988) *Sovitaan-projektin kokemuksista. Sovittelun mahdolli-suuksista vaih-toehtona rikosoikeusjärjestelmässä Vantaan Sovitaan-projektin koke-musten val-ossa*, 1/1988 (Helsinki: Sosiaalihallituksen julkaisuja).

Iivari, J. (1991) *Rikosten ja riitojen vaihtoehtosovittelu refleksiivisen oikeuden konseptiossa. Sosiaali- ja terveyshallitus*, 12/1991 (Helsinki: Tutkimuksia), with English summary: Mediation of Crimes and Disputes in the Concept of Reflexive Justice.

Iivari, J. (2001a) *Rikos- ja riita-asioiden sovittelun valtakunnallinen organisointi*, Työryhmämuistioita 2000:27 (Helsinki: Sosiaali- ja terveysministeriö).

Iivari, J. (2001b) 'Challenges of organising victim-offender mediation in Finland', *Newsletter of the European Forum for Victim-Offender Mediation and Restorative Justice*, October 2001, Vol. 2, Issue 2.

Iivari, J., Kuoppala, T. and Säkkinen, S. (2008) *Mediation in Criminal and Civil Cases 2008 National Statistical report 5/2008* (Helsinki: National Institute for H4ealth and Welfare).

Iivari, J. (2010) *Justice in the Shadow of Justice. An Evaluation Study of the Imple-mentation of the Act on Mediation in Criminal Cases* (Helsinki: National Insti-tute for Health and Welfare) Report 5/ 2010.

Järvinen, S. (1993) *Rikosten sovittelu Suomessa. Sovittelukäytännöt ja vaihtoeh-tois-uuden arviointi*, STAKES (tutkimuksia 21) ja Oikeuspoliittinen tutkimuslaitos (julkaisuja 116) (Helsinki: STAKES).

Mielityinen, I. (1999) *Rikos ja sovittelu. Valikoituminen, merkitys ja uusintari-kollis-uus* (Helsinki: Oikeuspoliittinen tutkimuslaitos).

Pawson, R. and Tilley, N. (1997) *Realistic evaluation* (London: Sage, New Delhi: Thousand Oaks).

Salonen, J. (2004) *Rikos- ja riita-asioiden sovittelu Suomessa 2004*. Kuntakyselyn tulokset. STAKES in Aiheita 22.11. 2004 (Helsinki: STAKES).

Salonen, J. and Iivari, J. (2004) *Evaluation of the "Let's Talk – Social Mediation for Refugee Communities in Europe" Project*, IOM International Organisation of Migration, IOM Helsinki Report 78/2004.

Takala, J.-P. (1998) *Moraalitunteet rikosten sovittelussa* (Helsinki: Oikeuspoliit-tinen tutkimuslaitos).

Teubner, G. (1988a) 'Evolution of autopoietic Law', in Teubner, G. (ed.) *Autopoietic Law: A New Approach to Law and Society* (Berlin/New York: De Gruyter), pp. 217-241.

Teubner, G. (1988b) *Refleksiv ret. Utviklingsmodeller for rette i sam-menliknende perspektiv*, i 'Refleksiv ret'. Redigeret af Asmund Born, Nils Breds-dorf, Leif Hansen, Fin Hanson, Nyt fra samfundsvidenskaberne.

6 Depicting the development of victim-offender mediation

Empirical research on restorative justice in Germany

Sönke Lenz, Elmar G.M. Weitekamp and Hans-Jürgen Kerner

1 Introduction

1.1 Context: state of affairs

In order to understand the development of victim-offender mediation [VOM] in Germany we have to consider the effects of two movements. The first is the development of mediation itself, its goals and its application in practice. The second is a general change in German law.

1.1.1 VOM in practice

Twenty years ago, VOM in Germany was a movement from the grassroots. It was more a vision carried out by committed individuals than an organised plan. Out of their experience with their practical work such as within juvenile courts and juvenile court assistance, prosecutors, judges and probation officers were thinking of alternatives in the sentencing of offenders. They thought that offenders should not primarily, at least not only, face a sentence but also examine the way in which they could make good what they had done to the victim and, in a wider perspective, to society at large.

Victims should not just be seen in their roles as witnesses or as accessory prosecutors. The change in the attitude towards the victims' needs is in general a central criterion to the development of the restorative justice philosophy. Through VOM, victims receive a decision-making role that supports their participation in the process. Analyses have shown, on the one hand, that victims generally do not have feelings of revenge but are mainly interested in compensation. On the other hand, they want to know why the particular crime happened to them and not to others. And they want in many cases, too, to express feelings of fear or anger or to make fully clear to the offender how the crime had a lasting impact on their lives. They feel a strong need to communicate these issues and therefore need a place where their voice will be heard (Pfeiffer, 1994: 91-116; Sessar, 1992, 1999).

With this in mind, all over Germany and mainly from 1985 to 1989, people started initiatives to get VOM projects off the ground. These first steps were based on individual efforts: they were all quite different from each other considering the persons involved and their relationship to different authorities or private associations, the structure of the projects and their implementation into local case law (see for instance Bannenberg, 1993; Dölling and Henninger, 1998: 203-365). Every project adapted the main idea and made it suitable for its own setting. Four of the projects showed enough practical experience to be chosen as so-called model-projects, which meant they received monetary grants and were empirically evaluated.[1]

During the 1990s, a movement started in order to standardise VOM work in Germany and to give it more theoretical focus. The first statistical surveys tried to take into account every aspect of the VOM outcome. Data on the experience of practitioners, involved in the daily work, were collected and led to the compilation of rules for good practice into a handbook on VOM, the so-called *TOA-Standards*.[2] This handbook codified the requirements with regard to quality control, the organisational level of the projects, the educational level of the mediators and the process of mediation.[3]

In the year 1992, the German Federal Government (as represented by the Federal Ministry of Justice) and relevant committees of the Federal Parliament opted to establish a nationwide central office, the *TOA-Servicebüro* (literally translated: Victim-Offender Mediation and Conflict Resolution Service Office).[4] Its tasks are to monitor and improve the quality of VOM work, and to certify an equal level of education for mediators. The office is a project of the so-called *DBH Association*[5] (German Association for Social Work, Penal Law and Crime Policy).

Social scientists and researchers from criminological departments all over Germany further founded an informal scientific cooperation network, the so-called German VOM Research Group, based on research experience with model-projects.[6]

Shortly after the start of the model-projects, Germany experienced a rapid rise in the number of new VOM projects. This foundation boom (Schreckling, 1991: 13; Bannenberg, 1993: 86; Wandrey and Weitekamp, 1998: 130) mainly lasted from 1985 to 1995. It was then joined by a large number of small-caseload projects in particular from Eastern Germany after the unification. The results from a national survey showed that 134 VOM projects existed in 1989, 226 projects in 1992 and 368 VOM projects in 1995 (Wandrey and Weitekamp, 1998: 133). The

---

1   Braunschweig: Pfeiffer H. (1989), Reutlingen: Kuhn (1989), Munich/Landshut: Hartmann (1995) and Cologne: Schreckling (1991), cf. infra for a discussion on the research results.

2   TOA-Servicebüro (1998: 12). TOA means *Täter-Opfer-Ausgleich*, the prevailing and official German term for VOM.

3   A thoroughly revised, updated and extended version has been published recently: see -TOA-Servicebüro 2010.

4   Its homepage is to be found under http://www.toa-servicebuero.de

5   Formerly Deutsche Bewährungs-, Gerichts- und Straffälligenhilfe, now Fachverband für Soziale Arbeit, Strafrecht und Kriminalpolitik (http://www.dbh-online.de).

6   Core members of the German VOM Research Group are: Britta Bannenberg at the University of Giessen, Dieter Dölling at the University of Heidelberg, Arthur Hartmann at the University of Applied Sciences in Public Administration Bremen, Wolfgang Heinz at the University of Konstanz, Dieter Rössner at the University of Marburg, Hans-Jürgen Kerner and Elmar G. M. Weitekamp at the University of Tübingen.

amount of cases dealt with increased from 2,100 in 1989 to 9,100 cases in 1995 (Wandrey and Weitekamp, 1998: 131). The total number of VOM projects at present in Germany cannot be counted on an official basis due to a lack of comprehensive surveys. However, the homepage of the TOA-Servicebüro in Cologne, as run by the private DBH, identifies more than 200 VOM projects.[7] Fact-finding at the VOM service office revealed that the most recent figure for the year 2006 amounted to 2,569 VOM cases for the State of Northrhine-Westfalia alone, which is the biggest State of the Federal Republic in terms of the number of inhabitants (some 18 million).

VOM work in Germany shows a big variety. On the one hand, we find smoothly running projects that are well-equipped and sufficiently staffed, with caseloads of over 100 up to several hundred cases per year. On the other hand, one can find small associations with caseloads of less than 30 VOM cases, small budgets and insufficient staff. Beside obvious differences, every VOM project in Germany faces the same general problem: during recent years, budget cuts (due to reductions in public subsidies) have led to a decline in the development of VOM. In some regions even some of the comparatively very successful projects have had to be closed (Hartmann and Kerner, 2004: 1).

1.1.2   The legal situation

All these practical developments in VOM influenced German youth law and in the long run the German general penal law as well. On the 1ˢᵗ of December 1990, VOM explicitly became part of revisions of sections 45 and 47 *Jugendgerichtsgesetz* (Youth Court Act or YCA). Since then, juvenile court judges and public prosecutors are authorised to divert any suitable case (including felonies) to a VOM project and eventually to fully dismiss the formal criminal procedure after a successful mediation has taken place (Hartmann and Kerner, 2004: 1). The law also provides other opportunities to initiate VOM and to take VOM into account. Especially Section 10 subsection 7 YCA gives the judge the possibility, in the final court verdict, the order to the young convicted offender to try hard to find a conflict resolution with the victim.

Exactly four years later, on the 1ˢᵗ of December 1994, a new VOM Section was added to the *Strafgesetzbuch* (Penal Code or PC).[8] Section 46a PC is divided into two parts: No.1 involves VOM, No.2 concerns financial compensation. The procedure in No.1 follows the steps of VOM with the exception that a mediator is not required in each and every case to make it legally valid. No.2 evaluates the legal duties for financial compensation. To avoid letting the offender get away with paying relatively small amounts of money, when and if his means surpass the amount of concrete damage done to the victim, he can receive a fully miti-

---

7   To be accessed via the bar "Konfliktschlichter in Ihrer Region" at: http://www.toa-servicebuero.de
8   The Penal Code represents the framework for mediation possibilities (cf. Rössner and Klaus 1998, 49). VOM work has not taken full advantage of its strengths up until now (Dölling, 1998: 19). Withdrawing from the VOM procedure and turning or returning to standard legal court procedures is possible at any stage, especially if the victim feels uncomfortable with the private solution.

gated sentence or even a conviction without a formal sentence only when he has achieved what amounts to 'a significant amount of personal payments or personal restrictions'. If the offender has achieved less than required by Section 46a No.2, the offender may still be given mitigation in sentencing through the discretionary court decision pursuant to Section 46 paragraph 2 PC, which deals with general considerations for meting out a sentence. The law does not set a formal limit in terms of the legal characteristics of the offence (misdemeanour or felony) for administering Section 46a in the one or other variant. However, there is a material limit for a declaration of guilt without imposition of any sentence in that the court must not grant this kind of privileged treatment when the sentence to be meted out would amount to more than one year of deprivation of liberty or more than 360 day units of a fine (Section 46a PC, last clause).

The last major legal step taken so far in Germany was the implementation of amendments to the *Strafprozessordnung* (Federal Code of Criminal Procedure or CPP) in 1999. The main regulations concerning defendants tried under adult rules can now be found in Section 153a CPP. With regard to diversionary solutions available to prosecutors and courts, either during preliminary procedures or outside the formal trial, the main difference compared to Sections 45 and 47 YCA is that normally the conflicting parties can only profit from diversion if a misdemeanour offence is at stake. Under very special circumstances, however, even some offences, which are legally to be handled as felonies, may lead to diversion if their concrete impact is actually not very serious (Section 153b CPP, relying in an analogue manner on PC regulations on formal sentencing options for the trial judge). The affiliated Section 155a CCP was intended to encourage the use of VOM in everyday criminal justice practice (Hartmann and Kerner, 2004: 2). Prosecutors and judges are requested by law to screen every case as early as possible and at every stage of the penal procedure (even later on during appeal) to see whether it would be suitable for VOM. They are also expected to instruct the parties actively about relevant options in cases where the persons involved do not have suitable knowledge, if any at all, on what is available to them. With Section 155b CCP, data and information exchange between prosecutors, the courts and (private) VOM projects received a legal basis in terms of general privacy and data protection laws (Hartmann and Kerner, 2004: 2).

1.2 Research: an overview

A substantial amount of research activities has been carried out in the field of VOM in Germany. From the beginning of the first pilot-projects, various studies were started. Relevant VOM publications fall into three main categories.

Publications in the first category deal with the research projects on single VOM projects. The four model-projects in Braunschweig, Reutlingen, Munich/Landshut and Cologne have been mentioned above. Research was carried out in other cities such as Hannover (Pfeiffer, 1997), Nürnberg/Fürth (Dölling and Hartmann, 1994, 2000) and Aschaffenburg (Dölling and Hartmann, 1997, 2000). To go into detail about all these particular VOM projects would go beyond the scope of this chapter; we will therefore focus on the model-projects (cf. infra, 2.1).

After certain projects were documented, the idea to create a broader ranging picture of the German situation was mooted. So the second main category of VOM publications relates to surveys. In order to get a solid overview of VOM projects, the initial surveys on VOM projects evaluated the distribution of VOM projects, their modes of implementation and their alleged success rates. The *DBH Association* had supported the conceptualisation and implementation of VOM projects since 1982. A research project was conducted in 1990 under its aegis. Its goals were to find out how widespread VOM projects were in Germany at that time, and to what extent different persons or professional groups accepted them. The research focused on the institutions directly involved in VOM projects: lower courts, prosecutors' offices, probation departments, youth welfare offices and non-governmental organisations. The research concentrated on West Germany and covered 1,251 institutions (Schreckling et al., 1991: 150-195). Bannenberg (1993) refers to the findings of this survey. In 1996, Wandrey and Weitekamp (1998) conducted a survey, encompassing both the old and the new States of Germany, that covered 368 VOM projects.

The third category of VOM publications refers to data-based studies. The biggest source for VOM database material is the German VOM survey that has been running since 1993 and is conducted by the German VOM Research Group. It is a collaborative documentation of VOM cases that are reported to the German VOM Research Group by VOM projects taking part in the data collection procedures of their own volition. In return for delivering their yearly data, participating VOM projects receive an analysis of their local data set in the context of VOM developments in Germany. In 2002, Bannenberg and Rössner (2002) added a couple of new results to the figures of the German-wide research from 1996, about single States and the 1997 report of the VOM statistics. Bals et al. (2005) conducted a research project that focused on adult criminal law cases in the State of Northrhine-Westfalia. The focus of the project was an efficiency report comparing the work of independent VOM services, social services of the courts and legal aid services. The VOM statistics, as collected by the German Research Group on VOM, are the basic source for most of the VOM research in Germany. They are partially funded by small federal grants, as awarded by the Federal Ministry of Justice.

2   DESCRIPTIVE-INVENTORY RESEARCH

2.1   The model-projects

The VOM project in *Braunschweig* was one of the first projects of the four VOM model-projects in Germany. The responsible agency was the department of juvenile court assistance. The project was founded in 1985 and was sponsored by the Department of Justice of the German State of Lower Saxony. In fact there were four different research projects implemented in Braunschweig.

The first study was realised by Christoph Pelster who carried out a semi-stand-ardised paper-and-pencil interview with social workers. The research took place between July 1987 and January 1989, during which 1,474 cases were carried out by the department of juvenile court assistance and more than a third (502 cases) proved to be suitable for VOM (Pelster, 1990: 26). The majority of these were assault and theft offences, therefore mediation agreements ranged from compensation and repairing the damage to oral and/or written apologies. From January 1988 to October 1988, Pfeiffer (1992) interviewed members of the youth service offices and the police involved in VOM cases.
In the third study Rattay and Raczek (1990) conducted interviews with all victims and offenders who took part in VOM meetings from January 1988 to January 1989, in order to evaluate their acceptance of VOM. The last Braunschweig study conducted by Bilsky and colleagues studied the efficiency of the Braunschweig VOM project in general. As a characteristic feature, the authors emphasised their findings on the good cooperation with the local police department (Bilsky et al., 1990).

The model-project in Cologne was also founded in 1985 as a registered society and started its work in January 1986. The financing was supplied by the 'E. & L. Oelbermann Foundation' for two years and was later taken over by the Department of Justice of Northrhine-Westfalia in cooperation with the city of Cologne. The accompanying research was carried out by one researcher and lasted from February 1986 to winter 1988. During that period, the project received 260 cases in total of which 246 cases were evaluated (354 offenders and 363 victims). One third of the offences comprised simple assault and damage to property, fraud accounted for 18% of the cases and 16% involved theft (Schreckling, 1991: 36). Half of the offenders were young adults, 41% of the sample were juveniles and 9% were adults (Schreckling, 1991: 38). More than half the victims belonged to the legal age groups of juveniles and young adults (Schreckling, 1991: 40). Almost every victim and nearly every offender was willing to go to the VOM meeting after being contacted via mail or telephone, but not all meetings were successful: in one third of the meetings the basic conflict between the parties reoccurred. Still, 68% of the offenders and 66% of the victims reached a settlement (Schreckling, 1991: 79). After two years of evaluation, all practitioners in the field of juvenile criminal law in Cologne considered the model-project as established.

The model-project in Reutlingen started in 1985 as a registered society too and was financially supported by the Federal Ministry for Family Affairs, Senior Citizens, Women and Youth for two years. The accompanying research was carried out by one single researcher, who analysed files from 1985 and 1986 from the juvenile court assistance department. In addition the 204 VOM cases, which had been mediated in Reutlingen between June 1985 and December 1987, were part of the evaluation (Kuhn, 1989: 93). Out of the 204 cases, the most common offences were theft (32%), assault (29%) and damage to property (22.5%). Most of the offenders were (as expected) juveniles, 26.5% were young adults and 3% adults.[9] In 50% of the cases involving personal victims (157 cases), it was possible to have a VOM meeting in the presence of a mediator who was a social worker. The success rate among such cases was 81%, which means that the meetings eventually led to a full agreement on how to settle the conflict. Depending on the offences, the compensation between the conflicting parties was mostly material (41%). In 18% of the mediated cases, victim and offender agreed on a joint activity or the victim accepted a gift from the offender. The agreements had a positive effect on the court proceeding: 152 cases were successfully closed and dismissed.

The last model-project combines two Bavarian cities namely Munich and Landshut, which both offer the possibility of VOM for juveniles and young adults. The project is a registered society (*Brücke e.V.*) and is carried by the *Stadt- und Kreisjugendring* [KJR][10] and by the society itself. The Bavarian Ministry for Family Affairs, Senior Citizens, Women and Youth supported the project financially from 1987 to 1989. The Landshut staff was composed of members of the youth welfare service. The project in Munich also had members of the community among its staff. The prosecution officer decided whether a case was suitable for VOM. One researcher evaluated the project by means of file analysis (1987 and 1988). The results for Munich showed that 337 cases were selected for VOM. Assaults made up the largest share of the cases (47.5%), 18.7 % involved aggravated bodily harm, 29.7% concerned theft and 10% damage to property. Out of 317 victims, 45.5% suffered from material damage and 46% from physical harm (Hartmann, 1995: 201). The mediation process can be divided into three sections: VOM sessions with a mediator present, meetings through private initiative and no mediation. Almost half of the successful mediations (i.e. leading to an agreement) came about with professional guidance; 33.5% of the successful cases were settled without VOM; and 18% of the cases were settled via a private initiative by the conflicting parties. The most common regulation was financial compensation, followed by symbolic regulations.[11]

The caseload in the Landshut project was 142 cases. The most frequent offence was theft (almost 50%), followed by assault (22.5%) and a relatively high percentage of trespassing (11.3%) (Hartmann, 1995: 210). From the 107 victims, 55.4% suffered from material damage and 32.4 % were bodily injured. The results from the meetings were positive. Like for Munich, the success rates could be divided into three sections. The success level of meetings with a mediator was 80.2%, without VOM 12.5%, and in 7.5% of the successful cases the regulation was found on a private basis (Hartmann, 1995: 215). The most frequent form of regulation was

---

9   The adult offenders had been involved in group conflicts.
10 The KJR is a voluntary union of democratic youth organisations and has the legal status of a corporation under public law.
11 According to the author, this entails a regulation where no material value was discussed (Hartmann, 1995: 245).

financial compensation, followed by symbolic regulation in 28.3% of the cases (Hartmann, 1995: 246).

2.2   Stock hold surveys

The German DBH-Association that supported and escorted the conception of VOM and the projects in Germany since 1982, conducted a nation-wide survey about the development of VOM in 1990. Its goals were to evaluate the spreading and the acceptance of VOM in Germany. The research was focused on the institutions directly involved in VOM decisions, namely lower courts, prosecution offices, probation offices, youth welfare offices and voluntary respectively charity organisations. In order to receive a proper feedback, the research team decided to mail out a short standardised questionnaire. One short questionnaire was sent to courts and prosecution offices, and entailed the VOM structure of the site and their eventual direct involvement in the VOM procedure. The second questionnaire was devised for Youth Welfare offices and voluntary or charitable organisations with items about the caseload, institutional background and the success of VOM settlements. After a period of one month, the return rate of the data covered 1,251 institutions (Schreckling et al., 1991: 154).

The evaluation showed that, in 1990, 42.6% of the institutions were informed about or even involved in VOM activities. The youth welfare and youth service offices were the best informed institutions. VOM was not well known or practised in the group of voluntary organisations. Most prevalent were VOM initiatives in the district courts of eight German cities (Schreckling et al., 1991: 160). Three thirds of the institutions participating in the survey were willing to promote VOM in their district or even initiate it.[12]

In 1994, Wandrey replicated the 1990's survey, covering the years 1989 up to 1992. The amount of VOM institutions increased in that period with about 40% and the caseload doubled. He found a boom of newly launched programmes in VOM (Wandrey, 1994: 10). The VOM organisation level can be described as follows: a lot of projects had dealt with up to 10 cases a year, while 10 VOM projects reported a caseload with more than 100 cases a year (Wandrey, 1994: 11).

In another study, Hartmann (1995: 185-299) verified a gap between ideal and reality for Bavaria with data from 1992. He found a need for education and information in his sample. The structural framework to establish these measures had not been built yet, which led to the inefficient caseload of many projects.

In 1996, the VOM Research Group started a follow-up research to the nationwide stock holds from 1989 and 1992. The VOM service office contacted VOM projects as well as youth welfare and youth service offices and probation offices. Overall, 368 projects responded to the inquiry of the Research Group, but only 261 project descriptions were detailed enough to be included in the analyses. Conclusions

---

12   Bannenberg referred to these results in her empirical study. She confirmed the high figures of VOM institutions, but especially for 1990 she concluded that fewer institutions had experience with VOM depending on the varying caseloads (Bannenberg, 1993: 269).

firstly entailed that the boom of newly launched VOM programmes continued: the amount of VOM projects again increased about 63%. This applied for the total amount of caseload too, which increased compared to the last survey by 78% (Wandrey and Weitekamp 1998: 131). A dynamic development was found with regard to the whole spectrum of German criminal law: the huge majority was operating in the field of penal law relating to young offenders (72%) and a small group operated in the field of adult penal law (14%). In 1992, there were only six projects working in both sectors, compared to fifteen projects or 14% of the 1996 survey (Dölling and Henninger, 1998: 203 ff.).

2.3   Data-based studies

Bannenberg and Rössner (2002) combined the findings of the 1996 survey with figures from the 1997 VOM statistics and concluded that about 9,000 cases had been processed through VOM in Germany. An additional 3,000 cases from the State of Brandenburg and roughly 1,600 cases from the State of Saxony-Anhalt, who were at that point in time not part of the collected VOM statistics, could be added, based on information by the respective Ministries of Justice. Regarding the organisational structure of VOM projects, they discovered a dynamic change: apart from traditional providers of VOM services like youth departments (59%) and court assistance services (15%), a third type of organisation came into play, namely independent operating institutions or NGOs (26%). These independent institutions played a major role in the practical VOM work. The 1996 survey revealed that over 50% of the human resources were used in independent institutions.

The number of cases in the 1997 VOM statistics mounted to 9,000 (5,300 offenders and 4,750 victims). The most frequent offence group is assault (including mayhem) with almost 50% of the caseload, followed by damage to property (14%), and a relatively high percentage of theft and fraud (10%) (Bannenberg and Rössner, 2002: 292). Because of the kind of offences, victims mostly suffered bodily harm (59%). After having had a VOM meeting, 85% of juvenile and young adult offenders and 78% of adult offenders reached a full settlement with their victims (Bannenberg and Rössner, 2002: 293). The content of settlements ranged from apology to compensation for personal damage, and compensation and joint activity with the victim (Bannenberg and Rössner, 2002: 293). After having met, 68% of the offenders and 66% of the victims achieved a fully satisfying settlement (Schreckling, 1991: 79).

In 2003, Bannenberg referred to another publication of the German VOM Research Group, covering the years 1993 to 1999 (Bannenberg, 2003: 21). These statistics again showed a big variety of offences for which VOM took place. However, the focus was on assault and mayhem. One third of the victims suffered from great injuries, which led to ambulant or in-patient treatment. Assault offences made up 60% in all age groups. Projects working with juveniles and young adults handled 10% of the cases in the field of robbery and blackmail. The first offenders constituted the majority, 35% of the offenders had a prior criminal record. 81% of the offenders were willing to join a VOM meeting compared to 63% of the victims. The results of the meetings were positive: in 86% of the mediated cases, the conflict parties achieved a full settlement. In another 4% of cases they came to at least partial settlements that seemed to be successful for them under given circumstances (Bannenberg, 2003: 22).

Bals et al. (2005) conducted a study on VOM projects for adult offenders in North-rhine-Westfalia. The evaluation period covered February 2002 till March 2004. The research focused on: (a) a file analysis: roughly 3,000 cases had been ana-lysed to obtain a broad view of the application of VOM; (b) questionnaires; and (c) interviews with public prosecutors, judges, mediators and with victims and offenders who had participated in a VOM meeting. One of the main focal points of the study was to clarify whether the willingness of victims and offenders to join a VOM meeting depended structurally from the kind of programme. This was indeed the case, when comparing 12 independent institutions with 18 Gerichts-hilfen, which are specialized offices related to the prosecution authorities and working for prosecutors and courts, run by social workers, and which may be translated literally as Court Aide Offices (Bals et al. 2005: 199ff).

Dölling and Hartmann, in 2003, analysed the likelihood for juvenile offenders to re-offend after participating in a VOM in juvenile court proceedings. The cases cover defendants who had taken part in the VOM model-project in Munich and Landshut. The control group of defendants who had not taken part in VOM were chosen from the same jurisdictions (Dölling and Hartmann, 2003: 210). The selection of control variables for the multi-variable analysis followed two princi-ples: a) variables which significantly correlated with the number of further official diversions; b) variables that occurred with different frequency in the VOM group and in the control group (Dölling and Hartmann, 2003: 222). The research in general revealed a favourable influence of VOM on re-offending, but the selected cases offered no other explanatory variable on that issue (Dölling and Hartmann, 2003: 228).

3   THE GERMAN VOM STATISTICS

Since 1991, the German VOM Research Group tried to improve the evaluation on VOM. The previous evaluations were only supplied by model-projects and the results were therefore not compatible with each other because every project used its own evaluation methods. However, many projects, which were not part of the model-projects, showed interest in sharing their data. It seemed therefore pos-sible to bring this knowledge to a nationwide level or, in other words, to collect VOM data on a national level for Germany.

Therefore, the German VOM Research Group developed a standardised ques-tionnaire that enabled the VOM projects to record their work. The questionnaire was developed through three steps. First, the methodological experiences of the model-projects were collected. With this information about questionnaires and counting methods, the German VOM Research Group created a questionnaire test-version that had been pre-tested in twelve projects. Based on that outcome, the final questionnaire was established.[13] The standardised questionnaire was available from March 1993 onwards via the VOM service office and remained the same until present (2007), with the exception of some little changes. In total, it contains 60 items to describe any case and is concerned with VOM on four different levels:

- *Organisational level*: questions about status and type of organisation: is the project specialised in VOM or do they mediate other conflicts or work in related areas? What code of law (age group) is the work based on?
- *Case level*: contains questions about the historical sequel of the conflict and about VOM, how many persons (victim, offender, third party) or institutions are involved in the conflict. On which level of proceeding was VOM started and who initiated it (e.g. prosecutor, judge)? And lastly, (to what extent) did the offender fulfil the VOM agreements?
- *Victim level*: contains particularities of victims, and questions about kind and seriousness of the victimisation, material damage and the physical and psychological harm. Lastly, it contains information about the question if the victim is willing to participate in a VOM attempt.
- *Offender level*: contains particularities of offenders, questions about the content of the crime, if the offender was ever punished before and if there was a relationship between victim and offender. Similar to the victim level it is inquired if the offender is willing to join a VOM attempt. Further questions concern the proceeding of the actual meeting if there is a mediator present or whether the conflict parties meet on a private basis. Further on questions were asked about the success of the meeting, in particular whether or not victim and offender achieved a full settlement. In addition information about the content of the agreement was gathered and the last items of the questionnaire clarified how the prosecutor or the court eventually handled the cases (proceeding quashed or additional restrictions).

All German VOM projects are constantly invited to join in. But since participation in the VOM statistics is voluntary, only a fraction of projects have decided to participate in data collection.[14] After ten years of existence the VOM statistics operate with 30,300 cases in total (Kerner et al., 2005a: 4). Those cases are, however, not representative in strict statistical terms, for all cases and all details dealt with in practice all over Germany in all the years. But, on the one hand, until now nobody can say anything about the 'true extent' of VOM in the whole Federation, since there is a severe lack of official sources and data. And, on the other hand, irrespective of how many projects actually participated over the years, and irre-

---

13   A report can be found in TOA-Servicebüro, 1993: 29 ff.
14   Apart from the so-called City States of Hamburg and Bremen, all German States were represented. However, the majority of cases reported to the VOM Research Group originate from 'old' Western States (up to 90%).

spective of where they were located geographically, the same basic data structures could always be found in the analyses. This leads to the conclusion that the VOM statistics data set depicts at least the main features and procedures and outcomes of all VOM endeavours in Germany.

The Institute of Criminology of the University of Tübingen took on the task to adjust and to interpret the data and to publish them on behalf of the German VOM Research Group. The researchers in Tübingen provide each project with an individual summary and output of their cases. The Federal Ministry of Justice receives in addition, in exchange for its support, a comprehensive annual report. Out of these annual stocktaking reports, the Tübingen team composes longitudinal studies for the Ministry of Justice, in order to provide material for law evaluation and reform purposes. Two of those longitudinal studies have been published so far on the official Ministry website in German language. The one covers the years 1993 to 1999 (Kerner et al., 2003), the other – as a tenth anniversary issue – covers the years 1993 to 2002 (Kerner et al., 2005a).[15]

3.1   Selected results from the VOM statistics 1993-2002

3.1.1   Organisation does matter

One can differentiate between the types of organisation of VOM projects by the degree of specialisation. It depends namely on whether staff is responsible for VOM only or has other duties in other working fields. Specialised projects have social workers who work only in the field of mediation. In semi-specialised VOM projects, the mediators have other functions as well, but they concentrate their work on VOM. Integrated projects work in the field of mediation and cooperate with the courts for writing dossiers as part of the youth court aid work.

When the German VOM statistics started, the number of integrated working projects was relatively high and the most common form of organisation (58.8%; semi-specialised: 15.7%; specialised: 25.5%). After ten years, and even in the most recently evaluated data, this picture has changed completely: now the specialised working projects are in the majority (73.3%; semi-specialised: 20%; integrated: 6.7%). This development is attributed to the experience that the organisation level has certainly an effect on the working quality and upon the complexity of the cases that can be mediated: the higher the specialisation, the better the work that can be done.

3.1.2   Target group

Since VOM in Germany started under the Youth Court Act, 90% of the projects were working with juveniles and young adults (18 to 21 year old persons). When the legal framework for VOM was established in the Penal Code, projects started to specialise in working with adult offenders. While in the years from 1993 to 2002 cases covered all age groups, the majority of the cases were still juveniles

---

15   The reports for the years in between were compiled for internal use only and they cannot be shown here due to copyright issues.

and young adults. Now, mainly because of dramatic changes in the financial support for VOM projects, it is more suitable for them to work with all age groups, and in 2002 the number of juvenile and young adult offender cases was in total 2,537 and for adult offender cases 2,148 (Kerner et al., 2005a: 9).

3.1.3 Offence categories

We know from previous surveys that especially the 'bodily injury' offences are very often considered inherently suitable for a VOM by the prosecutors' office. During the first ten years of VOM statistics, the most frequently mediated cases involved 'bodily injury' cases[16] with almost 60% of the mediated cases belonging to this category, followed by 'theft and fraud'[17] with almost 11%, 'robbery/extortion'[18] with some 6% and 'criminal damage'[19] with 0.7% (Kerner et al., 2005a: 51, 2005b: 33; see also Hartmann and Kerner, 2004: 5). The official German Police Crime Statistics differ from that picture significantly.[20]

---

16 The category 'bodily injury' as used here is a composite variable, containing the following single offence categories according to the German Penal Code: § 223 Körperverletzung (simple assault), § 224 gefährliche Körperverletzung (dangerous assault), § 225 Misshandlung von Schutzbefohlenen (abuse of dependent persons), § 226 schwere Körperverletzung (assault with long lasting consequences e.g. impairment), § 227 Körperverletzung mit Todesfolge (assault with fatal consequences), § 229 fahrlässige Körperverletzung (negligent wounding), and § 340 Körperverletzung im Amt (criminal wounding as committed by a public employee in the course of his duties).

17 The category 'theft and fraud' as used here is also a composite variable. It contains the following single offences according to the German Penal Code: § 242 Diebstahl (ordinary theft), § 243 besonders schwerer Fall des Diebstahls (theft under aggravating circumstances, like breaking and entering), § 244 Diebstahl mit Waffen (theft while carrying firearms or other weapons), § 263 Betrug (fraud), § 263a Computerbetrug (fraud using a computer), § 265 Versicherungsmissbrauch (damaging or destroying objects with the intent to commit insurance fraud), § 265a Erschleichen von Leistungen (fare dodging on public transport, sneaking into cinemas, football matches etc. by evading payment, and the like), § 265b Kreditbetrug (fraudulent manipulations to get financial credit), § 266 Untreue (injury to a third party through abuse of trust), § 267 Urkundenfälschung (falsifying or faking documents), and § 266a Vorenthaltung und Veruntreuen von Arbeitsentgelt (not paying the employer's share of the employees social security benefits etc. to the federal schemes, or misusing the relevant financial means).

18 The category 'robbery/extortion' as used here is also a composite variable. It contains the following single offences: § 239a erpresserischer Menschenraub (holding hostage with violence in order to extract ransom), § 239b Geiselnahme (holding another person captive with the use of violence or threat in order to press someone else to do or omit certain behaviour, like taking a customer hostage after a failed bank robbery with the intent to have the police provide the offender/offenders with a car for escape), § 249 Raub (ordinary robbery, like purse snatching with bodily force), § 250 schwerer Raub (robbery under aggravated circumstances, e.g. using a firearm or another weapon), § 252 räuberischer Diebstahl (using a weapon or other means of force when caught by the victim or another persons upon committing an act of theft or aggravated theft), §253 Erpressung (extortion) and § 255 räuberische Erpressung (extortion with the use of physical violence or weaponry or by severely menacing the victim, e.g. threatening fatal consequences if the victim will not comply with the orders given by the offender).

19 The category 'criminal damage to property' as used here is a composite variable. It contains the following single offences: § 303 Sachbeschädigung (standard criminal damage to foreign objects) and § 304 gemeinschädliche Sachbeschädigung (damaging objects belonging to the public or having important public functions).

20 Theft/fraud: 47.5%; assault/mayhem: 6.5%; and robbery: 0.9% of all offences as recorded by the police in Germany (cf. Bundeskriminalamt, 2003: 28).

3.1.4   Meeting of victims and offenders

Normally the parties have to meet personally either in a secure, mediated situation or, if there is only a limited conflict, on a private basis to come to terms with each other. According to the VOM statistics, VOM attempts in the presence of a mediator are the most common way to settle the conflict, followed by cases where the parties either met fully alone in private or at least initially before contacting a mediator. Parties rarely met in private in addition to a running mediation procedure. Table 1 depicts the situation for a ten-year period. On the one hand, one should note that the percentage of professionally mediated cases would be even higher if only those cases where meetings occurred were taken into consideration. On the other hand the table shows, in the long run, that this type lost some of its prominence. The reasons for this shift are not known yet.

Table 1   Preparedness of victims and offenders to join VOM procedures, and preferred types of meetings (Germany, 1993 to 2002)

	Results in %									
	1993	1994	1995	1996	1997	1998	1999	2000	2001	2002
VOM meeting with mediator	60.0	60.6	58.3	53.0	55.6	58.7	59.1	51.7	48.7	48.4
Private meeting during VOM attempt	6.3	4.5	5.5	5.5	5.3	5.1	6.9	6.5	7.2	5.9
Private meeting before VOM attempt	8.0	7.5	10.4	10.5	11.1	10.4	10.1	10.4	10.3	11.7
Victim refuses VOM	10.5	12.9	12.1	15.8	14.4	16.8	14.8	13.8	20.5	6.7
Offender refuses VOM	1.9	1.1	1.6	2.0	1.6	1.7	1.6	5.5	1.9	13.5
Other factors of refusal	13.3	13.4	12.1	13.1	11.0	7.3	6.3	11.9	11.4	13.9
Total	100.0	100.0	100.0	99.9	99.0	100.0	98.8	99.8	100.0	100.1

Having met, it is important how the conflict parties finally settle. The figures are positive in this regard (see also Bannenberg, 2003: 22). The evaluation over a ten-year period clarifies that both parties mostly strive to achieve a full settlement once they consented to join the endeavour. They may eventually, however, also be content with a partial settlement, if they come to realise that this is the maximum to be gained in the concrete case. On average, in 85% of the cases in which the parties joined a VOM attempt, a full settlement was achieved and in a further 3.6% a partial one. Failed VOM cases accounted for on average 11.1% between 1993 and 2002 (Kerner et al., 2005a: 85).

3.1.5   Content of VOM agreements

Table 2 presents the content of VOM agreements. The total may add up to more than 100% since sometimes the parties agree on more than one issue. Apart from obvious VOM agreements, like compensation for personal suffering or damage (which has always been an important part of mediation), VOM in practice seems to be also able to create new agreements that go beyond strict court regulations.

This may include a symbolic gift to the victim or the transfer of assurance contracts from the offender to the victim. As far as an apology is concerned this may be, on the one hand, just an 'emerging' part of a broader solution, based mainly on material restitution or harm compensation. But practitioners' reports do show, on the other hand, that sometimes the parties finally reach an emotionally rewarding state of affairs where an apology on the part of the offender prevails above all other aspects, and leads the victim to renounce his original claims for restitution or compensation in part or even totally. In other cases victims and offenders agree on what is called joint activities, e.g. community work on behalf of parochial organisations or joint weekend excursions where the offender takes responsibility for an impaired victim.

Table 2   Content of VOM agreement as reached eventually by victims and offenders (Germany, 1993 to 2002)

	Results in %									
---	1993	1994	1995	1996	1997	1998	1999	2000	2001	2002
Apology	59.1	58.1	72.0	66.7	74.5	72.2	83.5	67.5	68.1	69.8
Gift for victim	5.6	3.0	6.7	3.5	4.4	4.9	8.8	4.9	4.7	4.9
Return of stolen goods	1.2	4.0	2.1	3.0	3.1	3.3	3.6	1.9	2.5	2.3
Compensation for personal suffering	20.2	21.8	21.1	20.2	19.0	15.9	21.8	15.3	17.0	13.6
Work for victim's benefit	6.3	5.7	6.5	6.1	4.0	7.0	9.1	7.4	5.8	5.7
Joint activity	5.0	5.7	8.3	5.4	5.4	4.7	6.0	3.3	2.5	2.8
Compensation for damage	37.3	30.4	27.2	33.9	27.5	27.4	34.6	26.7	25.0	25.1
Other solutions	15.3	16.2	13.0	10.6	11.3	11.1	18.0	11.4	12.4	13.6
No agreement deemed necessary any more	6.7	10.7	5.9	5.4	5.2	5.2	9.9	8.6	8.6	8.3

3.2   Developments of VOM in Germany (2003 to 2005)

3.2.1   Structural organisation
According to the structural organisation of VOM, it was to be expected that the previous picture would not change too much in recent years. Indeed, specialised services dealing with VOM in everyday practice continue to dominate on average during the three years taken into consideration (75.1%), whereas partly specialised services came to 14.3% and integrated services to 10.6%.[21] Details can be found in Figure 1.

---

21   All upcoming figures were originally made by Anke Eikens and were translated by Elmar Weitekamp.

Figure 1   Organisational form of the victim-offender mediation institutions

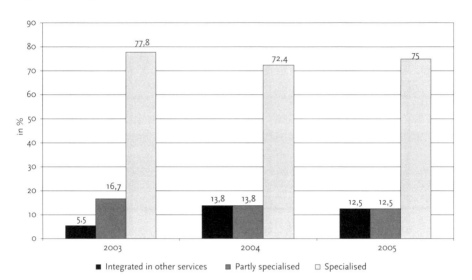

3.2.2   *Point of entry into the procedures*

The German VOM statistics also evaluate at what point of the criminal procedure endeavours to bring victims and offenders together are being initiated, and who is the one to take the official initiative for starting relevant activities.

As far as the first question is concerned, data for the years 2003 to 2005 also follow the former German tradition and there is practically no real variance: on average 87.8% of the endeavours start during the preliminary investigations; 6.8% start after the offender is formally charged with one or more offences; 0.9% happen during trial time, and 1.2% originate later, i. e. after a (first) formal conviction.

Regarding the second question, it is clear that the vast majority of VOM attempts are still initiated by the prosecutors' offices. Behind this official initiative, however, other persons or institutions may have been substantially active in order to give the responsible prosecutor the idea that the case might be suitable to deviate from traditional manners leading to a formal charge and then the main public trial. The VOM Research Group received several comments of that nature from police authorities or individual police officers, claiming that German police, in taking victims' needs more serious than previously, were also more inclined to seek case indicators for VOM and make relevant notes for the prosecution. As Figure 2 clearly shows, at least in the last three years of the VOM statistics this 'hidden role' of the police has become more evident in case management. On the other hand, for reasons that are not clear at all, the formerly important role of the social workers in Youth Court Aid Services and in Adult Court Aid Services seems to have lost momentum.

Figure 2   Initiation of VOM-attempt (main categories)

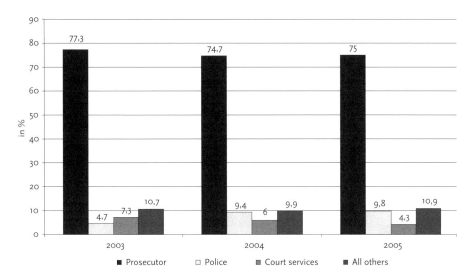

The category 'all others' in Figure 2 refers to persons or institutions contributing only a small part to the whole picture. These were, in order of declining percentage on the average of the three years, judges (2.3%), offenders themselves (2.0%), victims themselves (0.8%) and probation officers (0.6%).[22]

3.2.3   Background of offenders and victims

As far as the legally defined age group of offenders is concerned, those services dealing with all age groups have declined further, as Figure 3 depicts clearly: from 42.5% in 2003 to 34.4% in 2004, and to 28.6% in 2005 (average 35.2%). Most services tend now to concentrate on a more clear cut clientele, be they young offenders up to 20 years of age (juveniles and young adults called 'adolescents' following the YCL) with an average of 41.3%, or be they full adult offenders from 21 years of age upwards with an average of 23.5%, both adding up to 64.8 % of the whole clientele of all services.

---

22   The remaining 5.2% are composed of diverse sources such as social welfare authorities, defence attorneys, victim support associations, VOM services as contacted by participants instead of the police, etc.

Figure 3   Intended group for victim-offender mediation according to legal age categories

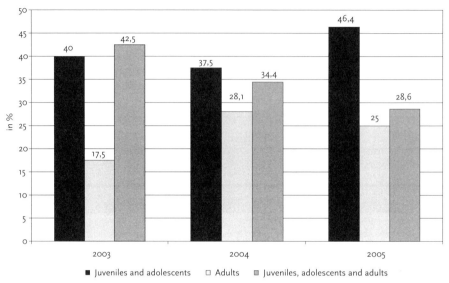

Juveniles and adolescents   □ Adults   Juveniles, adolescents and adults

The age distribution of offenders and victims looks structurally similar which means that the bulk of cases tends to arise among persons of the same age group. However, the average age of the offenders involved in VOM cases has always been lower on average than the age of the victims. This is also true for the years 2003 to 2005. As Figure 4 depicts in details, the most prevalent offender age category is represented by those young persons dealt with in the German Youth Court System, an age category containing the legal categories of juveniles (aged 14 to 17) and the young adults called adolescents (aged 18 to 20). According to German Penal Law the lower age limit of penal responsibility is 14 years of age. So nobody below 14 can be treated according to formal penal procedural rules of the CPP. The few youngsters included in the 0.6% in Figure 4 are therefore neither 'defendants' nor 'culprits'. As case details behind the VOM statistics show, they were 'collaborators' with older comrades or members of a street corner clique, and they and their parents had consented eventually to join in voluntarily (or 'induced' by local youth authorities) when it came to VOM procedures.

Figure 4   Age of offenders and victims (average 2003-2005)

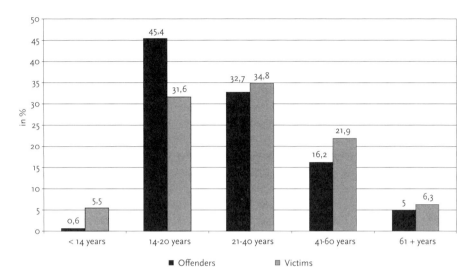

The distribution of nationalities among offenders and victims in VOM cases shows a strong predominance of German nationals. Structurally similar to those of previous years, the VOM statistics for 2003 to 2005 show that among the offenders 74.3% and among the victims 76.3% were Germans, whereas 25.5% respectively 23.7% were non-Germans. However, the trend seems to show a continuous decline of non-Germans.[23] The reasons are not yet clear: in part the declining trend may be attributable to general developments in the committing of offences by different nationalities and/or ethnic groups, and to different effects of victims' reporting behaviour, and eventually police clearance endeavours and effectiveness.[24]

3.2.4   The offences
Figure 5 summarises the main criminal law offence categories that led to VOM procedures in the years 2003 to 2005. The structure here basically resembles that of former years: the majority of the cases dealt with are assaults, followed by cases of criminal damage to property and cases of property offences (including fraud), while robbery and extortion cases remain relatively small.

---

23   Between the year 2002 as reference year and 2005 as the last year in consideration, non-German offenders diminished in VOM procedures from 31.4% to 21.6% and non-German victims diminished from 32.7% to 20.2%.
24   According to German Police Crime Statistics data on all 'persons suspected of a crime or a misdemeanour' the percentage of non-Germans was as follows: 2002: 24.4%, 2003: 23.5%, 2004: 22.9% and 2005: 22.5%. There is no information available at all about the nationality of victims, and only some pieces of information on age and sex of victims for selected offences.

Figure 5   Structure of offences in cases of victim-offender mediation –
summarised main categories

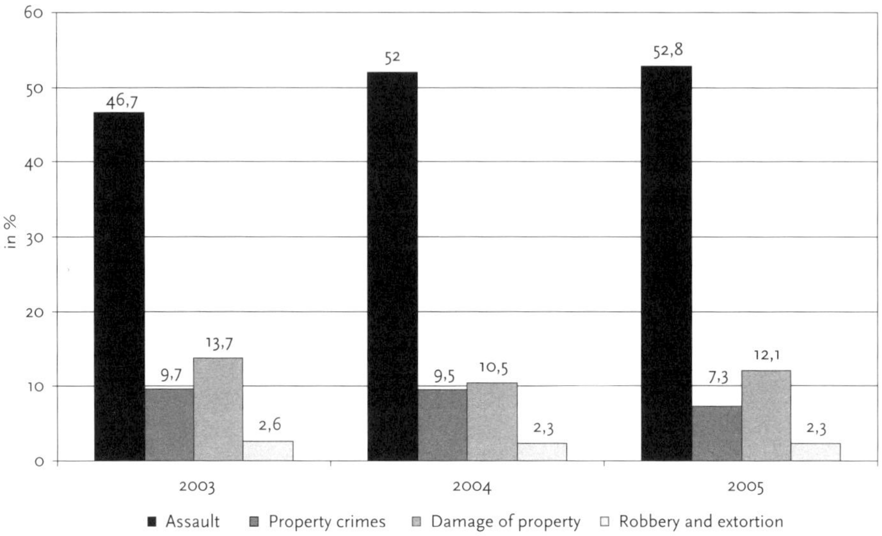

Broken down according to the juvenile and adolescent category on the one hand, and the adult category on the other hand, the results look very similar, with the exception of robbery and extortion cases which are, while generally low, nevertheless considerably lower for adults (1.2%) compared to those for juveniles and adolescents (3.3%).

3.2.5   Consequences for the victim
Figure 6 considers not the legal offence category implied but the actual consequences of the criminal act for the victim. It indicates the harm or damage suffered predominantly through the victimisation. As one can see it is, as in previous years, mostly physical harm that victims suffered from. Psychological harm and material damage made up around 20% each of the remaining part.[25]

---

25   The percentage values do not add to 100%; this is usually due to cases where the kind of harm or damage was not delineated clearly enough in the files.

Figure 6   Suffered harm through victimization

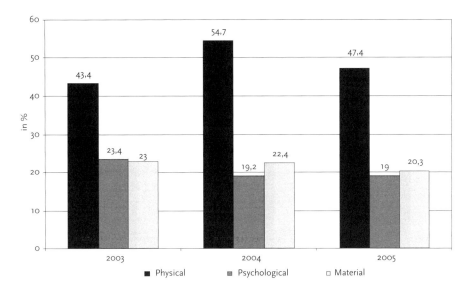

Upon closer examination we find that, as in former years, the majority of the physical harm was 'light' (60.8% on the average) which means that the victims did not need medical care or only out-patient treatment by a medical doctor. Around a third of the victims (32.3% on average) suffered 'medium' harm, which means that they needed repeated out-patient medical treatment or had to stay for one or a few days in the hospital. On average 6% of the victims were 'severely' harmed which means they had to spend many days in hospital and in some cases to undergo post-hospital treatment procedures as well. Only some 0.9% of the victims included in VOM procedures were 'permanently' affected by the offence, which means they had, for example, been disfigured or disabled. Nevertheless, taking the last two categories together, it seems worth noting that the German juvenile and/or adult criminal justice systems regularly have some 7% very serious cases of physical harm among all relevant cases included in VOM procedures.

3.2.6 Willingness to participate
Figure 7 looks at the results of contacting the victims and offenders with regard to their willingness to participate: on average almost 70% of the victims agreed to VOM compared to almost 83% of the offenders. This is basically in line with results of previous years, but it is possible to detect in the long run a slowly declining trend among victims.

Figure 7   Results of contacting victims and offenders without considering persons who could not be reached

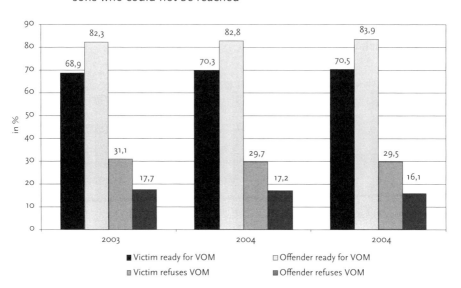

After clearing the willingness of victims and offenders to join in principal, the question arises in practice whether the parties really feel a kind of 'conflict' which needs to be dealt with as such and, in particular, requires a personal meeting if not repeated meetings, especially in the presence of a trained mediator. In Germany the VOM services tend to come to the conclusion, after considering case details and after consulting with the parties, that a more or less considerable part of the cases can be handled successfully just by talking to the persons involved separately, finding out their predominant wishes and eventually reaching a solution suitable for both the victim and the offender. As one may assume, such an approach is used more frequently when it comes to property offences such as theft or embezzlement compared to personal offences such as assault or injury. The results of the VOM statistics for 2003 to 2005 indicate the same. Since there are no structural differences in individual years, only the averages are presented here: out of all property offences 49.8% had been solved without personal meetings; the respective percentage values were for criminal damage 40.4%, for robbery and extortion 35.5%, and for assault and injury only – but nevertheless significant – 31.4%.

3.2.7   Outcomes

According to Figure 8, the results of VOM procedures, either via negotiating the outcome through the VOM services or via personal meetings in presence of a mediator, can be considered mostly a success: around 83% of the involved offenders and victims reach, on average, a full agreement as to what the final solution of the conflict should look like, and around another 4% come at least to a consensus that full agreement is impossible but that each side could live with a less than perfect solution.

Figure 8   Results of mediation in terms of agreements among victims and offenders

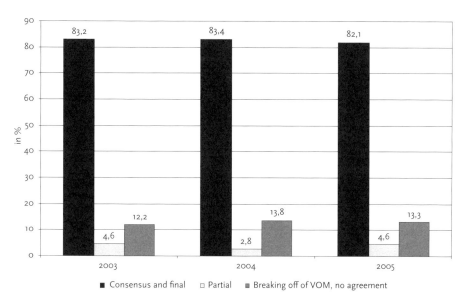

This leaves an average of 13.1% where eventually either the victim or the offender or both of them broke off rather suddenly (and sometimes with strong emotional involvement still) 'their' VOM procedure or just terminated it after a while without much remaining conflict among them after realising that a fully suitable agreement would remain beyond reach, at least for the near future. It is interesting to note, in more detail, that successful VOM results were reached in all of the robbery and extortion cases which could otherwise be considered the most difficult ones, whereas the percentage was a bit lower in the other case categories: on average 95.6% regarding assault and injury, 94.6% regarding property offences and 93.8% regarding criminal damage.

Figure 9 depicts the categories of agreements victims and offenders did eventually reach. One of the most remarkable results of these mediation agreement outcomes is the fact that the apology did not lose its predominant place among all kinds of solutions but nevertheless declined strongly in percentage between 2003 and 2005. As opposed to this, solutions such as payment of damages or offenders working for the benefit of victims or different (not specified) individually negotiated 'other solutions' did rise in those years.[26]

---

26 The data set of the VOM statistics does not allow for testing possible causes for this phenomenon.

Figure 9   Details of mediation agreement between victims and offenders

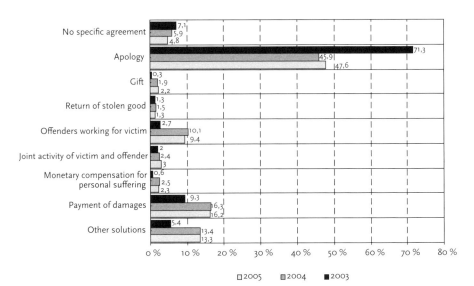

As Figure 10 makes clear, the eventual fulfilment of VOM agreements supports the general notion of appropriateness and success of VOM. Complete or eventually only partial (but consented) fulfilment combined with pending cases (hopefully coming to a positive end) made up for 99.2 % on average for the years 2003 to 2005. The respective (definite) failure rate of around 0.8% is sufficiently small to be ignored.

Figure 10   Fulfilment of agreements

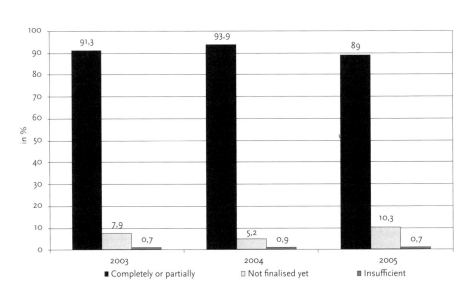

4   CONCLUSION

The results presented above of VOM in Germany speak for themselves and show that the development in general, and the results reached in practice in particular, can be considered predominantly as a success story. Some shortcomings definitely exist and improvements could be made and are sometimes necessary, but the overall picture is satisfactory.

As far as research on VOM is concerned, nearly all studies are cross-sectional. Even the VOM statistics remain basically cross-sectional, since they represent separate results for separate study years under a comparative perspective. Only true longitudinal studies taking into account the development of the same cases over time (Rössner, 2007) would produce more precise information about long term effects of VOM on offenders, victims and communities as well as recidivism rates and levels of satisfaction with VOM. Also, other types of research approaches seem necessary such as action-research, process evaluation studies and meta-analyses of different study outcomes over time and for different case particularities.

REFERENCES

Bals, N., Hilgartner, C. and Bannenberg, B. (2005) *Täter-Opfer-Ausgleich im Erwachsenenbereich. Eine repräsentative Untersuchung in Nordrhein-Westfalen* (Mönchengladbach: Forum Verlag Godesberg).

Bannenberg, B. (1993) *Wiedergutmachung in der Strafrechtspraxis. Eine empirisch-kriminologische Untersuchung von Täter-Opfer-Ausgleichsprojekten in Deutschland* (Mönchengladbach: Forum Verlag Godesberg).

Bannenberg, B. (2003) *Täter-Opfer-Ausgleich. Wiedergutmachung im Strafrecht. Grundgedanken, Rechtsgrundlagen und empirische Ergebnisse* (Bonn: Bundesministerium der Justiz).

Bannenberg, B. and Rössner, D. (2002) 'Die Wirklichkeit des Täter-Opfer-Ausgleichs (TOA) in Deutschland – Eine Zwischenbilanz', in Kühne, H.-H. (ed.) *Festschrift für Klaus Rolinski zum 70. Geburtstag* (Baden-Baden: Nomos Verlagsgesellschaft), pp. 287-302.

Bilsky, W., Netzig, L. and Petzold, F. (1990) *Praxis und Perspektiven des Täter-Opfer-Ausgleichs in Braunschweig – Konzeption, Durchführung und Ergebnisse einer Delphistudie mit Jugendgerichtshelfern und anderen TOA-Praktikern* (Hannover: Projekt Waage).

Bundeskriminalamt (ed.) (2003) *Polizeiliche Kriminalstatistik, Bundesrepublik Deutschland 2002* (Wiesbaden: Eigenverlag Bundeskriminalamt).

Dölling, D. (ed.) (1998) *Täter-Opfer-Ausgleich. Eine Chance für Opfer und Täter durch einen neuen Weg im Umgang mit Kriminalität. Kurzfassung des 1997 vorgelegten Gutachtens der Forschergruppe Täter-Opfer-Ausgleich* (Mönchengladbach: Forum Verlag Godesberg).

Dölling, D. and Hartmann, A. (1994) *Forschungsbericht zu dem Modellversuch TOA im Erwachsenenstrafrecht der Staatsanwaltschaft bei dem Landgericht Nürnberg/Fürth* (Heidelberg: Institut für Kriminologie).

Dölling, D. and Hartmann, A. (1997) *Forschungsbericht zu dem Modellversuch TOA im Erwachsenenstrafrecht der Staatsanwaltschaft bei dem Landgericht Aschaffenburg* (Heidelberg: Institut für Kriminologie).

Dölling D. and Hartmann, A. (2000) *Endbericht zu den Modellversuchen TOA im Erwachsenenstrafrecht der Staatsanwaltschaften bei den Landgerichten Aschaffenburg und Nürnberg/Fürth* (Heidelberg: Institut für Kriminologie).

Dölling, D. and Hartmann, A. (2003) 'Re-offending after victim offender mediation in juvenile court proceedings', in Weitekamp, E. and Kerner, H.-J. (eds.) *Restorative Justice in context. International Practice and Directions* (Cullompton: Willan Publishing), pp. 208-228.

Dölling, D. and Henninger, S. (1998) 'Sonstige empirische Untersuchungen zum TOA', in Dölling, D. (ed.) *Täter-Opfer-Ausgleich in Deutschland. Bestandsaufnahmen und Perspektiven* (Mönchengladbach: Forum Verlag Godesberg), pp. 203-365.

Hartmann, A. (1995) *Schlichten oder Richten. Der Täter-Opfer-Ausgleich und das Jugendstrafrecht.* Neue Kriminologische Studien, Band 13 (München: Fink Verlag).

Hartmann, A. and Kerner, H.-J. (2004) 'Victim-Offender-Mediation in Germany', *Erces Online Quarterly Review*, Vol. 1, No. 2, pp. 1-21.

Kerner, H.-J., Hartmann, A. and Lenz, S. (2005a) *Der Täter-Opfer-Ausgleich in der Entwicklung 1993-2002* (Mönchengladbach: Forum Verlag Godesberg).

Kerner, H.-J., Hartmann, A. and Lenz, S. (2005b) *Der Täter-Opfer-Ausgleich in der Entwicklung, 1993-2002*, online publication of the Federal Ministry of Justice. Available at: http://www.bmj.bund.de/media/archive/883.pdf

Kerner, H.-J., Hartmann, A., Lenz, S. and Stroezel, H. (2003) *Der Täter-Opfer-Ausgleich in der Entwicklung 1993-1999*, online publication of the Federal Ministry of Justice. Available at: http://www.bmj.bund.de/media/archive/517.pdf

Kuhn, A. (1989) *'Tat-Sachen' als Konflikt. Täter-Opfer-Ausgleich in der Jugendstrafrechtspflege. Forschungsbericht zum Modellprojekt 'Handschlag'* (Bonn: Schriftenreihe der Deutschen Bewährungshilfe e.V., Band 14).

Pelster, C. (1990) *Täter-Opfer-Ausgleich in Braunschweig. Ergebnisse der schriftlichen Befragung von Jugendgerichtshelfern* (Hannover: Projekt Waage).

Pfeiffer, C. (1994) 'Wiedergutmachung und Strafe aus der Sicht der Bevölkerung', in Kerner, H.-J., Hassemer, E., Marks, E. and Wandrey, M. (eds.) *Täter-Opfer-Ausgleich. Auf dem Weg zur bundesweiten Anwendung?* (Bonn: Schriftenreihe der Deutschen Bewährungshilfe), pp. 91-116.

Pfeiffer, C. (1997) *Täter-Opfer-Ausgleich im Allgemeinen Strafrecht: Die Ergebnisse der Begleitforschung des WAAGE Projekts Hannover* (Baden-Baden: Nomos Verlagsgesellschaft).

Pfeiffer, H. (1989) 'Die Einbeziehung der Polizei in das Modelprojekt Täter-Opfer-Ausgleich in Braunschweig', in Marks, E. and Rössner, D. (eds.) *Täter-Opfer-Ausgleich: Vom zwischenmenschlichen Weg zur Wiederherstellung des Rechtsfriedens* (Bonn: Schriftenreihe der Deutschen Bewährungshilfe), pp. 65-76.

Pfeiffer, H. (1992) 'Täter-Opfer-Ausgleich unter Mitwirkung der Polizei. Erfahrungen aus dem Modellversuch in Braunschweig', in BMJ (ed.) *Täter-Opfer-Ausgleich. Zwischenbilanz und Perspektiven* (Bonn: Bundesministerium der Justiz), pp. 169-172.

Rattay, H. and Raczek, W. (1990) *Täter-Opfer-Ausgleich in Braunschweig. Zur Akzeptanz des TOA durch die Beteiligten. Eine Interviewstudie* (Hannover: Projekt Waage).

Rösssner, D. (2007) 'Wirklichkeit und Wirkung des Täter-Opfer-Ausgleichs in Deutschland', in Schöch, H., Helgerth, R., Dölling, D. and König, P. (eds.) *Recht gestalten – dem Recht dienen. Festschrift für Reinhard Böttcher* (Berlin: De Gryter Recht), pp. 357–377.

Rössner, D. and Klaus, Th. (1998) 'Rechtsgrundlagen und Rechtspraxis', in Dölling, D. (ed.) *Täger-Opfer-Ausgleich in Deutschland. Bestandsaufnahme und Perspektiven* (Bonn: Forum Verlag Godesberg), pp. 49-120.

Schreckling, J. (1991) *Täter-Opfer-Ausgleich nach Jugendstraftaten in Köln- Bericht über Aufbau, Verlauf und Ergebnisse des Modellprojekts „WAAGE"* (Bonn: Forum Verlag Godesberg).

Schreckling, J. Marks, E. and Franzen, W. (1991) 'Bericht über eine Rundfrage der Deutschen Bewährungshilfe e.V. bei Institutionen der Strafrechtspflege zur Verbreitung und Akzeptanz des Täter-Opfer-Ausgleichs', in Schreckling, J. (ed.) *Bestandsaufnahmen zur Praxis des Täter-Opfer-Ausgleichs in der Bundesrepublik Deutschland* (Berlin: Bundesministerium der Justiz, Reihe recht), pp. 150-195.

Sessar, K. (1992) *Wiedergutmachen oder Strafen* (Pfaffenweiler: Centaurus).

Sessar, K. (1999) 'Punitive Attitudes of the Public: Reality and Myth', in Bazemore, G. and Walgrave, L. (eds.) *Restorative Juvenile Justice: Repairing the Harm of Youth Crime* (Monsey: Criminal Justice Press), pp. 287–304.

TOA-Servicebüro (ed.) (1998) *TOA-Standards* (Köln: DBH-Fachverband für Soziale Arbeit, Strafrecht und Kriminalpolitik).

TOA-Servicebüro and Bundesarbeitsgemeinschaft Täter-Opfer-Ausgleich e.V. (eds.) (2010): *Standards Täter-Opfer-Ausgleich* (Köln, DBH-Eigenverlag, ISSN 0947-5249)

Wandrey, M. (1994) 'TOA 1992: Licht und Schatten. Trendmeldungen zur TOA Praxisliste', *TOA Intern*, Issue 3, pp. 10-51.

Wandrey, M. and Weitekamp, E. (1998) 'Die organisatorische Umsetzung des Täter-Opfer-Ausgleichs in der Bundesrepublik Deutschland – eine vorläufige Einschätzung der Entwicklung im Zeitraum von 1989-1995', in Dölling, D. (ed.) *Täter-Opfer-Ausgleich in Deutschland. Bestandsaufnahmen und Perspektiven* (Mönchengladbach: Forum Verlag Godesberg), pp. 121-143.

7 The spontaneous bottom-up rise of mediation with youth offenders

Empirical research on restorative justice in Italy

Anna Mestitz

1 INTRODUCTION

In Italy, restorative justice [RJ] is a little known concept and it is mainly associated with victim-offender mediation [VOM] in the juvenile criminal justice system. In the second half of the 1990s the great interest in RJ was demonstrated by the spontaneous bottom-up rise of mediation activities with youth offenders and the creation of new local VOM services. Although no specific legal provisions for VOM have been implemented, juvenile public prosecutors and judges use different norms to apply RJ and to refer the cases to these new VOM services. Indeed, paradoxically, a law decree of 2002 permits the justice of peace to carry out VOM with adult offenders but it is hardly ever applied, as cases are not referred to VOM services but rather judges personally try to conciliate the conflicting parties.

So far in Italy no family group conferencing, sentencing circles or other similar RJ practices are operating. For this reason this chapter only focuses on services and groups dealing with VOM for youth offenders.[1] Moreover, as we shall see, very few research programmes have addressed RJ and VOM.[2] Because VOM practices are in fact limited to the juvenile criminal justice system, the functioning of this system is first briefly sketched to illustrate the context in which VOM was introduced in Italy. Then, some notes regarding its implementation are presented, followed by a description of the legal framework within which VOM can be adopted. Finally the main results of empirical research are reported and discussed.

1.1 Context: state of affairs of VOM for juveniles

1.1.1 Overview of the Italian juvenile criminal justice system[3]

The system of first instance courts (i.e. first level of jurisdiction) is the main context in which juvenile criminal justice is administered. It is quite separate from that of adults and includes 29 juvenile courts (*Tribunali per i minorenni*) through-

---

1 Cf. infra, 1.1.2. Implementation of RJ and VOM.
2 Even though RJ as a concept is not well-known, probation is considered to be an RJ practice, cf. infra.1.1.3. Legal framework.
3 For an analytical description see Mestitz (2000).

out the country as well as an identical number of prosecution offices (*Procure della Repubblica per i minorenni*).[4] Juvenile courts and prosecution offices are generally located in the same buildings. Both are supported by 29 units of the national welfare service of the judicial administration (*Servizi sociali minorili*, hereafter 'court social service'), often also located in those buildings. Not infrequently, these buildings also include the prisons and other correctional institutions for juveniles. This proximity allows for very close collaboration among the network of institutions providing for the juvenile justice system.

Magistrates, namely prosecutors and judges[5], acquire information on juveniles with the help of both public court social services (belonging to the Ministry of Justice) and public local social services (i.e. belonging to local governments: municipalities, provinces or regions). Both categories of social services also collaborate to assist juvenile defendants during the proceedings. Additionally, social workers are instrumental for the execution of most sentences and other tasks, such as supervising the minors on probation, a circumstance in which they play the role of probation officers. As we shall see later, the institute of probation may include orders allowing for restorative practices, such as VOM, which are applied with educative and diversion aims. For these practices, social workers frequently seek collaboration from volunteer associations as well as rehabilitation communities in the territory. Social services were introduced in Italy only in the 1960s and are still understaffed in some Southern regions. This situation is relevant to the slow implementation of VOM, given that social services often have to play an active role in offering and promoting mediation.

Juvenile criminal courts are concerned exclusively with crimes committed by offenders aged 14 to 18 (offenders under 14 years of age cannot be charged). According to the principle of mandatory criminal action, the prosecution office must examine all crimes reported and cannot drop the cases (the judge is tasked with this).[6] Before charges are made, courts must evaluate whether the offender

---

4   In the Court of Appeal, at the 2nd level of jurisdiction, there are 26 special 'juvenile sections' (*Sezioni minorili di Corte d'appello*) which are concerned with reviewing the judgment in fact and law. The sentences given by these sections may then be revised before the Supreme Court of Cassation only for the judgment in law.

5   It is important to note that the Italian career judges and public prosecutors belong to the same corps. As in France, they are both indicated by the term 'magistrates' (*magistrati*) and share the same recruitment, training and career. They can even move easily from the position of judge to that of public prosecutor and vice-versa in the course of their long career. One important difference with respect to the situation in France is that French prosecutors are hierarchically subordinated to the Ministry of Justice, while Italian ones are fully independent. Furthermore, in Italy the close connection between judges and public prosecutors is reflected in a confusion of their roles in public opinion. Di Federico (1998) outlined the manifold dysfunctional consequences deriving from the peculiar set up of Italian prosecution.

6   Because of the principle of mandatory criminal action foreseen by the Italian Constitution, the Constitutional Assembly decided that '*in order to avoid a discretionary or arbitrary, and therefore politically relevant, use of prosecutorial powers, ... it would be sufficient to prescribe that commencing criminal proceedings should be mandatory for all criminal violations*' (Di Federico, 1998: 375). The principle is closely connected to the principle of legality, but the nature of this connection is differently interpreted in different countries. The principle cannot be applied in practice, thus each

is responsible and in full possession of his 'understanding and mental faculties' (*capace di intendere e volere*).

With respect to the different phases of the criminal proceeding, three different judging forums may be distinguished: in the investigative phase, a single career judge (*giudice dell'indagine preliminare*)[7]; in the preliminary hearing, a panel of three judges, including one career judge and two lay judges[8] (*giudice dell'udienza preliminare*); in the juvenile criminal court (*tribunale minorile penale*) a panel of four judges, including two career judges and two lay judges.

The majority of criminal cases are either dismissed by the judge of the investigative phase and/or decided by the judge of the preliminary hearing. Thus, only a minority of cases proceeds to trial in the juvenile criminal court. As a result, in the implementation of RJ practices and VOM the prosecutors and the first two judging forums are those mainly involved.

In conclusion, the juvenile justice system is functionally connected with, and in various ways dependent on, a complex network of subjects and institutions including: juvenile courts and prosecution offices, both court and local social services, judicial police for juveniles, voluntary work associations and rehabilitation communities, where the juvenile offenders may be placed for the execution of different sentences (probation, rehabilitation, placement outside the home). Magistrates perform a dominant role not only in the courts and prosecution offices, but in all groups which collaborate in the working of the juvenile justice system, as well as in the central Department for Juvenile Justice (hereafter DJJ) at the Ministry of Justice which provides for the organisation and management of court social services and the correctional institutions. It is therefore no surprise that RJ and VOM could not have been developed in this context without the active contribution and the central role played by the magistrates.

1.1.2   *Implementation of RJ and VOM*

In the first half of the 1990s, the new trend focusing on RJ was promoted by a very small group of juvenile magistrates in Turin (North-Western Italy) who published some relevant articles on the hypothesis of applying RJ, thereby opening a new scenario in juvenile criminal justice. A few main steps undertaken in the period 1992 to 1995 were crucial to the implementation of VOM in the Italian juvenile justice system.

Italian public prosecutor carries out discretionary choices about whom, what and how she/he will prosecute (Di Federico, 1998).

7   The judge of preliminary investigation decides if the evidence collected in the investigative phase is sufficient to initiate the proceeding or not. The public prosecutor cannot decide to terminate any investigation without a decision by the judge.

8   As in other European countries, juvenile lay judges are recruited among 'experts' in disciplines relevant to the juvenile phenomena, such as psychology, social work, sociology, criminology, psychiatry and so on (Mestitz, 2000).

The first article describing VOM and its application in France, written by a judge of the juvenile court of Turin (Bouchard, 1992),[9] stressed the need for increasing the diversion of juveniles from the criminal justice system, and indicated proba-tion as the normative framework allowing for the application of mediation in the juvenile criminal proceeding.[10] A few months later the same author, in the same journal, criticised the strategies and the policies pursued by the central DJJ and particularly the scarce attention to the 'mediation-reconciliation' strategy which was defined as 'one of the main pillars of juvenile criminal law in the next dec-ades' (Bouchard, 1993: 152). The author underlined the total lack of application of two provisions of the institute of probation, that is, the reparation of damages caused by the crime, and conciliation between victim and offender. Later, a third article, again by the same author, was published in the official journal of the juvenile and family magistrates association, stressing that 'restorative practices as mediation' had developed quickly even in some Eastern Europe countries, but Italy remained substantially reluctant to undertake the experiment (Bouchard, 1994).

In the same issue of the journal where this last article appeared, an unusual article by his colleagues, magistrates of the juvenile court and prosecution office of Turin, was also published. It was unusual because, exceptionally, the authors' names were replaced by the following premise: 'We present a document prepared by the magistrates of the juvenile court and prosecution office of Turin. It pro-poses a new path for the juvenile criminal process through the so-called victim-offender mediation and the reparation of damage caused by the crime' (Juvenile magistrates of Turin, 1994). Taking into account the journal where this article was published, the absence of the authors' names and the fact that the authors were the most representative and authoritative group in the juvenile justice arena, the cited article may be considered as the *manifesto*, the formal declaration of intent, for the application of RJ and VOM in Italy.

On these premises, it comes without surprise that the first Italian VOM service was founded in Turin in the following year (1995) and temporarily located inside the juvenile prosecution office. Then, over a period of five years, eight new local VOM services were gradually and spontaneously created in other sites (Table 1): in 1996 new services were created in Trento, Catanzaro, Bari, Rome (this last service was created in 1996 but closed in 1999, so it is not included in Table 1), in 1998 in Milan, in 1999 in Sassari, in 2000 in Cagliari and Foggia.

Later in 2003 a new service was created in Bologna and after 2005 in Palermo, Florence, Ancona and Brescia. In the same years some court social services began directly to manage mediation meetings in Bolzano, Salerno, Perugia, L'Aquila, Naples, Venice and Caltanissetta (Ciuffo et al., 2005). In May 2007, by counting

---

9   The French influence on the Italian judicial system is very strong, mainly in Turin because of its geographical proximity to France.

10   Article 28 of DPR 448/88 (code of juvenile criminal procedure). DPR means *Decreto del Presidente della Repubblica* (decree by the President of the Republic). For the legal framework, cf infra 1.1.3. Legal framework.

both the 10 existing local mediation services and the 10 groups managing VOM inside court social services, it seems that 20 mediation services/groups were operating, but the situation is rapidly changing as new services and groups become operative.

For the last ten years the DJJ itself has relied on its website to encourage the experimental application of VOM[11] and became a partner in an AGIS project founded by the European Commission,[12] thus confirming a strong interest in developing VOM across the country.

Table 1   The first 8 local VOM services established in Italy by date of foundation (1995 to 2000)

Sites of VOM services	Dates of foundation	Promoters and founders
Turin (Northern Italy)	1st foundation 1995; 2nd foundation 2000	Juvenile magistrates; members of court and local social service
Trento (Northern Italy)	1st foundation 1996; 2nd foundation 1999	Juvenile magistrates; members of court and local social services
Catanzaro (Southern Italy)	1st foundation 1996; 2nd foundation 2002	Juvenile magistrates; members of court and local social services
Bari (Southern Italy)	1st foundation 1996; 2nd foundation 2001	Juvenile magistrates; members of court and local social services
Milan (Northern Italy)	1998	Lay judges, researchers, university professors
Sassari (Sardinia)	1999	One lay judge
Cagliari (Sardinia)	2000	2 juvenile magistrates, 1 lay judge
Foggia (Southern Italy)	2000	Juvenile magistrates; lay judges; members of court and local social services

Source: Mestitz (2004b).

Juvenile lay judges and social workers often participated in the creation of local mediation services and, in some cases, were themselves volunteer mediators. The creation of VOM services was often stimulated and actively organised by juvenile professional magistrates as is shown by two facts:

1) In the beginning, almost all VOM services were located in the same buildings of the juvenile courts and/or prosecution offices (i.e. Turin, Bari, Trento and Milan)[13] or in the same location of the court social service (i.e. Catanzaro). Then four VOM services (in Turin, Bari, Trento and Catanzaro) changed their

---

11   See 'minori' section in the website of the Italian Ministry of Justice, www.giustizia.it.

12   See Casado and Willemsens (2006), Casado Coronas (2008) and http://www.euforumrj.org/ Projects/projects.AGIS3.htm

13   For example from January 1995 to May 2000 the VOM service in Turin was named *Ufficio Mediazione* and was located in the juvenile prosecution office; in May 2000 it was renamed *Centro mediazione penale minorile di Torino*, becoming an institution of the city government. This model

location after receiving funding by local governments (see '2nd foundation' in Table 1).

2) At the establishment of a new local VOM service, formal documents such as 'letters of intent' (i.e. *protocolli d'intesa* or *accordi di programma*) were underwritten – starting from 1998 – by local institutions such as: the juvenile court and the prosecution office, court social service, local social service, interregional juvenile offices of the Ministry of Justice, municipalities, provinces and/or regions. The letters of intent provided VOM services with financial and human resources. In fact, mediators (and other personnel) are human resources of the institutions or administrations which signed the above-mentioned letters (Ministry of Justice, municipality, province or region) and are allowed to carry out part-time mediation in the VOM services. Such formal letters of intent have been signed in almost all mediation services so now they represent the main 'model' of collaboration. They are very useful not only to move part-time civil servants into the mediation services but also to get resources such as offices, furniture, computers etc. and funding. For this reason, a second foundation based on the new model of collaboration was needed for the first VOM services created in Turin, Trento, Catanzaro, and Bari.

The organisational models and the funding of the VOM local services are different, but three common elements can be traced in: i) the active role of magistrates and lay judges in their foundation; ii) the mediation activity is carried out by part-time mediators; iii) the collaboration and the agreement of the court social workers is needed. There is only one exception: the VOM service founded by a group of researchers at the University of Rome, which can be considered a 'deviant' model. This initiative failed, as the service was closed after three years (1997 to 1999) during which only twenty cases were referred. According to some members of the group, the failure was the result of a silent boycotting by court social workers and juvenile magistrates. This seems to confirm the unwritten rule that a strong agreement with both categories is needed to make a VOM service work in Italy. These events show the ambiguous nature of the powerful role exerted by magistrates, as well as the many contradictions and ambiguities in the juvenile justice system dominated by the 'religio-familistic values' which gave rise to a 'precariously institutionalised form of justice' – as Lemert (1986: 510-511) argued two decades ago – apparently, very hard to overcome.

1.1.3   Legal framework

We must distinguish between VOM as practiced for adult offenders, and that for youth offenders.

1) *Adult offenders.* In the adult criminal justice system the institution (DPR 274/2000) of the justice of peace (a lay judge) has made it possible to use VOM for misdemeanours, but very frequently the judges themselves try to concili-

---

was also followed by the VOM service in Trento which until February 1999 was located inside the juvenile prosecution office and then became an institution of the autonomous province of Trento.

ate the conflicting parties. This can be understood in the light of the fact that justices of peace are paid on the basis of the number of cases they manage. Probably for this reason they refer only a few cases to mediation services.

2) *Youth offenders.* Although so far there is not a specific norm providing for VOM, nor is the term mediation mentioned in the code of juvenile criminal procedure (DPR 448/1988)[14], it includes two norms used by magistrates to apply VOM and restorative practices: article 9 (personality assessment) and article 28 (probation). In the investigative phase public prosecutors currently use article 9 by asking court social services to attempt mediation. The court social services can carry out the mediation directly or ask a local VOM service to do so.[15] Then the mediation result is communicated to the public prosecutor. If the mediation concludes with a positive agreement, the public prosecutor asks the judge to dismiss the case or to give judicial pardon. Probation (article 28) differs from similar institutes for minors in other countries as it is based on the suspension of the trial, not of the sentence. The judge (usually the judge of the preliminary hearing) may refer the case on probation according to article 28 to the court social service and/or to a local VOM service with the aims of 'conciliation', 'reparation' or 'mediation'. When the outcome of the mediation is positive, the judge proceeds to dismiss the case; when it is negative the suspension ceases and the case proceeds along the normal judicial path.

1.2   Empirical research on VOM: an overview

In 1998, the DJJ of the Ministry organised the first seminar on VOM in Rome in order to provide magistrates and professionals working on mediation with the opportunity to meet and discuss their first experiences. At the time, the majority of the Italian VOM services had just been established (see Table 1). Thus preliminary data on some VOM practices underway were presented (data about Bari, Milan, Turin, Trento, and Catanzaro) and later published in a book edited by the DJJ itself (Ufficio Centrale Giustizia Minorile, 1999). The contributors of the book outlined the characteristics of services by describing briefly the institutional environment in which VOM services were implemented. Some relevant information was missing, however, such as the normative and theoretical background as well as basic elements concerning the process of implementation. Moreover, information from each VOM service was not gathered and presented in a standardised fashion. Additionally, each contribution emphasised different features of the local services. As a consequence it was not possible to systematically compare the characteristics of VOM services. All the local surveys presented by members of VOM

---

14 An overview of the legal framework concerned with VOM with youth offenders is outlined by Patanè (2004).

15 This happens only if there are VOM groups able to mediate inside the court social services.

services[16] can be classified as *descriptive-inventory research* (Ufficio Centrale Giustizia Minorile, 1999; Scaparro, 2001).

No *action-research* has been carried out in Italy so far. Perhaps some of the research activities of the Milan VOM group may be qualified as action-research, a project providing both descriptive and evaluative information. However, only a few preliminary results have been published (Ceretti et al., 2001).

As to *evaluative research*, a number of theoretical contributions (mainly by jurists, philosophers and others) have been published, but any research comparing RJ projects to other criminal justice practices has not been carried out. I have been involved in empirical research in juvenile criminal justice for about twenty years so I can confirm that it is not at all easy to carry out evaluative research in this area in Italy because of the laws protecting privacy in general and that of juveniles in particular, and because of the difficulty to obtain authorisation by the DJJ to collect empirical data. Moreover, when this difficulty can be overcome one meets the big problem of data reliability. No evaluative research is available on relevant issues such as the possible influence of RJ on recidivism, the impact on judicial decisions and judicial functioning, or the acceptance of RJ by the judiciary and the general public. The available evaluative research conducted so far deals with the following issues in the juvenile justice system:[17]

1) probation, VOM and the role of social workers;
2) probation and RJ practices;
3) VOM services and practices.

2   EVALUATIVE RESEARCH

2.1   *Research on probation, VOM and the role of social workers*

The first Italian *exploratory evaluative research* on VOM was funded by the Department of Psychology of the University of Rome 'La Sapienza' with only € 5,000.[18] It was carried out by a group of 3 researchers (social psychologists) directed by Gaetano De Leo, full professor of Psychology and law.[19] Research results were published both in Italian (Baldry, 1997; Scardaccione et al., 1998) and English (Baldry, 1998; Baldry et al., 1998).

The sample was pre-selected by the DJJ which gathers information and statistics on probation cases on the national territory. There were 90 VOM cases in a period

---

16   Regarding the VOM service in Bari see: Coppola De Vanna and De Vanna (1999); regarding that in Catanzaro: Briguglio (1999); regarding Milan: Ceretti et al. (2001); regarding Turin: Buniva (1999); regarding Trento: Zanfei and Fortuna (1999).

17   As we will see in more detail, certainly so far the disciplinary group most involved in empirical research in this field is that of social psychologists.

18   The authors described the research as evaluative.

19   Unfortunately, on 31 December 2006 we suddenly lost our friend and colleague De Leo, one of the most outstanding scholars in the field of psychology and law.

of one year and a half,[20] thus 90 questionnaires were sent to the court social work-ers in charge of each case (Baldry, 1998). In the first part of the questionnaire items included descriptive variables on the probation (duration, results, etc.), the juvenile offenders' characteristics (age, gender, family) and the crimes. In the second part questions dealt with details on the mediation activity and meet-ings. Research showed that in the period concerned, VOM was not widely imple-mented, and lacked structure and organisation. Only 51 cases out of 90 resulted in a VOM, while 39 cases did not go to mediation. The offenders' age was on average 17 and gender predominantly male (84 out of 90). Additionally, the study reports that social workers felt that they were not well-prepared for the job, nor did they have the time to do it, given their other commitments in addition to VOM. Moreover, little attention was given to the victims' interests and needs as in most cases the focus was on young offenders. Interestingly, for the majority of the cases (59.5%), mediation did not involve a direct meeting with the parties, because, as reported by Baldry (1998), social workers acting as mediators frequently asked the offenders to write a letter of apology.

The main limitation of this first research regards the selection and small size of the sample. Nevertheless, the role of the group of the University of Rome in dis-seminating VOM should be acknowledged, as should the group's effort to create also the voluntary experimental VOM service in Rome which operated for three years from 1997 to 1999.

2.2   Research on probation and RJ practices

Research conducted on probation in the first half of the 1990s in Bari showed relevant findings concerning RJ and VOM practices. The project was part of a wider project aimed at monitoring the application of the new Code of Criminal Procedure in adult and juvenile courts.[21] This last area included a group of com-parative researches on the application of probation, which were undertaken with different methods in various cities.[22] The research was funded by the Research Institute on Judicial Systems of the National Research Council [IRSIG-CNR][23] with about € 15,000. It was carried out by two researchers: the author of this contribution (social psychologist) with the collaboration of Marilena Colamussi (jurist, researcher at the University of Bari). Results were published only in Italian (Mestitz and Colamussi, 2000).

Data were collected from a sample of juveniles on probation recorded by the court social service from 1991 to 1996. A representative random sample of 190 cases was selected out of the total of 553 cases of probation registered in that period

---

20 According to the English publication (Baldry, 1998: 735), but according to the Italian article the period considered was two years and 5 months, from January 1991 to June 1993 (Baldry, 1997: 215).

21 A special law (n. 17 of 17 January 1992) had assigned this monitoring to the CNR (National Research Council) and particularly to IRSIG-CNR which carried out different projects in the period 1993-1996 (Di Federico et al., 1995).

22 They were carried out in Milan, Bari and Palermo (Mestitz, 1997).

23 Cf. supra, footnote 21.

by the court social service. The method included filling out 190 data sheets (one per case) from the court social service records and conducting in-depth interviews with social workers, magistrates and lay judges. Results showed significantly that in the first half of the 1990s probation was applied with reference to the RJ model in the large majority (81.1%) of cases (Table 2) and direct mediation through victim-offender meetings also began to be used in a small percentage of cases (9.1%). Nevertheless, mediation was frequently formal and indirect as the two main restorative practices adopted in Bari were: (a) symbolic financial compensation to charity and welfare institutions, churches included (51.3%) and (b) different forms of reconciliation with the victim (49%). Among the latter, writing letters of apology to the victim was the most used strategy (35.7%).

Table 2   Details of 154 probation cases where RJ practices were adopted in Bari

Restorative practices	N	%
symbolic payment to charity and welfare institutions	79	51.3
letter of apology to the victim	55	35.7
victim-offender mediation meetings	14	9.1
financial compensation to the victim	6	3.9
Total	154	100

Source: Mestitz and Colamussi (2000: 253).

On the one hand, the critical issue of this research is that, being a local case, results cannot be generalised to other juvenile courts and social services. On the other hand, previous research on the Italian juvenile justice system had always shown very different practices in each jurisdiction, precluding broad generalisations.

A recent research, again on probation, entirely funded by IRSIG-CNR with about € 16,000, was carried out in Bologna. The research was coordinated by the author of this contribution who developed the project with Simona Ghetti (developmental psychologist, researcher at IRSIG-CNR) and Laura Angelini (psychologist, during her on-the-job research training). Results have been published in Italian (Ghetti and Angelini, 2007; Mestitz, 2007a, 2007b). Data were collected by means of a data sheet from the universe of youth in probation in the years 1998, 2000 and 2002 (205 cases) recorded by the court social service in Bologna (which operates over the entire region of Emilia-Romagna including nine provinces). Then a questionnaire was administered to all social workers, public prosecutors, juvenile professional and lay judges of Bologna in order to explore their opinions on the application of probation. Surprisingly, RJ strategies and VOM were applied in only two cases in the period under study and in only three cases from 2003 to May 2007. Probation projects made by court social service focused on a few routine activities. The questionnaires show that magistrates share correct information on RJ and VOM, while the majority of social workers do not. The practical application of probation is guided by shared beliefs and ideologies: mainly the basic position 'favourable/not favourable' with regard to probation and presumably also to VOM. The long time needed to sentence the case emerged as the most critical element. Even if the 'due process in reasonable time' has been established by article 6 of the European Convention of Human Rights, and recently accepted by article 111 of our Constitution, the slowness of justice heavily damages all social, political and economic life in Italy. In the area of juvenile justice this is particularly serious because for adolescents the correctional aim can be obtained only when a short time interval between the deviant action and the reaction of the institutions occurs (Mestitz and Colamussi, 2000).

2.3   Research on VOM services and practices

The above-mentioned first research on probation in Bari (Mestitz and Colamussi, 2000) stimulated in 2001 a new project aimed at exploring the organisation and management of the nine local VOM services established in the country at that time. This was a smaller part of a wide project on 'Judicial public policies' of IRSIG-CNR funded by the Ministry of University and Research. The subproject on VOM in juvenile courts was funded with about € 15,000. The research was split into two parts and carried out as two independent researches in 2002 and 2003 by the author of this contribution and Simona Ghetti.

The first research was conducted by collecting data on all nine local VOM services by means of two different questionnaires (self-administered by participants): one was filled out by VOM services coordinators (including the one in Rome), and one by the universe of mediators (50 out of 55 participated). It was the first Italian research permitting the collection of comparable and homogeneous data on the organisation, structure and resources of the existing VOM services. Results have been published in Italian and English (Mestitz, 2002, 2004a, 2004b) and are partly used in this chapter.

The second research was also carried out by means of questionnaires (self-administered or completed by phone) interviewing 60% of the universe of juvenile magistrates working in seven cities where VOM services existed (namely 36 judges and public prosecutors participated). Results have been presented in Italian (Ghetti, 2004) and in English (Mestitz, 2002; Mestitz and Ghetti, 2002, 2005b; Ghetti and Mestitz, 2003).

Subsequently, a national survey on VOM was carried out by the 'Study and Research Group' in the DJJ and results were presented by Isabella Mastropasqua (philosopher), the head of the group, and her collaborator Elisabetta Ciuffo (psychologist), who made an exhaustive summary in Italian (Mastropasqua and Ciuffo, 2004). The summary was published as a chapter in the same book including the two above cited researches (Mestitz, 2004a). Some preliminary results were presented also in English in a report at an international seminar (Mestitz et al., 2003). Data on mediation cases were collected by using a questionnaire which was completed by court social workers carrying out victim-offender meetings. In particular 34 participants filled out 321 data sheets on each juvenile offender who participated in a VOM meeting in the first semester of 2002. The group from the DJJ continued to collect data on VOM but so far (2008) only results regarding the year 2003 have been made available (Ciuffo et al., 2005). The information reported in the next sections is extracted from the results of these research activities.

2.3.1   Discussion of the results

Figure 1   Crimes committed by youth offenders referred to mediation
(321 juveniles in the first semester of 2002)

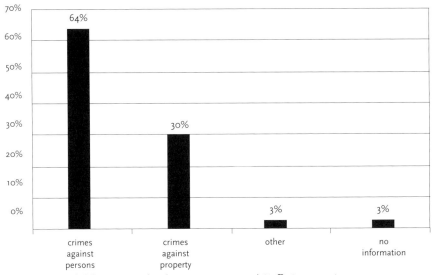

Source: personal elaboration on data by Mastropasqua and Ciuffo (2004: 125).

Of the 321 youth offenders referred to mediation analysed by Mastropasqua and Ciuffo (2004: 125), the majority (64%) committed crimes against persons, far fewer (30%) against property (Fig. 1). Considering that in Italy, as elsewhere, the majority of juveniles commit crimes against property, these findings clearly show that magistrates not only select the offenders to be referred to VOM on the basis of their crimes, but also that they prefer to refer those who commit crimes against persons. On the other hand Ghetti (2004: 96) stressed that 93% of magistrates' answers in the questionnaires show that they choose first on the basis of the crime, and 65% of this group indicated that other key elements were the existence of a previous relationship between the victim and offender and cases where the victim is a clearly identified person.

If we compare the two above-mentioned categories of crimes with the results of mediation, a very interesting phenomenon emerges, which, surprisingly, was not noticed by the authors of the report, i.e. (as may be seen in Table 3) the percentages of successful mediation are reversed: only 20% of crimes against persons conclude the mediation with an agreement, while 71% of those against property conclude positively. In other words, a less superficial analysis of data collected by the DJJ shows that VOM is more successful with crimes against property than with those against persons, but the latter are those preferred by magistrates for VOM.

Why do juvenile judges and public prosecutors prefer referring the youth who commit crimes against persons for VOM? A couple of shared beliefs/ideologies among magistrates, mediators and social workers seem to play an important role in choosing criteria for VOM: (a) the victim must be a person, thus victims as public or private groups, societies etc. are disregarded; (b) victim and offender must have a previous relationship, so that the mediation can allow them to overcome the conflict generated by the crime.

Table 3   Crimes committed by 321 youth offenders referred to VOM in the first semester of 2002 and successful results of mediation

Crimes	Referred to VOM		Positive results	
	F	%*	f	%**
Against person	204	64	41	20
Against property	97	30	69	71
Other/no information	20	6,2	11	55
Total	**321**		**121**	

*   Percentages calculated on column total (321 cases referred to VOM).
**   Percentages calculated on line total for each crime category (f in the first column).
    For example 41 positive results are 20% of 204 crimes against persons.

Source: personal elaboration on data by Mastropasqua and Ciuffo (2004: 125).

Finally, an interesting finding was that in 2003 only 189 youth offenders (46% of the total of 412 referred to mediation) participated in a mediation meeting: in 45% of cases the meeting did not occur due to the unwillingness of the offender and in 55% to that of the victim (Ciuffo et al., 2005: 20).

2.3.2   Organisation and distribution of the VOM services
As reported above, in the last decade, Italian VOM services were created bottom-up from spontaneous initiatives mainly promoted by juvenile magistrates (public prosecutors and judges) and they generally stem from the collaboration of different institutions: judicial authorities, court and/or local social services, NGOs, local government administrations etc. based on formal 'letters of intent'.[24] In May 2007, there were 20 services and/or groups offering VOM in Italy. Twelve local VOM services are randomly distributed over the territory: seven are located in the North (Turin, Milan, Trento, Bologna, Florence, Brescia, Ancona), three in the South (Foggia, Bari, Catanzaro) and two on the island of Sardinia (Cagliari, Sassari). Moreover, eight VOM groups operating inside the court social services

24 These documents were published in the journal *Minorigiustizia* n. 2/1999.

manage mediation meetings in Bolzano and Venice in the North, Perugia and L'Aquila in Central Italy, Salerno, Palermo, Naples, and Caltanissetta in the South (Ciuffo et al., 2005).

In recent years local mediation services and new groups of court social workers offering mediation have increased. In 2008 only nine juvenile courts out of the total 29 cannot apply VOM. Unfortunately their distribution across the country is very uneven, in some places excellent, while in other places lacking, as in Rome (where no VOM service was created after the failure of the first experiment in 1999). This is due to both the spontaneous nature of the development of VOM groups and to the lack of intervention on the part of a central institution in the process of distribution on the territory. It can be added that so far a few referrals for VOM with adult offenders are sent only to the Turin, Bari and Trento mediation services by the justice of peace.

We analysed the main organisational issues relevant for VOM: funding and coordination of VOM services, referral agencies, human resources of VOM services and training of mediators (Mestitz and Ghetti, 2005b).

Funding and coordination of VOM services

VOM services are generally structured as public services; this happens both inside the court social services and the new local mediation services funded by one or more local governments (municipalities, provinces, regions, districts etc.).

Table 4   Funding local VOM services in Italy.

VOM services	Funding by local administrations
Bari, Catanzaro	Regions
Trento, Sassari	Provinces
Cagliari	Municipality and province
Foggia, Milan, Turin	Municipalities and regions

Source: Mestitz (2004b: 58).

In the majority of European nations, local governments contribute to fund VOM services and programmes by participating in their organisation. In Italy they do not 'contribute' to, but totally fund VOM activities as the Ministry of Justice does not supply financial resources. The DJJ contributed financially only to the training of the first groups of mediators in Turin and Milan.

In many European countries the executive branch (often the Ministry of Justice as in France, Netherlands, Norway, Italy, Catalonia) defines public policies concerned with VOM (Mestitz and Ghetti, 2005a). Sometimes there is a special central organisation, funded by the executive branch, which coordinates and supplies financial support to private groups and NGOs offering VOM (such as in Austria, Germany, Sweden and Poland). The Italian DJJ of the Ministry of Justice acts, as other Ministries of Justice, promoting VOM, supplying guidelines for the legal application of VOM, and preparing national surveys on it but, as opposed to other

Ministries, it has no function in supervising local VOM services, does not fund VOM activities and its contribution in terms of human resources is limited to lending few part-time personnel.

A comparative overview of 15 EU nations (Mestitz and Ghetti, 2005a) showed that basically three categories of services offer VOM activities: public services (national and/or locals), private NGOs (including volunteers) and mixed systems of public and private services. Countries where all VOM services are private represent one pole of a continuum (England and Wales), while at the opposite pole nations or parts of federal states where VOM services are all public, are grouped (Austria, Netherlands, Catalonia in Spain). The mean position is occupied by the majority of EU nations, Italy included, which rely on mixed systems including both court and local social services as well as private and/or voluntary NGOs. In Italy only some services work exclusively with VOM, whereas the majority also work with mediation in other fields such as family, school, social mediation. More recently some services have begun to carry out VOM meetings with adult offenders.

Referral agencies

The main referral agencies are prosecution offices and courts. They play a direct and key role in promoting VOM: the juvenile prosecutor may refer the youth offender to the court social service to attempt some mediation activity.[25] Similarly the judge of the preliminary hearing or the juvenile criminal court may refer the cases to the court social service and VOM service. As mentioned above, the prosecution must examine all crimes referred since it is governed by the principle of mandatory criminal action, and she/he asks the judge either to dismiss the case or to make a decision if there is evidence of a crime.

Three empirical researches agree that the majority of cases, about ¾, are referred to VOM services during the investigative phase by the prosecution, while only one fourth is referred by the judge of the preliminary hearing for probation (Ghetti, 2004; Mestitz, 2004b; Mastropasqua and Ciuffo, 2004). According to Ghetti (2004), both male and female juvenile magistrates refer juveniles to VOM services on the basis of the crime they committed (93% males, 92% females); interestingly, female magistrates refer fewer cases to VOM than male magistrates, who rely also on two other criteria: 40% take into account if the juvenile is a first offender (15% female magistrates), 27% take into account offender age (interestingly no female magistrates consider this aspect).

In terms of receiving requests for mediation, there is widespread consistency among mediators and coordinators, regardless of the VOM service they work at: juvenile prosecutors and/or judges usually send a request for mediation in the initial phase of the proceeding. Once mediation is performed, VOM services inform the juvenile magistrates of its success or failure. Some interesting differences among VOM services emerge as only some mediators are provided with information regarding the final sentence. The lack of information on the outcome of VOM had some impact on the mediators' job satisfaction as there was a statistically sig-

---

25   Very often, mediation is indirect, such as sending a letter of apology.

nificant difference in job satisfaction between mediators who knew the sentences of the cases (Catanzaro, Milan, Turin) and those who did not, or who knew that the mediation had no impact on the sentence. Communications among magistrates and mediators are not always easy; some mediators report: (i) difficulties in coordinating VOM activities with the juvenile justice system, (ii) the lack of correspondence between the outcome of the mediation and the sentence of the case, (iii) the absence of an official communication to mediators about the sentence from the prosecutor or the judge (Mestitz and Ghetti, 2002).

Human resources
As reported above, the facilitators of the meetings between victim and offender may be both court social workers acting as mediators and mediators working in the local VOM services. The time invested in VOM is not significant as the majority of mediators in local mediation services work part-time only a few hours per week: 46% works 6-10 hours per week, 28% from 2½ to 5 hours and only 24% 11 hours and more (Mestitz, 2004b).
The research further showed that the most of the Italian mediators are public servants, often employed part-time by VOM services or voluntary professionals. In particular, social workers and lay judges represented the majority of mediators (62%) and about one third of all mediators were volunteer professionals (doing mediation in their spare time, unpaid), including lawyers, psychotherapists and juvenile lay judges (Mestitz, 2004b). Finally, one fifth of all the mediators come from the local social services and one fourth from the court social services. The mediators' age ranges from 27 to 68 years (mean age 44), but the majority are young (62% between 28 and 38 years) and have a university degree (68%).
No good practice standards or complaint procedures, nor requirements for recruitment and training have been established so far. For some years the guidelines (mainly dealing with the legal framework) for applying VOM have been available on the website of the Ministry of Justice.[26]

Training of mediators
The vast majority of Italian mediators (76%) received formal training before the beginning of their mediation activity, while 71.1% were trained both before and after beginning the mediation activity. An exception to this is the VOM service in Catanzaro where only one mediator participated in some training before starting work on the project, while others learned in the field (apprenticeship or on-the-job-training). In general, mediators of each local VOM service organised their training autonomously.
According to research findings the length of training of mediators – different in the various local VOM services – was on average 315 hours corresponding to 30.8 days (7 hours per day) (Mestitz, 2004b), while the training of court social workers and other personnel of the DJJ lasted a mean of 180 hours (Mastropasqua and Ciuffo, 2004). Nevertheless, during an international conference, the head

---

26   www.giustizia.it/minori.

of the DJJ reported that social workers of the DJJ undergo a '30 hour training' period (Cavallo, 2007: 7). This shows the absence of national standards and clarity regarding training.

A strong cultural homogeneity emerges as almost all mediators underwent the same training with few exceptions. In fact the most widely represented 'model' of mediation is that proposed by Jacqueline Morineau (1998) as she trained (in France and/or in Italy) mediators of all Italian VOM services with the exception of those in Catanzaro and Trento. This latter group defines its model as 'non directive' and follows the French approach of Michel Lobrot. The Bari group reported that the training model by Morineau was elaborated and improved under the new label 'Mediterranean model'. This model has been adopted also in Sardinia by mediators in Sassari and Cagliari, because they were trained by the Bari mediators. However, it is interesting to note that Morineau's model – in Italy defined as the 'French model' – has 'not made a significant impact on the French experience' (Milburn, 2005: 311-312). In Italy, on the contrary, it seems to have had a significant influence as it spread by imitation from one group to another. The influence of this model also emerges from the practice of co-mediation, which is adopted by all VOM services, and the widely shared opinions among the majority of mediators: 66% of them report that the objective of VOM is to establish communication and a relationship between victim and offender. To a lesser extent they also agree on the following aims: facilitating the sharing of feelings and emotions between victim and offender (36%), making the offender responsible (34%) and providing support to the victim (26%) (Mestitz, 2004b).

2.3.3   Mediation practice

In all Italian VOM services, mediation practice is based on co-mediation and occasionally even three or more mediators carry out the meetings. Sometimes there are more than two victims and offenders and sometimes parents and/or social workers participate during the mediation meetings. The amount of time spent in each intervention of VOM ranges from 7 to 18 hours (according to 50% of the answers) or more than 19 hours (20%), as reported by mediators. An average of three meetings is needed to complete each intervention. The mean number of meetings between victim and offender differs considerably in each VOM service: one in Turin and Milan; three in Catanzaro, Trento and Sassari; four in Bari and Cagliari; and five in Foggia (Mestitz, 2004b).

Number of cases dealt with

To calculate the number of cases dealt with, we cannot rely on national quantitative data, thus it was only possible to compare referrals to local VOM services and the number of juveniles referred to prosecution offices in those provinces where a VOM local service is operative (Mestitz, 2004b). Research data from four provinces where a VOM service existed (Bari, Catanzaro, Turin and Trento) show for instance that in 1999 cases referred for VOM were about 7% of the total criminal cases referred to the four prosecution offices concerned.

By 2000, this percentage had grown to 8% as two new VOM services (Cagliari and Foggia) were established, but the VOM services in Milan and Sassari did not supply data on referrals. Thus the percentage of 8% is in fact certainly higher. However, the mediators seem to have a very light workload: the majority of them (60%) dealt with a mean of 15 cases per year, which is less than two cases per month (1.4 case). This is the result of both the part-time practice and the limited use of VOM (Mestitz, 2004b).[27]

An overview of all 942 cases referred for VOM in the period 1995-2001 can be found in Table 5. Data were supplied by directors of eight VOM services by means of questionnaires. Unfortunately data from the Bari VOM service are missing as the director supplied only the total number of referrals, thus column totals and mean column percentages reported in the two last lines are within parentheses as they are only rough indications. Percentages of successful and unsuccessful VOM have been calculated on the totals of cases carried out, while percentages of mediations not carried out have been calculated on the total of those referred.

Table 5   Total cases referred to VOM in the period 1995-2001

VOM services	Years	Referrals	VOM carried out	Successful VOM (agreement)		Unsuccessful VOM (no agreement)		Mediation not carried out	
				N	%	N	%	N	%
Bari	1996-2001	222	-	-	-	-	-	-	-
Cagliari	2000-2001	40	40	36	90.0	-	-	3	7.5
Catanzaro	1995-2001	174	155	118	76.1	37	23.9	19	10.9
Foggia	2000-2001	13	8	6	75.0	2	25.0	5	38.5
Milan	1998-2000	120	75	62	82.7	3	4.0	53	44.2
Rome	1997-1999	20	15	10	66.7	5	33.3	5	25.0
Turin	1995-2001	318	152	122	80.2	30	19.7	166	52.2
Trento	1999-2001	35	35	21	60.0	14	40.0	-	-
Totals*	**1995-2001**	**942**	**(480)**	**(375)**	**-**	**(91)**	**-**	**(251)**	**-**
Mean percent.	**1995-2001**	**-**	**-**	**-**	**(75.8)**	**-**	**(24.3)**	**-**	**(29.7)**

* Partial totals are within parentheses as data from Bari VOM service were missing.

Source: Mestitz (2004b: 73).

It is clear that the attempt to carry out mediation fails for a sizeable minority of cases (on average 29.7%). There is, however, a remarkable variability in this percentage among different VOM services. Whereas mediation was successfully conducted in about 90% of the cases in the Cagliari and Catanzaro services, this was true for only about 50% of the cases in Turin. It is not clear why the observed dif-

---

27   Unfortunately, no recent data are available.

ferences among services exist. One possible explanation could lie in differences among the strategies used to approach and select victims and offenders: different styles may result in different agreement rates of victims and offenders to participate in the mediation. Another possible explanation is that the differences in rates of agreement across services do not reflect a characteristic of the service *per se*, but a characteristic of the territory in which the service operates (e.g. geographical differences in crime, trust in institutions, etc.).

VOM and crimes

As indicated above, official data on crimes committed by juvenile offenders referred to VOM in 2003, reported by Ciuffo et al. (2005), reveal some peculiar findings regarding the distribution of crimes in 412 cases (Table 6): the highest percentage of crimes is concerned with offences against persons (more than 58%) and the majority of victims were individual persons aged 11-80 years with a peak between 14 and 20 years (86%). In about half the cases (49%), victims were persons known by offenders.Very rarely were victims public or private legal entities. It can be added that similar results have been reported in Turin for the time period 1995 to 98: 70% of offences committed by juveniles referred to mediation were crimes against persons (Buniva, 1999). In Milan, between 1998 and 2000, the majority of crimes were also against persons: assault (55 out of 107 cases referred to VOM service), threat and injuries (30 cases) (Ceretti et al., 2001). The over-representation of offences against persons (Table 6) shows the pre-selection made by juvenile public prosecutors and judges, as they reported that in selecting cases for referrals to VOM, they gave precedence to offences committed within a pre-existing social relationship between victim and offender (Ghetti, 2004, cf. supra).

The national survey mentioned (Ciuffo et al., 2005) shows that: (*i*) the percentage of VOM carried out and positively concluded with an agreement is 88.3%, (*ii*) victim and offender mean participation rates are: 64.6% of offenders and 45% of victims agree to participate in the mediation meetings (Table 6). It can be observed that the percentages of offenders' agreement do not vary significantly while victims' agreement strongly varies according to the crimes committed, being 27.5% for crimes against persons and 73.1% for crimes against property (Table 6).

Different percentages resulted from previous local research where victim and offender participation rates were analysed. According to Ceretti and colleagues (2001) who examined those rates in the Milan VOM service between 1998 and 2000, victims agreed to participate in mediation 52.5% of the times, whereas offenders agreed 93% of the time. Data concerning Turin (in the period 1995 to 1998) are somewhat different: victims agreed to participate 67% of the times, whereas offenders agreed 79% of the times (Buniva, 1999). These differences may be due to the mediators' different practices of approaching victims and offenders.

Table 6   412 cases referred to VOM in 2003: 189 meetings of mediation actually made, victims' and offenders' agreement to meet and crimes committed by juvenile offenders referred for mediation ('other' and 'missing data' not included)

Crimes	Cases referred to VOM	VOM meetings	Offender's agreement		Victim's agreement	
			N	%*	N	%*
Against persons	251	90	162	64.5	69	27.5
Against property	134	80	83	61.9	98	73.1

* Percentages of agreement have been calculated separately on each category of crimes.

Source: Ciuffo et al. (2005: 9).

3   INTERNATIONAL RESEARCH PROJECTS

In concluding this overview, it is worth mentioning briefly two international research projects initiated by Italian promoters. The first one, *Victim-Offender Mediation: organisation and practice in the juvenile justice systems*, was promoted and coordinated by the author of this chapter at IRSIG-CNR and funded by the European Commission Grotius II Criminal Justice Programme (project 2002/GRP/029) for about € 70,000. It lasted from November 2002 to January 2004 and aimed to compare the organisation and management of VOM in 15 European countries (14 EU and Norway). The two partners in the project were Christa Pelikan (Institut für Rechts- und Kriminalsoziologie, Vienna, Austria) and Inge Vanfraechem (Research Group on Juvenile Criminology, Dept. of Criminal Law and Criminology, Catholic University of Leuven, Belgium). By using common guidelines aiming to collect empirical data and information, a number of relevant issues were examined in a comparative perspective:
1) legislation and legal provisions for the application of VOM;
2) organisational structure of VOM centres;
3) categories and profiles of juvenile offences;
4) models, approaches, and theoretical framework of VOM;
5) professional characteristics and job evaluation of mediators.

At the end of the project, 15 national reports on these topics were presented and discussed at the final seminar in Bologna in September 2003. Two years later a book with chapters widely re-written from the original national reports was published (Mestitz and Ghetti, 2005a). Some results of this work have been mentioned above.

The method of establishing common guidelines for national reporters was very useful for collecting standardised information, even if not all participants developed the issues at the same level and some of them did not follow the general guidelines. The different scientific background of participants was one of the main difficulties.

The second project *MEDIARE, Mutual Exchange of Data and Information About Restorative Justice*, began in June 2003 and was concluded in June 2004. It was funded by the European Commission Grotius II Criminal Justice Programme (2002/GRP/037) and coordinated by a magistrate, Luigia Mariotti Culla from the Department of Penitentiary Administration of the Ministry of Justice, together with Transcrime (University of Trento). The two partners in this project were: the Austrian Neustart organisation (Probation, Mediation, Social Work) (Vienna) and the Department of International and European Affairs of the Ministry of Justice (Paris). The aims of the project were: (1) to conduct a comparative study of norms and application of mediation in 3 countries: Italy, Austria and France; (2) to analyse the state of application of Recommendation R(99)19 in Council of Europe nations; and (3) to exchange visits in Austria and France in order to compare mediation practices.
Unlike previous international projects coordinated by researchers, in this project the coordination was in the hands of the magistrates from the Ministry of Justice and the only researchers were those from Transcrime (University of Trento). Results of the project were presented at the final seminar held in Rome in June 2004 (Ministero della giustizia, 2004). An outline of the ideal VOM good practices emerged from the (very superficial) comparison of those applied in Italy, Austria and France.

4   Concluding remarks

The national and international research projects mentioned in this chapter show that many efforts have contributed to shed light on various aspects of VOM in Italy. Nevertheless, the phase of spontaneous – and sometimes precarious – initiatives essential for introducing VOM in Italy is ongoing and can rapidly change the general overview. In fact in recent years many new VOM local services and VOM groups of court social services have begun their activities. This means that further evaluative research efforts (and financial investments) are needed to collect more standardised data, diffusing VOM standardised procedures, exploring the attitudes of victims and offenders participating in the mediation meetings and, more generally, elaborating RJ applicative models. As far as the methodology is concerned, research results show that questionnaires with open and closed questions are a valuable tool for systematic and consistent data collection and longitudinal analyses, both of which are essential for focusing on development and change over a given period of time.

In concluding, I wish to focus on two different aspects: the diffusion of VOM in Italy and the perspectives of research.

On a positive and optimistic note, I would like to point out that even if the role of VOM in altering the Italian juvenile justice landscape is still quantitatively marginal, it does seem that the creation of VOM services is contributing to the promotion of restorative practices and to a cultural change in the Italian juvenile justice system. At the national level this is shown by the promotion of VOM on the website of the DJJ of the Ministry of Justice, by the conference on the subject organised by the same DJJ in Rome (December 1998), by the publication of the book containing the reports presented at this conference (Ufficio Centrale Giustizia Minorile, 1999), by the research activities of Ghetti, Mastropasqua, Ciuffo and myself described above, by a recent research project, funded by the European Commission, deepening the good practices of RJ in some European countries (Mestitz and Colamussi, 2010), and, last but not least, by the national data of the DJJ. At the international level in the period from 2002 to 2004 two European Commission Grotius projects were promoted and completed. In 2007 and 2008, the DJJ participated in the third European AGIS project awarded to the European Forum for Restorative Justice (Casado Coronas, 2008). The DJJ is also working on a new bill for mediation. All these activities confirm the general attention given to the subject. As a consequence, our hope that in the near future a further expansion of VOM in Italy appears much more grounded than in the past.

At the same time, I cannot be silent about the other side of the coin regarding research developments. It suffices to stress two relevant and unpleasant points.

(1) In recent years we have witnessed increasing activity on the part of the magistrates and other personnel of the DJJ (i.e. social workers, educators) in research initiatives, in collecting data and in addressing requests for funds to the EU Commission for research. In fact these initiatives do not deal with empirical evaluative research activities because magistrates and social workers do not possess the necessary methodological skills in the social sciences to conduct empirical research. This is, obviously, detrimental to systematic empirical research or even for a more modest data collection on relevant phenomena such as VOM.

(2) The abovementioned activity is accompanied by a parallel decrease in any independent research initiative by university scholars and public researchers. What happens in fact is that researchers need the authorisation of the DJJ to undertake research tied to the juvenile judicial system at the national level, but in recent years to get those authorisations has become more and more difficult.[28] Paradoxically, the DJJ has no money to fund research but can obstruct any research initiative carried out independently by universities or the National Research Council using their own research funds.

As a consequence of this trend in enforcing the power exerted by magistrates in this area, no new empirical research has been conducted in Italy after those, mentioned above, which we finished in 2004 (Mestitz, 2004a). The various VOM services and groups do not collect data or reflect on their own results and as yet,

---

28   I would say 'impossible' looking at my experience in the last years after the publication of our book on VOM (Mestitz, 2004a): I presented a couple of projects without asking any funding but I did not receive any answer.

there is no any central coordination body. The DJJ is trying to adopt this role more and more, but without providing any funding and scientific support, this aim seems very difficult to realise. On the other hand, the data collection on VOM initiated by the DJJ is very slow and it is also based on incorrect methodological criteria. The DJJ would be able to play the role of research coordinator if two conditions were met: (1) if the DJJ agrees to be assisted for research aims by a team of social science researchers competent in questionnaire design, data collection and data analysis; and (2) if this group of expert and experienced researchers are given the opportunity to update (or change) the questionnaires used so far to collect VOM data and solve their relevant methodological problems.

If these shortcomings are not addressed, the lack of expertise required to conduct empirical research will not guarantee in the future any reliable scientific result, but only those so-called 'research results' that are filtered by magistrates from the Ministry of Justice itself.

A relevant direction to develop empirical research in Italy is to explore the relationship between the type of crime and the success of VOM and the influence of restorative measures, as probation and VOM, on recidivism, by examining the population of young adults who were dealt with – as juveniles – by means of the VOM and RJ. In addition, a questionnaire administered to victims, offenders and mediators before and after each direct meeting can be very useful for shedding light on mediation practices and on the motivation and satisfaction of participants to VOM meetings. The basic conditions to achieve these aims are: (1) the authorisation to conduct such research and (2) the correction of the policy of the last three Italian Governments (Berlusconi,Prodi and again Berlusconi) which drastically reduced State expenditure and funding of universities and research institutes over recent years.

REFERENCES

Baldry, A. (1997) 'Vittima e autore di reato nella giustizia penale minorile. Indagine su campione', in Mestitz A. (ed.) *La tutela del minore, tra norme, psicologia ed etica* (Milano: Giuffré), pp. 212-221.

Baldry, A. (1998) 'Victim-Offender Mediation in the Italian Juvenile Justice System: the Role of the Social Worker', *British Journal of Social Work*, 28, pp. 729-744.

Baldry, A., De Leo, G. and Scardaccione, G. (1998) 'Victim-Offender Mediation in the Italian Juvenile Justice System: A First Attempt of Definition', in Boros, J., Munnich, I. and Szegedi, M. (eds.) *Psychology and Criminal Justice* (Berlin: De Gruyter), pp. 377-384.

Bouchard, M. (1992) 'Mediazione: dalla repressione alla rielaborazione del conflitto', *Dei delitti e delle pene*, 2/92, pp. 191-202.

Bouchard, M. (1993) 'Alcune riflessioni sulle linee di politica giudiziaria dell'Ufficio Centrale per la Giustizia Minorile', *Dei delitti e delle pene*, 2/93, pp. 143-156.

Bouchard, M. (1994) 'Dove va la delinquenza dei giovani, dove va la giustizia minorile?', *Minorigiustizia*, 4/1994, pp. 10-18.

Briguglio, C. (1999) 'L'esperienza dell'Ufficio per la mediazione a Catanzaro', in Ufficio Centrale Giustizia Minorile (ed.) *La mediazione penale in ambito minorile: applicazioni e prospettive* (Milano: Franco Angeli), pp. 186-190.

Buniva, F. (1999) 'L'esperienza dell'Ufficio per la mediazione a Torino', in Ufficio Centrale Giustizia Minorile (ed.) *La mediazione penale in ambito minorile: applicazioni e prospettive* (Milano: Franco Angeli), pp. 111-120.

Cavallo, C. (2007) *An introduction to Restorative Justice*, paper presented at the International Conference 'Restorative Justice in Europe: needs and possibilities' (Lisbon, May 10-12). Available at: www.euforumrj.org/Activities/seminars.Lisbon.htm

Casado Coronas, C. (2008) *Restorative Justice: An Agenda for Europe. Supporting the Implementation of Restorative Justice in the South of Europe* (Leuven: European Forum for Restorative Justice). Available at: www.euforumrj.org/Projects/projects.AGIS3.htm

Casado, C. and Willemsens, J. (2006) 'Third AGIS project awarded to the European Forum', *Newsletter of the European Forum for Restorative Justice*, 7(3), pp. 1-3.

Ceretti, A., Di Ciò, F. and Manozzi, G. (2001) 'Giustizia riparativa e mediazione penale: esperienze e pratiche a confronto', in Scaparro, F. (ed.) *Il coraggio di mediare* (Milano: Guerini e Associati), pp. 307-354.

Ciuffo, E., Mastropasqua, I. and Pelliccia, M.T. (eds.) (2005) *Rilevazione sulle attività di mediazione penale minorile. Anno 2003*, unpublished report (Roma: Dipartimento giustizia minorile, Ministero della giustizia).

Coppola De Vanna, A. and De Vanna, I. (1999) 'L'esperienza dell'Ufficio per la mediazione a Bari', in Ufficio Centrale Giustizia Minorile (ed.) *La mediazione penale in ambito minorile: applicazioni e prospettive* (Milano: Franco Angeli), pp. 130-136.

Di Federico, G. (1998) 'Prosecutorial independence and the democratic requirement of accountability in Italy. Analysis of a deviant case in a comparative perspective', *British Journal of Criminology*, 38, 3, pp. 371-387.

Di Federico, G., Gaito, A., Margaritelli, M., Sechi, P. and Seghetti, A.V. (1995) 'Il monitoraggio del processo penale. Potenzialità e limiti delle analisi statistiche', *Working papers IRSIG-CNR*, 5 (Bologna: Lo scarabeo).

Ghetti, S. (2004) 'Cosa pensano i magistrati minorili della mediazione penale?', in Mestitz, A. (ed.) *Mediazione penale: chi, dove, come e quando* (Roma: Carocci), pp. 89-109.

Ghetti, S. and Angelini, L. (2007) 'Messa alla prova e sistema giudiziario minorile: risultati dell'indagine sul campo', in Mestitz, A. (ed.) *Messa alla prova: tra innovazione e routine* (Roma: Carocci), pp. 40-73.

Ghetti, S. and Mestitz, A. (2003) *Victim-Offender Mediation with Juvenile Offenders: Perceptions of Public Prosecutors and Judges*, paper presented at the International Conference of the American and European Psychology-Law Society (Edinburgh, 2003 9-12 July).

Juvenile magistrates of Turin (1994) 'Proposte per una risposta penale riparatoria', *Minorigiustizia*, 4, pp. 26-33.

Lemert, E.M. (1986) 'Juvenile justice Italian style', *Law & Society Review*, 20(4), pp. 509-543.

Mastropasqua, I. and Ciuffo, E. (2004) 'L'esperienza della mediazione penale nei servizi della Giustizia Minorile. Indagine su un anno di attività', in Mestitz, A. (ed.) *Mediazione penale: chi, dove, come e quando* (Roma: Carocci), pp. 111-134.

Mestitz A. (ed.) (1997), *La tutela del minore, tra norme, psicologia ed etica* (Milano: Giuffré).

Mestitz, A. (2000) 'Managing Juvenile Criminal Justice in Italy', in Fabri, M. and Langbroek, P. (eds.) *The Challenge of Change for Judicial Systems* (Amsterdam: IOS Press), pp. 221-234.

Mestitz, A. (2002) *A first survey on Victim-Offender Mediation in Italy*, paper presented at the International Conference on 'Conferencing, Circles and Restorative practices' (Minneapolis, USA, August 8-10). Available at: www.restorativepractices.org

Mestitz, A. (ed.) (2004a) *Mediazione penale: chi, dove, come e quando* (Roma: Carocci).

Mestitz, A. (2004b) 'I centri locali per la mediazione penale', in Mestitz, A. (ed.) *Mediazione penale: chi, dove, come e quando* (Roma: Carocci), pp. 44-88.

Mestitz, A. (ed.) (2007a) *Messa alla prova: tra innovazione e routine* (Roma: Carocci).

Mestitz, A. (2007b) 'La gestione della messa alla prova tra innovazione e routine', in Mestitz, A. (ed.) *Messa alla prova: tra innovazione e routine* (Roma: Carocci), pp. 74-105.

Mestitz, A. and Colamussi, M. (2000) 'Messa alla prova e restorative justice', *Minorigiustizia*, 2, pp. 223-288.

Mestitz, A. and Colamussi, M. (2010), 'Probation and victim-offender mediation: good practices of Restorative Justice in Italy', in J.I. Prieto Lois and M. Gonzales Vazquez (eds.) *Good Practices of restorative Juvenile Justice* (Xunta de Galicia: A Coruña), pp. 176-193.

Mestitz, A. and Ghetti, S. (2002) *Juvenile magistrates and Victim-Offender mediation: the communication System*, paper presented at the 2nd Conference of the European Forum for Victim-Offender Mediation and Restorative Justice 'Restorative justice and its relation to the criminal justice system' (Oostende, October 10-12). Available at: www.euforumrj.org

Mestitz, A. and Ghetti, S. (eds.) (2005a) *Victim-Offender Mediation with Youth Offenders in Europe. An Overview and Comparison of 15 countries* (Dordrecht: Springer).

Mestitz, A. and Ghetti, S. (2005b) 'Victim-Offender Mediation and Youth Offenders: the Italian experience', in Mestitz, A. and Ghetti, S. (eds.) *Victim-Offender Mediation with Youth Offenders in Europe. An Overview and Comparison of 15 countries* (Dordrecht: Springer), pp. 321-345.

Mestitz, A., Ghetti, S., Ciuffo, E. and Mastropasqua, I. (2003) *Victim-Offender Mediation with juveniles in Italy*, paper presented at the International Seminar on the EU Grotius project 'Victim-Offender Mediation: organization and practice in the juvenile justice systems', unpublished (IRSIG-CNR, Bologna, September 19-20).

Milburn, P. (2005) 'Mediation and reparation for young offenders in France: an overview', in Mestitz, A. and Ghetti, S. (eds.) *Victim-Offender Mediation with Youth Offenders in Europe. An Overview and Comparison of 15 countries* (Dordrecht: Springer), pp. 311-319.

Ministero della giustizia, Dipartimento Amministrazione Penitenziaria (2004) *M.E.D.I.A.Re. verso il futuro. Atti del seminario transnazionale conclusivo del progetto M.E.D.I.A.Re.* (Roma: ISSP).

Morineau, J. (1998) *L'esprit de la médiation* (Ramonville Saint-Agne: Erès trajets).

Patané, V. (2004) 'Ambiti di attuazione di una giustizia conciliativa alternativa a quella penale: la mediazione', in Mestitz, A. (ed.) *Mediazione penale: chi, dove, come e quando* (Roma: Carocci), pp. 19-40.

Scaparro, F. (ed.) (2001) *Il coraggio di mediare* (Milano: Guerini e Associati).

Scardaccione, G., Baldry, A. and Scali, M. (1998) *La mediazione penale. Ipotesi di intervento nella giustizia minorile* (Milano: Giuffré).

Ufficio Centrale Giustizia Minorile (ed.) (1999) *La mediazione penale in ambito minorile: applicazioni e prospettive* (Milano: Franco Angeli).

Zanfei, A. and Fortuna, P. (1999) 'L'esperienza dell'Ufficio per la mediazione a Trento', in Ufficio Centrale Giustizia Minorile (ed.) *La mediazione penale in ambito minorile: applicazioni e prospettive* (Milano: Franco Angeli), pp. 177-185.

8 Evidence based policies?

Empirical research on restorative justice in the Netherlands

John Blad and Katrien Lauwaert

1 INTRODUCTION

1.1 Context: state of affairs[1]

This chapter provides a survey of empirical research on victim-offender mediation [VOM] and family group conferencing [FGC] in a criminal justice context in the Netherlands, where a number of restorative practices have been developed. However, not all of them qualify as VOM or FGC. Although they do contain restorative elements, some of the practices do not fit the definitions of victim-offender mediation[2] or conferencing[3] in a criminal justice context, for various reasons. The procedure may, for instance, be almost exclusively focused on the administrative arrangement of financial reparation through a third person and to a great extent lack the aspect of communication between the parties about what has happened. Or the cases may be mainly civil and not criminal in nature. The three most important examples of this broader scope are: claims settlement,[4] HALT [Het ALTernatief, cf infra] and community mediation.

Claims settlement focuses on compensation of the victim by the offender, and is quite administrative in nature. It applies in principle to all offences. If, in the investigation stage, the victim has indicated that he would like to receive compensation and the suspect has been found, the police attempt to arrange for payment between the parties at as early a stage as possible. Where the case proceeds to prosecution, the Public Prosecution Service [PPS] likewise tries to organise damage settlement between the parties. The sum is paid to the police or the PPS and then credited to the victim's account. Claims settlements resulting in a payment to the victim lead, in less serious cases, to the dismissal of the case against the

---

1   The information in this section is largely drawn from Miers and Willemsens (2004), more specifically from the section on the Netherlands (p.87-97) prepared by Katrien Lauwaert.
2   Victim-offender mediation is defined as a process in which victims and offenders communicate with the help of an impartial third party, either directly or indirectly via the third party, enabling victims to express their needs and feelings and offenders to accept and act on their responsibilities.
3   Family group conferencing can be defined as a method of resolving the effects of a crime by bringing together a large number of stakeholders with a facilitator.
4   In Dutch, 'claims settlement' is called 'schadebemiddeling'.

offender. In more serious cases, successful claims settlements can be taken into account in sentencing. Claims settlement is regulated by the Directive regarding the Care of Victims. Although this Directive also allows for conflict resolution, this is practiced only very occasionally.[5]

It is interesting to note that claims settlement was preceded by a project – in 1990 only in Amsterdam, it was extended later – aiming at the settlement of disputes called *dading*. This term 'dading' refers to a civil law contract, concluded between the lawyers of victim and offender, without the latter meeting each other face-to-face.[6] The 'dading' project implied that this contract could be sent to the public prosecutor, who – as a rule – would not prosecute on the grounds that the contract had settled the conflict. After the formal introduction of claims settlement, questions arose about the relation between claims settlement and dealing with claims by way of the civil 'dading' contract.

After 1995, experiments were implemented to find out more about the need for a separate use of 'dading'. One problem brought forward by the PPS was that they felt that they did not have sufficient information about the degree of compliance with the civil law settlements, which implied loss of control over the way the criminal conflict was dealt with.

In 1998, a one-year experiment with an adapted form of 'dading' was set up by the Minister of Justice in six judicial districts for misdemeanours involving adult offenders. A member of the prosecution service staff would select the suitable cases, after which a facilitator contacts offender and victim. If both agree to participate, the staff member presents a draft agreement to the parties. If they agree on it and the offender executes it within the set time limit, the prosecutor will drop the case. If the agreement is not executed, or not satisfactorily, the case can be prosecuted. This adapted model implied full control by the PPS and no involvement of lawyers (unless parties wanted to consult them). The final report on this experiment (Spapens and Rebel, 1999) was reason for the Minister of Justice to decide that there was no need to maintain a separate procedure of 'dading' in the criminal justice context and that the conceptual differentiation between claims settlement, 'dading' and other forms of 'mediation' should be dropped. From then on the terminology became 'criminal damage and conflict regulation'.[7] Notwithstanding these decisions, the term 'dading' regularly pops up amongst practitioners and in research, apparently in reference to the adapted form under

---

5   Empirical research projects concerning claims settlement practices at police level in the late 1980s and early 1990s were reported in Zeilstra and van Andel (1989, 1990) and Van Hecke and Wemmers (1992). The evaluations were ordered by the Ministry of Justice and carried out by its Research and Documentation Centre (WODC).

6   In Dutch civil law the term 'dading' – which literally means 'settlement' – has disappeared and has been replaced by the concept of the 'vaststellingsovereenkomst' which is a contract in which the rights of the contracting parties are established.

7   Memorandum of the Minister of Justice, sent to parliament by letter of 18 February 2000, nr. 778915/99/PJS. In this memorandum, the 'decision' was also made to reserve the term 'mediation' to the context of civil law only (page 5).

control of the PPS. As a consequence of the blurring of definitions, the quantitative dimensions of the use of 'dading' cannot be researched.

Because both the actual civil law settlement ('dading') and the criminal law settlement of damage and conflict regulation (also, although unjustifiably, called 'dading') clearly have some characteristics of restorative justice (e.g. victim and offender *can* meet in person and have some say in how the case will be dealt with) the relevant research is included in this chapter.

The HALT programme[8] is a voluntary diversionary measure for juveniles between 12 and 18 years old. It started in 1981 and was one of the first Dutch programmes clearly containing restorative elements. However, mediation or conferencing in the sense of setting up an elaborate and phased communication process between victim and offender is practiced only in a minority of cases within HALT. One experiment with conferencing within this context has been included in the research discussed in this chapter.

HALT offers juvenile offenders an alternative to a civil or a penal law disposal. Cases suitable for settlement are referred by the police to the HALT centres. Staff members at the HALT centre endeavour to reach an agreement with the juvenile, his parents and, if possible, with the victims. The offender undertakes unpaid work or participates in an educational project. If possible, these have a direct link to the offence committed. Apologising to the victim is often part of the HALT procedure. If the juvenile cannot repair the damage done, a financial settlement for the damage, in full or in part, will be arranged. The offender will meet the victim directly only when he works to repair the damage or when he apologises in person. The offences falling within the programme are those that would get light sentences. In practice, the programme primarily targets vandalism, shoplifting and petty crime. If a settlement is reached and fulfilled, the young offender is not prosecuted.

As mentioned above, a meeting between victim and offender in the sense of mediation rarely takes place, but apologies are often made. An evaluation study showed, amongst other results, that in a population of 1,000 young offenders, randomly assigned to either HALT or no intervention, no relevant differences in later conduct, e.g. levels of recidivism, could be found.[9] But for specific groups of juveniles the HALT intervention worked well in preventing or reducing future misconduct, especially when apologies were made (Ferwerda et al., 2006).[10] In the further development of the HALT project, apologies by young offenders was given more attention in the programme.

---

8   For more information on HALT, see www.halt.nl

9   That is to say, no other intervention than being apprehended and having a report made up. Strictly speaking this is also an intervention.

10   The research was commissioned by the Research and Documentation Centre of the Ministry of Justice and carried out by a private research agency. The report is in Dutch (www.WODC.nl) but has a summary in English.

Community mediation will not be elaborated upon in this chapter because the topic of these mediations is mainly of a non-criminal nature. A small part of the cases dealt with in community mediation can be qualified as criminal offences, mainly misdemeanours under municipal law. These criminal offences are usually too minor to justify official action by the police and the judicial authorities. Nevertheless, these small offences are a burden on community life that should be dealt with and against this background informal mediation between neighbours came into existence. The focus is on dealing with problems at an early stage so as to prevent escalation of conflicts and to restore communication between the parties. A conflict will not be taken into mediation if official legal proceedings of any kind – civil or criminal – have been initiated.

The community mediation programmes are set up by a collaboration of local organisations. Community mediation started in 1996 and developed rapidly into a nationwide network of mediation programmes. At the beginning of 2004, 51 projects were operational. Each project is run by about 10 to 18 volunteers, who carry out the mediation, and a professional coordinator. Conflicts are mediated after self-referral by the neighbours involved, referral by other people from the neighbourhood or by third parties such as the police or housing corporations. Mediations are carried out by teams of two citizens, sometimes close neighbours, acting as mediators.[11] They first have separate interviews with the parties involved and, if possible, they meet.[12]

1.2   Brief overview of mediation and conferencing in the Dutch context

Besides criminal law settlement (3.1), we will elaborate in this chapter upon mediation and conferencing in the context of Neighbourhood Justice Centres (2.2), police mediation (2.3), restorative mediation (3.2), family group conferencing with juveniles (3.3) and the 'victim-offender conversations' (3.4), although the restorative character of the latter can be doubted.[13]

---

11   These citizens receive only a short training in simple mediation techniques.
12   An interesting, because comprehensive, research report on community mediation practices is Peper et al. (1999). This research looked into 5 neighbourhood mediation projects functioning in Rotterdam, Zwolle and Gouda. The projects were set up from 1996 on. The research was financed and commissioned by the Ministry of Justice and the Ministry of Home Affairs and conducted over the period 1996 to 1999. The researchers were staff members of the Law Faculty of the University of Rotterdam. The research was a combination of action-research and evaluative research. The goals of the project were formulated as follows: to give theoretical support to the practitioners carrying out the neighbourhood mediation and to act as a soundboard for them; to make an analysis of the process of mediation; and to make an evaluation of the effects of the neighbourhood mediation. A combination of quantitative and qualitative research methods was used. The process and the results of community mediation were evaluated positively and the report led to the Dutch Government's decision to implement community mediation on a national scale.
13   We have not included them in our chapter because, first, victim-offender mediation was set up nationally in 2007 and second, there is empirical research available that supports their 'restorative' impact for victims.

Different forms of mediation or conferencing are part of the activities of a number of Neighbourhood Justice Centres (in Dutch: 'Justitie in de Buurt', or JIB). Neighbourhood Justice Centres [NJCs] were introduced in four Dutch cities in 1997 as part of the Policy on Large Cities ('Grootstedenbeleid'). By the beginning of 2004, the number of offices has grown significantly to 27.

In a NJC office, PPS staff work together with staff from other organisations (such as the police, Child Protection Service, Probation Service and Victim Support) to tackle local crime problems. The aim of NJC is to contribute to the overall safety and feelings of security in certain communities with serious security problems. NJC offices are mainly situated in inner city areas and areas with a relatively poor socio-economic position. The focus is on persistent forms of nuisance, the less serious forms of crime and the ensuing problems regarding the quality of life.

Different kinds of restorative processes are practised: preventive mediation (in situations of conflict to prevent escalation to criminal conduct), claims settlement (concerns only financial reparation), conflict mediation (focuses on conflict in the aftermath of an offence) and family group conferencing. The restorative process can be organised before or during criminal proceedings and the result can have an impact on the further handling of the case. In neighbourhoods where a community mediation project exists, the NJC sometimes refers cases to community mediation to be dealt with informally.

Police officers are also known to use informal mediation techniques on many occasions in which they intervene and an interesting qualitative research – discussed in Section 2.3 – has been done to understand more about this practice.

Restorative mediation ('herstelbemiddeling') normally takes place after sentencing. It is concerned with non-material or symbolic reparation. The aim is explicitly not to influence the criminal process but to help victims and offenders cope with the psychological burdens of crime and victimisation. It intends to assist victims and offenders in coming to terms with the pain of the victim and with the feelings of guilt of the perpetrator. By removing feelings of bitterness or revenge and by acknowledging moral guilt, the quality of life of the persons involved is improved and the reintegration of the offender in society may be stimulated. Victims and offenders can enrol in the restorative mediation scheme either on their own initiative or through referral by authorities. The mediator[14] holds separate preliminary interviews with the sentenced offender and the victim. Only when both parties agree to continue, will direct mediation take place.

Restorative mediation was set up jointly by Victim Support and the Probation Service. The project operated between 1997 and 2003 in two jurisdictions. The four mediators, employed by the organising bodies, were professionals trained at the Netherlands Mediation Institute. Restorative mediation took place mostly in more serious offences, such as robbery, cases involving lethal violence, vio-

---

14 In this particular project the – initially two – mediators were also the project managers, which may not have been a very wise decision: partly because of a lack of administrative data, the project was later cancelled.

lence causing injury and lethal traffic accidents. Since the formal termination of this project in 2003, restorative mediation continues on an informal basis, particularly in the context of penitentiary institutions. It looks like practitioners involved would replace this terminology of 'restorative mediation' with the officially launched (terminology of) 'victim-offender conversations' (see Section 3.4).

Various kinds of family group conferencing with juvenile offenders have been set up since 1998 in several projects, of which the most important have been evaluated. Many, but not all of these projects use the conferencing model of 'Real Justice', which has a strictly scripted character[15] and an informal closing-part to facilitate reconciliation and reintegration. The report we will discuss evaluates 'Real Justice conferences' across a wide range of projects in various contexts.

Victim-offender conversations are the latest development: these facilitated talks between victim and offender have the aim primarily to assist the victim and are not intended to have any consequence in terms of how the case of the offender is dealt with by the criminal justice authorities. This model was launched nationally in 2007. They differ from victim-offender mediation in that they focus on delivering a special service to victims and not to offenders. The responsibilisation of the offenders remains limited to offering them the opportunity to apologise for the criminal act.

From this short survey, it is clear that a number of different restorative practices are being developed in the Netherlands. Restorative justice does not, however, figure as a priority on the Dutch political agenda. In a time of serious budgetary cutbacks and criminal justice policy dominated by law and order, victim-offender mediation and family group conferencing have remained a marginal phenomenon. Moreover, recent policy developments render it doubtful whether the Dutch government will really embark on a restorative justice course.

1.3   Legislative context

In the Netherlands, there are as yet no statutory rules with regard to victim-offender mediation or family group conferencing. Claims settlements can take place in the context of the Directive for the Care of Victims.[16] HALT has a legal basis in Article 77e Criminal Code. It is also regulated by the Directive on HALT[17] and by a Decree.[18]
In 2002, the Board of Procurators-General issued a viewpoint articulating a positive attitude towards restorative justice programmes. The PPS is willing to

---

15   This is different from the New Zealand family group conferencing model, which is not scripted.

16   The *Aanwijzing Slachtofferzorg* was issued in 1995 and amended in 1999 (*Staatscourant* 1999: 141).

17   The *Aanwijzing HALTafdoening* was issued by the board of Procurators-General in 1999 (*Staatscourant* 1999: 82).

18   The *Besluit aanwijzing HALTfeiten* was issued in 1995 (*Staatscourant* 1995: 62).

take restorative processes into account during the criminal proceedings if they respond to the requirements of voluntariness (of all participants), transparency (of the procedure) and professionalism (of the persons in charge of the process). No guarantees can be given in advance concerning the impact of the restorative process on the criminal justice decisions.

In 2009 a government bill with regard to changes in the Code of Criminal Procedure was passed by parliament, which included a new par. 51h that states that rules can be issued with regard to mediation between suspects and victims. The intention is not to provide statutory rules, but only for regulation through a ministerial Decree. These changes to the Code of Criminal Procedure were gazetted in early 2010 and will probably come into force this same year.

1.4 Research

The research that is available can be divided into two categories. First, descriptive research takes stock of the modalities of mediation and conferencing that exist in specific professional contexts or settings. Secondly, there is evaluative research into the practices of 'dading' (criminal law settlement), restorative mediation ('herstelbemiddeling'), various family group conferencing projects with juvenile offenders and the latest development of victim-offender conversations. Action-research in the field of restorative justice has not been done in the Netherlands.

In what follows, we start with the inventory that was made of the mediation practices before, during and after criminal proceedings (2.1), and continue (2.2.) with the available knowledge about the existence of victim-offender mediation or conferencing practices in the context of Neighbourhood Justice Centres ('Justitie in de Buurt' or JIB). After that, we look at what is known about mediation practices by the police (2.3).

These studies – with the exception of the police study – are all characterised by a 'bird's eye view', which means that sometimes the results seem rather shallow. It is not clear which practices fall under which title, because they are often vague or inadequately described. Fortunately, this is not the case with the more in-depth and often participatory evaluative studies that exist with regard to restorative practices as such. These will be discussed in the latter part of the chapter, under criminal law settlement (3.1); restorative mediation (3.2); family group conferencing (3.3); and victim-offender conversations (3.4).

2 DESCRIPTIVE RESEARCH

2.1 Inventory of mediation before, during and after criminal proceedings

2.1.1 Set-up of the research

In May 2000, a descriptive-inventory research was concluded on forms of mediation before, during and following criminal proceedings in the Netherlands

(Spapens, 2000).[19] It was commissioned by the Ministry of Justice because at that time different types of 'mediation' had become operational, but there was no concise and accessible survey of the different types of mediation which were practiced in relation to criminal justice. The information in the report was drawn from project descriptions and other written material, supplemented by a limited number of interviews with experts and persons involved in the different mediation projects.

2.1.2   Research results

After a short historical account on how mediation in criminal cases came about in the Netherlands, the report describes and analyses the different forms of mediation. The rest of the report examines three practices more elaborately: community mediation, claims and dispute settlement by the PPS, and restorative mediation. Interesting is the analysis of all types of penal mediation according to their objectives, the status, position and role of the mediators and the relation to the criminal procedure.

Concerning the objectives of the restorative practices, the report states that financial reparation of damages forms the basis of most forms of mediation in the Netherlands. In claims settlement by the police and the prosecution department, most of the time the intervention remains limited to that aspect, although in principle conflict regulation is also possible. 'Conflict regulation' should be understood as a procedure – after an offence – in which the intervening officer tries to get the parties to agree on a number of rules for their future interactions. In this chapter, it is also referred to as 'dispute settlement'. HALT also aims to have an educational effect. In community mediation, mediation by the Neighbourhood Justice Centres and 'dading', conflict regulation has priority on regulation of the damages. Restorative mediation aims firstly at dealing with feelings of pain and guilt caused by the offence. Although not an official objective, the idea that mediation might contribute to lightening the load of the criminal justice system plays a role in all the forms of mediation practiced (with the exception of the 'restorative mediation' project, cf. infra).

In most mediation practices, mediators are not professional mediators but PPS officers or staff members of other judicial agencies. In community mediation, mediators are volunteers. The report[20] moreover indicates that only in restorative and community mediation are mediators independent in the sense that they do not represent one of the parties or the public interest. In all other forms of mediation, mediators are staff members of the police or other justice agency (e.g. the prosecution service or HALT). As a consequence, in almost all cases there is a certain pressure on the offender, since refusal to participate or an unsatisfactory execution of the agreement can still lead to prosecution.

The mediator can have different roles according to the practice in which he functions. In community and restorative mediation, mediators act as facilitators. They

---

bring parties together and guide the process by stimulating parties to come to a solution by themselves. They do not take sides.

In claims settlement by the police or the prosecution service and in HALT, mediators act as representatives of the victim and/or the public interest. On behalf of the victim, the mediator tries to obtain financial compensation from the offender for the damages suffered, as far as possible. The interests of the offender are only taken into account in as much as the mediator prevents the victim from claiming disproportionate repair from the offender. Strictly speaking, this cannot be considered to be real mediation.

Mediators may also act as advisors, but again this does not represent a pure form of mediation. The advisor takes a certain position and proposes solutions, but the parties do not have to accept them. This is what happens when Neighbourhood Justice Centres handle mediation (where claims settlements are not involved) or by the police, in 'dading' and in conflict regulation by the prosecution service.

Regarding the relationship to the criminal proceedings, community mediation is outside the realm of criminal justice or at the very beginning of the continuum, usually before a criminal offence has been committed. At the very end of the continuum, i.e. after conviction, restorative mediation may take place. The majority of the mediations are conducted when a police report has been drawn up but before the case goes to the PPS or to court. This is the case for mediations in the framework of HALT, claims and dispute settlements by the police and the prosecution department, NJC and 'dading'. Mediation in the framework of NJC can also happen before a criminal offence has been committed and when a criminal offence has taken place but no police report has been drawn up.

This profile of the different forms of mediation shows that, qualitatively, community mediation and restorative mediation are probably the most 'pure' forms of mediation. Quantitatively however, they are by far outnumbered by claims settlement by the police and the prosecution service.

Although all the interventions mentioned above are commonly referred to as mediation (or 'bemiddeling') in the Netherlands, it is obvious that some of them lack the basic features of what is internationally considered to be mediation, such as neutrality of the mediator and restrictions of the scope for intervention by the mediator (Brenninkmeijer and Bonenkamp, 2003). The research report recognised this problem.

The Minister of Justice has attempted to introduce at least some clarity in the terminology. In a letter to parliament[21] he indicated a separation of claims settlement, i.e. financial settlement of damages, from settlement of disputes – in which the focus is on handling the conflict between parties. Unfortunately, the minister at the same time indicated that 'for clarity' he wanted the term mediation to be reserved for the field of civil law. The English word mediation is so widely used in every day language – and not differentiated from the Dutch word 'bemiddeling' –

---

21   Kamerstukken II 1999-2000, 25452, nr. 8. For more elaborate comments on this letter, see Groen-huijsen (2000).

that it would have been more realistic to accept the international usage of mediation for the domain of criminal law as well.

2.2   Modalities of mediation in Neighbourhood Justice Centres (NJC)

2.2.1   Set-up of the research

In 2003, a private research bureau conducted a research project on the mediation activities in the NJCs (Slump, 2003).[22] The project was commissioned by the Ministry of Justice. The research report starts by providing an inventory of mediation activities of NJCs in the Netherlands. It then gives an in-depth descriptive account and an evaluation of mediation activities of 4 pre-selected NJCs. The methodologies used are telephone interviews, the study of a limited number of mediation dossiers (5 or 6 per NJC) and registered information, face-to-face interviewing of NJC staff and a small satisfaction inquiry through telephone interviews (9 in total) with victims and offenders who participated in mediation.

2.2.2   Research results

In 13 of 23 NJCs interviewed, mediation was practised. In 10 NJCs this mediation involved not only financial settlement of the case (claims settlement) but also conflict resolution and/or emotionally coming to terms with what happened. The research further focused on the mediation practice of these 10 NJCs. The services practice mediation before as well as during the criminal proceedings. The initiative to refer to mediation always comes from the prosecutor's office. The cases are selected according to the damages and specific target groups (such as juvenile offenders, victims and offenders with a prior relationship or, more specifically, cases of domestic violence and neighbour conflicts). Other selection criteria include the offender admitting guilt or that the case can be proved, or counter-indications (e.g. the offender has no fixed address or one of the parties has mental problems). Most cases concern minor offences.

Although the report suggests that a PPS staff member is often involved in setting up the mediation, it also emphasises that the mediation process is not a solo operation of the prosecutor's office. External organisations or individuals are often involved in the preparation (mainly Victim Support and Probation) or asked to lead the process (external mediators). In almost all cases the result of the mediation is written down in an agreement. In all cases there is at least some personal contact between the officer and the parties (besides contacts by phone and possibly in writing). The report does not indicate whether the mediation involves face-to-face contact between the parties.[23]

In almost all NJCs, recording of the outcome of the mediation is incomplete or

---

22   The research report is written in Dutch.

23   Note that we are describing the organisational setting and process. With regard to substance and dynamics of the mediation or the conference that follows, there are no (known) differences with conferences in other settings. But it must be stressed that the descriptions of what really took place are often quite unclear.

even non-existent. In all of the 10 NJCs, mediation could have consequences for the decision regarding whether or not to prosecute, or sentencing. Overall, the number of cases referred to mediation is low.

From the in-depth description of 4 NJC-offices, we learn that it is impossible to develop mediation in an NJC office without the support of the prosecutor's office of which the NJC is a part. Other factors are also crucial for a good development of mediation in NJC, such as the collaboration with different justice organisations, a thorough description of the process and protocol, and training of mediators and referrers. The report suggests that these conditions were mostly absent.

The interviewed participants (victims and offenders) showed great appreciation for the fact that mediation was an option for them. According to most of the people interviewed, the strength of mediation lies in the fact that not only the damages, but also the emotional aspects of the case are dealt with. The role of the mediator, especially the more personal approach, was evaluated positively. Parties were satisfied with the result of the mediation but felt that it should have been initiated sooner.

2.3   Exploring police mediation

2.3.1   Set-up of the research

An interesting study, finished in 2003, explored mediation in police practice (Van Stokkom et al., 2003).[24] Although small scale, this study is interesting because of its exploratory design which is different to most other empirical studies on VOM or conferencing in the Netherlands. It builds on cases, which provides an interesting qualitative insight into what the police mediation work is really about. Moreover, it is one of the few studies not financed by the Ministry of Justice for purposes of evaluating whether projects should be continued. The study was financed by the police of Amsterdam-Amstelland and a police foundation.

The initiator of the project[25] was a researcher and police psychologist who was fascinated by the professional way in which police officers mediated in long-lasting and complicated conflicts. This police practice was all the more interesting because mediation is not considered to be a fixed police task in the Netherlands. Police chiefs prefer to concentrate on law enforcement and criminal investigation. Mediation in their view should be done by other agencies. Nevertheless, day-to-day work often pushes police officers into a mediation role for various reasons.

First of all, the police often have a 'dustbin function'. They pick up tasks that have been left by the regular social services. More and more frequently, police are being confronted with incidents requiring intervention. Often drug addicts, mentally disturbed people or isolated elderly people are involved. It is the task of the police to spot the problems, provisionally provide help and to refer those involved to other agencies. But often those other agencies lack the capacity to deal with

---

24   The book is only available in Dutch.
25   Frans Denkers initiated the research. After he passed away in 2000, the study was finalised by the authors of the report.

these cases and so the incidental help function becomes a permanent task, which encourages the police to contribute to the search for solutions.

A second factor stimulating police mediation is the more pragmatic and problem-oriented approach adopted during the 1990s. Pragmatic police officers realise that prosecution is not an adequate solution for every conflict or incident. They are convinced that society is better off when citizens find solutions themselves. Finally, the police were given more room for initiative, which also provides more space for mediation.

Besides analysing the type of mediation police officers practice, the focus of the research was on two main questions. Firstly, in which way do police officers consider mediation as a meaningful police task? Secondly, to what extent does police mediation respect basic principles commonly attributed to mediation, such as voluntariness of participation and impartiality of the mediator?

Fifteen semi-structured interviews were conducted with police officers. They belonged to different geographical areas and different sections of the Dutch police force. Most of them regularly conducted mediations.

2.3.2 Research results

The report presents the verbal reconstruction by the interviewed police officers of eleven cases in which they conducted mediation activities. This material indicates three categories of police mediation.

'Spontaneous mediation' is often triggered by emergency situations or hopeless cases of long-lasting conflicts between man and wife, between families or neighbours. The police officers try to restore the peace and to normalise the social relationships between the parties involved. This is often done in collaboration with social services.

'Group talks with neighbours' are conducted to resolve problems of vandalism, bullying and discrimination. These talks provide an opportunity for neighbours to let off steam and to suggest solutions themselves. They vary from conversations in the entrance hall to group conferences in a community centre.

'Offender-victim confrontations' most resemble what is generally understood by victim-offender mediation. It is a more structured form of mediation in which separate conversations with victims and offenders are conducted in order to find out whether a meeting in person could be realised in a meaningful way.

Now, why do police officers consider mediation to be important? The interviews show that breaking through communication blockades between persons is one of the main motivations, because this allows people to speak to each other about problems and to find solutions themselves. The police officers emphasise that citizens need to take responsibility: they have to gain insight into their own and others' unlawful behaviour and mediation helps to achieve that. Police officers also want to mediate in order to resolve long-lasting conflicts in the long term, especially when other agencies fail, when the safety of persons is at stake and when they consider prosecution will only temporarily stop the problem or conflict. They hope that not only the parties, but also the police force will gain from these interventions. A successful mediation can prevent the intervention team from being sent over and over again to recurrence of the same problematic situation, which is – according to them – an enormous waste of energy. Finally, their motivation is very pragmatic. They will only invest time in mediation when they estimate that an adequate solution or restoration of the relationships is feasible. They stick to their role of public servant and do not want to act as social workers or therapists.

The second main question in the project was how the mediation practice relates to other, public-oriented police tasks. In those other tasks, police officers are used to present possible solutions and to exercise authority. The question was whether police mediation respects basic rules such as being impartial, not using pressure on parties and having people come up with solutions themselves. The interviews show that police officers have trouble letting go of their dominant and authoritative attitude. Often they lead the participants to a solution. They sometimes warn people of the 'big stick' of criminal punishment if they will not participate in the mediation. Not all information discussed during the mediation is kept confidential. The researchers therefore conclude that police officers introduce their own touch to mediation. Police primarily remain faithful to their law enforcement obligations, such as providing security.

Police officers encounter different kinds of obstacles in their mediation work. First of all, they feel police management does not provide sufficient support. They are encouraged to refer the cases to other agencies for mediation. This is however not always possible. People often prefer to work with the policeman on the beat (and not another professional they do not know) or they have lost confidence in the social services. Sometimes social services have given up. And it happens that situations are too explosive and potentially dangerous for the police to suspend an intervention and just refer the case. It is also difficult for police mediators to account for their work. The output may be much appreciated by the population, but it is not easy to measure in statistics. Mediation is very time-consuming and, when work pressure is high, it is certainly not a priority.

The researchers conclude that mediation activities enhance the quality of police work. It is a long-term investment: obtaining long lasting solutions for conflicts and problems saves time later on. Moreover, the mediation work is very visible to the public, which is in line with the goals of local policing such as the development of a more approachable and accessible police.

3 EVALUATIVE RESEARCH

3.1 Evaluation of experiments with criminal law settlement

As indicated above, the first 'dading' experiment of 1990 was a challenging attempt to civilise the resolution of criminal offences and their consequences by a contract under civil law. The adapted version – criminal law settlement of damage and conflict, also called 'dading' – still includes some restorative justice characteristics and seems to survive, although policy decisions in 1999 favour the less costly (and also less communicative) claims settlement (cf. supra).

Spapens and Rebel (1999) – researchers at the University of Tilburg – evaluated six experimental projects in criminal law settlement ('dading') which had been set up in 1998 in six judicial districts. Three models of implementation had been tried out: settlement operating from the public prosecutor's office, from the Neighbourhood Justice Centres and from legal advice centres ('bureau voor rechtshulp'). The projects lasted twelve months. The Ministry of Justice financed the programmes as well as the evaluations.

The research followed the programmes as soon as they started. Information was gathered through interviews with the professionals carrying out the criminal settlement as well as other professionals – mainly lawyers – involved in the programmes; registration of data on the cases treated; and questionnaires filled in by victims and offenders.

The agents carrying out the criminal law settlement (e.g. lower public prosecution personnel and legal advisors) did not receive specific training. The overall number of cases was low and considered disappointing. In 108 cases a settlement procedure was started. This resulted in 43 settlement agreements. Therefore the experiment hardly had any influence on the rate of dismissals. On average, however, the time taken to dispose of cases through settlement was short and victims and offenders considered this to be an important advantage.

Operating criminal law settlements from the public prosecutor's office proved to have most advantages in terms of efficiency. Comparatively, the prosecutor's office could offer the highest number of potentially suitable cases. Moreover, the settlement task could be combined with 'claims settlement' in the framework of the Directive for the Care of Victims, which can be a fulltime job. In the Neighbourhood Justice Centres the project functioned well, but as they operate in a smaller geographical area, the number of suitable cases coming in is not high enough to justify fulltime allocation of staff.

3.2 Evaluation of restorative mediation

3.2.1 The first evaluation in 2000
Restorative mediation started in 1997 in the jurisdiction of The Hague. A first evaluation was conducted in 2000 (Van Barlingen et al., 2000a). It was financed by the Ministry of Justice and carried out by a private research bureau. Besides a description of what restorative mediation is about, the interim evaluation report focused on bottlenecks that appeared while developing the programme and on the opinions of clients concerning the set-up, the value and the significance of restorative mediation.

One serious bottleneck encountered by the project managers was the lack of support and co-operation by the organisations that set up the project, namely the Probation Service and Victim Support. The deliberate choice to conduct the programme on a neutral site outside the lead organisations themselves (in order to avoid any appearance of partiality towards clients) seemed to worsen this problem. Lots of energy went to repeated efforts to create support for the project. Although these efforts generated positive reactions, the number of referrals remained low. The report suggests that the referrers were very hesitant to actively suggest restorative mediation to their clients. This seemed primarily to be due to the tendency of social workers to protect and identify with their client. They were inclined to be somewhat paternalistic and to make choices for their clients rather than discuss options with them.

During the initial two and a half years of the project, 118 requests came in, which lead to 121 'actions' of the project. These resulted in 19 direct mediations and 25 indirect mediations. In 14 additional cases, the participants indicated that, although no mediation took place, being involved in the project had been a positive experience. In sum, 17 requests were rejected by the project managers, in view of the admission criteria they designed;[26] in 15 cases no contact with the second party was established; and in 20 cases the request was withdrawn. The remaining number of cases was not yet completed at the time of writing the report.

The opinions of clients concerning the value, set-up and significance of restorative mediation was investigated by examining all available client files as well as ten interviews with clients. The researchers concluded that restorative mediation does respond to a need of victims and offenders. Both groups generally valued the process positively. They indicated that it helped them to cope with the effects of their victimisation. After this first evaluation, a second project was set up in the jurisdiction of Den Bosch in 2001.

3.2.2 A second evaluation in 2002

A second evaluative research on restorative mediation was commissioned by the Ministry of Justice for purposes of decision-making regarding the continuation of the project after a run of five years (1997 to 2002). It was conducted in 2002 by a private research bureau (Homburg et al., 2002).[27] The main purpose of the study was to investigate whether and, if so, under which conditions, restorative mediation should be continued and become a structural component of the criminal justice administration.

A mainly descriptive part focused on the referrals to restorative mediation, the course and the results of the mediation processes conducted. It was based on the data available in the project's registration system in the period between 1 January 2001 and 5 September 2002. From the 168 referrals received in this period, a more in-depth analysis was done of 49 randomly selected cases in which there had been a meeting between victim and offender.

More than two thirds of the 168 enrolments were made by offenders who wanted to apologise, to allay the victim's fears, to make it clear that they intended to better

---

26 Such as: the offender is 'not really' prepared to listen to the victim, or the victim has too strong vindictive feelings (p. 30).

27 The report is published in Dutch but contains an English summary.

their life, to relieve their feelings of guilt, to ask for forgiveness or to find closure. In a few cases the aim of the offender – contrary to the aim of the scheme – was to influence the criminal proceedings. Victims who applied for restorative mediation wanted to hear apologies, find answers to questions about the crime, find closure, forgive, let the offender know what damage he had done or let him know that they did not blame him. The Probation Service referred about half of all cases to the project, followed by Victim Support, self-referral by victims or offenders and referrals by the Prison Mental Health Service. Of a total of 161 cases, 16% concerned lethal violence, almost 30% violence leading to injury, almost 9% lethal traffic accidents and almost 9% robbery.

The result of an enrolment could, according to the researchers, include the withdrawal by the applicant, rejection by mediators, non-participation by the recipient, indirect mediation and a direct or face-to-face meeting between applicant and recipient. In the period indicated above, face-to-face meetings took place between the offender and the victim in one sixth of the enrolments. The chance for the referral to end in a meeting between victim and offender was much higher when the victim was the applicant. When the offender was the applicant, there was a higher rate of withdrawals by the applicant and a higher rate of refusals to participate by the recipient.

Through a written questionnaire, potential referrers were asked about their knowledge of the project, their experiences with the project as well as their opinion of it. Questionnaires were sent out to a random sample of 300 staff members of the three main referring organisations in the two jurisdictions where the project was operational (Probation Service, Victim Support and the Prison Spiritual Welfare Service). One hundred and twenty-eight of them responded.

Positive findings included that most respondents were aware of the existence of the restorative mediation scheme and were well-informed about the value the scheme could have for their clients. According to the respondents, for victims the added value vis-a-vis other types of support concerns mainly the possibility to start or accelerate the process of coming to terms with the event. For offenders, the respondents indicated that the main added value is that offenders are much more aware of what their act meant for the victim.

More problematic findings showed that a large group of the respondents were not, or not sufficiently, informed about the methodology of the scheme and their role as referrers (almost half of the respondents) nor about the results of the project (more than half of the respondents). Of those aware of the existence of the scheme, more than 40% indicated that it was not a recurrent part of their work activities. For those for whom it was a recurrent topic, this mostly meant that they spoke about it when a client seemed to be a suitable applicant for restorative mediation. The project was structurally integrated in the working processes for only 5% of the respondents who knew about it. Improving knowledge about different aspects of the projects was seen as the major possibility to improve their integration in the referring organisations.

Apart from the information already gathered, nine interviews with key inform-ants were conducted as part of evaluating whether the project should be contin-ued. Key issues were: arguments for and against the continuation of the project; conditions for continuation; where in the criminal justice context the project should be embedded; the expected demand for the project; and an estimation of the costs involved if the project were to be implemented nationwide.

From the start of the project onwards, the emphasis was on the development of the mediation methodology. Although more attention was given to registration of information about the cases after the first evaluation, the organisational or management aspects of the scheme remained underdeveloped. When the second evaluation was conducted in view of continuation or more structural implemen-tation of the project, this became problematic. Not enough project information (such as descriptions of the work processes and clear information on the results) was generated to support a decision to continue with objective and quantitative arguments. If the scheme was to be continued, the development of these aspects was considered to be essential. The decision to be taken had to be grounded on substantial qualitative arguments for which there was, however, no operational information. Those arguments included the increase of attention for the victim in criminal justice contexts; the need for rehabilitation of the offender; the intro-duction of a mediation culture focusing on dealing with guilt and pain instead of punishment and retribution; and the prevention of recidivism. Most of those interviewed felt that the scheme addressed a need that had, up until then, not been met.

So far, the restorative mediation project had functioned as a more or less inde-pendent scheme with the Probation Service performing an official role as sec-retary and budget holder. When considering the possible future organisation of the scheme, three main types of organisation emerged: continuing as an inde-pendent scheme, linking up with an existing organisation (Probation Service or Victim Support) or linking up with a new organisation bringing various types of mediation under one roof. The last option seemed to have the most advantages in the long term. In the short term, linking up the scheme to Victim Support seemed most advantageous. Criteria taken into account included: accessibility for victims and offenders; the organisational relationship with the main referrers; the development of methodology; the possibility of using volunteers to do some of the work; the availability of proper management, and management and opera-tional costs.

It is estimated that on a national level, the annual number of cases potentially suitable for restorative mediation according to the criteria and the model chosen in this project is 4,100. Based on the current system this would require 80 media-tors. The average cost per mediation was estimated at around €840.

3.2.3 Restorative mediation in practice after the evaluations
In November 2003 the Ministry of Justice decided – in a more general context of drastic cutbacks – not to continue the restorative mediation project. Reasons given were: the high costs of restorative mediation, the fact that it was mainly

offender-oriented (the requests for mediation mainly came from offenders); the rather low rate of victims willing to participate; and the fact that the project was not well enough embedded in the organisations which set it up (Victim Support and the Probation Service).[28]

In 2007, some form of restorative mediation still existed, both in the context of juvenile offender institutions and in penitentiary institutions for adults, as an activity set up and maintained by mediators – calling themselves 'restorative mediators' – supported by the administrations of these penitentiary institutions. There is no scientific research available concerning this development, on that is consciously linked to the attempt to develop a restorative detention regime.

From recent publications by practitioners involved (Jansen, 2007; Van Rhijn and Van Genabeek, 2007), we learn that in the last three years at least 75 cases with adults have been taken up, as well as around 120 cases with juvenile offenders and their victims. Most often the restorative mediation involves 'shuttle mediation' and the writing of letters of apology. In 10% of the finalised cases with adults, involving serious crime such as aggravated assault, a face-to-face meeting took place (Van Rhijn, 2007).

3.3   Evaluation of family group conferencing with juvenile offenders

There are three major publications to be discussed: the first two are reports initiated by independent researchers and which analyse the same projects in consecutive time periods. The last and most recent report resulted from research done for the major initiator of restorative conferencing according to the 'Real Justice' model in The Netherlands, by researchers working for an affiliated foundation. This is not to say that their research was in any way biased. It must be noted on beforehand that the last report (Section 3.3.3) analyses completely new (and more) material, *partly* derived from projects that were also investigated by the first two researches. The case-material in the last report had not been investigated yet, so the number of cases could in principle be accumulated to have an indication of the total amount of 'known' conferences held.

3.3.1   The 2004 report
A number of projects have been set up since 1998 and they are all variations on the family group conferencing model working with juvenile offenders. A two-year research study focused on seven of these projects. The Ministry of Justice commissioned and financed the project, which was carried out by a researcher at the University of Utrecht (Hokwerda, 2004).[29]

Data collection took place over a period of 15 months (1 September 2001 to 1 December 2002) and provided a description and evaluation of the working method of

---

28   *Beleidsbrief Slachtofferzorg aan de Tweede Kamer*, Ministerie van Justitie, Directie Preventie, Jeugd en Sancties, 27 november 2003 (Policy letter concerning Victim Care by the Minister of Justice to parliament).

29   The research report was written in Dutch.

the projects as well as the effects of the conferences. In order to gather qualitative and quantitative information, different research tools were used. During the data collection period, 52 conferences were organised over the seven projects. On 50 of those conferences, research information was gathered through questionnaires. Questionnaires were completed by mediators, victims, offenders and other parties who attended the meetings to support the offender. Additionally, 19 of the conferences were observed and 14 were taped and transcribed for analysis. Police files were examined in order to provide data on recidivism. Finally, the information gathered was completed through (informal) conversations with mediators and project leaders, participation in project meetings and the study of project documentation.

The seven family group conferencing projects have been set up by different agencies such as the police, the prosecutor's office, HALT, Bureaus for Youth Care, the Council for Youth Protection and schools. The conferences are led by facilitators with different titles ('coordinators' or 'discussion leaders') that belong to these organisations, all of whom received training. The list of agencies and persons who can refer cases to the projects is quite diverse, and include Victim Support and the organising agencies.

The overall procedure is more or less the same, but there are differences as to who leads the session, who is allowed to participate and the relation to the criminal justice process. In five of the projects, the conferences do not have a formal role or position in the criminal proceedings. Nevertheless, the coordinators try to organise the conference as soon as possible after the facts so that the public prosecutor or the youth judge will receive a report of the conference and can take this into account in his decision. Two projects embed the conference in the formal decision-making process: in one project, the conference is part of a HALT measure. In the second, it is seen as a replacement for a caution by the public prosecutor.

For the conferences organised in schools, it is not clear to what extent the programmes are dealing with criminal offences, but they were nevertheless included in the research.

In total, 337 people participated in the conferences, comprising 100 offenders, 71 victims, 107 supporters of the offenders and 59 supporters of the victims. The number of participants varied from 2 to 24. The average age of the offenders was 15 (ranging from 10 to 18); the average age of the victims was 33 (ranging from 11 to 79). The cases generally concerned rather minor offences: assault (39%), damaging property (25%), theft (14%) and bullying/threat (14%). The vast majority of the crimes were committed by groups. The delay between the day of the offence and the day of the conference varied greatly, with averages for every project varying between 52 days and 262 days.

The majority of the participants said that the conference met their expectations and that they were satisfied with the outcome. Reasons to participate mentioned by the offenders were that they regret what happened and they felt a need to explain things to the victim. The victims indicated that they felt a need to tell the offender about how they experienced the incident and about what the consequences had been for them. They also gave as a reason that conferences gave them the opportunity to ask questions about what happened and why.

In 58% of the cases an agreement was written down; in the other cases the agreements were only made orally. In most cases apologies were offered to the victim (92%). Additionally, the agreements mainly concerned reparation or compensation of the damage; fixing rules of conduct between victim and offender; and promises concerning future law-abiding behaviour of the offender. According to the author, there was a striking absence of provisions to monitor the execution of the agreement and no facilities to address non-compliance of the agreement.

Slightly over 50% of the offenders had a criminal record prior to the conference. In the year following the conference, the majority of the offenders (66%), and a big majority of the first offenders (87%), did not appear again in the police records. The researcher remarked, however, that no conclusions could be drawn concerning the effect of conferencing on recidivism based on this study because of the low number of cases studied and the lack of a control group of offenders to compare them with.

Based on this evaluation study, the Minister of Justice decided in November 2003 to continue a number of existing family group conferencing programmes for juvenile offenders and to set up new similar pilot schemes. At the same time, further research on the effect of conferencing on recidivism rates and on the cost-effectiveness of the schemes was to be conducted. This could be used in decision-making on the desirability and the financial feasibility of a nationwide implementation and of expansion of the schemes to young adult offenders.[30]

3.3.2   The 2006 report

After the conclusion of Hokwerda's research, the Research and Documentation Centre of the Ministry of Justice commissioned a second investigation which lasted one year.[31] The Hilda Verwey-Jonker Institute was commissioned to carry out the research and the report was published in 2006 (Steketee et al., 2006). One of the main reasons to commission this second research was to gain information about recidivism after participation in a restorative project. This is reflected by the central research question, i.e. the possible effects of 'restorative mediation'[32] and the degree to which these effects are caused by the organisational model of the project or the stage of the criminal procedure in which the project is set up.

The report firstly contains a literature review about what psychological and pedagogical theories say about moral development of children in relation to restorative

---

30   *Beleidsbrief Slachtofferzorg aan de Tweede Kamer*, Ministerie van Justitie, Directie Preventie, Jeugd en Sancties, 27 november 2003 (Policy letter concerning Victim Care by the Minister of Justice to parliament).

31   This new research concerned six pilot-projects; of these, 4 were also investigated by Hokwerda (2004).

32   The term 'restorative mediation' is used here as the translation of the Dutch word in the title of the research, which is 'herstelbemiddeling'. The term must be taken to cover both conferencing and mediation.

justice, and feelings regarding fair administration of justice. The second part is a report on the results of monitoring the six projects for the year under study. Thereafter, a description follows of the results of the separate projects and the evaluation of these results by mediators and participants. The fourth part concerns the questions with regard to measuring recidivism and ways in which it can be measured. The fifth part focuses on longer term general effects and the last part is an analysis of time investment.

For the empirical elements, the researchers issued questionnaires to mediators and participants (victims, offenders and members of their social network). Furthermore they analysed documents produced by the projects (e.g. about the projects design) and those resulting from restorative conferences.

The literature review resulted in support for restorative justice as a promoter of moral development of young offenders (Steketee et al., 2006: 31) on the basis of notions related to procedural fairness (theory) and the pedagogical value of holding young people accountable for the consequences of their conduct. Also, the participation of family members is considered to be of great importance (Steketee et al., 2006: 109).

The monitoring of the six projects resulted in systematic information about 87 cases in which a restorative conference[33] took place, as well as 150 'non-response' cases.[34] Mediator reports were available for all cases. Of all participants, 64 offenders and 55 victims and 114 members of respective social networks returned the questionnaire. Mediators were asked to report about the follow-up of 30 conferences.

In 50% of the cases that did not result in a conference ('non-response'), the offenders refused; in 25% the victims. In one of every eight non-response cases, an alternative way to seek reconciliation was followed, e.g. writing a letter of apology or offering flowers. The cases that did not result in a conference often involved offenders belonging to an ethnic minority. The report suggests that this may be due to the circumstance that these minorities have less knowledge of or affinity with restorative practices.

The criminal offences that led to conferences often involve bodily injury (assault). Other offences are vandalism and other violations of public order, threats and theft with or without the use of violence. Offences that were committed in a group more often lead to a conference than offences committed by an individual offender.

The juvenile offenders were usually male, and between 14 and 17 years of age, and born in the Netherlands. Three quarters of the victims were boys under eighteen years of age, of Dutch nationality; the youngest victim was ten, the oldest 91.

In about 66% of the cases, the restorative conference resulted in an agreement, but in only 33% of them it consisted of a written agreement. Compliance with

---

33   Most projects in this study use the conference model of 'Real Justice'.
34   The term is used here to indicate that a conference could not be arranged.

the agreement was left mostly to the participants: in most cases nothing was decided about supervision or about the consequences of non-compliance. The report presents no data on the degree to which agreements were complied with, but implicitly suggests that the compliance rate is very high. No complaints of victims or mediators about non-compliance are reported.

The evaluations of both participants and mediators of the cases resulting in restorative conferences are predominantly positive, although victims tend to be a bit sceptical and are waiting to see future developments before giving a final evaluation.

With regard to the key issue, at least for the Minister of Justice, of recidivism the report concludes that the researchers had to omit this part of the study for technical reasons: 'Because police records were inadequate ... it was impossible to accumulate unambiguous information about the characteristics, dimensions and degree of recidivism of the random sample' (Steketee et al., 2006: 13).

Looking at long-term effects of the conference, the report concludes that victims and offenders, contacted by the mediator[35] after a time lapse of three months, are still quite positive about the experience: 'The offender's social network reports a behavioural change in their son or daughter. This behavioural change usually obviates recidivism. The victims are less fearful than before and they are satisfied that there has been no reoccurrence of the offence' (Steketee et al., 2006: 13).

In terms of time investment, the conclusion is that on average each case takes about eight or nine hours of work. Those cases resulting in a conference take about fifteen hours, but sometimes much more when there are several victims and/or offenders.

3.3.3   Real Justice conferences 2000-2006

The 'real justice' model was introduced in the Netherlands in 2000 by the civic organisation now called 'Eigen Kracht Centrale' (EKC). The research was carried out by experienced researchers working for the affiliated foundation 'Wesp Jeugd-zorg' on the basis of case registrations by the (voluntary) facilitators (also called 'coordinators') of Real Justice conferences, trained by the EKC.

The Real Justice conferences are offered as a service whenever citizens are engaged in conflicts of any kind, legally defined or not. Conferences can in principle be organised outside and besides criminal proceedings or can be linked with criminal proceedings. Most conferences, however, involve juvenile offenders: from their introduction onwards, Real Justice conferences have found supporters in the youth agencies of criminal justice, namely the police, the Child Protection Service, the Juvenile Care services (including juvenile probation), the HALT service and the specialised public prosecutors for juvenile cases.

Since 2000, some estimated 800 cases have been received by the coordinators, most of whom are working in the organisations mentioned. The research report,

---

35   Mediators made contact after the conference in less than 50% of the cases.

titled 'Let's just interact normally', gives information on 542 of these cases.[36] All 542 cases had reached a conclusion before 2007. The facts of the cases are given as well as data with regard to the process of the conferences, the participants and the results of the conferences. The content of the 'restorative plans', the degree of compliance with the plan and the degree of satisfaction of the participants are analysed. The substantial basis of the research consists of 542 fact-sheets received from the coordinators, 1,052 returned questionnaires concerning participant satisfaction (48%), 201 (original) restorative plans (70%) and 120 follow-up reports (37%).

Cases presented
In line with the purpose of the Real Justice conference, the cases concern some wrongful action, be it an offence or another kind of misconduct. On average per case there were 1.2 wrongful actions to be discussed with a view to redressing the damaging consequences. These wrongful actions most often implied physical contact between offender and victim, often assault. Threats, intimidations, destruction and vandalism, stealing, bullying and robbery were also dealt with, but in much smaller numbers.
In 67% of the cases victim and offender knew each other before the incident. In 61% of all cases presented to the coordinator, a Real Justice conference had actually taken place. In 39% of all presented cases, no conference could be held: the report gives details about these 'no conference cases'.

No-conference cases
In almost half of the cases in which no conference was held, this was due to the refusal of the victim and/or his social network to participate. Sometimes fear of negative consequences, such as intimidation or escalation, is the reason for refusal, but sometimes victims felt no need to participate because they had already 'closed' the incident. In 19% of the 'fail-cases' the offender refused. Sometimes the incident had simply taken place too long ago or had been resolved in another way.
In 47% of the no-conference cases, the misconduct was physical assault and in 15% threats and intimidations. On average 1.8 offenders were involved, mostly of Dutch origin and aged between 13 and 18. On average 1.2 victims were involved, victims were more likely to be men than women and also were mostly aged between 13 and 18. About one-third of the victims (32%) are adults. In 60% of the no-conference cases victim and offender knew each other before the incident.

Conference cases
In total, 329 conferences took place (61%), predominantly about matters of physical assault (45%) and destruction or vandalism (12%). On average 2.4 offenders were involved in the conference, mostly Dutch youngsters between 13 and 18

---

36 Of the remaining number of cases no records were available. The report is in Dutch and does not have an English summary (Van Beek and Gramberg, 2007).

years of age. Victims were more often male than female and mostly (64%) of the same age group as offenders. Again, most victims and offenders knew each other before the incident (71%).

On average 8.1 people were present at the conference, excluding interpreters and the coordinator: 4.9 persons on the part of the offender, and 3.2 on the victim's side. The number of the participants varied between 4 and 28. The social network of the victim varied more than the social network of the offender: the latter is more likely to be accompanied by parents; the victim is more likely to bring friends and partners. At least 5% of all participants were there in a professional capacity: policemen, social workers, teachers. In 70% of all conferences everybody who had agreed to come, did participate. In the other cases an average of 1.3 persons did not show up for various reasons. The mean duration of a conference is one hour and a half.

Results

Most conferences that take place result in the intended 'restorative plan' (92%) and in 94% of the conferences apologies are made. In two-thirds of the conferences that ended without a plan, the participants felt no need to make one and were satisfied with the apologies. In one-third of the conferences not resulting in a plan, there were negative reasons for this, which are not further explained in the report.

On average, the restorative plans – which are written agreements – contain 1.3 'engagements' and 2.3 'intentions'. Engagements are more firm and easier to check with regard to compliance than intentions, for instance to 'be good'.

Engagements most often imply financial compensation for damages and apologising, but sometimes also involve doing work and living up to clear rules of conduct. For the participants – who most often have an ongoing relationship – the most important function of the conference is designing a future in which they can 'interact normally'.

Compliance and satisfaction

Directly after the conclusion of a conference, participants were asked to fill in a questionnaire to present their evaluation. Participants could do that on the spot or later at home and send in the form. Most participants were satisfied with the experience and the average mark given to the conference was 7.8 out of 10. The way the coordinators conducted the process was evaluated with the average mark of 8 out of 10.

Only 5% of the participants felt that they had not been able to contribute to a resolution of matters discussed. Of all participants, 75% felt that they had contributed fully and 20% that they had contributed partially to the resulting restorative plan. Of all participants, 93% indicated that they had been able to say all they wanted to communicate; 6% indicated this was partially so.

In 120 conference cases, the coordinator contacted the principal participants to inquire how things went three months after the conference had taken place. According to offenders and victims most of the restorative plans were well executed. Of the offenders 84% replied that they had complied with the agreements and of the victims 77% felt that the agreement was completely, and a further 20% that the agreement was partially met. Three per cent of the victims indicated there was no compliance at all with the agreement made.

93% of the offenders and 90% of the victims were satisfied about the conference: the report does not distinguish satisfaction with the process from satisfaction with the outcome. Most victims and offenders felt that good relations had been restored as a result of the conference. Most offenders said that their conduct had actually changed; only seven of all offenders involved felt that the conference had not worked in any way.

Comparison of conference with no-conference cases
Why does a presented case lead to a conference? It is clear that there are not many differences between cases in which a conference takes place and those in which it does not. Types of offenders and types of victims do not differ categorically between the two.

The authors conclude, in comparing conference cases with no-conference cases, that the type of offence or misconduct is not an explanatory variable. But when the cases are presented from the context of schools and when the referring organisation is the police, more conferences are carried out. In the first case, the interest lies in normalising ongoing relationships and in the second case, the fact that the police could also bring the case to the public prosecutor seems to be an explanatory factor. Striking in this regard is that 97% of the cases presented by schools led to a conference.

3.4 Victim-offender conversations

Since the autumn of 2004, experiments have been done in a number of regions in a project called 'victim-offender conversations'. The primary aim of these projects is to help victims to cope with the experience of victimisation. The experiments have been evaluated with regard to the process of these conversations, not with regard to their outcomes and effects (Hissel et al., 2006).

This project is not a restorative justice practice as such because there is no intention to have a victim-offender mediation or a conference, nor to give the offender an opportunity to accept and assume his responsibility: the term 'mediation' is explicitly absent from the name of the project. It is intended to be merely an additional service to victims in the context of criminal justice and to be appreciated as such. The report gives an impression of the dimensions that surface in a predominantly victim-oriented initiative. Moreover, the model of these victim-offender conversations seems to be, for the Dutch Government, the now preferred way of implementing Article 10 of the European Union Framework Decision on the Standing of Victims in Criminal Proceedings (2001/220/JHA). It can however be argued, as we do, that these conversations do not conform to the obligations that this Framework Decision imposes.[37]

---

37 See Blad (2007).

The experiment was initiated by Victim Support and subsidised by the Ministry of Justice. The research was carried out by a private research bureau in the first financed period of the project (October 2004 to January 2006), by way of interviews with experts, project staff and volunteers of Victim Support. Working reports drawn up by the volunteers and staff were analysed and 14 victims (of the 36 victims who participated) were interviewed.

The initiative for this project was taken because it was believed that victims would be able to cope better and sooner with the consequences of the offence if they could have a talk with the offender. The project design implied that the volunteers of Victim Support, who usually receive and aid victims who turn to Victim Support, would indicate to their clients that the possibility exists to have a facilitated conversation with their offender. If the victim at any moment in the process of assistance indicates that he would indeed want to meet the offender, the project coordinator[38] opens a file, finds the offender (if known at all) and if the offender agrees, the Victim Support volunteer will prepare the victim. A 'network-partner'[39] will prepare the offender for the meeting in separate talks. The project coordinator (a trained mediator) organises and convenes the victim-offender conversation.

In actual practice, the role of the coordinators appeared to be more dominant: they were often directly addressed by victims and organised the conversation without the help of volunteers. Sometimes they also have preparatory talks with offenders. The project coordinators use a checklist of criteria to judge the suitability of victims and offenders for the intended conversation.[40]

The volunteers of Victim Support have indicated that they find it hard to mention to the victim the possibility of having a conversation with the offender. Often they do not offer this information and wait for the victim to come up with the desire to speak to the offender. As a result the number of conversations that actually took place remained quite low.

Offenders can also request a victim-offender conversation: these requests reach Victim Support either directly or indirectly through its network-partners (including Probation Service).

The preparatory talk with the victim is intended to help the victim identify what he wants to find out from the offender. After the start of the conversation, the victim is first to speak about the impact of the offence and ask questions. The offender is then given the opportunity to present apologies and answer the questions. The report notes that, in practice, the victims were largely allowed to structure the conversation as they wished (Hissel et al., 2006: 56).

---

38 Five coordinators are in place: one for each region.
39 Network-partners are other para-judicial organisations such as the Dutch Probation Service, Youth Probation and the police.
40 In view of the background and motivation to organise the project, it seems a bit odd that the first criterion used to judge whether a victim is a suitable candidate for a meeting with the offender is that the victim has by and large come to terms with the victimising event: 'He or she has passed the first stages of repression and emotional re-experiencing of the event.'

The aim of the project was to organise 250 meetings in five regions in a pilot period of 15 months, to give 250 victims the occasion to have a conversation with their offender. At the time the research report was made, 208 requests for a victim-offender conversation had been registered: 116 coming from offenders and 92 coming from victims. These requests led to actual conversations in 70 cases. Fifty-three cases were taken up but not yet concluded.

Of the cases where the request came from the victim, 39% resulted in a meeting and 1% (one case) in a communication between victim and offender without a meeting. In cases requested by offenders, 29% resulted in a meeting, 19% in indirect communication.[41]

An important bottleneck in the project's implementation appeared to be the fact that in less than a third (31%) of the assistance-meetings that volunteers of Victim Support had with victims, the possibility of talking with the offender was mentioned. In sum, 110 victims were informed of this facility: 36% of them responded positively.[42]

Of the 33 victims that were interviewed by the researchers, 14 had actually had a conversation with the offender and 19 had not. The interviewed persons were victims (or their relatives) of offences which had a deep impact upon their lives: serious crimes and traffic accidents with serious consequences, assault, sexual offences, (attempted) manslaughter or murder, hostage, robbery and violent threat.

Two thirds of the conversations took place before trial. The report notes that victims wanted to have the conversation for various reasons: they were afraid of a new confrontation – elsewhere and in a less secure environment – with the offender (in cases where there was a previous and/or ongoing relation), the victim wanted to prevent a repetition of the event or to get 'on speaking terms' again. Other reasons given were that they wanted to confront offenders with what they had done and that they wanted the offender to be law-abiding in the future. Other aspects of victims' expectations were: getting questions answered, receiving a sincere apology, preventing an escalation and reducing fears and frustrations.

Most victims who had the conversation were satisfied with both the talk and the results, directly after the talk and in the longer term of several months. Evaluating after some time – three to six months – they experienced a reduction of anxiety and fear and said that the talk had helped them to come to terms with the event. Getting a clearer picture of who the offender was as a person had been

---

41 The report uses the Dutch terminology of 'shuttle mediation' ('*pendel bemiddeling*') when a direct victim-offender conversation is no longer intended. It must be noted that the term 'mediation' is applied very loosely and as a 'catch-all' term for interventions that do not impose but propose something.

42 It is unclear – from the report – whether 'responded positively' means that they in fact requested a conversation (p. 48). It seems that most of the requests by victims reached project coordinators in other ways than through the channel of victim assistance. This is considered as problematic because the model implied that the requests should be channeled through the volunteer victim assistance workers.

helpful for many victims. Two victims however were disappointed by the fact that their offender had not been prosecuted.[43]

Victims who did not have the desired talk with the offender saw no positive results of the (failed) attempt to meet. They felt disappointed, powerless and in some cases let down by Victim Support or the offender. Some still wanted to meet the offender several months after the failed attempt.

No information has been collected for this report about how participating offenders experienced the offer or the actual conversation. Also, no research has been undertaken into the impact of successful conversations upon sentencing.

In a policy letter of 16 August 2006, the Minister of Justice announced that victim-offender conversations would be rolled out nationally. This national implementation – both for juveniles and adults – is based on three principles: first, that these conversations will be on a voluntary basis only; second, that they will not have any influence on the criminal procedure; and third, that there will be a report about the conversations to the PPS. The public prosecutor may then take this report into account when demanding punishment in court.[44] The second and the third principle together induce a lot of uncertainty about the legal status of the conversations – and the reports about them – and illustrate that these conversations do not conform with the Framework Decision of 2001.

4   CONCLUSION AND REFLECTIONS

Empirical research on victim-offender mediation and family group conferencing in the Netherlands is not abundant. It does cover, however, to a great extent the existing victim-offender mediation and family group conferencing practices. Overall, a mix of research instruments has been used such as face-to-face and telephone interviewing, use of written questionnaires, observation of family group conferences, analysis of registered data, programme descriptions and other written material and analysis of police files to track recidivism.

Participant satisfaction is a recurring topic in all of the evaluation studies. To a lesser extent, we found information on effectiveness of the procedure in terms of time-saving and financial cost, as well as on the effect of victim-offender mediation and family group conferencing on the further criminal procedure and on recidivism.

---

43 Although this is not mentioned, nor substantiated, in the part of the report that gives the results of the victim interviews, the summary states that victims can also feel disappointed when they feel their offenders have been punished less severely than expected because of the fact that the conversation had taken place.

44 These principles are highly unsatisfactory and clearly exclude serious victim-offender mediations – that is why this terminology is avoided – leading to agreements. In this way, the empowering potential of victim-offender mediation is annulled. The policy is laid down in a letter of the Minister of Justice of 18 August 2006, nr. 5400790/06/DSP.

Descriptive-evaluative research is predominant. A pattern can be detected according to which new victim-offender mediation and family group conferencing projects are started up with financial support of the Ministry of Justice. Right from the start of the project or after a few years of functioning, the same Ministry of Justice commissions an evaluation to support decisions regarding the continuation of the project, its extension or discontinuation. The evaluations are carried out by university researchers or private research bureaus and provide quantitative as well as qualitative information. The reports are made public.

This pattern brings up different issues for reflection. It is commendable that the Ministry of Justice invests in setting up mediation and conferencing schemes and in evaluating them. The research reports show that monitoring projects from the start clearly enhances the quality of registration of data which facilitates evaluation and steering of the project. Evaluation of certain projects not followed up from the start proved difficult in certain respects because no adequate information was available.

At the same time, monitoring projects from the start can become problematic when it is done on a short term basis and when it leads to an evaluation involving decision-making on continuation of a project. On several occasions, projects were started up and monitored during a (more or less) one-year period. The report on the functioning of the project during this year subsequently formed the basis for policy decisions. It is clear that a new practice needs more than just one year to develop and stabilise. It is therefore questionable whether it is sound policy to take decisions on such short-term project developments. Putting in place working methods, building up support from the public and from professionals involved (e.g. as referrers) takes more time. Moreover, it is very difficult to develop a critical mass of cases in one year that can provide a sound basis for making statements about the practice. Conclusions in some of the reports were therefore based on (very) low numbers of cases and very small samples of interviews with victims and offenders. And although these conclusions were often formulated with due reservation by the researchers, they were in the end used as a basis for evaluative decisions. As can be learned from our discussion of the research, many projects have been discontinued in spite of being relatively successful, only to be followed up by new experiments which generally do not find their reason for introduction in the shortcomings of the previous project but in changing interests of those policy makers and/or politicians in positions of responsibility, for example the Justice Department.

To give an example: the latest report on family group conferencing with juvenile offenders omitted to research 'recidivism after taking part in a conference', stating that one would at least need a time span of two years and several other conditions to do so. Although measuring effects on recidivism was the key reason for this research, this focus seems to have disappeared and now victim-offender conversations – instead of mediation and conferencing with restorative ambitions with regard to all stakeholders – are presented as the preferred national model. Moreover, this model of victim-offender conversations appears to imply the end of family group conferencing with juveniles – in spite of their success – by way of imposing the 'triade' structure of a facilitated conversation between victim and offender only. It is the intention that conferencing will disappear and agreements between victim and offender are not encouraged and have no formal meaning for criminal proceedings. Future research will have to explore the extent to which there are differences between policies and practices as they develop or continue to exist in the field of justice.

References

Blad, J.R. (2007) 'Slachtoffer-dadergesprekken als vorm van rechtshandhaving', *Justitiële Verkenningen*, 3/07, pp. 50-68.

Brenninkmeijer, A.F.M. and Bonenkamp, H.J. (eds.) (2003) *Handboek Mediation*, 2ᵉ herziene druk (Den Haag: SDU Uitgevers).

Ferwerda, H., Van Leiden, I., Arts, N. and Hauber, A. (2006) *Halt: Het alternatief? De effecten beschreven* (Arnhem: Advies- en onderzoeksgroep Beke).

Groenhuijsen, M.S. (2000) 'Mediation in het strafrecht. Bemiddeling en conflict-oplossing in vele gedaanten', *Delikt en Delinkwent*, pp. 441-448.

Hissel, S.C.E.M., Jansen, M., Soethout J.E. and Tromp, E. (2006) *Procesevaluatie slachtoffer-dadergesprekken*, publicatienr. 1377. (Amsterdam: Regioplan).

Hokwerda, Y.M. (2004) *Herstelrecht in jeugdstrafzaken. Een evaluatieonderzoek van zeven experimenten in Nederland* (Den Haag: Boom Juridische Uitgevers).

Homburg, J., Jonker, I. and Soethout, J. (2002) *Eindevaluatie herstelbemiddeling. Eindrapport* (Amsterdam: Regioplan Beleidsonderzoek).

Jansen, J. (2007) 'Herstelgerichte ontwikkelingen in Nieuwegein', *Tijdschrift voor Herstelrecht*, 7(2), pp. 54-62.

Miers, D. and Willemsens, J. (eds.) (2004) *Mapping Restorative Justice. Developments in 25 European countries* (Leuven: European Forum for Victim-Offender Mediation and Restorative Justice).

Peper, B., Spiering, F., De Jong, W., Blad, J.R., Hogenhuis S. and Van Altena, V. (1999) *Bemiddelen bij conflicten tussen buren. Een sociaal-wetenschappelijke evaluatie van experimenten met buurtbemiddeling in Nederland* (Delft: Eburon).

Slump, G.J. (2003) *Bemiddelingsmodaliteiten bij Justitie in de Buurt* (Amsterdam: DSP-groep).

Spapens, A.C. (2000) *Bemiddeling tussen dader en slachtoffer. Bemiddelingsvormen voor, tijdens en na het strafproces* (Den Haag: Ministerie van Justitie, Directie Preventie, Jeugd en Sanctiebeleid).

Spapens, A.C. and Rebel, J. (1999) *Evaluatie experimenten dading. Eindrapport* (Tilburg: IVA).

Steketee, M., Ter Woerds, S., Moll, M. and Boutellier, H. (2006) *Herstelbemiddeling voor jeugdigen in Nederland* (Assen: Van Gorcum).

Van Barlingen, M., Slump, G.J. and Tulner, H. (2000a) *Tussenevaluatie herstelbemiddeling* (Amsterdam: DSP).

Van Barlingen, M., Slump, G.J. and Tulner, H. (2000b) *Interim evaluation of restorative mediation*, unpublished.

Van Beek, F. and Gramberg, P. (2007) *'Gewoon normaal tegen elkaar doen', Herstel-bijeenkomsten Echt Recht 2000 – 2006* (Voorhout: Stichting WESP).

Van Hecke, T. and Wemmers, J. (1992) *Schadebemiddelingsproject Middelburg* (Arnhem: Gouda Quint).

Van Rhijn, A. and Van Genabeek, M. (2007) 'Forensisch Centrum Teylingereind. Op weg naar een restoratieve inrichting?', *Tijdschrift voor Herstelrecht*, 7(2), pp. 63–71.

Van Rhijn, A. (2007) 'Een kei met datum: Herstelbemiddeling in de P.I. Nieuwegein 2004-2007', *Tijdschrift voor Herstelrecht*, 7(4), pp. 53-61.

Van Stokkom, B., Toenders, N. and Hogenhuis, S. (2003) *Bemiddeling in de politie-praktijk. Een herstelgerichte aanpak van overlast en slepende conflicten* (Dordrecht: Stichting SMVP Producties).

Zeilstra, M.I. and van Andel, H.G. (1989) *Evaluatie van het schadebemiddelings-project bij de Leidse politie* (Den Haag: WODC).

Zeilstra, M.I. and van Andel, H.G. (1990) *Informatieverschaffing en schadebemid-deling door de politie. Evaluatie-onderzoek van een experiment bij slachtoffers van misdrijven in Alkmaar en Eindhoven* (Arnhem: Gouda Quint).

LEGISLATION

Art. 77e Criminal Code

Aanwijzing Slachtofferzorg, college van procureurs-generaal 29-7-1999, Staats-courant 1999, 141.

Aanwijzing HALT-afdoening, college van procureurs-generaal, 13-4-1999, Staats-courant 1999, 82.

Besluit Aanwijzing HALT-feiten, Staatscourant 1995, 62.

Kamerstukken II 1999-2000, 25452, nr. 8.

Beleidsbrief Slachtofferzorg aan de Tweede Kamer, Ministerie van Justitie, Direc-tie Preventie, Jeugd en Sancties, 27 november 2003.

Beleidsbrief Slachtoffer-dadergesprekken aan de Tweede Kamer, Ministerie van Justitie, DSP, 18 augustus 2006.

Wetsvoorstel 30 143 Wijziging van het Wetboek van Strafvordering ter versterk-ing van de positie van het slachtoffer in het strafproces, nr. 1, 9 juni 2005 e.v. Aangenomen op 17 december 2010 en gepubliceerd in het Staatsblad 2010, 1.

9 From local trial projects to state owned services

Empirical research on restorative justice in Norway

Ida Hydle and Siri Kemény

1 INTRODUCTION

The mediation and reconciliation service (Konfliktrådet) in Norway is a product of the debates of the 1970s and 1980s on criminal policy. In 1976, Professor Nils Christie held his renowned lecture about the professionals in general, and the legal experts in particular, 'stealing the conflicts' from their rightful owners. Christie argued that the participants', i.e. the victims' and the offenders', rights to their own conflicts should be restored. Christie's idea and the political current at the time converged into the realisation of the mediation and reconciliation services, later named the National Mediation Service [NMS] (see also Kemény, 2000).

1.1 Context: state of affairs

1.1.1 Legal situation

The Act of 15 March 1991 No. 3, relating to mediation and conciliation by the NMS, regulates both criminal cases, i.e. victim-offender mediation [VOM], and mediation in civil cases (such as family group conferencing [FGC], group mediation as well as VOM as a supplement to the criminal procedure). Through the act, all inhabitants in Norway are offered these two sorts of services. Mediation services are governmental institutions, with mediators, in every municipality.

Referral to VOM is mainly a diversionary measure decided upon by the prosecuting authorities. It is regulated in the Criminal Procedure Act and by the Circular issued in 1993 by the Director General of Public Prosecutions. The circular also mentions the possibility of applying VOM as a special condition with a suspended sentence. This possibility was made explicit in the Criminal Code in 2003. In 2001, The Execution of Sentences Act was passed by Parliament. Chapter 5 deals with community sentences, and it provides for the possibility of applying VOM as part of the community sentence (implying VOM in combination with work for the community, education or other activities). The contents of community sentence are decided upon by the probation service. It should also be mentioned that a pilot project has been organised to offer mediation as a supplement to punishment after sentencing in serious cases of violence (Hydle, 2004). More and more mediation is being applied in cases involving violent offences.

1.1.2   Availability of VOM and FGC

Since 1994, VOM and mediation in civil cases have been generally available to all citizens. The mediation services were organised as municipal public services, under the auspices of the Ministry of Justice. In 2004, the NMS was reorganised into governmental institutions. FGC has been taken up on an experimental level since 1999. It has been evaluated and is now regularly used (Falck, 2006). In Norway, direct mediation is the rule: indirect mediation is almost non-existent.

There are 22 regional NMS offices in Norway, with one coordinator and 650 local mediators in total. All of them deal with both VOM and mediation in civil matters, and they work with adults and juveniles alike: there are no services dealing exclusively with VOM or exclusively with adults or with juveniles. The mediation services are autonomous institutes. The NMS is a relatively centralised government institution. The local mediators who are appointed in the municipalities are supposed to take care of the local community aspect.

The mediation services are independent, public services. They are organised with one or more coordinators and a number of volunteer mediators. The mediation services are supervised by the general office of the NMS and the Ministry of Justice. The prosecuting authorities at the police level refer criminal cases. In addition, since 2003 the probation services have referred cases in which VOM is to be part of the community sentence. When VOM is a special condition with a suspended sentence, the courts make the referral.

Volunteer or lay mediators bring the parties together. The mediators have to apply to become a mediator and they are carefully chosen. All mediators have to attend training according to certain standards. The mediators have their expenses covered, and they also receive a small, symbolic payment for their work (2007: 130 N.Kr. (15.5 Euro) per hour). Each service receives funding according to the number of inhabitants and the level of activity.

The regulations for mediation issued in 1992 by the Ministry of Justice lay down standards of good practice. The coordinators have developed a good practice standard in the form of a 'code of ethics', issued in 1996, and it has since been revised and further developed. It is not possible to lay a formal complaint about the agreement or outcome of mediation. However, it is regulated by law that the parties can withdraw from the agreement within one week of signing. An agreement can of course be re-mediated if the parties agree upon this, e.g. if the offender needs more time to fulfil his obligations. Complaints about mediators should be addressed to the coordinator. Complaints concerning the mediation service are handled by the Head of the general office.

The training scheme of the mediators has been evaluated and revised several times. The National Mediation Service is responsible for the content and quality of the training. A national plan for the training of mediators has been adopted, and a national team of instructors (coordinators) has been appointed. The instructors represent different regions of the country. The elementary four days' training stresses the practical part of being a mediator. This is done mainly through role-plays. The legal provisions and the rules for conduct are well implemented during the training and also at the compulsory up-dating courses twice annually.

Mediators are supervised on a more or less regular basis and 'quality controlled' through questionnaires filled in by the mediators after sessions.

FGC is available at 10 out of 22 mediation services. Due to lack of money it has not been possible to give sufficient training to all mediators, but the NMS has adopted a 3 days basic training in the FGC method. The experiences with FGC are very promising so far and will no doubt be incorporated as a method by all the mediation services.

In 2007, 9,120 cases were referred to the mediation services. This is the highest number referred to the mediation services since its inception. Of these cases, 4,513 (49%) are criminal cases, but a large number of the civil cases are offences where the perpetrators are under the age of consent (15 years) and thus per definition civil and not criminal. The most typical offences and crimes mediated were violence (18%), destruction of property (17%), shoplifting (15%), theft (11%), bullying, defamation and menace (12%) and financial offences (6%).

Ninety-five percent of the agreements reached through mediation were complied with. The different kinds of outcomes in mediation were: work for the victim (13%), financial compensation (37%), work and financial compensation combined (4%), reconciliation (35%) and various other agreements (11%). In 69% of the cases referred, mediation or an FGC took place. This means that both victim and offender participated in a face-to-face meeting.

Only the offenders' age and gender were registered, not those of the victims. Seventy-three percent were male offenders and 27% were female. In 2007, 2% of the offenders were under the age of 12; 21% were between 12 and 14 years; 31% were between 15 and 17 years of age; 15% between 18 and 24 years; 8% between 25 and 34 years; and 23% were more than 35 years old.

1.2   *Research: an overview*

In general, empirical research carried out in the field of VOM and FGC is sparse. Only a few research institutes have taken an interest in contributing to the general development of restorative justice [RJ] – such as the Department of Criminology and the Sociology of Law and the Department of Women's Law, both at the University of Oslo; the Norwegian Centre for Child Research; the University of Trondheim; Norwegian Social Research [NOVA]; Agder University and the Institute of Dialogue and Conflict Management in Kristiansand, Stiftelsen Arkivet (Agder). Some researchers (mostly originally practitioners) have on their own initiative and interest designed research projects that deal with VOM, conferencing (particularly with youth groups) and FGC, i.e. mediation with the involvement of family and the community network and often Child Welfare Services. The research that has been or is being carried out in Norway is mainly of three kinds:

1. Descriptive-inventory (empirical/developmental) (some of these projects are of an evaluative nature).
2. Action-research (empirical/developmental/evaluative and with the researcher taking actively part in the action/process/change).
3. Evaluative research.

2   EMPIRICAL RESEARCH PROJECTS

The following overview of finished or ongoing research is presented according to the type of research.

2.1   *What has become of the mediation services?*

This is a systematic evaluation from the experimental period of the mediation and reconciliation services in the 1980s. In spite of its critical conclusions (mainly with regard to the small number of cases being referred), the Act concerning mediation was passed by Parliament (Nergård, 1990).

2.2   *Mediation in NMS – what happens? Community mediation in Norway – what is happening?*

What happens when parties meet each other in mediation? What concerns them and what do they focus on? Is it to punish, to take revenge, to show their pain, to rant and rave, to settle accounts – or perhaps to reconcile? These were the main questions in a descriptive-inventory, qualitative research project (Mørland, 1995a, 1995b, 1995c). Mørland observed 13 cases, ranging from the 'typical' case for mediation, i.e. adolescents who had committed property damage and theft, to cases of slander among adults. Twenty-seven of the 29 people, ranging from the age of 14 to 82, were interviewed some time after the mediation. Two thirds of the participants expressed that meeting the other party was the most important issue: to express their views, to listen, to receive help, to talk together, and perhaps demystify some myths about each other, to facilitate an approach between the parties. The wish for a visible, material settlement was secondary to most of them, especially the complainants[1].

2.3   *Evaluation of the NMS organisation*

The organisation of the NMS has been evaluated in two separate studies. The first was a descriptive evaluative study of the organisation of the Norwegian NMS, based upon studies of the legal framework, statistical material from the NMS, written interviews with coordinators, mediators, cooperating agencies and interviews in a national meeting of coordinators. More than half of the cases mediated are adolescent criminal cases that the police and public prosecution consider relevant. More than 70% of the complainants are satisfied with the outcome of mediation, and 96% of the agreements are fulfilled. The costs of the NMS are low in relation to the high degree of satisfaction and fulfilment; costs to society are low compared with the costs within the criminal justice system (Alexandersen, 1996).

---

1   For further reading see Mørland (1992, 1994a, 1994b).

The second study was of a descriptive evaluative nature and looked at the basis for and the development of the organisation of the Norwegian NMS, based upon studies of the legal framework, statistical material from the NMS, interviews (written as well as oral) with coordinators, mediators, representatives from the police, the prosecuting authorities on different levels and the Ministry of Justice. Also participant observation in meetings (national and local) of mediators and coordinators was applied. The theoretical framework is based upon the perspective of Christie (1977) in 'Conflict as property', i.e. the relativity of crime, crime as a social, cultural and political construction in complex societies and the perspectives of Mathiesen (1978) and Cohen (1985) focusing on the potential growth of punitive control using the NMS. The findings focus on the NMS as part of the criminal justice system. Yet, at the same time, their function has a civil justice, i.e. societal, nature. However, prevention of juvenile crime and crime control seems to be dominating in the use of the NMS, not the broader alternative of a general conflict solution in the communities, i.e. the punitive dimension of the NMS is enhanced. Criminal cases are most frequently referred and the NMS act as 'rapid court' solution for juvenile crime (Dullum, 1996).

2.4   Close-ups of mediation at the NMS

This is a descriptive-inventory study of the extent to which cases of violent conflicts can be handled in the NMS. By observations during conference and open, semi-structured interviews of parties, family members and mediators/facilitators in 7 cases, Kemény further qualified the following issues: the question of cases' eligibility, the question of restoration and the premises thereof if there is no reconciliation, as well as the need for quality control of the mediators (Kemény, 1998; Krogstad, 1999).

2.5   Between reconciliation and prevention

The purpose of this work was to explore the prevailing values in the mediation service, and how these influenced the organisation of the general activity of the service. The author also investigated whether the prevailing values influenced the mediation itself. The practice of the mediation service of Tromsø was analysed according to two idealised types of mediation service: an ideological and a pragmatic model. These models were to a great extent based upon the variability of values and historical development of the services. In the pragmatic model, the local community is seen as a tool for the crime prevention work of the police and the legal system. The ideological model focuses on the local community as an agent represented by the NMS. Mediation of conflicts strengthens the community and prevents the professionalised handling and thus alienation of people. The study was carried out as fieldwork at one mediation service ('case study'), applying the tools of interviews and observation (Håkonsen, 1998, 1999). The author shows how the pragmatic model prevails because the police were more or less forced by the Prosecutor-General to refer cases of youth shoplifting. The mediators were also influenced by these contextual conditions and were not able to change the model.

2.6 A pilot programme of peer mediation in schools

The purpose of this pilot programme was to apply experiences from the local mediation services to develop means and ways to introduce peer mediation in schools. Forty-five schools, 13 mediation services and 3,500 pupils took part in the project that lasted from 1995 to 1997. The action inventory project was evaluated by using questionnaires, interviews and observations. During the project, findings were communicated to the participants, i.e. pupils and teachers. In this way the researcher took an active part in the project development. Thus this work should be classified as evaluative action-research. The main finding was an overall positive effect of peer mediation. It was recommended that peer mediation should be integrated into the general syllabus of primary and secondary schools (Hanssen, 1998).

2.7 Comparative analysis of the mediation services in Norway and Denmark

This is the only comparative RJ work at present in Norway. The former experimental period in Norway as well as the present established situation is compared culturally and politically to the present situation in Denmark, which is still at an experimental stage. The possibilities of establishing a permanent mediation service in Denmark is discussed, particularly with a focus on cases of violence (Raahave, 1999). A trial project on organised meetings between parties in rape cases has been successfully launched in Denmark and now established on a permanent basis (Madsen, 2006). This may also be tried out in Norway.

2.8 The pupil as resource

The project coordinator of the National Programme for Peer Mediation has published three reports (Andberg, 2001a, 2001b). The reports take the form of manuals for the implementation of peer mediation and they also present a method for self-evaluation of the programme. The method has been developed by key participants in the programme, together with an external evaluation researcher.[2]

2.9 Immigrant women and informed mediation (conflicts in marriages)

This is a descriptive evaluative research focusing on how mediation and legal counselling may be combined and applied for the benefit of women from ethnic minorities. Through practical experience with legal counselling for immigrant women, the aim has been to improve awareness and knowledge in the NMS of

---

2 More information on the evaluation project of school mediation: http://www.skolenettet.no/moduler/templates/Module_Article.aspx?id=17855&epslanguage=NO).

immigrant women's rights. Another aim is to contribute to women's law studies concerning cultural problems as well as gender-related communication. Legal
safeguards are focused upon. There is a presupposition of gender differences
in communication patterns. The data were gathered from a selection of cases
handled in the NMS, and further analysis and evaluation was based upon the
aforementioned aims of the study (Thomsen, 2002). In the cases referred both
to legal advice and to the NMS, there were clear differences in the ways in which
the lawyers and the mediators handled the cases. The legal categorisation of the
questions that arose was more or less resolved during the mediation. The method
of mediation included more issues than were relevant to the case.

2.10   'Street mediation' and conferencing

This is an innovative intervention that aims at working constructively with disaf-
fected and excluded young people in Oslo (many of whom are from ethnic minority communities) as well as with other interested young people and agencies on
the issues of conflict resolution, mediation and alternatives to violence. The project
organises 'extended groups' (*stormøter*, i.e. conferencing) of 10-35 participants
involved in conflicts. The model is based on Polynesian rituals for reconciliation
and the FGC model from New Zealand, as well as the Group Conferencing model
from Australia (Transformative Justice Australia, TJA) (McDonald and Moore,
2000). The organisation of the meetings is based upon Tomkins' (1995) theory
of emotional affect: the transformation from the collective realisation of shared
rage and from negative affects to shared vulnerability, and the shared interest in
the community. The preparatory work took 70% of the overall time and involved
identifying suitable accompanying persons, organising preparatory meetings as
well as motivating participants to take part in the main conference (Bitel, 2002;
Dale, 2002, 2006). Hydle evaluated this project as a short-term research project
after two years of practical work together with a PhD student, Espen M. Foss who
is continuing to work with some of the street mediation groups on a participatory
filming project. The results are good and interesting. Young people (e.g. 16 – 18
year olds) have adopted the methodology as their own, and work hard to continue
in their local environment to improve non-violent conflict transformation. They
claim that they have learned to talk another language and seem conscientious
about the advantage of non-violent solutions to conflicts. The professional crime
prevention bureaucracy, however, seems unwilling to admit the advantages of
young people themselves taking over and assimilating good methodologies and
practices within violence and crime prevention (Hydle, 2007).

2.11   Mediation/conferencing as a supplement to criminal procedure; cases of
serious violence

This was a three-year developmental project running from 2001 to 2004, based
on the findings of previous investigations (such as Alexandersen, 1996; Dullum,
1996; Kemény, 1998). One project coordinator and 12 trained facilitators organ-

ised meetings between victims and imprisoned or formerly imprisoned offenders as well as support persons from both sides. The project was based on cooperation between NMS and the state prosecutor, the prison authorities and the probation service (Fadnes, 2002). The results were evaluated, according to quantitative and qualitative measures, such as number of participants and cases in addition to detailed descriptions of situations, conversations and opinions (Hydle, 2002a, 2004). The project was also a basis for research on the culture of conflict dialogues. This study is a linguistic anthropological study of conflict discourses, related to differences in rituality and dialogism between the criminal and restorative justice in Norway. Theoretically the study is based on Bakhtin's culture theory of dialogism, as explained by Linell (1998, 2005), and Foucault's framework of power and government (Hydle, 2002a, 2002b, 2002c; Hasund and Hydle, 2007).

2.12 Conflict handling and networking in the community

This descriptive-inventory research project focuses on the multitude of premises for community counselling. Apart from the invitation to the parties involved in the conflict to include some of people who are close to them and whom they trust, the aim is to visualise some of the more hidden parties in the conflict. Such hidden parties may be for example professionals in state or municipal agencies or other invisible agents like rules, laws, shops, factories, being partly responsible for the origin or the development of the conflict. Another aim is to describe the various ways in which reconciliation in these kinds of group conferences can be achieved. This study is based upon results from previous studies (see 1.2.3), and includes new observations, questionnaires for various participants as well as cooperation with different municipal groups and organisations (Mørland, 2001). The study showed the clear advantage of this approach and has contributed to a shift in the practice of the NMS moving from a dialogue between the two conflicting persons towards a conferencing approach with all involved taking part.

2.13 Delegation of prosecutorial authority to refer cases for mediation to the police sergeant level

This was a three-year developmental project initiated by Parliament and launched by the Ministry of Justice. It was tried out on a small scale some years ago, without success. The lack of success was at least partly due to insufficient planning and organisation. A developmental project has been re-established, on the initiative of parliamentary representatives. Seventy-one police districts in rural areas are participating in this project for a period of three years. The aim is to test whether there will be an increase of criminal cases referred to mediation, and if it is possible to shorten the time spent on preparatory proceedings, by letting police sergeants also formally decide upon referral to mediation instead of the prosecuting authority at the police level. The project started in January 2003 and is currently (2008) being evaluated.

3   DISCUSSION AND CONCLUSION

In addition to the projects mentioned, several developmental/innovative projects have been undertaken, and are continuously being undertaken, mostly by the coordinators at the mediation services (e.g. Strøm, 2000). Often the projects are initiated and launched by the mediation services, and evaluative reports are produced. It is not unusual that the mediation service workers manage to raise funds for specific projects and purposes, for example, for mediation in ethnic conflicts. Thus, the boundary between 'pure' research projects and evaluation of developmental, trial or action projects is not fixed. We regard this as both desirable and inevitable. If 'pure' research is defined as research that has a clear and explicit statement of theoretical and methodological approaches and superior analytical/scientific (be it social scientific, cultural scientific or humanistic scientific) accountability, the projects of Dullum (1996), Hydle (2004) and Hasund and Hydle (2007) would qualify as research. However, the majority of the projects mentioned could be further developed or elaborated, and are therefore relevant for more research and evaluation.

Quite a bit of innovative work has been done and is being done in the field of restorative justice. However, the most intriguing question for RJ advocates still remains: What is the context and content of the overall resistance against RJ – in spite of the amazing amount of positive evaluations at all levels? What is needed in terms of arguments for the criminal justice system and the citizens in general that it will pay, financially as well as methodologically, to apply restorative justice on a broader scale? By what means can research (i.e. esteemed research institutes) contribute to a favourable development in this respect? Seen from the Norwegian angle, the following topics should be focused upon: cost-effectiveness, standardised data collection (to make comparison and cross-cultural studies possible), theoretical research linked to the philosophy of law (this philosophy should be discussed and challenged; what are the responsibilities and tasks of the criminal justice system?), measures in the form of action-research to improve the visibility of restorative justice in society in general and in the criminal justice system in particular.

REFERENCES

Alexandersen, G. (1996) *Evaluering av konfliktrådsordningen* (Sandvika: Agenda utredning og utvikling AS).

Andberg, K. (2001a) *Eleven som ressurs i skolen* (Oslo: Norwegian Board of Education).

Andberg, K. (2001b) *Evaluering av skolemegling* (Oslo: Norwegian Board of Education).

Bitel, M. (2002) *Mainstreaming diversity: building bridges to young people in conflict*, unpublished (London-Oslo: Partners in evaluation).

Christie, N. (1977) 'Conflicts as property', *British Journal of Criminology*, pp. 1-15.

Cohen, S. (1985) *Visions of Social Control* (London: Polity Press).

Dale, G. (2002) *Konflikt i gatelys – aktiviteter, resultater og utfordringer i Gatemeglingsprosjektet*, unpublished (Oslo, Norwegian Mediation and Reconciliation Service).

Dale, G. (2006) *Fra Konflikt til Samarbeid. Grunnbok i konfliktarbeid med ungdom* (Oslo: Cappelen Akademisk).

Dullum, J. (1996) *Konfliktrådene* (Oslo: University of Oslo, Department of Criminology).

Fadnes, G. (2002) 'Statusrapport og presentasjon: Megling i alvorlige voldssaker', *Opp og avgjort*, Vol. 2, pp. 6-7.

Falck, S. (ed.) (2006) *Hva er det med familieråd? Samlerapport fra prosjektet: 'Nasjonal satsing for utprøving og evaluering av familieråd i Norge'* (Oslo: NOVA Rapport 18/06).

Hanssen, E. (1998) *Elever kan selv. Evaluering av Utviklingsprogram om skolemegling*, Report no. 50 (Trondheim: Norwegian Center for Child Research).

Hasund, I.K. and Hydle, I. (2007) *Ansikt til ansikt. Konfliktrådsmegling mellom gjerningsperson og offer i voldssaker* (Oslo: Cappelen Akademisk).

Hydle, I. (2002a) 'Anthropological reflections on restoring justice in Norway', in Walgrave, L. (ed.) *Repositioning Restorative Justice* (Cullompton: Willan Publishing), pp. 296-312.

Hydle, I. (2002b) *Case studies in Norwegian punitive and restorative practices – revisiting the Manchester School.* Paper presented at the 7th European Association for Social Anthropologists' Conference (Copenhagen August, 14–17).

Hydle, I. (2002c) *The magic of personal encounters; dialogicity in Norwegian 'conflict councils'* Paper presented at the 7th European Association for Social Anthropologists' Conference (Copenhagen August, 14–17).

Hydle, I. (2004) *Prosjektet 'Megling i voldssaker' ved Konfliktrådet for Hordaland. Evalueringsrapport* (Høgskolen i Agder).

Hydle, I. (2007) 'Gatemeglingsprosjektet.i Oslo Røde Kors – en evaluering', *NOVA Skriftserie*, 7/07.

Hydle, I. and Hasund, I.K. (2004) 'Evaluating a Norwegian Restorative Justice project: mediation as supplement to punishment in serious violence cases', *Newsletter of the European Forum for Victim-Offender Mediation and Restorative Justice*, July 2004.

Håkonsen, C. (1998) *Megling i konfliktråd – mellom forsoning og forebygging*, (Tromsø: University of Tromsø, Department of social sciences).

Håkonsen, C. (1999) 'Butikkjedene I konfliktrådssaker – en maktfaktor', *Opp og avgjort*, Vol. 1, pp. 4-6.

Kemény, S.I. (1998) *Nærbilder av saker meglet i konfliktråd* (Oslo: University of Oslo, Department of criminology).

Kemény, S.I. (2000) 'Policy Developments and the concept of restorative justice through mediation', in The European Forum for Victim-Offender Mediation and Restorative Justice (ed.) *Victim-Offender Mediation in Europe. Making restorative justice work* (Leuven: Leuven University Press), pp. 83-121.

Krogstad, B. (1999) 'Megleren – konfliktrådets krumtapp og akilleshæl', *Opp og avgjort*, Vol. 1, pp. 12-13.

Linell, P. (1998) *Approaching Dialogue. Talk, interaction and contexts in dialogical perspectives* (Amsterdam: Johns Benjamins).

Linell, P. (2005) *Essentials of Dialogism. Aspects and elements of a dialogical approach to language, communications and action.* Available at: http://www.tema.liu.se/tema-k/personal/perli/Linell_Essentials-of-dialogism_050625.pdf

Madsen, K. (2006) *Hvor ku'du gøre det?* (Copenhagen: Rigshospitalet). Available at: www.rigshospitalet.dk/rh.nsf/AttachmentsByTitle/JMC.CfV.M%C3%A6 gling/$FILE/JMC.CfV.M%C3%A6gling.pdf

Mathiesen, T. (1978) *Den skjulte disiplinering. Essays om politisk kontroll* (Oslo: Pax Forlag).

McDonald, J.M. and Moore D.B. (2000) *Transforming Conflict – in work places and other communities* (Melbourne: Transformative Justice Australia).

Mørland, L. (1992) *Kjønn og konfliktløsning* (Oslo: Universitetet i Oslo).

Mørland, L. (1994a) *'...a bridge over trouble...'?: refleksjoner over megling i konfliktråd: hva skjer?* (Oslo: Universitetet i Oslo, Department of pedagogic sciences).

Mørland, L. (1994b) 'Et levende konfliktråd i nærmiljøet?', *Opp og avgjort*, Vol. 1, p. 3.

Mørland, L. (1995a) 'Bridge over troubled water?', *Opp og avgjort*, volume 1, pp. 16-17.

Mørland, L. (1995b) *Megling i konfliktråd: hva skjer?* (Kristiansand: Høyskoleforlaget).

Mørland, L. (1995c) *Et allsidig konfliktråd – en styrke for nærmiljøet?* (Kristiansand: Report NMS).

Mørland, L. (2001) 'Finnes støttepilarene i lokalmiljøet?' *Opp og avgjort*, Vol. 2, p. 13.

Nergård, T. (1990) *Hvordan har det gått med konfliktrådene?*, (Oslo: Diakonhjemmets sosialhøyskole).

Raahave, D. (1999) *En komparativ analyse af den norske og den danske konfliktrådsmodel* (Copenhagen: University of Copenhagen, Department of Law).

Strøm, B. (2000) 'Flerkulturelle meglere', *Opp og avgjort*, Vol. 2, pp. 6-10.

Thomsen, E.H. (2002) 'Indvandrerkvinder og informeret mægling', *Opp og avgjort*, Vol. 1, pp. 16-17.

Tomkins, S.S. with Demos, E.V. (ed.) (1995) *Exploring affect: the selected writings of Silvan S. Tomkins* (Cambridge: Cambridge University Press).

10 The quest for sustaining research

Empirical research on restorative justice in Poland

Beata Czarnecka-Dzialuk

1   INTRODUCTION

1.1   *Context: state of affairs*

1.1.1   *Victim-offender mediation in Poland*

Victim-offender mediation [VOM] practice in Poland dates from mid-1995, when the first cases were mediated as a pilot study of the experimental programme for juvenile offenders, developed and led by the Committee for Introducing Victim-Offender Mediation in Poland (from now on 'the Committee'). In the beginning the Committee acted within the framework of 'PATRONAT' – an NGO for helping prisoners and their families, dealing with adult offenders. Later it became an independent NGO and it is now called the Polish Centre for Mediation [PCM].[1]

The experimental programme had been operational in five family courts and was later expanded to involve three other courts. Nowadays, after legal amendments, VOM is generally available in adult offender cases (since September 1998) as well as in juvenile cases (since mid-2001). However, it would be difficult to evaluate its availability in practice, as it depends on the activity of mediators in the specific region of the country. There are 719 independent mediators accredited by all Courts of Appeal – volunteers are paid a fixed sum per case and undertake mediation work in addition to their daily professional activities. There are five institutions accredited by all Courts of Appeal. It is hard, however, to know the exact number of active mediators as there are no data on the number of cases they each deal with. We may assume that only some of them are mediating: in some court districts where many mediators are registered, only a few are active as mediators. There are 40 mediation services organised in different towns under the auspices of the PCM. Each of them has one or a few mediators who are acting on a voluntary basis. There are also three mediation services led by another NGO, namely DOM (Lower Silesian Mediation Centre). Officially, the Family Consultation and Diagnostic Centres are also authorised to conduct mediation: family mediation (in the cases concerning guardianship, divorce and other issues from the domain of family law) as well as victim-offender mediation in juvenile cases (there are 64 such centres). The PCM only started family group conferences in 2005. Until

---

1   In January 2008 it had 1,168 members. It is worth noting that PCM organises training for prospective mediators as well as advanced mediators; 1,529 mediators have been trained by PCM.

2007, there were just a dozen or so in juvenile offender cases; PCM also conducted ten restorative conferences in three correctional institutions.

1.1.2 Legal framework

The specific articles on VOM can be found in both the Code of Criminal Law [CCL] and the Code of Criminal Procedure [CCP] of 6 June 1997.[2] These are very general in nature, allowing for referral to VOM under certain circumstances. The results of VOM would be taken into account when deciding upon the case, especially when deciding on conditional discontinuance of the proceedings or suspension of the penalty, or when other penal measures are imposed (in the decision to apply exceptional mitigation of the penalty).[3]

According to art. 23 a. CCP,[4] the court, and in preparatory proceedings a state prosecutor and the police (as this section applies also to the police), may, on its own initiative or with the consent of the parties, refer the case to a trustworthy agency or person in order to conduct a mediation procedure between the suspect and the injured party (§1). §2 states that the mediation procedure should not last longer than a month; its duration is not counted towards the length of the stage of criminal proceedings called preparatory proceedings (that should be completed within a certain time period prescribed by the law, namely one to three months). It means that the public prosecutor or the police need no longer be concerned that because of mediation, this time could be exceeded.[5]

The CCP contemplates that mediation may be used following a private accusation (art. 489 §2). Such proceedings may be instituted only in cases in which there is not sufficient public interest to engage the prosecution. It is therefore confined to offences such as slander and personal affronts that may involve personal issues but do not cause bodily injury. The fact that prosecutors have no interest in these cases may explain why many of them consider mediation to be the appropriate

---

2   Journal of Laws, no. 88, item 535-555; the CCP was amended by the Law of 10 January 2003 – Journal of Laws, no. 17, item 155.

3   Respectively articles 53 §3, 60 §2.1 and 66 §3 CCL.

4   Art. 23 a. §1. The court, and in preparatory proceedings a state prosecutor, may, on their own initiative or with the consent of the parties, refer the case to a trustworthy agency or person in order to conduct a mediation procedure between the suspect and the injured party. §2. The mediation procedure should not last longer than a month; its duration is not counted in the length of time of the preparatory proceedings. §3. The mediation procedure cannot be conducted by a person, to whom, in the specific case, the circumstances stated in art. 40 and 42 apply, by a professionally active judge, defending lawyer, legal counsellor, nor by applicants to these professions or other persons employed in the court, in the state prosecutor's office or in any other agency authorised to prosecute offences. §4. Having conducted the mediation procedure, a trustworthy agency or person shall prepare a report on its course and results. §5. The Ministry of Justice shall set forth, by ordinance, conditions to be met by agencies and persons authorised to conduct mediation, the method of appointing and removing them, the scope and terms of giving them access to the case files, as well as the manner and the course of the mediation procedure, keeping in mind the need of effective realisation of this procedure.

5   Not counting the mediation duration in the length of preparatory proceedings was introduced only in 2003; lack of such prescription in the first prescriptions of 1997 appeared to be one of the obstacles to applying mediation in practice.

response. The judge may set a time limit for the parties to complete the mediation and the Code indicates how the judge should proceed when the parties reach an agreement: it may lead to the discontinuation of the proceedings. In practice, mediation in proceedings involving private accusation is not very common (Niełaczna, 2007).

Some questions were left to be regulated by the Ministry of Justice, which was done in the Regulation of 14 August 1998. After amending it in June 2003[6] according to art. 23a §5 CCP, the scope of the Regulation became wider and included: conditions to be met by agencies and persons authorised to conduct mediation, method of appointing and removing them, the scope and terms of giving them access to the case files, as well as the manner and the course of the mediation procedure.

The law of 24 July 2003 has added art. 162 §1 to the Penal Executory Law (art. 1 p. 109), providing that when deciding on conditional release, the court must take the result of mediation into account.

The most recent ministerial draft of the CCP of 2007 proposes certain changes in respect to mediation. It guarantees the confidentiality of mediation and provides that a mediator cannot be questioned as a witness in court or by a prosecutor. Moreover, the protocol on mediation could contain only activities undertaken by the mediator, for example, concerning the date and place of meetings, and the presence of participants, but no comments are permitted regarding the parties' behaviour during the process.

As for juvenile offenders, the amendment of the Law on Juvenile Responsibility of 26 October 1982, adopted by the Parliament on 15 September 2000,[7] enables the family court at every stage of the proceedings, acting on the initiative of or on an agreement between the parties, to refer the case to mediation. The result of mediation is to be taken into consideration in passing the sentence (art. 3a §1 and 2).[8] Its scope is slightly wider than that of the regulation concerning mediation in adult offender cases. It also deals with certain norms and procedures for conducting mediation and the question of the obligatory training of mediators (including standards for training mediators). The regulation provides for the principle of impartiality (§6.3), voluntary participation (§11) and confidentiality (§12). It further provides for neutral venues for the mediation and guidance about the manner in which mediation should be conducted: two separate meetings with both sides and a 'face-to-face' meeting after they have agreed to proceed. Juveniles are represented by their parents, who, in Polish law, are their legal representatives. The regulation further requires the mediator to help the parties to formulate an agreement and to monitor its completion (Niełaczna, 2007).

---

6   Regulation of the Minister of Justice of 13 June 2003 on mediation proceedings in criminal cases, Journal of Laws of 26 June 2003, No. 108, item 1020.
7   Journal of Laws no. 91, item 1010.
8   §3 of art. 3a points out the questions to be regulated by the Minister of Justice; this was done in the Regulation of the Minister of Justice on mediation proceedings in juvenile cases of 18 May 2001, Journal of Laws no. 56, item 591.

1.2   Research: an overview

Even though the interest in mediation continues to grow, little research has been carried out. The first completed research concerned the abovementioned experimental programme of mediation in juvenile offender cases. It was carried out between 1997 and 1999 at the Institute of Law Studies of the Polish Academy of Sciences, by Professor Dobrochna Wójcik and Beata Czarnecka-Dzialuk, with the help primarily of mediators from the PCM and also of other collaborators, specially trained in interviewing and in examining court files. Results are available on several topics: profiles of juvenile offenders and their offences, the process of mediation (the course of mediation on the basis of participatory observation of mediators), evaluation of mediation by the parties and by the mediators, and recidivism. Research into the mediation programme was based on feedback from the mediators (a purpose-specific questionnaire), on surveys addressed to the juvenile offenders and the victims, as well as on the court files. The research was rather complex, therefore it is hard to classify it only as 'action-oriented' or 'evaluative'.

Another research project concerning VOM in adult cases was carried out in the Institute of Justice by the Ministry of Justice in 2001. Its main task was to examine the efficiency of mediation and its benefits for the justice system, procedural problems connected with mediation proceedings, the duration of mediation proceedings, fulfilment of the agreement, as well as to collect general information on the type of offences, offenders and victims. Judges were interviewed to gain additional information. The research was led by one person in the Institute (Professor Dobrochna Wójcik) with the help of two colleagues who examined the court files. Another research project on the practical implementation of mediation in adult and young offender cases is currently (2008) being led by judge Agnieszka-Rękas for her doctoral thesis. Its goals are to analyse whether the legal prescriptions are suitable and whether they are applied correctly in practice (in order to propose legislative changes); to examine the benefits of mediation for the parties as well as for the justice system (i.e. whether mediation allows for speeding up the proceedings); to examine the cost-effectiveness of mediation; and to compare the agreements with the final court decision about the case. Nearly 400 court files have been examined; the results have to be elaborated.

There are also other research projects carried out as part of master theses at various universities, which usually deal with small samples and only cover one or two problems. An additional source of information is offered by smaller research projects done by judges, public prosecutors and mediators that were published in the quarterly 'Mediator'.

2   DESCRIPTIVE-INVENTORY RESEARCH

2.1   Background

The preliminary evaluation of mediation during the first months of its existence was conducted at the Ministry of Justice on the basis of information collected from the Presidents of District Courts by Marzena Kruk.[9] Information was collected on the number of referrals, completed mediations and details about the agreements.[10] Since September 1998, statistical (court) data, based on the reports sent by the courts and collected by the Administration Department of the Ministry of Justice, contain the basic information relating to cases that were transferred to mediation. The data presented in the following paragraphs originate from these two sources.

2.2   Organisation of the services

As already mentioned, there are 14 mediation centres that are members of the PCM and three that are members of the Lower Silesian Mediation Centre (Dolnośląski Ośrodek Mediacji – DOM). The majority of the mediators in the country are not connected with any of these centres. They act independently, principally at their place of work or in the victims' or offenders' residence (initial meetings are conducted in the parties' residence and a face-to-face meeting generally in a neutral venue). As mentioned, the Family Diagnosis and Consultation Centres are authorised to conduct mediation in juvenile cases. Other services may deal with adult as well as with youth offenders.

The services/mediators may act at any stage of the proceedings in the case of youth offenders (also after sentencing). In adult cases they may act at the level of the prosecutor or a judge/court. Since 2003, the Penal Executory Code mentions in art.162 that when deciding on conditional release, the result of mediation is to be taken into account, but it does not mean that mediation after sentencing is accepted: officials from the Ministry of Justice and from the Headquarters of the Prison Service understand that the legislator referred to mediation that was carried out before the sentence. There were, however, some cases of mediation after sentencing carried out on an experimental basis. It has been indicated that mediation could be used as an element in programmes of integration (Niełaczna, 2007).[11]

The mediation services are run by private organisations (NGOs). Neither the mediation centres nor the mediators are formally related to the justice system. Employees of the justice system (including probation officers) are not allowed to be mediators (art. 23a §4 CCP).

---

9   Who was then responsible for mediation matters at the Ministry of Justice.
10   The results have been published in Kruk, 1999; Waluk and Kruk, 2001; and Kruk, 2000.
11   Art. 89 §1 and 2, Art. 95, The Penal Executory Code.

Referrals in adult cases in practice mostly come from the court and only some of them from the public prosecutors. In juvenile cases, it is the family court or a family judge that decides on the referral. Since 2003, the police may also refer cases for mediation. No data are available on how often these possibilities are being used.

The actual meeting between parties is facilitated by volunteer mediators, i.e. mediators who are undertaking the mediation work in addition to their daily professional activities. Among mediators, the professions represented the most are teachers and schoolmasters (36.2%), psychologists (17.5%), jurists (but not practising in the legal professions – art. 23a §4 CCP) (12.7%).

The services are funded by different sponsors in specific towns – either NGOs or private foundations – and some expenses are often covered by local authorities. Good practice standards are elaborated by the PCM and complaint procedures are foreseen for members of the PCM through a special arbitration commission. Legal provisions concerning mediation in adult cases do not require trained mediators, unlike the provisions concerning mediation in juvenile cases. According to the Regulation of the Minister of Justice of 18 May 2001, the training consists of theoretical as well as practical topics. The scope of topics is defined by the Regulation which also defines requirements concerning institutions and persons that lead the training. The first 5-day training session was organised in mid-1995 by the Committee for Introducing Mediation in Poland (now the PCM) with the help of the German Heinrich Böll Foundation from Cologne. The trainers for the first course were specialists from Germany and from the Polish Negotiation Centre. Later on, the PCM started to organise training sessions itself. About 700 mediators have completed those PCM training sessions. There were also second-level training sessions for receiving the certificate as well as special 'training of trainers' initiatives. The group of 16 trained mediators have started to teach. There were also training courses on mediation that last a few days, organised by the Helsinki Foundation for Human Rights with the help of American expert Bill Lincoln, and organised by DOM with the help of the PCM.

2.3   Mediation practice

The regulation of the selection of mediators in adult offender cases is not satisfactory in some regards. The abovementioned Regulation of the Minister of Justice contains certain conditions for being a mediator: he or she must be over 26 years of age; have no criminal record; and have Polish citizenship, proper life experience, the ability to solve conflicts, the knowledge needed for handling mediation, especially in the field of psychology, education, sociology, re-socialisation and the law. There is no formal requirement to complete any training to become a mediator in adult offender cases. Only in juvenile cases is there a formal requirement to complete special training according to the Regulation of 18 May 2001 mentioned above. However, initial and ongoing training, support and some supervision are the normal practice of some organisations.

The referrals in adult cases come mostly from the courts, at the stage of preparing the trial, while the public prosecutors rarely use the possibility to refer the case before they apply to the court for a particular disposal. There are no self-referrals, but the parties may apply to the public prosecutors or to the court to refer their case to mediation. The requirement of the CCP is formulated in such a way that it appeared to be necessary for the referring agency to obtain the consent of the parties before referring the case to mediation (which means they need to be heard and have this option explained to them, which may prolong the proceedings and which is often perceived as an additional complication). The mediator will inform victims and offenders about mediation and of their rights and will ask whether they agree to take part in mediation.

The regulation on mediation in juvenile cases as well as the one on mediation in adult cases lay down the sequence of the phases of mediation by specifying what the mediator has to do: obtain certain information from the court files, contact the parties, organise separate preliminary meetings with victims and offenders and the face-to-face meeting (according to regulations, indirect mediation is allowed but it happens very seldom in practice), then monitor the fulfilment of the agreement if it was concluded and write the report for the court on the mediation proceedings and its results.

The regulation delineates the responsibilities of mediators, particularly informing all participants of the voluntary aspect of mediation, as well as the presentation of the essence and the rules of mediation, and the roles and rights of the parties participating in mediation.

As for the contents of VOM, the material harm and financial aspects of the cases are not primary concerns, and as the research concerning mediation in juvenile cases has proven, the emotions are really important. The agreement – in juvenile as well as in adult offender cases – must be in writing. It has to contain the essence of the agreement, the timeframe of fulfilment and it must be signed by the victim and the offender (and if they are under 18 also by the parents). The mediator signs the agreement as well and later checks whether the agreement is fulfilled and informs the referring agency. There is no regular follow-up. The result of mediation is to be taken into account by the referring agency: if it is the public prosecutor they may submit an application to the court, for example for conditional discontinuation of the proceedings. The court should take the result of mediation into account when deciding about the case: its discontinuance or exceptional mitigation if a penalty is imposed.

As there is no clear system of collecting data about mediation cases, the numbers reported by the courts in the court statistics and by the judges to the Ministry of Justice differ: the numbers in the court statistics are a bit lower. According to the data collected by the Ministry, the number of adult offender cases that were referred to mediation by the courts has increased from 366 in 1999 to 5,052 in

2006.[12] The rate of agreement for the whole period 1999-2006 is about 60%. The public prosecutors in the first years referred few cases to mediation, but this number increased as well, namely from only 42 in 1999 to 1,447 cases in 2006.[13] It should be noted that the rate of agreement is very high, higher than in the cases directed to mediation by the court: in 1999 it was 80%, in 2002 up to 88%, while in 2006 it amounted to 78%.

The most frequent feature in an agreement (according to the court statistics) is an apology: its rate rose from over 30% in the first years up to 49% in 2002, and thereafter remained around 45%. Then there are 'various forms' (e.g. obligation to certain behaviour) that rose from 26% in 1999 to 46.5% in 2002 and in 2006 it consisted of about 30%. The percentage of financial restitution for the victim has changed from 27.3% in 1999 to 34.3% in 2000 and went down to 13.4% in 2006. The percentage of payments for some social purpose was 5% in 1999, 8.6% in 2003 and in 2006 it went down to 3.1%. Community work or for the benefit of the victim was only marginally present in agreements (about 1% each) (Kruk, 2007). Although the family court judges showed interest in mediation at the time of the experimental programme, the number of mediations in cases of juvenile offenders is low after mediation was introduced in the youth law. In 1999, 50 cases were referred to mediation and in 37 of these an agreement was reached. In 2000 there were 63 cases with 49 agreements, and in 2001 there were 42 cases and only 29 were completed (with agreements in 19 cases). In 2002 there were 42 cases, but in 2003 already 145 and in 2006 cases raised up to 366. The percentage of agreements was high; in 2006 it was about 80%.

In the first years nearly half of the mediations in juvenile offender cases were conducted at the Family Diagnostic and Consultation Centres, but in 2003 there were 37 cases mediated there, whereas for that year 108 were led by mediation centres and individual mediators.

Obstacles to developing mediation practice include lack of financial resources (the remuneration the mediators receive per case is rather low) and the lack of mediators who meet the requirements concerning training contained in the regulation. Even if numerous persons have already been trained in a suitable manner, some procedures for certification are needed. The issue was raised that, while introducing mediation in Poland, not enough care was given to creating organisational circumstances nor for preparing criminal justice practitioners and society to make use of it (Rękas, 2003). Incomplete and unsuitable regulations discourage and hamper prosecutors and judges from the use of mediation in criminal proceedings. The legislator's failure to address such matters as definition or statement of purpose of mediation, the principles of mediation and a lack of legal guarantees in order to respect the rules of mediation or requirements of the special training for mediators generated many difficulties in the implementation and further practice of mediation (Niełaczna, 2007).

---

12   723 cases in 2000; 800 in 2001; 929 in 2002; 1,838 in 2003; 3,569 in 2004 and 4,440 in 2005.
13   211 cases in 2004 and 721 in 2005.

3   THE FIRST EXPERIMENTAL PROGRAMME OF MEDIATION IN JUVENILE
     CASES: EVALUATIVE AND ACTION-ORIENTED RESEARCH

3.1   Background information

The aims of this research project were to provide information for the youth law reform; to enable the mediation programme to be verified and improved before it was introduced to all Polish family courts; to gain experience that would help to develop more adequate guidelines for mediation of criminal cases involving adults; and to estimate the possible role of mediation within, or as an alternative to the justice system.

Methods of evaluation were: on the one hand, collecting data concerning mediation proceedings, characteristics of offences, offenders, victims and mediation outcomes (using court files); on the other hand, interviews with mediators and participants in order to receive feedback.[14] The research was carried out from July 1997 to the end of 1999. It was made possible through a grant allocated by the National Committee for Scientific Research and was directed by the Institute of Law Studies of the Polish Academy of Sciences.

The policy context in particular included seeking new methods of dealing with youth offenders and introducing these methods into the youth law, as a revised law was being prepared at the time. Ministry of Justice officials took part in discussions on the experimental mediation programme and were kept informed about the preliminary results of the research.

Partners in the research were mediators from the PCM and mediation participants. The report was published in a book in Polish, with an English summary (Czarnecka-Dzialuk and Wójcik, 2001). The team who conducted the research consisted of two researchers (full-time positions), mediators and collaborators (students and PCM volunteers) trained in interviewing. There were regular meetings of the whole team (mediators, researchers and also judges taking part in the experimental programme of mediation) in order to discuss current problems. As a result, the research was expanded to include more complicated cases (more serious offences, cases with many parties and many punishable acts) and to be conducted in three additional family courts in order to get more cases and to use the interest of local self-government, judges, communities and mediators. It was observed during the research that the judges taking part in the experiment influenced other judges, and that victims and offenders even applied to have their cases submitted to mediation.

At the same time, some members of the research team took part in legislative work on the regulation regarding mediation, using the research results as arguments in the discussions on the draft provisions. Attention was focused on implementing the standards of mediation, especially using the late 1990s draft Council

---

14   The research was drafted as a part of the experimental programme of mediation in juvenile cases. The character of the research was in fact more complex, including elements of both action-oriented and evaluative research.

of Europe Recommendation concerning Mediation in Penal Matters, presented by experts in Poland at a seminar co-organised with the Council of Europe.

3.2   The results of the research

3.2.1   Profile of the cases

First, some data should be presented concerning the profile of the offenders and their acts. The majority had committed property offences (66.5%) and a further 31% committed personal crimes. Most of them were not grave acts and some could be classified as 'very petty' cases that would probably have been dropped by the judge anyway. However, there were also felonies which were very serious in terms of degree or type of violence, their deliberate nature and influence of alcohol. The sample consisted of 174 juveniles.

It was found that the number of violent offenders among the juveniles referred to mediation was significantly higher than among the total population of juvenile offenders and that young females were significantly more likely to perpetrate acts against the person, such as light bodily injury, violation of personal inviolability (by striking or in another manner – shoving, pushing), participation in a fight or beating or threats. The girls were also more likely to show indifference to the victims than the boys. In approximately one-fifth of the cases some negative factors coincided (showing symptoms of social dysfunction, alcohol or other intoxicants, aggressive behaviour, dropping out of the school system, dysfunctional families), which may impede the juveniles' adaptation to society and may be conducive to their return to criminality.

Among victims, the number of males was three times higher than that of females, and in 12 cases an institution was victimised. The victims of male juveniles were more frequently males (of whom approximately 50% were minors), while those of female offenders were mainly females who were usually their peers. The research did not lend support to the contention that mediation was more – or less – likely to be successful when there was a relationship between the offender and a victim.

3.2.2   Mediator's view on mediation

The feedback from the mediators provided insight into the mediation process. Mediators emphasised the emotional aspect of mediation. The intensity of emotions was similar for both parties (an average level for about 60% of the participants and a high level for 20%; the rest expressed no clear emotions). The types of emotions differed: the most frequently reported emotions of the victims included anger (25%), anxiety (20%), fear of the offender (10%) and a deep sense of harm (13.5%). The offenders experienced anxiety (33%), fear and concern about the decision of the family court (22%), shame (25.5%) and anger (only 2.6%). As a rule, the emotional intensity subsided towards the end of the face-to-face meeting.

The mediators reported that the vast majority of the offenders (nearly 93%) and victims (over 72%) did not show hostility, aggressiveness or (verbal) domination over the other party. About 4% of offenders and 9% of victims did show hostility and aggressiveness, and an attempt at dominating the other party was made by about 3% of offenders and nearly 19% of victims (usually the adult victims).[15] In the opinion of the mediators, the attitudes of parents who participated in mediation and their cooperation with mediation were in most cases appropriate. However, some of them were inclined to whitewash the behaviour of their children or dominate them and did not allow them to play an autonomous role in mediation.

3.2.3   Participants' view

Nearly one-third of victims reported that it was important that the offender should apologise to them and show regret. For over 13%, it was important just to meet the offender and to deal with the conflict that occurred between them. Thus, the moral redress was no less important than the compensation for material damage, indicated as the most important by one out of four of the victims.

Fifty-eight percent of victims stated that the experience of mediation had changed their opinion of criminality and the family court. Ninety percent of them expressed satisfaction with their participation in mediation as well as with the performance of the agreement. Similarly, the juvenile offenders changed their attitudes towards the victims (65%) and no longer thought that all the victim wanted was to take revenge. They also understood that their act had caused harm. Ninety-five percent of the youth offenders expressed their satisfaction with their participation in mediation as well as with the agreement. As for the merits of taking part in mediation, for over 34% of juveniles the most important element was avoiding a court trial; for about 22% that the case was definitively ended; and nearly 13% thought that they had avoided a worse sanction, whereas 14.5% of juveniles stated that they had 'learned something' and that they would not re-offend. Nearly 13% saw peacemaking with the victim as having merit.

3.2.4   Results of the mediation process

The results of mediation are the following: of all 174 offenders, 29 (16.7%) did not take part in mediation. The most frequent reason was the lack of consent from the parents of victimised children (9 cases); a further four adult victims did not agree to take part in mediation. In eight cases the parties failed to turn up for the mediation session despite repeated invitations from the mediator.

Of the total of 145 juveniles who took part in mediation, 137 (92.5%) negotiated and accepted the terms of compensation, however seven of them failed to perform the accepted obligation. One hundred and thirty youth offenders (94.9% of those who had signed the agreement) did satisfy their terms. For eight juveniles an agreement could not be reached. In one-third of cases, the agreement consisted of apologies to the victim, 57.8% of juveniles made financial reparation and 10% performed various services for the benefit of their victims.

The most frequent decision of the family court was to discontinue the case (87.9%). With respect to 6.8% of juveniles the following educational measures were applied: admonition, parental supervision, supervision by the probation officer and in one case placement in a correctional institution. It was decided

---

15   All these figures are based on the questionnaires filled out by mediators.

not to start proceedings against 5.3% juveniles. Regarding re-offending, 14.4% of offenders stood trial in the follow-up period (at least one year to 2.5 years after completion of the mediation process). This ratio is not high compared to the results of other studies on traditional measures that were carried out earlier: in those studies the percentage of juveniles whose criminal cases had been discontinued and who were later convicted reached 22.3% (Kołakowska-Przełomiec and Wójcik, 1990: 151). The repeat offenders were more likely to come from dysfunctional families and showed signs of social dysfunction.

4 MEDIATION IN ADULT CASES: EVALUATIVE RESEARCH

4.1 Research sample

The research on mediation in adult cases is of a qualitative nature. All cases transferred to mediation in 1999 were examined (about 350 court files). A group of judges, both those who have referred cases to mediation and those who have not, were interviewed.[16] Recidivism was examined, defined on the basis of new convictions.

The research started in mid-2000. It was drafted in the Institute of Justice and was paid from its budget. The results were to be presented to the Ministry of Justice. Marzena Kruk and Professor Dobrochna Wójcik led the research, with the help of two experienced collaborators. As far as the methodological problems are concerned, the most important was data protection, which is an obstacle for the researcher when contacting the mediation parties.

Its results were published in autumn 2004 (Kruk and Wójcik, 2004). The research results show the variety of the types of offences. However, the cases most frequently referred to mediation were those of offences against family and guardianship (36.6%, namely ill-treatment of family members (28.8%) and nonpayment of support (7.6%), followed by offences against life and health (21.9%, and half of them were beatings and taking part in assaults and causing serious harm). Only 14.1% of the cases were property offences. Furthermore, 13.8% of the cases consisted of offences against honour and personal inviolability and 9.2% against individual autonomy and sexual abuse.

Cases referred to mediation in 1999 did not reflect the general structure of convictions according to type of offence. The same tendency of over-representation of certain cases compared to similar cases convicted in court was observed while analysing court statistics in 2002: 34% of the referred cases are offences against family and guardianship. There are also more cases of offences against life and health (26.6%) and against individual autonomy (16.9%). Furthermore, there is a decrease of cases of property offences (to 10.1%), indicating an under-representation of these cases.

---

16 The plan was to interview the parties to mediation also, but technical possibilities were lacking.

4.2   The mediation process

As far as the mediation process is concerned, the research results show that mediators in 1999 did not have enough knowledge about all aspects of mediation, so in many cases there were some discrepancies with principles and rules of mediation mentioned in international documents. For example, only in about 31% of cases preparatory meetings were held separately with the parties followed by face-to-face meetings; in the remaining nearly 70% either a preparatory meeting or a face-to-face meeting were not conducted. It was assumed that only in half of the cases mediation was conducted in a proper (i.e. a safe, neutral and comfortable) place: 38.4% of cases took place in the mediation centre; 14.0% took place in the court; 14.0% at parties' home; 2.8% in the mediator's flat; and 30.8% in other places, mainly at the mediator's work place.

4.3   Mediation results

Despite these imperfections in the mediation method, the results of the mediation proceedings were quite good. For 347 examined files, an agreement was signed in 228 cases (65.7%). In 56 cases (16.1%) the mediation was not conducted, mostly because one or both parties did not show up at the proposed meeting (without giving the reason). In 61 cases (17.6%), the mediation did not result in an agreement.[17]
The terms of agreement were most often apology: apology only in 17.5% of 228 cases which ended in an agreement; apology and payment in 38.6% of cases; apology and obligation to therapy in 11.1% of the cases; and a combination of different obligations in 32.9% of the cases.
Most often court's decisions were: conditional discontinuance of the proceedings (36.3%); termination of the proceedings (23.8%); suspended sentence of deprivation of liberty (23.5%); and a fine (5.5%). Court's decisions after mediation were evidently more lenient when the mediation resulted in an agreement.
The reconviction rate in respect to cases submitted to mediation was not high: 21.4% of perpetrators were reconvicted up to year 2002. The period to examine the reconviction rate after sentence was much longer than in the official statistics. According to the statistics, the general rate of reconviction of all adult offenders was, at that time, about 30%.

4.4   Judges' views

The interviews with the judges were done in 2004 by the Institute of Justice. The goal of this research was to examine the interest of judges in mediation; the level of their knowledge about its idea, rules and principles; the assessment of its usefulness; and their opinion on modification of existing legal prescriptions, bearing in mind their deficiency and generality. The respondents were either judges

---

17   In two cases, no data were available on the mediation results.

that directed cases to mediation in 2003 (101 judges, this group was called M+), or belonged to the group of those who did not refer cases (203 judges, called M-). Both groups were not differentiated by factors such as age and sex, but those who worked in the criminal court for less than five years significantly rarely directed cases to mediation. The vast majority of judges from both groups had knowledge of the legal regulations on mediation (90 and 80% respectively). However those who had more information on mediation through publications, conferences and discussions, referred cases to mediation more often than the others. The general attitude towards mediation differs per group: 76.6% of M+ judges accepted mediation and only 47.4% of those from M- group. In the latter, 1/5 partially accepted mediation and 1/3 did not like mediation at all.

When asked about the reasons for not directing cases to mediation, the judges from each group answered differently. Those who never directed cases to mediation stated that mediation prolongs the proceedings; it is inefficient and parties are not interested; there is a lack of mediators and a lack of cases suitable for mediation; and there are no clear legal regulations. Judges from the other group (M+) indicated more concrete reasons, such as the lack of the parties' consent to take part in mediation; their absence on the proposed meetings; long distances from the parties' residence; or the lack of mediators.

A similar difference could be found regarding the question of what should be done to make the criminal justice practitioners interested in mediation. Respondents from the M+ group talked about the necessity of advertising the benefits of mediation in society, of informing the parties about the possibility of mediation and only 10% suggested changing legal regulations. Also 10% of those belonging to the M- group suggested such changes, but 40% had no idea how to increase the use of mediation.

5   CONCLUSION

Summarising the research results, it should be stressed that the research on mediation in youth and adults cases proves that mediation is highly effective: an agreement was reached in over 60% of adult cases and in nearly 80% of the youth cases; over 90% of agreements were carried out in youth cases.

The fact that mediation functions outside the justice system, although in close collaboration with it, should be regarded favourably (for instance, this external position makes it easier to explain to the parties the principles of voluntariness of mediation and neutrality of the mediator). However, mechanisms of substantive supervision over those organisations and mediators should be put in place.

There is a need to conduct continuous research. Especially important would be evaluative research to examine whether the practice complies with the legal regulations and whether the legal regulations are in line with good practice. Furthermore, the question arises whether the mediation practice follows the acknowledged rules and recommendations.

The basic problems include a lack of financial resources and the issue of data protection, which is an obstacle for the researchers regarding contacting the mediation parties.

There further is a need to design a functional documentation system that would collect more detailed data concerning mediation proceedings. The question then arises as to what information should be included and who should collect these data.

Last but not least, there is still a lack of theoretical research on the concept of restorative justice. Maybe this is not the priority, as it seems more urgent to analyse and solve practical problems, but still this gap in theoretical research should be taken into account.

REFERENCES

Czarnecka-Dzialuk, B. and Wójcik, D. (2001) *Mediacja w sprawach nieletnich w świetle teorii i badań* (Warsaw: Typografika).

Kołakowska-Przełomiec, H. and Wójcik, D. (1990) *Selekcja nieletnich przestępców w sądach rodzinnych* (Warszawa, Ossolineum).

Kruk, M. (1999), 'Jak funkcjonuje w Polsce instytucja mediacji między poszkodowanym a młodocianym i dorosłym przestępcą', *Mediator,* 10 (2/99), p. 8.

Kruk, M. (2000), 'Pierwsze doświadczenia mediacji pomiędzy ofiarą i sprawcą przestępstwa', *Palestra,* 4, p. 158.

Kruk, M. (2007), *Funkcjonowanie instytucji mediacji w sprawach karnych w Polsce. Analiza kryminologiczna*, doctoral thesis (Warsaw: library of the Institute of Law Studies of the Polish Academy of Sciences).

Kruk, M. and Wójcik, D. (2004), *Postępowanie mediacyjne w sprawach karnych. Wyniki badań empirycznych* (Warszawa: Instytut Wymiaru Sprawiedliwości).

Niełaczna, M. (2007), *The mediation and restorative justice movement in Poland*, unpublished (Warsaw).

Rękas, A. (2003) 'Mediacja w praktyce wymiaru sprawiedliwości – szanse i zagrożenia', in *Konferencja naukowa: Mediacja w polskiej rzeczywistości* (Warszawa: Biuro Rzecznika Praw Obywatelskich).

Waluk, J. and Kruk, M. (2001) 'Problemy wprowadzania mediacji w Polsce. Mediacja w prawie karnym – pierwsze doświadczenia', in Senat Rzeczypospolitej Polskiej (eds.) *Probacyjne środki polityki karnej – stan i perspektywy* (Warsaw: Dział Wydawniczy Kancelarii Senatu), pp. 279-290.

11 Variations on a theme

Empirical research on restorative justice in England and Wales

James Dignan

1 INTRODUCTION: PUTTING RESTORATIVE JUSTICE RESEARCH IN CONTEXT[1]

The task of providing an overview of restorative justice [RJ] research in the United Kingdom presents a major challenge, which results from two main sources of complexity. The first relates to the multiplicity of legal jurisdictions that co-exist as separate entities within the territory of the United Kingdom itself. Constitutionally, the United Kingdom comprises four separate countries: England, Wales, Scotland and Northern Ireland. Legally, three almost entirely separate legal jurisdictions operate within the territory of the United Kingdom since, although England and Wales share the same law and legal procedures, both Scotland and Northern Ireland have retained their own separate legal systems. As a result, there are important differences between the adult and youth justice systems that operate in the three principal jurisdictions. For the purpose of this paper, the main focus is on RJ research in England and Wales.[2]

A second source of complexity relates to the changing policy context within which RJ initiatives operate within each of these jurisdictions, which has had important implications both for the kind of empirical research that has been undertaken, and also its desirability in the eyes of potential funders. Very briefly, when the earliest RJ initiatives were introduced in England during the mid-1980s, there was a strong emphasis on the need to divert offenders away from prosecution and also imprisonment. This 'minimum intervention' philosophy enjoyed strong support not only from criminal justice practitioners (especially those working with young offenders) but also (for rather different reasons) from the government of the day. Since the mid-1990s, however, this approach has been eclipsed by a much more interventionist philosophy in which the primary aim is to take effective action early on in order to prevent offending and re-offending. This has been referred to as a policy of 'neo-correctionalism' (Pitts, 1999; Cavadino and Dignan, 2006). Official attitudes towards RJ have also shifted radically over this period. During

---

1 This chapter draws on two previous reports: Dignan and Lowey (2000) and Bottoms and Dignan (2004). The chapter was completed in 2004 in response to an earlier deadline, and has been subject to further relatively minor updating during October 2007 to briefly take account of subsequent developments in preparation for this volume.

2 See Dignan (2007a) for a brief overview of the various different ways in which RJ processes have been used in England and Wales, Scotland and Northern Ireland.

the mid-1980s they could best be described as lukewarm and sceptical, but since the mid-1990s, as we shall see, elements of an RJ approach have been adopted as a significant, albeit subordinate, part of the developing neo-correctionalist strategy (since the latter's primary focus is on the prevention of offending). Moreover, in July 2003, the government published a consultation document in which it set out its plans to extend the use of RJ interventions at various stages within the criminal justice (Home Office, 2003).[3]

1.1   Legislative context: stand-alone initiatives

Not surprisingly, this changing policy context has also affected the legislative context within which RJ initiatives have to operate. When they were first introduced in the mid-1980s, there was no specific legal basis or framework within which they might operate. But equally, there was nothing to stop interested practitioners working in juvenile justice teams or within agencies, like the probation service or the police, from adopting new procedures or techniques, often involving North American style victim-offender mediation [VOM] or the negotiation of reparative outcomes. This resulted in a short-term proliferation of *ad hoc* local initiatives, most of which were small-scale, experimental projects. Most were not in any way integrated within the mainstream criminal justice system, but co-existed, often rather precariously, on its margins, and are therefore best described as 'stand-alone' initiatives. Some of these early VOM and reparation schemes received short-term financial support from the Home Office (see for details, Davis et al., 1989; Marshall and Merry, 1990; Davis, 1992), and a number of evaluations date from this era, as we shall see in Section 2.

One group of projects (mostly focusing on juvenile offenders) operated at the pre-court stage, often in conjunction with a police caution, as an alternative to prosecution. Most schemes of this type were concerned with juvenile offenders only, but one – the Kettering Adult Reparation Bureau – was devised for adult and young adult offenders and, after a successful pilot in the midlands town of Kettering (see Dignan, 1991, 1992), was extended to the entire county of Northamptonshire.[4] A second group of projects was court-based, and either operated on adjournment between conviction and sentence or offered mediation and/or reparation as part of a sentence. In addition, a very small number of projects[5] accepted referrals at all stages of the criminal justice process from caution to post-sentence, including the

---

3   Key elements in the strategy include the introduction of conditional cautions for adult offenders, promoting the development of restorative cautioning (see below), making reparation an additional purpose of sentencing and promoting the development of RJ initiatives within both youth and adult criminal justice systems. The commissioning of further research to test and evaluate the use of RJ as both a diversionary measure, and also in connection with sentencing disposals forms, another key part of the strategy.

4   See also Hughes et al. (1995) for a more general discussion of the diversionary context in which the Unit operated during the early 1990s.

5   The best known of which was the Leeds Victim-Offender Unit, previously known as the Leeds Mediation and Reparation Scheme (see Wynne, 1996).

period prior to an imprisoned offender being released from custody. Moreover, the use of mediation has not been confined to the criminal sphere as it has also been extensively adopted as means of dealing with a wide variety of other disputes between neighbours or those living within the same neighbourhood.[6]

The experience with New Zealand-style family group conferencing has been rather more limited to date, at least within an English criminal justice context. Once again most such projects have operated on a small-scale stand-alone basis since the late 1980s. The early experience with this type of approach has largely echoed that of the early mediation and reparation projects, with most schemes operating experimentally on the margins of the regular criminal justice system. Again as with VOM, however, the family group conferencing approach has also been adopted more widely, in this case within a child protection setting, where it has become established on a somewhat more secure footing (see Challiner et al., 2000; Dignan and Marsh, 2001).

A third form of RJ process that also deserves a mention within the context of 'stand-alone' initiatives relates to the adoption of an Australian variant of the conferencing approach. This police-led conferencing model was originally pioneered in Wagga Wagga in New South Wales, and because of this is sometimes referred to as the 'Wagga' model, though it has subsequently spread to a number of other Australian jurisdictions – notably Canberra and Sydney – and also the United States, and Canada. Within England, the Thames Valley police force,[7] which covers the English counties of Oxfordshire, Berkshire and Buckinghamshire, began to introduce the 'scripted conferencing' model in the mid-1990s (see Pollard, 2000; Young, 2001) as the standard way of dealing with 'low tariff' offences that would previously have been dealt with by means of a police caution. Following the election of the 'New Labour' government in 1997, the Thames Valley approach attracted the interest of the government and, as we shall see, has subsequently influenced the development of some of the more recent 'mainstream' RJ initiatives in England and Wales.

Prior to 1997, the attitude of successive English governments towards most of these early RJ initiatives could at best be described as agnostic, following a brief flurry of interest during the mid-1980s when short-term funding was provided for a small number of schemes and also for their evaluation. This sceptical approach inhibited the development of RJ, particularly in comparison with some other common law jurisdictions, notably New Zealand and some Australian states. In 1997, however, there was a change of government, and the Labour Party – after eighteen years in opposition – embarked on a programme of radical reform, particularly with regard to the youth justice system (see for details Bottoms and

---

6   Although this particular aspect of the topic lies beyond the scope of this paper, the use of mediation in the context of neighbour disputes, together with the findings of an empirical evaluation are described in Dignan et al. (1996). Another field in which RJ approaches have been attempted is in responding to bullying and conflict management in schools, an evaluation of which was undertaken by the Youth Justice Board (2004).

7   A small number of other police forces in England and Wales adopted the same model soon afterwards, but the Thames Valley initiative was the first and remains the best known.

Dignan, 2004; Dignan, 2007a, 2007b) but also embracing many aspects of the adult criminal justice system.

1.2 Legislative context: 'mainstream' initiatives

The most important changes in the present context involved the introduction of a number of key elements of an RJ approach as part of the mainstream response to youth justice offending in England and Wales. Initiatives that were intended to 'mainstream' RJ approaches to youth offending focused on three distinct phases of the criminal justice process: pre-prosecution; at first conviction; and as a sentencing option for offenders who are punished following a second or subsequent conviction. The reforms involved significant changes to the legislative framework within which RJ initiatives now operate and were brought about principally by the Crime and Disorder Act 1998 and the Youth Justice and Criminal Evidence Act 1999. Moreover, important changes were also made to the non-statutory guidelines regulating pre-prosecution warnings that are administered by the police (Home Office/Youth Justice Board, 2002).

A simplified flow chart of the current English youth justice system is provided in Figure 1,[8] though this account will only deal with those aspects that allow RJ interventions to operate as mainstream initiatives within the youth justice process. Under the pre-1998 youth justice system, the main pre-court alternative to prosecution consisted of a non-statutory cautioning system that applied to both young and adult offenders. This was a fairly permissive[9] and explicitly diversionary system, though formal cautions were citable in court in the event of any later proceedings. With regard to young offenders under the age of 18, however, this old-style cautioning system has been replaced by a much more restrictive statutory regime in which a young offender who fails to desist can normally expect at best[10] to receive a single 'reprimand' and then a 'final warning', followed by prosecution.

---

8   The flow chart is taken from Cavadino and Dignan (2007). Interventions that provide scope for RJ approaches to operate as mainstream interventions are shown in italics, and these alone are described here.

9   The cautioning system was regulated by non-statutory guidelines issued by the Home Office. Although the guidelines were amended in 1994 in an attempt to discourage the practice of 'repeat' cautioning and cautioning inappropriately (e.g. for very serious offences), the system still afforded considerable discretion to the police.

10   Though if an offence is sufficiently serious it may result in a prosecution without going through any intermediate procedures.

Figure 1   The English youth justice system in outline

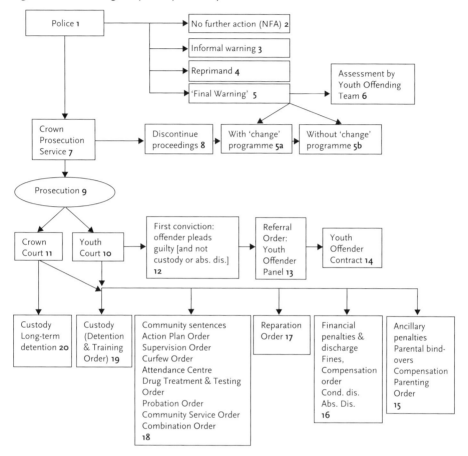

Under the new system, the reprimand (Box 4) is a formal oral warning that is intended to be issued by a police officer to a first time juvenile offender provided the offence is minor and the juvenile is judged to have only a low risk of further offending. Only a single reprimand may be delivered in respect of a particular offender, which means that any further offence should be followed by either a final warning or a prosecution, depending on the seriousness of the offence and the perceived risk of further offending.

The final warning is intended to provide a fast and more effective response to early offending behaviour, and to ensure that appropriate action is taken at this early stage to confront the young person with their offending behaviour. Where an offender is to be issued with a final warning (Box 5), the police are required to refer the case to the local youth offending team (Box 6),[11] which in turn is expected to assess the offender's suitability for a compulsory 'rehabilitation' or 'change' programme (Boxes 5a and 5b). The principal aim of this programme is to confront and address the offender's behaviour.

With regard to the delivery of reprimands and final warnings, the official guidance (Home Office/Youth Justice Board, 2002) endorses, and indeed strongly encourages, the use of restorative processes, where appropriate, based on experience gained in the Thames Valley police area. One option that is endorsed – termed a 'restorative warning' – includes the involvement of a young offender's parents and any other influential adult where appropriate, and seeks to ensure that the victim's views are also conveyed. The second main option, termed restorative meeting or conference, includes the presence and direct participation of the victim and, possibly also, the victim's supporter(s).

The second phase of the criminal justice process at which the possibility for undertaking RJ initiatives has been introduced is at the point of first conviction. Here, a radically different procedure was introduced for young offenders who are prosecuted for the first time, who plead guilty as charged when they appear in the youth court, and who in the opinion of the court should not receive either a custodial sentence or an absolute discharge (both of which disposals are rare for first-time defendants). In such circumstances the youth court is now normally obliged to deal with the case by passing a sentence known as a 'referral order'. This order requires the young offender to attend a meeting of the 'youth offender panel' or 'YOP' (Box 13); the length of the order is specified by the court at the time of the referral to the YOP, and can last from three to twelve months.

The YOP is convened by the local youth offending team (YOT), which also supplies one member of the three-person YOP panel, the other two being lay persons drawn from an approved list. In addition to the offender and his/her parents, any victim of the offence may also be invited (but not obliged) to attend the panel meeting, the purpose of which is to conclude a contractual agreement (Box 14) binding the young offender to an agreed 'programme of behaviour' for the duration of the referral order. The aim of this programme must be the prevention of re-offending. If no agreement can be reached, or a contract is made but subsequently breached, the young offender will be returned to court to be sentenced for the original offence. If an agreement is reached, however, the panel is responsible for monitoring it and, provided the offender complies with it, the referral order is then discharged.

The aims of the referral order procedure are strongly influenced by RJ thinking in four important respects. First, the decision-making process itself is intended to be both inclusionary and party-centred, in order to encourage and facilitate participation by those most directly involved in the offence and its consequences. This is also reflected in the adoption of a 'quasi-conferencing' model in place

---

11   Youth offending teams were established in 1998 as multi-agency bodies comprising representatives from police, probation, social services, health and education.

of the traditional adversarial judicial decision-making model. Second, the decision-making forum is community-based and has involved the recruitment and training of a new cohort of volunteer 'community representatives'.[12] Third, both the process itself and also its outcomes are intended to be 'restorative'. This is reflected firstly in the provision of a forum in which the views and wishes of victims can be articulated (whether directly or indirectly) and addressed; and secondly in the expectation that offenders will undertake some form of reparation to either the victim or the community. Fourth, there is also a strong emphasis on the importance of 'reintegrating' offenders back into the community by the time the process is concluded. For where an offender successfully completes the programme, the referral order is discharged when the offender is 'signed off'. This has the effect of 'purging' the offender of the offence (which is then considered spent).

Finally, elements of the RJ approach also feature in a number of the sentencing options that are available to youth courts, including reparation orders (Box 17), action plan orders, and as an additional condition that may be attached to a supervision order (Box 18). The emphasis, in all of these measures, is on making offenders accountable for what they have done by requiring them to undertake some form of reparation for either their victim or the community. However, the Crime and Disorder Act also stipulates that before any reparative interventions – of whatever kind – are imposed, the views of the victims should be sought and relayed to the court. And offenders can only be ordered to make direct reparation to victims who have consented to this (which amounts, in effect, to a limited veto). As for the content of any reparative interventions, the main emphasis is on practical reparative activities[13] that should, if possible, be related to the offence, and also letters of apology, though there is also scope for VOM to take place.

There are a number of other broadly reparative penalties available to the courts, including community service[14] and compensation orders, but these are not included in this paper because they do not involve any kind of restorative decision-making process since they are imposed on offenders by the court when passing sentence in the normal way.

2   RESTORATIVE JUSTICE RESEARCH IN ENGLAND AND WALES

Most of the RJ initiatives that have been introduced over the last quarter of a century have been researched – often as a condition of any funding that may have been provided – and, consequently, there are now a good many published

---

12 See Crawford and Newburn (2002) on this particular aspect of the new procedure.

13 Offenders cannot be ordered to make financial compensation as part of a reparation order, though this can be ordered separately as an ancillary order.

14 Now known as 'community punishment orders' after they were renamed by Section 44 of the Criminal Justice and Court Services Act 2000.

research studies. The most significant of these are set out in tabular form in the Appendix, which provides basic information relating to the initiative that has been researched, including the type of RJ intervention that is employed, and also its scope. Brief details are also provided of the research itself, including the names of the researchers, the methods they employed, the duration of the research and also citation details for any publications, all of which are listed in the bibliography. As can be seen from the Appendix, many of the studies employ a variety of research methods and, for that reason, it is not feasible in this report to employ a thematic approach according to the methodology that is used. Nor would it be feasible, or particularly instructive, to attempt to document all of these studies in detail, particularly since some of them are highly complex in terms of their research design and, in some cases, encompass other aspects in addition to the RJ intervention. Instead, this paper will highlight examples of the more important studies that are selected either on the basis of the methods they employ or the significance of their findings, or both. As in the previous section, research relating to stand-alone initiatives is presented first, and is sub-divided according to the type of RJ intervention that is employed, followed by research into some of the 'mainstream' RJ initiatives.

2.1 Research focusing on 'stand-alone' restorative justice initiatives

2.1.1 Victim-offender mediation and reparation initiatives

Among the early 'stand-alone' initiatives, some of the initial research studies were almost as exploratory and innovative as the projects they were researching themselves. A good example is the research conducted by David Smith and colleagues in connection with the first court-based mediation and reparation scheme, which was developed by South Yorkshire Probation Service (Smith et al., 1985, 1988). The project itself was pioneering inasmuch as it set out to test the feasibility of VOM in respect of four local high crime areas, and in the context of middle-ranking offences where the offender was remanded on bail prior to trial. The research was conducted over a fifteen-month period (between September 1984 and December 1985) and adopted a relatively unsophisticated descriptive research design. Its main component consisted of a series of semi-structured interviews with victims and offenders who had been contacted by the project (irrespective of whether they had met with one another) within its first five months of operation. The research findings took the form of a series of accounts conveying the views of both victims and offenders, which provided tentative support for the proposition that real communication is possible between both parties even where it takes place 'in the shadow of the law' (Mnookin and Kornhauser, 1979). They also suggested that, in some cases at least, a degree of reconciliation is possible even in the absence of reparation, or with only a symbolic reparative gesture. However, the research also raised doubts about whether recourse to mediation as a matter of routine would be feasible in view of the time and resource constraints that it entails.

One of the earliest research studies to examine pre-court mediation and reparation schemes adopted a somewhat similar descriptive approach involving interviews with a small number (42) of young people who had been involved in various
forms of informal offence resolution and, in some cases also, their parents (Blagg,
1985). The main purpose of Blagg's study was to investigate the meaning of reparation in the context of diversion from prosecution. The study concluded that,
used in the right context and with careful preparation, reparation could be a
meaningful experience for young offenders but cases involving interaction with
authority figures (for example where the victim is the representative of an institution) could be problematic and therefore require sensitive handling.

Although most of the 'stand-alone' RJ initiatives are relatively small scale, this has
not always been the case with research projects that have been commissioned to
investigate them. Thus, one early study conducted by Gwynn Davis and a team of
colleagues set out to review the operation of all VOM and reparation schemes in
England and Wales during the period October 1985 to September 1986 (Davis et
al., 1987). This aspect of the project was also largely descriptive in its aims and was
mainly based on a questionnaire survey sent out to all[15] known schemes including
pre-court, court-based and community-based neighbour dispute schemes. The
returns from this survey were used to identify a smaller group of 17 schemes for
a more in-depth and analytical survey based on observations, interview data and
analysis of project records. The initial survey findings are now largely of historical interest only, though the approach that was adopted – involving an evaluation
of multiple projects by a single team of researchers using a common set of criteria – provides the first example of a type of research that is referred to in this
report as 'meta-evaluation'. Several other examples will feature in the following
paragraphs.

Among the projects selected for in-depth investigation were several that were run
by juvenile liaison bureaux[16] in the county of Northamptonshire, which was an
early pioneer of pre-court mediation and reparation initiatives in England (Davis
et al., 1988, 1989). Their operation was subjected to detailed and, at times, critical examination, focusing on the proclaimed aims of the project and the extent
to which these aims were achieved in practice. One of the main criticisms was
that, although the schemes described themselves as being mediation and reparation schemes, many of them could more accurately be described as straightforward diversion schemes, since their principal aim in reality was to avoid the
use of imprisonment for offenders and also, where possible, to keep them out of
court altogether. Consequently, interventions that were felt to be more intrusive
and demanding, such as mediation and reparation, tended to be used only selec-
tively, for example in cases where the police were thought unlikely to agree to a

---

15   There were thought to be 41 such schemes at the time of the initial survey.
16   Juvenile liaison bureaux (or cautioning panels, as they were sometimes known) were non-statutory
     multi-agency initiatives mainly comprising police officers and social workers that came to be asso-
     ciated with the 'minimum intervention' era referred to in the introduction. They were disbanded,
     however, following the replacement of juvenile cautions by reprimands and final warnings.

straightforward caution. Such findings are not altogether surprising in view of the diversionary aims of the juvenile liaison bureaux themselves, and the 'minimum interventionist' context in which many of the early mediation and reparation projects were adopted. But they did have a damaging effect on the image of such projects, by suggesting that victims' interests in particular might be subordinated to those of offenders.

A second meta-evaluation which, like the first, was also funded by the Home Office, used local teams to monitor a number of pre-court and court-based standalone initiatives, including four schemes that were themselves Home Office funded for a short period (Marshall and Merry, 1990). This largely descriptive research study set out to monitor the development of the projects, describe their operation and assess their impact upon victims and offenders and also on criminal justice agencies. A number of positive findings were reported, including the fact that many victims appeared to welcome the opportunity to meet their offender, and that most who experienced the process of mediation were sufficiently satisfied with it that they would take part in it again or recommend it to others. However, a number of problems were also identified, including low referral rates, criminal justice processes that do not allow sufficient time to undertake the mediation process and a failure to maintain basic restorative aims. Taken as a whole, the findings suggested that it is difficult to introduce RJ initiatives – at least where they take the form of stand-alone schemes – as part of the regular criminal justice system because of a combination of philosophical differences and conflicting operational procedures.

Although most of the early mediation and reparation initiatives in England and Wales were focused on juvenile offenders, one exception was the Kettering Adult Reparation Bureau, which was one of the first in Britain to use mediation and reparation in conjunction with the diversion from prosecution of adult and young adult offenders. The evaluation of this scheme also broke new ground in several respects. It was one of the first English RJ research studies to incorporate an action-research component (Dignan, 1991, 1992);[17] it was also one of the first to incorporate a quasi-experimental methodology[18] in order to measure the diversion rates and reconviction rates of those who were referred to the project; and a preliminary attempt was made to assess the cost-effectiveness of the project. The three-year evaluation project (1986 to 1989) concluded that it was possible to develop an 'even-handed' approach in which reparation and mediation could be used in conjunction with the diversion of adult offenders from prosecution without necessarily sacrificing the interests of victims in the process. Moreover, it demonstrated that such an approach was viable – in terms of both referral rates and police support – even within the context of the existing criminal justice sys-

---

17 The project was based on an active collaboration between researcher and those responsible for running and managing the schemes. This involved the regular feedback of ongoing findings, which in turn were used in the monitoring, and development of the scheme's operation.

18 Offenders who were referred to the scheme were 'matched' with those from a nearby control area that fell outside its catchment area.

tem. Although the diversion rate for those who were referred to the project was found to be relatively high (60%) for a scheme of this kind, the effect on the reconviction rate was found to be broadly neutral, whether measured on the basis of a matched comparison sample or in terms of predicted reconviction scores.

All of the research studies that have been examined so far, including the two meta-evaluations, concentrated exclusively on the operation of VOM projects within England and Wales. A rather different research design was adopted by Umbreit and Roberts (1996), who set out to examine the development and impact of two VOM projects in England in the context of a much larger cross-national comparative study involving the use of common data collection instruments and analytical techniques in three different countries. The study involved four projects in the United States, four in Canada and two in England, using a quasi-experimental research design to compare the experiences and perceptions of those who had been involved in mediation (including both direct and indirect mediation) with those who were referred to mediation but who did not go through with it. Victims and offenders who participated in some form of mediation at either of the two English projects were more likely to express satisfaction with the justice system's response to their case, and to feel that the response had been fair, than those who were referred to the projects but never participated in them. However, the study also found (in common with many others) that the proportion of victims who participated in direct as opposed to indirect mediation in England is much lower than elsewhere.

The most recent, and also one of the best-known studies of stand-alone VOM projects is another meta-evaluation that was commissioned by the Home Office (Miers et al., 2001). This was a fifteen-month retrospective study of the effectiveness of seven stand-alone English RJ projects, two of which dealt principally with adult offenders, and the other five with juveniles. The principal aims of the study were to identify which elements, or combination of RJ elements, in the schemes were most effective in reducing crimes, and at what cost. The aims themselves reflect a continuing preoccupation on the part of the government with reconviction rates as one of the key yardsticks by which to measure the effectiveness of RJ interventions, even though it is by no means the only available indicator; nor, some would argue, is it necessarily the most appropriate. The research involved comparisons between the reconviction rates of those who had experienced an RJ intervention and control groups who had not.[19]

The findings of the evaluation were somewhat mixed, which again is not that surprising since the schemes themselves were very diverse and several had undergone significant changes during the period encompassed by the study. Only one of the schemes showed a significant impact on re-offending, both in terms of offence frequency and also in terms of offence seriousness. Interestingly, this scheme was also the one dealing with the highest risk offenders and the one that made the most effort to routinely involve victims. Perhaps not surprisingly, it was

---

19 In addition, the two adult schemes only involved comparisons between actual and predicted reconviction rates.

also the only scheme judged to be cost-effective in reducing further offending, even taking account of the higher costs associated with victim involvement. Other findings, however, made less comfortable reading for RJ advocates. For example, the juvenile stand-alone schemes did not have any significant impact on reconviction rates; nor were they judged to be cost-effective in this regard. Moreover, even among schemes that did receive high number of referrals, the rate of unambiguously restorative interventions (involving direct or even indirect) mediation was relatively low. As we shall see, this is also a feature of many of the more recent mainstream RJ initiatives.

2.1.2 Family group conferencing initiatives

Within a criminal justice context, the early experience of conferencing has followed a broadly similar pattern to the one outlined for VOM, with a very limited number of small-scale pilot projects operating on the margins of the regular criminal justice system. Some successes have been reported, particularly with regard to high levels of participant satisfaction. But similar developmental problems have also been encountered, including the difficulty in attracting high numbers of referrals, tensions between projects and mainstream criminal justice agencies and, in the case of at least one of the projects, difficulties in securing participation on the part of victims.

A number of family group conferencing projects for young offenders in England have been evaluated, including the London-based Victim Offender Conference Service (Liddle, 1999), the Hampshire Youth Justice Family Group Conference Pilot Project (Jackson, 1998), the Sheffield/Kirklees project (Crow and Marsh, 2000) and the Kent Intensive Support and Supervision Programme [ISSP] (Gilroy, 1998; Little et al., 2002).

The Victim Offender Conference Service was a pilot pre-trial project aimed at young people (aged 10 to 17) that operated briefly in Lambeth and Hackney. Although a total of 160 referrals was accepted, none of these resulted in a conference, and only a very small minority involved either direct or indirect mediation (4% and 13% respectively). Almost half of the cases involved work with only one party, usually the offender. Throughout the project, inter-agency tensions were compounded by entrenched working practices and differences in professional ethos.

The Hampshire project was more typical of recent family group conference developments in that it emanated from the successful implementation of family group conferences within a child welfare context in the same county. Those eligible for referral were repeat offenders who were deemed unlikely to respond to further cautioning. However, the project was slow to develop and encountered a familiar litany of problems. Referrals were slow to materialise, as a result of which the number of completed conferences (12 in the first year) failed to meet even the relatively low target initially adopted. This in turn caused problems for the type of evaluation that had been planned since the numbers were too small to allow for cases to be randomly allocated to experimental or control samples, as had originally been contemplated. Professional commitment was also difficult to sustain, and the role of youth justice staff in particular was unclear.

The Sheffield/Kirklees project also experienced developmental problems resulting in only a small number of referrals. Nonetheless, the conferences that were carried out seemed to be well received, with both professionals and families expressing positive views. Victims attended around half of the conferences, and their views were also reasonably positive. Despite the small numbers involved (18 in total), the research showed that family group conferences were certainly achievable in the English system, but that considerable development work was still needed.

The Kent ISSP scheme targeted a group of persistent young offenders facing a custodial sentence. The catchment group was restricted to 15 to 17 year olds (though younger ones were also eligible), who had been charged or cautioned on three previous occasions in the preceding 12 months, and who had served a custodial or community sentence (JUSTICE, 2000: 63; Little et al., 2002). The scheme was court-based, and operated in part as an alternative to custody, not court. Intervention in such cases took place between conviction and sentence. Alternatively, offenders could be referred at the point of release from custody or while an offender is on licence.

The scheme employed a 'family decision-making model' (essentially a family group conference), and the outcome formed part of the pre-sentence report to the court. However, the conferencing process constituted just one of seven possible intervention components to which a young person may be subject.[20] The project was evaluated, using a reasonably rigorous methodology based on the use of random assignment to either ISSP or one of two control groups (one operating within the pilot site, the other operating in an adjacent non-pilot area).

The final evaluation report (Little et al., 2002) disclosed a statistically significant reduction in the volume of crime committed by ISSP participants over a two-year follow-up period.[21] However, it was not possible to attribute the improvement to any particular intervention component, so it is not possible to say whether, for example, it was a product of the conferencing process or the increased supervision to which the young offenders were subject. Moreover, an interim evaluation identified a number of implementational problems (see JUSTICE, 2000: 63). They include reluctance by victims to participate, and time pressure constraints brought about by tight court schedules that made it difficult for victims to participate in the programme. It also proved difficult to promote meaningful restorative interventions with a group of offenders whose attitudes towards victims and their offending could often be problematic, and whose risk of re-offending and

---

20 The others included more intensive supervision by police and social service staff, availability of victim reparation and mediation in appropriate cases, the provision of mentoring (in the form of a role model) where appropriate, improved information sharing, better diagnosis, assessment and individual treatment plans and, finally, regular multi-agency reviews of cases.

21 As measured by arrest rates, and taking into account periods spent in custody. As expected, however, overall reconviction rates did not appear to be affected by the intervention.

associated needs often appeared to warrant alternative, more therapeutic, forms of intervention.

2.1.3 Police-led conferencing

The Thames Valley restorative cautioning initiative that was referred to in Section 1 above has also been independently evaluated (Hoyle et al., 2002). The scheme required the police to facilitate a structured discussion between those present, with the aid of a script, focusing on the harm that is caused by an offence and how this might be repaired. This was intended as an alternative to traditional cautioning sessions, which previous research had shown were often used to humiliate and stigmatise offenders and, particularly in the case of juveniles, to make them cry. An explicit aim of the process was to achieve the kind of 'reintegrative shaming' that John Braithwaite (1989) has espoused, by making the offender feel ashamed about what he or she has done while respecting them as an individual and encouraging them to put the offence behind them once the process is over.

The evaluation adopted a major action-research component in which the evaluators studied a number of cases in depth and identified deficiencies in the implementation of the restorative cautioning model in those cases. Some of the biggest deficiencies related to the use of restorative cautioning sessions by a number of police officers who appeared to pursue a 'policing agenda' – for example by reinvestigating the offence or seeking criminal intelligence – rather than following the authorised RJ script. These findings were fed back to the force during the developmental phase of the project and were reflected in follow-up training and in a revised script, the aims of which were to eliminate the deficiencies. The evaluators then conducted a more formal evaluation of the process and its outcomes, including a preliminary reconviction study using a combination of self-report instruments and official reconviction data from the police national computer.

The final evaluation reported that this remedial activity resulted in a much greater use of the restorative cautioning script, though significant deficiencies in facilitators' practice still remained. Thus, for example, whereas irrelevant or improper questions featured in over half the cases observed in the interim phase, this occurred in only a quarter of cases featuring in the final evaluation. Offenders, victims and their respective supporters were generally satisfied with the fairness of the process and the outcomes achieved. Once again, however, the overall rate of victim participation in the process was disappointing. From the figures provided in the report it appears to be around 16% overall, diminishing slightly over the three years of the project. However, the report did find that cautioning sessions that adhered most closely to RJ principles tended to produce the most positive outcomes including perceptions of fairness. In terms of reconvictions, the report tentatively suggested that about a quarter of offenders were helped by the restorative session to stop or reduce their active offending, though the sample was only small (56 offenders aged between 10 and 17). Thus, as the authors themselves acknowledge, a larger scale re-offending study is required in order to confirm the validity of this finding.

2.2   *Research focusing on 'mainstream' restorative justice initiatives*

As we saw in Section 1, several elements of the RJ approach were introduced by the youth justice reforms, and now form part of the mainstream response to youth offending in England and Wales. As a result of these changes, efforts to 'main-stream' RJ responses to youth offending have so far focused mainly on three distinct phases of the criminal justice process: pre-prosecution, at first convic-tion and as a sentencing option following subsequent convictions. Some research studies have now been completed and others are under way in respect of most of these mainstream initiatives. However, it is still very early days and so far the findings are for the most part, not surprisingly, both tentative and inconclusive.

2.2.1   *Restorative justice interventions at the pre-prosecution stage*

With regard to the reformed pre-prosecution system of reprimands and final warnings the primary emphasis, as we have seen, is on the need to address the offender's behaviour. However, pilot areas were advised of the importance of con-tacting victims, where possible, to establish their views about the offence and also the nature and significance of any harm or loss that may have resulted from it. They were also instructed to consider whether or not some form of direct contact with, or reparation to, the victim would be appropriate, and a number of different forms of possible reparation were identified. The reformed system was initially evaluated as part of a much larger and more comprehensive meta-evaluation of the pilot youth justice reform areas, which highlighted a number of shortcomings in the way final warnings were being implemented (summarised in Holdaway et al., 2001: 72ff; see also Holdaway, 2003). In brief, the evaluation found that in only 43% of the cases was a final warning change programme recorded as appropriate;[22] victims were contacted in just 15% of the cases and only 7% of vic-tims were involved in any kind of mediation or reparative activity (4% in direct reparation, which included mediation; and 3% in indirect reparation). Concerns were also raised about the relevance of the change programme in relation to the nature of the offence that had been committed.

A one-year reconviction study was also conducted in conjunction with the main pilot evaluation, which set out to compare the effectiveness of the new final warn-ing system compared with the old-style cautions it replaced (Hine and Celnick, 2001). The key finding from this study was that the final warning sample had outcomes that were statistically significantly better than those for the caution comparison group, even after controlling for differences between the two sam-ples. However, this seems unlikely to have been the result of any RJ interventions that may have formed part of the process since, as the main evaluation study had shown, only a minority of final warnings (43%) were accompanied by a change programme of any kind. And, while letters of apology featured prominently

---

22   The proportion of cases involving intervention programmes subsequently increased to 70%, though even this fell short of the target of 80% that was set by the Youth Justice Board.

among the activities that are associated with such programmes, direct victim participation in the programmes was extremely limited.

The final warning scheme was the focus of further research involving a total of 30 projects that were funded by the Youth Justice Board in order to develop and implement various final warning intervention programmes. These spanned a range of interventions that included, but were not restricted to, RJ interventions.[23] Just under half of the projects (43%) described themselves as RJ projects, and between them these accounted for over two thirds (71.5%) of the cases dealt with. Findings from this research (Holdaway, 2004) suggest that the degree of victim participation remains limited, even within projects that have been set up specifically to develop and deliver RJ interventions. Taking the final warning sample as a whole, the overwhelming majority of warnings delivered (80%) were of the 'standard' type. Only 16% could be categorised as restorative warnings (see above), in which specific reference to a victim is made when the police administer a warning. And just 4% could be categorised as restorative conferences (see above), in which the offender meets the victim, though others may also be present (Holdaway, 2004: 7). In total, victims were present at just 3.4% of warnings, three-quarters of which took the form of restorative conferences.

A total of 506 cases dealt with by RJ projects were also analysed (Holdaway, 2004: 29). Many of these involved young offenders who were assigned to take part in 'change' programmes in addition to receiving a final warning as described in the previous paragraph. Of these, one fifth (20%) of the total involved no RJ intervention of any kind. Over one quarter (27%) involved no more than a letter of apology.[24] Just 13% involved VOM and a further 12% involved some other form of direct mediation. Restorative conferences were held in just 5% of cases and family group conferences in 1% of cases. Of the remainder, 11% of cases involved indirect (community reparation) and 8% involved victim awareness related activities.

2.2.2   Restorative justice interventions at the point of first conviction

The introduction of referral orders and the setting up of youth offender panels that are supposed to be governed by RJ principles (defined by the Home Office (1997: 31-32) as 'restoration, reintegration and responsibility') also prompted a separate large-scale meta-evaluation led by Tim Newburn (Newburn et al., 2001a, 2001b, 2002). Once again, the findings from this study were rather mixed. The final report suggested that the pilots were broadly successful in setting up the youth offender panels including recruiting and training their members. And both magistrates and YOT staff appeared to support the RJ approach that was assumed to characterise the new process. However, the more detailed findings raised some serious doubts as to how 'restorative' the panels were in practice.

---

23 Other interventions included educational and careers advice, mentoring, methods of dealing with drugs and alcohol-related offences, parenting and so on.

24 The evaluation report commented critically on the routinised, non-specific and often rather pointless nature of this exercise which appeared to have had little impact on the young offenders themselves, despite being well-regarded by the YOT staff who supervised the activity.

For example, victims only attended a YOP in 13% of appropriate cases. And even if other more limited forms of input are included, such as allowing a statement to be read out at the panel or consenting to receive some form of reparation such as a letter of apology, the participation rate was still only 28%. This level of involvement is far lower than had been anticipated, and is also lower than in many comparable RJ initiatives from around the world, though it is broadly in line with other RJ initiatives in England and Wales. To some extent, of course, the low level of participation might reflect early teething troubles and problems in setting up such a completely new system for dealing with young offenders. And it may be significant that half of the non-attending victims who were interviewed said they had not been offered the chance of attending a panel meeting. Moreover, half of these indicated that they would have attended if they had known about it or been given a chance to attend. So it is possible that victim participation rates may improve over time, as also happened in New Zealand[25] following the introduction of family group conferences. Unlike New Zealand, however, the disappointingly low level of victim participation does not appear to be caused by inconvenience in the timing of the panels, since almost two-thirds were held after 5 p.m. and over one-third were scheduled to begin after 6 p.m.

One possible explanation for the relatively low level of victim participation may relate to difficulties that have been encountered in identifying, contacting and consulting with victims to see if they wish to participate.[26] Another is that working with victims is a new responsibility for most criminal justice practitioners and one that has not, as yet, successfully overcome some deeply entrenched cultural attitudes and assumptions about their role and remit.

As for the outcomes of the referral order process, the commonest compulsory element in the resulting youth offender contracts was some form of reparative activity, usually in the form of community reparation (42% of cases), followed by a written apology (38%). Direct reparation to victims or the payment of compensation occurred in only 7% of cases. Young offenders successfully completed their contracts in 74% of cases where a panel had met.

A subsequent study examined a six-month cohort of 250 referral order cases coming before a youth offender panel in Leeds in 2004 (Crawford and Burden, 2005). This study also found that only 15% of victims elected to attend panels, though those who did attend had a generally favourable view of the outcomes contained in the agreements and the presence of a victim was also thought to have had a significant impact on young offenders, notably with regard to understanding the effect of their behaviour on others, their determination to keep out of trouble and their capacity to put the offence behind them. Even where victims elected not to attend a panel, however, many reported significant benefits as a result of the procedure.

---

25 Though the initial victim participation rate (of slightly less than 50%) was substantially higher in New Zealand.

26 One set of difficulties relates to the way data protection legislation has been very restrictively interpreted, which in many areas has made it extremely difficult for victim contact details to be passed on from the police, who are classed as authorised data holders, to victim contact workers, who are not.

Thus, more than three quarters felt that contact with the service had provided them with the chance to have their say; half agreed that even the limited contact they had had with the YOT had helped them put the experience behind them and just over a fifth reported that the service had helped to allay fears about the offence.

2.2.3   Restorative justice interventions as optional sentencing measures for 'multiply convicted' young offenders

The remaining stage at which there is scope for RJ measures to operate as mainstream interventions for young offenders is in connection with court-ordered penalties such as reparation orders or action plan orders that are imposed on convicted young offenders. These were also evaluated as part of the large scale meta-evaluation of the pilot youth justice reforms conducted by Holdaway and colleagues (2001). The main research indicated not only that there was considerable disparity in the take-up of the orders in different YOTs around the country, but also that there was significant variation between YOTs in the way they delivered the new interventions and likewise in the extent to which they successfully adapted their programmes to meet the needs of both victims and offenders. The final report produced by this study also disclosed a relatively low rate of victim participation in the reparation order. Victims were contacted in around two-thirds of cases in which there was an identifiable victim and, of those who were contacted, exactly half consented to some from of reparation being made by their offender. However, only 9% of orders made were said to have involved mediation, and in the majority of cases (63%) reparation was ordered to be made to the community rather than the victim.

A separate process evaluation was also conducted in conjunction with the main evaluation of the youth justice pilot. Its aim was to investigate processes relating to victim contact work and the nature of the mediation and reparation work that was being undertaken under the auspices of the Crime and Disorder Act of 1998 (Dignan, 2000). This provided an overview of the main types of interventions, progress on implementing the measures and identified a number of good practice recommendations based on early experience in the pilot areas.

As with the final warning scheme, the reparative court-based penalties that were introduced by the Crime and Disorder Act of 1998 were also the focus of further research that was commissioned and funded by the Youth Justice Board (Wilcox and Hoyle, 2004). A number of projects were evaluated but, unlike the final warning evaluation, which was undertaken by a single team of evaluators based at Sheffield University, the other 46 RJ projects that were funded by the YJB were evaluated by local evaluators, who each provided data to a national evaluator based at Oxford University. The national evaluator was responsible for collating data about each area of work to which the development fund was relevant – RJ in this case – and a common template was produced for this purpose. Because the local evaluators were appointed in advance of the national evaluator, however, the task of coordinating the research was much more difficult than it might otherwise have been.[27]

The study's findings were broadly in line with those of other recent studies insofar as the bulk of the restorative interventions consisted of either community reparation (36%) or victim awareness (20%), with relatively few cases (13.5% of the total) involving direct meetings between the parties. Problems were also encountered by several of the schemes in engaging with victims, attracting sufficient number of referrals and undertaking meaningful RJ interventions within the rigid time constraints that are imposed by fast-tracking initiatives. However, the study suggested that fewer implementational problems were experienced where restorative interventions were delivered 'in house'[28] by members of the youth offending team than where they were delivered by independent projects, or by staff from independent agencies working within a youth offending team (known as the 'hybrid model').

2.2.4   *Restorative justice initiatives for adult offenders*

Most of the mainstream initiatives to date have targeted young offenders.[29] However, in August 2001, the Home Office commissioned a composite and complex meta-evaluation of three separate sets of projects that are designed to pilot the mainstreaming of RJ interventions for mainly adult offenders at various different stages of the criminal justice process. The projects themselves, operating across three large geographical areas, were also funded by the Home Office for eighteen months (from August 2001 until March 2003). A separately commissioned evaluation was undertaken by Joanna Shapland and a team based at the University of Sheffield (Shapland et al., 2007, 2008).

The first project, run by an organisation known as Connect, was based in London and offered conferencing and VOM for adult offenders and their victims in two magistrates' courts as part of a deferred sentence. The second project was run by the Justice Research Consortium [JRC][30] and offered conferencing in three separate sets of areas: London, Northumbria and Thames Valley. The London site involved five separate Crown Courts and mainly dealt with adults facing burglary

---

27   For example, the national coordinators had no control over the methodology that was employed by the local evaluators, and the quality of the data they provided was also somewhat variable (Wilcox and Hoyle, 2004: 5).

28   See Holdaway et al. (2001: 82) for a more detailed discussion of the different delivery models.

29   A partial exception relates to the introduction of a statutory conditional cautioning scheme for adult offenders under the Criminal Justice Act 2003, which was intended to supplement the existing non-statutory system of adult cautioning. The aim was to enable offenders who made a full admission to be diverted from prosecution and dealt with by means of a caution to which conditions would be attached requiring some form of reparative or rehabilitative activity to be undertaken. In the event, however, a pilot scheme in London failed to get off the ground because of technical difficulties relating to the restrictive wording of the legislation, which requires a full admission to be made before an offender may be offered a conditional caution (see Sherman and Strange, 2007: 83 for details).

30   The same consortium had previously been involved in the RISE (Re-Integrative Shaming Experiment) initiative in Australia.

and robbery charges prior to sentence. The Northumbria site offered conferencing for young offenders in connection with final warnings and for adult offenders who were cautioned.[31] And the Thames Valley site offered conferencing in respect of adult offenders who were recommended for or given community sentences, and also for prisoners who were approaching release from custody. A distinctive aspect of this project is that it adopted an experimental methodology (as in the Australian RISE initiative) involving the random allocation of offenders either to the experimental programme or to a control sample, which was dealt with in the normal way.[32] The third project was run by Remedi in South Yorkshire and offered VOM in respect of adult and young adult offenders[33] who were given either custodial or community sentences following conviction. All three projects aimed to pilot the delivery of RJ interventions as a regular part of the criminal justice process and in respect of a major throughput of cases, unlike most of the earlier stand-alone initiatives.

The methodology included observations, interviews, a process and outcome evaluation, and a longer-term reconviction study involving both experimental and control groups. The first interim report (Shapland et al., 2004) examined the implementation of the schemes up to autumn 2002, and concentrated on the problems the projects encountered in establishing themselves as 'regular players' alongside the already established criminal justice fraternity. Many of the difficulties – for example involving the need to secure an adequate supply of referrals and to elicit acceptance and cooperation on the part of more established players – were similar to those encountered by earlier stand-alone and mainstream initiatives.

The second interim report dealt with the extent of participation and what happened during conferencing and direct mediation. The proportion of victims who were willing to participate in RJ encounters ranged from 30% in adult probation cases and 36% of prison cases to 56% of London Crown Court burglary cases and 89% of referral order youth offender panel cases (Shapland et al., 2006: Table 3.3). Although most cases involved adult offenders, the level of victim participation was particularly high in cases involving juvenile offenders. When given a choice of RJ process, participants were more likely to opt for indirect rather than direct mediation or conferencing, though restricting the choice to a direct meeting only did not reduce participation rates. Discussion concerning outcomes[34] and the future were more likely to occur in conferencing than mediation sessions and follow-up monitoring of outcomes was only undertaken by the JRC in respect of conferencing cases, but not by the other two schemes.

---

31   However, the latter are not included in the random allocation trials, referred to below.

32   The Justice Research Consortium, which conducted the randomised control trials within this latter scheme, has also reported on some of its preliminary findings (see Sherman et al., 2005; Strang et al., 2006; Sherman and Strang, 2007).

33   Young adult offenders are those between their eighteenth and twenty-first birthdays.

34   Outcome agreements were concluded in a very high proportion (98%) of conference cases conducted by the JRC, 36% of which were completed in full and a further 52% of which were partially completed, leaving just 11% in which the agreement was not completed at all.

The third report contained findings relating to the attitudes of victims and offenders towards RJ (Shapland et al., 2007). Those who participated in conferencing or mediation were generally very positive about their experience. Where the RJ encounter took the form of a conference, 85% of victims and 80% of offenders indicated that they were very or quite satisfied with the JRC conference itself and, likewise with regard to the outcome, almost all participants thought that it was fair and only 12% of victims and 10% of offenders expressed doubts about any aspect of it. The small number of direct mediation cases conducted by the other two schemes also produced high levels of satisfaction on the part of both victims and offenders, though generally there were no outcome agreements and there was less likelihood of discussion about what might happen in the future, including steps the offender might take to stop re-offending.

3   CONCLUDING REMARKS

Elements of an RJ approach have featured reasonably prominently in a range of recent youth justice reforms and have now been introduced at various stages in the English criminal justice process. Consequently, RJ initiatives of one kind or another do now form part of the mainstream response to youth offending in England and Wales. And, in this sense at least, they are no longer confined to 'marginal, irregular and highly localised activities' (Dignan, 1999: 53). However, three important caveats are in order in assessing the current situation.

The first is that, as we have seen, the initiatives themselves draw on an eclectic mixture of approaches. These not only emanate from a variety of different jurisdictions but are also derived from a range of different philosophical and practice-based assumptions about RJ and the way it should be implemented.[35] Thus, there are clearly major differences between the three main types of RJ initiatives that are outlined in this paper.

The police-led and facilitated scripted conferencing model that is now being encouraged at the pre-prosecution stage draws consciously on an explicit 'crime control' perspective that is associated with John Braithwaite's (1989) theory of reintegrative shaming. It also related to Donald Nathanson's (1992, 1999) work on shame and pride within the context of his 'affect theory'.

As for the reparative interventions that are available under the Crime and Disorder Act, these draw in part on the principle of 'coerced restitution' that has also been associated in the past with the use of court-ordered compensation orders and community service orders. But they also draw to a lesser extent on the more recent development of extra-judicial forms of offence resolution that have come to be associated with the (ostensibly voluntary and non-coercive) practice of VOM.

---

35   See also Crawford (2002), who has made a similar and very pertinent observation specifically with regard to the introduction of referral orders themselves.

Both of these initiatives may be contrasted in turn with the potentially much more inclusive and consensual decision-making processes that might be expected to form part of the youth offender panel proceedings. However, this forum also appears to draw on a range of disparate precursors. The use of community volunteers in an 'extra-judicial' forum for determining 'dispositional outcomes' is somewhat reminiscent of both the Scottish Children's Hearings system and the Community Reparative Boards that have been developed in Vermont (see Dooley, 1995, 1996; Bazemore and Umbreit, 1998: 3; Dignan, 2005: 121-5, 148-54). However, the youth offender panels differ from both of these other forums by including provision for victim participation from the outset.[36] This particular aspect of the youth offender panel more closely resembles the New Zealand family group conference procedure, though the latter makes no attempt to involve members of the community in its conferencing process, which is facilitated instead by professional youth justice coordinators, who are employed by the Department of Social Welfare.

At the very least, the eclectic mixture of RJ approaches that has informed recent developments in England and Wales poses awkward questions as to their compatibility. It also raises serious doubts about the underlying coherence of the government's overall approach to RJ issues.

A second caveat relates to the strength of the government's commitment towards RJ since its confused and timid approach to date contrasts sharply with the much more ambitious and comprehensive youth conferencing reforms that have been introduced in New Zealand and, more recently, in Northern Ireland. The tentative and disparate initiatives that have been introduced in England and Wales form part of a wider set of youth justice reforms, not all of which are compatible with the RJ ethos of 'repairing the harm' that has been brought about by the offence. One very obvious example relates to the desire to speed up the youth justice process, in the interests of both efficiency and also to increase the effectiveness of any intervention by reducing the delay between the commission of an offence and its consequences for the offender. It is extremely difficult to reconcile the constant emphasis on fast-tracking and the use of statutory time limits with the need for patience and sensitivity if victims are also to be consulted and enabled to participate in RJ processes without being pressurised or excluded by time constraints.

A third caveat relates to the current state of play regarding the evaluation of RJ initiatives, which is still in its infancy. Most funded research has been predominantly offender-oriented, with a particular focus on the impact that RJ might have on reconviction rates. Much less emphasis has been placed on its possible impact on victims when formulating research strategies, and most studies to date have concentrated on a fairly narrow range of issues relating broadly to 'victim

---

36 Although victim participation was not encouraged initially, some community reparative boards do now welcome this, and others may refer cases for VOM in areas where this is available (Dignan and Lowey, 2000: 31).

satisfaction' ratings.[37] Methodologically speaking, much RJ research has been of variable quality, which means that many of the findings need to be treated with caution. When assessing the significance of RJ research from a policy-making perspective one of the biggest challenges is to determine the extent to which the 'outcome' findings can be attributed to the RJ process itself as opposed to factors relating to the manner in which it has been implemented within the wider criminal justice system.

REFERENCES

Bazemore, G. and Umbreit, M. (1998) *Conferences, Circles, Boards and Mediations: Restorative Justice and Citizen Involvement in the Response to Youth Crime* (Minnesota: University of Minnesota and Florida Atlantic University).

Blagg, H. (1985) 'Reparation and Justice for Juveniles', *British Journal of Criminology*, Vol. 25, pp. 267-279.

Bottoms, A.E. and Dignan, J. (2004) 'Youth Justice in Great Britain', in Tonry, M. and Doob, A.N. (eds.) *Youth Crime and Youth Justice: Comparative and Cross-National Perspectives*. Crime and Justice: A Review of Research, Vol. 31. (Chicago and London: University of Chicago Press), pp. 21-183.

Braithwaite, J. (1989) *Crime, Shame and Reintegration* (Cambridge: Cambridge University Press).

Cavadino, M. and Dignan, J. (2007) *The Penal System: An Introduction* (London: Sage Publications).

Cavadino, M. and Dignan, J. with others (2006) *Penal Systems: A Comparative Approach* (London: Sage Publications).

Challiner, V., Brown, L. and Lupton, C. (2000) *A Survey of Family Group Conference Use Across England and Wales* (Porthsmouth: University of Portsmouth Social Services Research and Information Unit and University of Bath Department of Social and Policy Studies).

Crawford, A. (2002) 'The Prospects for Restorative Justice in England and Wales: A Tale of Two Acts', in McEvoy, K. and Newburn, T. (eds.) *Criminology and Conflict Resolution*, (Basingstoke: Palgrave), pp. 171-207.

Crawford, A. and Burden, T. (2005) *Integrating victims in restorative youth justice* (Bristol: The Policy Press).

Crawford, A. and Newburn, T. (2002) 'Recent Developments in Restorative Justice for Young People in England and Wales: Community Participation and Representation', *British Journal of Criminology*, 43(3), pp. 476-495.

Crow, G. and Marsh, P. (2000) *Family Group Conferences in Youth Justice: A Study of Early Work in Two Pilot Projects in South Yorkshire* (Sheffield: Children and Family Research Group, Department of Sociological Studies, University of Sheffield).

---

37 See Dignan (2007b) for an overview of research findings relating specifically to restorative outcomes for victims.

Davis, G. (1992) *Making Amends: Mediation and Reparation in Criminal Justice* (London: Routledge).

Davis, G., Boucherat, J. and Watson, D. (1988) 'Reparation in the Service of Diversion: the Subordination of a Good Idea', *The Howard Journal*, Vol. 27, pp. 127-133.

Davis, G., Boucherat, J. and Watson, D. (1989) 'Pre-court decision-making in juvenile justice', *British Journal of Criminology*, Vol. 29, pp. 219-235.

Davis, G., Boucherat, J., Watson, D. and Thatcher, A. (1987) *A Preliminary Study of Victim Offender Mediation and Reparation Schemes in England and Wales*, Home Office Research and Planning Unit, Paper 42 (London: Home Office).

Dignan, J. (1991) *Repairing the Damage: An Evaluation of an Experimental Adult Reparation Scheme in Kettering, Northamptonshire* (Sheffield: University of Sheffield).

Dignan, J. (1992) 'Repairing the Damage: Can Reparation be made to work in the Service of Diversion?', *British Journal of Criminology*, Vol. 32, pp. 453-472.

Dignan, J. (1999) 'The Crime and Disorder Act and the Prospects for Restorative Justice', *Criminal Law Review*, pp. 48-60.

Dignan, J. (2000) *Youth Justice Pilots Evaluation: Interim Report on Reparative Work and Youth Offending Teams* (London: Home Office Research, Development and Statistics Directorate Occasional Paper).

Dignan, J. (2005) *Understanding Victims and Restorative Justice* (Maidenhead: Open University Press).

Dignan, J. (2007a) 'Juvenile justice, criminal courts and restorative justice', in Johnstone, G. and Van Ness, D. (eds.) *Handbook of Restorative Justice* (Cullompton: Willan Publishing), pp. 269-292.

Dignan, J. (2007b), 'The victim in restorative justice', in Walklate, S. (ed.) *Handbook of Victims and Victimology* (Cullompton: Willan Publishing), pp.309-331.

Dignan, J. and Lowey, K. (2000) *Restorative Justice Options for Northern Ireland: A Comparative Review*, Research Report 10, Review of the Criminal Justice System in Northern Ireland (Norwich: Her Majesty's Stationary Office).

Dignan, J. and Marsh, P. (2001) 'Restorative Justice and Family Group Conferences in England: Current State and Future Prospects', in Morris, A. and Maxwell, G. (eds.) *Restorative Justice for Juveniles: Conferencing, Mediation and Circles* (Oxford: Hart Publishing), pp. 85-101.

Dooley, M.J. (1995) *Reparative Probation Programme* (Waterbury, Vermont: Vermont Department of Corrections).

Dooley, M.J. (1996) *Restoring Hope through Community Partnerships: the Real Deal in Crime Control* (Lexington, KY: American Probation and Parole Association).

Gilroy, P. (1998) *The role of restoration, mediation and family group conferencing in the youth justice system*, paper presented to a Home Office special conference, (February 18-20).

Hine, J. and Celnick, A. (2001) *One Year Reconviction Study of Final Warnings*. Available at: http://www.homeoffice.gov.uk/rds/pdfs/reconvictstudywarn.pdf

Holdaway, S. (2003) 'The Final Warning: Appearance and Reality', *Criminal Justice* Vol. 3(4), pp. 351-67.

Holdaway, S. (2004) *The National Evaluation of the Youth Justice Board's Final Warning Projects* (London: Youth Justice Board). Available at: http://www.youth-justice-board.gov.uk/Publications/Scripts/prodView.asp?idproduct=181&eP=YJB

Holdaway, S., Davidson, N., Dignan, J., Hammersley, R., Hine, J. and Marsh, J. (2001) *New Strategies to Address Youth Offending: the National Evaluation of Pilot Youth Offending Teams,* Home Office Research, Development and Statistics Directorate Occasional Paper, no. 69 (London: Home Office).

Home Office (1997) *No More Excuses – A New Approach to Tackling Youth Crime in England and Wales.* Cm 3809 (London: Home Office).

Home Office (2003) *Restorative Justice: the Government's Strategy: A consultation document on the Government's strategy on restorative justice* (London: Home Office).

Home Office/Youth Justice Board for England and Wales (2002) *The Final Warning Scheme Guidance for the Police and Youth Offending Teams* (London: Home Office).

Hoyle, C., Young, R. and Hill, R. (2002) *Proceed with Caution: An Evaluation of the Thames Valley Police Initiative in Restorative Cautioning* (York: Joseph Rowntree Foundation).

Hughes, G., Leisten, R. and Pilkington, A. (1995) *An Independent Evaluation of the Northamptonshire Diversion Unit, Final Report,* unpublished.

Jackson, S. (1998) *Family Justice? An evaluation of the Hampshire Youth Justice Family Group Conference Project* (Southampton: University of Southampton).

JUSTICE (2000) *Restoring Youth Justice: New Directions in Domestic and International Law and Practice* (London: JUSTICE).

Liddle, M. (1999) *Evaluation of Victim Offender Conference Service: Final Report* (London: NACRO).

Little, M., Kogan, J., Bullock, R. and van der Laan, P. (2002) *ISSP: An experiment in multi-systemic responses to persistent young offenders known to Children's Services.* Available at: http:// www.dartington.org.uk/documents/ ISSP%20 Final%20Sep%2002.pdf

Marshall, T. and Merry, S. (1990) *Crime and Accountability: Victim/Offender Mediation in Practice* (London: HMSO).

Miers, D., Maguire, M., Goldie, S., Sharpe, K., Hale, C., Netten, A., Uglow, S., Doolin, K., Hallam, A., Enterkin, J. and Newburn, T. (2001) *An Exploratory Evaluation of Restorative Justice Schemes,* Crime Reduction Research Series paper 9 (London: Home Office).

Mnookin, R. and Kornhauser, L. (1979) 'Bargaining in the Shadow of the Law', *Yale Law Journal,* 88, pp. 950-997.

Nathanson, D. (1992) *Shame and Pride: Affect, Self and the Birth of Self* (London-New York: WW Norton).

Nathanson, D. (1999) 'Affect and Restorative Justice', in *Behaviour Online* – website discussion forum on shame and affect theory. Available at: www.behavior.com

Newburn, T., Crawford, A., Earle, R., Goldie, S., Hale, C., Masters, G., Netten, A., Saunders, R., Hallam, A., Sharpe, K. and Uglow, S. (2001a) *The Introduction of*

Referrals Orders into the Youth Justice System, First Interim Report, Home Office Research, Development and Statistics Directorate Occasional Paper, no. 70 (London: Home Office).

Newburn, T., Crawford, A., Earle, R., Goldie, S., Hale, C., Masters, G., Netten, A., Saunders, R., Hallam, A., Sharpe, K. and Uglow, S. (2001b) *The Introduction of Referrals Orders into the Youth Justice System, Second Interim Report,* Home Office Research, Development and Statistics Directorate Occasional Paper, no. 73 (London: Home Office).

Newburn, T., Crawford, A., Earle, R., Goldie, S., Hale, C., Masters, G., Netten, A., Saunders, R., Hallam, A., Sharpe, K. and Uglow, S. (2002) *The Introduction of Referrals Orders into the Youth Justice System, Final Report,* Home Office Research Study no. 242 (London: Home Office).

Pitts, J. (1999) 'New Youth Justice, New Youth Crime', *Criminal Justice Matters,* 38, pp. 24-25.

Pollard, C. (2000) 'Victims and the Criminal Justice System: A New Vision', *Criminal Law Review,* p. 5.

Shapland, J., Atkinson, A., Colledge, E., Dignan, J., Howes, M., Johnstone, J., Pennant, R., Robinson, G. and Sorsby, A. (2004) *Implementing restorative justice schemes (Crime Reduction Programme): a report on the first year.* Home Office Online Report 32/04 (London: Home Office). Available at: www.homeoffice. gov.uk/rds/pdfs04/rdsolr3204.pdf.

Shapland, J. Atkinson, A., Atkinson, H., Chapman, B. Colledge, E. Dignan, J. Howes, M. Johnstone, J. Robinson, G. and Sorsby. A. (2006) *Restorative justice in practice: the second report from the evaluation of three schemes* (Sheffield: Centre for Criminological Research). Available at: http://www.shef.ac.uk/ccr/

Shapland, J. Atkinson, A., Atkinson, H., Chapman, B. Dignan, J. Howes, M. Johnstone, J. Robinson, G. and Sorsby. A. (2007) *Restorative justice: the views of victims and offenders – the third report from the evaluation of three schemes.* Ministry of Justice Research Series 3/07 (London: NOMS). Available at: http:// www.justice.gov.uk/publications/research190607.htm

Shapland, J., Atkinson, A., Atkinson, H., Dignan, J., Edwards, L., Hibbert, J., Howes, M., Johnstone, J., Robinson, G. and Sorsby, A. (2008) *Does restorative justice affect reconviction? The fourth report from the evaluation of three schemes.* Available at: http://webarchive.nationalarchives.gov.uk/+/http://www.justice. gov.uk/restorative-justice-report_06-08.pdf

Sherman, L.W. and Strang, H. (2007) *Restorative Justice: the Evidence* (London: The Smith Institute).

Sherman, L.W., Strang, H., Angel, C., Woods, D., Barnes, G.C., Bennett, S. and Inkpen, N. (2005) 'Effects of Face-to-Face Restorative Justice on Victims of Crime in Four Randomized Controlled Trials', *Journal of Experimental Criminology,* Vol. 1, pp. 367-95.

Smith, D., Blagg, H. and Derricourt, N. (1985) *Victim Offender Mediation Project,* Report to the Chief Officers' Group (South Yorkshire Probation Service).

Smith, D., Blagg, H. and Derricourt, N. (1988) 'Mediation in South Yorkshire', *British Journal of Criminology,* Vol. 28, pp. 378-395.

Strang, H., Sherman, L.W., Angel, C., Woods, D., Bennett, S., Newberry-Birch, D. and Inkpen, N. (2006) 'Victims of Face-to-Face Restorative Justice Conferences: A Quasi-Experimental Analysis', *Journal of Social Issues*, 62(2), pp. 281-306.

Umbreit, M. and Roberts, A.W. (1996) *Mediation of Criminal Conflict in England: an assessment of services in Coventry & Leeds* (St. Paul: Minnesota: Centre for Restorative Justice and Mediation).

Wilcox, A. and Hoyle, C. (2004) *The National Evaluation of the Youth Justice Board's Restorative Justice Projects* (London: Youth Justice Board).

Wynne, J. (1996) 'Leeds Mediation and Reparation Service: Ten Years' Experience with Victim-Offender Mediation', in Galaway, B. and Hudson, J. (eds.) *Restorative Justice: International Perspectives* (Monsey, New York: Criminal Justice Press – Amsterdam: Kugler Publications), pp. 445-461.

Young, R. (2001) 'Just Cops Shameful Business? Police-led Restorative Justice and the Lessons of Research', in Morris, A. and Maxwell, G. (eds.) *Restorative Justice for Juveniles: Conferencing, Mediation and Circles* (Oxford: Hart Publishing), pp. 195-226.

Youth Justice Board (2004) *National Evaluation of the Restorative Justice in Schools Programme* (London: Youth Justice Board). Available at: http://www.yjb.gov.uk/Publications/Resources/Downloads/nat%20ev%20of%20rj%20in%20schoolsfullfv.pdf

Appendix: UK (England and Wales) overview of restorative justice research (up to 2007)

RJ initiatives – brief details

Name of initiative and/or location	Type of initiative	Form of RJ intervention	Scope
South Yorkshire probation service	Exploratory Stand-alone	VOM & reparation	1 x court-based schemes (adult)
Northampton Juvenile Liaison Bureau	Exploratory Stand-alone	VOM & reparation	1 x pre-prosecution (juvenile)
Early English mediation & reparation projects	Exploratory Stand-alone	VOM & reparation	9 x pre-prosecution schemes (juvenile) 15 x court-based schemes (adult)
Northampton Juvenile Liaison Bureau	Exploratory Stand-alone	VOM & reparation	1 x pre-prosecution (juvenile)
Home Office-funded early mediation & reparation projects	Exploratory Stand-alone	VOM & reparation	3 x pre-prosecution (juvenile) 6 x court-based schemes (mixed age)
Kettering Adult Reparation Bureau	Developmental Stand-alone	VOM & reparation	1 x pre-prosecution (adults & young adults)
Northamptonshire Diversion Unit	Developmental Stand-alone	VOM & reparation	1 x pre-prosecution (all age groups)
Reparation and Mediation Schemes Coventry & Leeds	Developmental Stand-alone	VOM & reparation	1 x court-based (all age groups) 1 x pre-prosecution, court-based and post-sentence
Various established restorative justice schemes	Developmental Stand-alone	Various, including mediation, reparation & conferencing	7 x RJ projects, 2 dealing mainly with adult offenders, 4 with juveniles
Hampshire Youth Justice FGC Pilot Project	Exploratory Stand-alone	New Zealand style family group conferencing	1 x pre-prosecution (juveniles)
Thames Valley Police Restorative cautioning initiative	Quasi-systemic	Police-led conferencing approach	1 x force-wide pilot project
Reparative sentences	Mainstream	Reparation possibly including VOM	4 x nationwide youth justice pilot projects

RJ empirical evaluation overview			
Evaluator(s)	Type of evaluation	Duration	Report(s)
Smith, D., Blagg, H. and Derricourt, N.	Simple evaluation Descriptive: feasibility study	15 months	Smith et al., 1985; 1988
Blagg, H.	'Simple' evaluation Descriptive	12 months	Blagg, 1985
Davis, G., Boucherat, J., Watson, D. and Thatcher, A.	Meta-evaluation Descriptive: aims & operation	One year	Davis et al., 1987; 1988
Davis, G., Boucherat, J., and Watson, D.	Simple evaluation Descriptive: aims & operation	One year	Davis et al., 1989
Marshall, T. and Merry, S.	Meta-evaluation Descriptive & evaluative (qualitative & quantitative)	Not recorded	Marshall and Merry, 1990
Dignan, J.	Simple evaluation Descriptive Action-research Evaluative: process, outcome, reconviction, cost-effectiveness	3 years	Dignan, 1990; 1992
Hughes, G., Leisten, R. and Pilkington, A.	Simple evaluation Descriptive Evaluative: policy analysis	6 months	Hughes et al., 1995
Umbreit, M. and Roberts, A.	Meta-evaluation (comparative) Descriptive Evaluative: policy analysis	Not recorded	Umbreit and Roberts, 1996
Miers, D., Maguire, M., Goldie, S., Sharpe, K., Hale, C., Netten, A., Uglow, S., Doolin, K., Hallam, A., Enterkin, J. and Newburn, T.	Meta-evaluation Descriptive, process and outcome evaluation; Retrospective reconviction analysis and cost-effectiveness analysis	15 months	Miers et al., 2001
Jackson, S.	Simple evaluation Descriptive Process & outcome evaluation (quantitative & qualitative)	2.5 years	Jackson, 1998
Hoyle, C., Young, R. and Hill, R.	Simple evaluation Action-research Process and outcome evaluation (quantitative & qualitative) including reconviction study	3 years	Hoyle et al., 2002
Dignan, J.	Meta-evaluation Qualitative process evaluation to enhance 'good practice'	6 months	Dignan, 2000

Appendix: UK (England and Wales) overview of restorative justice research
(up to 2007) (continued)

RJ initiatives – brief details

Name of initiative and/or location	Type of initiative	Form of RJ intervention	Scope
Reparative sentences and new pre-trial final warnings	Mainstream	Reparation possibly including VOM	4 x nationwide youth justice pilot projects
Final warnings	Mainstream	Includes reparation and, possibly also VOM	4 x nationwide youth justice pilot projects
Referral Order	Mainstream	Conference-style youth offender panels	11 x nationwide youth offender panel pilot projects
RJ projects funded by the Youth Justice Board	Developmental Mainstream	Various RJ approaches including community reparation, VOM & conferencing	42 x projects
Referral Order	Mainstream	Conference-style youth offender panels	1 x case study based on a single YOT in Leeds
Home Office funded adult RJ initiatives	Developmental Mainstream	Various styles of conferencing plus VOM	3 x projects, one offering VOM, the other two conferencing

RJ empirical evaluation overview			
Evaluator(s)	Type of evaluation	Duration	Report(s)
Holdaway, S., Davidson, N., Dignan, J., Hammersley, R., Hine, J. and Marsh, J.	Meta-evaluation Descriptive Process & outcome evaluation (quantitative & qualitative) Cost benefit analysis	2 years	Holdaway et al., 2001
Hine, J. and Celnick, A.	Meta-evaluation Reconviction study Quasi-experimental comparative statistical analysis	1 year	Hine and Celnick, 2001
Newburn, T., Crawford, A., Earle, R., Goldie, S., Hale, S., Masters, G., Netten, A., Saunders, R., Hallam, A., Sharpe, K. and Uglow, S.	Meta-evaluation Descriptive Action-research Process & outcome evaluation (quantitative & qualitative) Analysis of cost data	18 months	Newburn et al., 2001a; 2001b; 2002
Wilcox, A. with Hoyle, C.	Meta-evaluation Process and outcome evaluation (mostly quantitative but with limited qualitative evaluation) Limited reconviction analysis	18 months	Wilcox and Hoyle, 2004
Crawford, A. and Burden, T.	Qualitative study of the impact of the referral order process on young people and victims	6 month cohort from 1/4/04 to 30/9/04	Crawford and Burden, 2005
Shapland, J., Atkinson, A., College, E., Dignan, J., Johnstone, J., Robinson, G. and Sorsby, A.	Meta-evaluation of Canberra (RISE) style experimental model (administered by JRC). Process and outcome evaluation plus reconviction study	5 years ongoing from Sept 2001	3 sets of interim reports: Shapland et al., 2004, 2006, 2007. Final report pending

12 Empirical research on restorative justice in Europe: perspectives

Inge Vanfraechem and Ivo Aertsen

This book provides an extensive and quite complete overview of empirical research on restorative justice in nine European countries. The country reviews were preceded by the discussion of a specific attempt to collect evaluative research data on the basis of a common template (Chapter 2). The authors pointed out the difficulties in undertaking such an endeavour, referring to the considerable differences in research methodology, in restorative practices and in language. Another, more extensive template was used as the framework for analysing the empirical research as presented in the nine country chapters of this book. Authors were asked to give systematised information on descriptive-inventory research, action-research and evaluative research available in their country. In this concluding chapter, we evaluate whether such a common design proved to be a sufficient and adequate tool to collect research data on restorative justice in Europe, as well as what peculiarities arose when comparing the countries' research results. We conclude with some reflections on further research needs in a European context.

1 THE AVAILABILITY OF RESTORATIVE PRACTICES AND RESEARCH THROUGHOUT EUROPE

From the outset of this study, countries have been chosen on the basis of the availability of restorative practices, such as victim-offender mediation [VOM] and family group conferencing, as well as a certain number of research projects on the topic.[1] After organising the initial seminar in 2002 and the subsequent discussions held in the working groups of the COST Action A21,[2] the chapters were broadened, updated and elaborated until an extensive overview of the state of affairs with regard to empirical research in those countries was attained.

---

1   Our involvement in the work of the European Forum for Restorative Justice (www.euforumrj.org) as well as literature reviews on the topic helped us to select those countries as well as the authors (see, for instance, European Forum for Victim-Offender Mediation and Restorative Justice, 2000; Miers, 2001; Walgrave, 2003; Weitekamp and Kerner, 2003; Aertsen et al., 2004; Miers and Willemsens, 2004; Mestitz and Ghetti, 2005; Willemsens and Walgrave, 2007).
2   Cf. supra, Chapters 1 and 2.

1.1   Restorative practices

As expected, VOM as a restorative justice practice proved to be far more common in Europe than conferencing, the latter only being available in Belgium, the Netherlands, Norway and the UK, and limited for the most part to youth offenders. Both practices – VOM and conferencing – have been legislated in the majority of countries (mostly, but not only, as a diversionary measure), but divergence remains with regard to the availability of practices throughout the countries and the level of implementation (inside or outside the criminal justice system; at the level of the police, public prosecutor, judge or during the executive phase of the sentence). While the emergence of VOM and conferencing seems to have been stimulated mostly with regard to youth offending, practices nowadays seem to be evolving more rapidly for adult offenders. Nevertheless, the reality in most European countries is that victim-offender mediation or conferencing are far from being provided as a 'generally available service' as defended in Council of Europe regulations.[3]

From our overview it appears, on the one hand, that some countries interpret the definition of restorative justice in a broad sense and include mediation practices with regard to, for example, neighbourhood disputes, conflicts within the family or school context or tensions with social minorities such as refugee communities. Besides mediation and conferencing, other practices – depending on definitional options and opinions – include damage settlement (the Netherlands); community service and commitments in the form of a 'written project' for juveniles (Belgium); and different types of community oriented boards (the UK). On the other hand, some countries clearly limit restorative justice to VOM, as is the case in Finland, Italy and Poland.

In general, even though conferencing is available to a lesser extent (namely in fewer countries and mostly for youth offenders), it is has been evaluated proportionally more often than VOM. This may have to do with its later occurrence in practice (when research was already more developed with regard to mediation, thus leading to more experience in the field of restorative justice research). The special attention for conferencing might also be related to the extensive research done in Anglo-Saxon countries such as Australia, New Zealand and the US, which offers a basis for European researchers to start from.

1.2   Research on VOM and conferencing

The selected countries also vary a lot as to the availability of research: some countries have carried out different types of research on various topics and practices (such as Belgium, Finland, the Netherlands and the UK); other countries mainly rely on descriptive research (such as Germany, Italy and Poland); while Aus-

---

3   Council of Europe Recommendation No. R(99)19 concerning mediation in penal matters, and European Commission for the Efficiency of Justice (CEPEJ – 2007) Guidelines for a better implementation of the existing recommendation concerning mediation in penal matters.

tria and Norway seem to balance between those two categories, having mainly descriptive and evaluative research on VOM, but also covering challenging issues such as domestic violence or 'street mediation'.

General experience in the field of restorative justice seems to influence the type of research that has been carried out. In the beginning of the development of restorative practices in any given country, research was apparently mostly limited to descriptive-inventory studies, providing basic data on the organisation of the services, the number of cases, features of the cases and participants, etc. In this initial phase, action-research proved to be useful in starting and developing inno- vative practices in close cooperation between researchers and practitioners. Con- comitantly, evaluative research includes topics such as satisfaction of participants, and job perception and satisfaction of mediators. When VOM and conferencing become more established practices, research tackles more in-depth questions and uses more complex techniques to investigate the research issues.[4] Understanda- bly, as practice is growing, more data become available allowing for more complex analyses. The higher number of cases and the spread of services throughout the country invite the use of more sophisticated research models, including experi- mental and quasi-experimental designs, working with comparative or matched control groups and – in a few cases – random assignment of subjects to control and experimental groups. Research results then include the effect of VOM and conferencing on re-offending and a comparison of their outcomes with the output of the criminal justice system.

One of the mayor problems researchers in all countries are confronted with is the access to appropriate data. Researchers are often quite dependent on authorities and service providers in order to be able to identify cases and to contact respond- ents. Rules about privacy protection apply – for obvious reasons – in most places. Ethical concerns always have to be taken care of and constitute one of the most important reasons why experimental research is so difficult to realise in this field. We found that restorative justice practices in several countries are not yet very well documented. Because of the lack of objective, uniform information on the state of affairs, it is often risky to make generalisations and theoretical interpre- tations about the phenomenon of 'restorative justice'. Both at the national and international level, basic data collection on restorative justice practices and pro- grammes is of utmost importance. In this respect, 'monitoring' should be dis- tinguished from 'evaluation' (Shapland, 2008). What the significance can be of adopting a nation-wide model of systematic registration is well demonstrated in the case of Germany (Chapter 6). It shows, for example, how representative (or selective) VOM cases dealt with are compared to real crime figures or cases proc- essed through the court system.

---

4   With regard to evaluation issues, see, for example, Kurki (2003) and Walgrave (2006).

In terms of research methodology, and taking into account the variability in background and approaches as well as the many problems often met in programme development, interesting perspectives for restorative justice research are offered by the model of 'realist evaluation'. Finland (Chapter 5) has offered an example of the applicability of this model when investigating the use of mediation in cases of domestic violence. Instead of focusing on just one dimension, realist evaluation encompasses elements of the wider societal context, the actual mechanisms behind the intervention and the outcomes. Features of this approach are, amongst other things, that process and impact evaluation are combined, that intended as well as unintended effects are studied, and that theories on effectiveness of interventions can be tested (why and how does it work?). When comparing different evaluative studies, however, it makes sense to select studies on the basis of more stringent criteria (e.g. Sherman and Strang, 2007; see also Chapter 2). Some authors have argued for combining the use of, for example, Campbell standards with the realist evaluation approach (Van der Knaap et al., 2008).

Looking at European countries, it becomes clear that different types of institutions have been involved in restorative justice research: research institutes under or affiliated with Ministries of Justice or Welfare, university institutes or a consortium of universities, and other independent or private institutions. Very seldom is a more permanent or structural partnership between service providers on the one hand and research institute(s) on the other hand available. A 'grey zone' of research exists in the various efforts made by students, and by restorative programmes themselves, to provide systematic data (e.g. in annual reports) and case studies, to discuss specific topics and to carry out evaluations (e.g. through the use of assessment forms at the end of each case). We opted to mostly leave out these evaluations, because it would be impossible to collect all these data in a comparable way. Nevertheless, they form a very useful and necessary compilation of primarily descriptive data, which should not be neglected if one wishes to get a more in-depth view on nation-specific evolutions. It is recommended that each country centralises relevant research by students and data collected by restorative justice organisations and makes it available for further analysis. Furthermore, for research projects in general, including English summaries in research reports would enhance the knowledge in Europe (and beyond) of the research that has been carried out.

Another interesting feature concerns the relationship and mutual influence between research and policy-making. In some countries, theory and research, and in particular the work by some academics, have exerted a considerable influence on restorative justice developments and policies. Conversely, even when most of the research is carried out quite independently, criminal policy does influence the research set-up in various ways:
(1) by creating the policy context for implementing restorative practices and determining their position and resources vis-a-vis monitoring and research;

(2) by defining research priorities and providing funding for independent research;
(3) by providing the necessary data, and access to them, to be examined;
(4) by outlining the research questions, which is especially the case in evaluative research when policy makers want to get an answer to a concrete question;
(5) by using the research results as a basis for deciding whether to continue restorative justice programmes and their funding, or as a support or justification of specific crime policies;
(6) and by establishing more permanent partnerships with research institutes in order to follow-up and assist the field of restorative justice.

For most European countries, an increasing connection between restorative justice programmes and criminal justice or youth justice policies can be observed. Interestingly, there is one exception to this tendency, namely Finland, where both restorative justice programmes and research are situated within a framework of social welfare policies, in good understanding with criminal justice. Furthermore, although in some countries research on restorative justice has a clear impact on policy-making, the inverse is also true: sometimes the impact is non-existent or empirical research findings are systematically ignored. Political agendas on crime do not always display the highest degrees of rationality.

2   DISTINCTION BETWEEN VARIOUS TYPES OF RESEARCH

The template for collecting country-specific research outcomes included three types of research: descriptive-inventory, evaluative and action-research. Rather than strictly defining these categories beforehand, we created subheadings which would provide the authors with some guidance as to the elements that may be included. The seminar and various discussions proved to be fruitful in disentangling what heading covered what kinds of research. In general, these three main headings did seem to cover most of the empirical research in Europe. Nevertheless, the distinction between them was not always self-evident or clear-cut.
Descriptive research covers basic data, such as the number of mediations and participants, and set-up of organisations. At the same time, researchers may evaluate such numbers by reflecting critically on, for example, whether mediation is an integrated practice or remains rather marginal compared to the total number of cases within the justice system, and whether the organisation is set up in an 'efficient' manner (which is then to be defined within the research). Evaluative research, from its side, needs to describe basic information and collect figures to have a starting point for the proper evaluation.
The peculiarity of action-research entails the close relationship between researchers and practitioners, in one way or another. Not a lot of literature is available on the matter and research reports do not always explicitly state what is understood by action-research. Throughout the chapters, action-research seems to entail the following elements: a close link to the setting-up of pilot projects (hence the term

used in Austria: 'accompanying research'); a merger between action and evaluation, or at least the systematic inclusion of evaluative moments in the development of action; and the close relationship between researchers and practitioners, with researchers involved in the implementation of practices and/or practitioners involved in the evaluation of the programme (hence the term 'participatory research' in Finland). Given the existence of recurrent problems in many countries at the level of developing and implementation policies, the potential of action-research in assisting the setting-up of innovative practices should be recognised, even valorised. However, the methodology of action-research should be refined and more attention should be paid to this method in international gatherings and publications.

Because of the difficulty of adhering to the template and to strict categories, some authors in this volume opted to present research in a more chronological manner (most notably Finland and the UK). For other authors, re-working the chapter did offer possibilities for integrating the researches into the headings. In any case, definitions vary across research reports, which may be related to cultural issues (Willemsens and Walgrave, 2007: 489) as well as to experience in both practice and research. Issues to do with defining the various types of research do not only relate to research but also to the restorative practices of VOM and conferencing themselves. Even though we had defined terms such as restorative justice, VOM and conferencing beforehand, the chapters show that a wide variation exists in practice (see also Raye and Warner Roberts, 2007).

The concept 'restorative justice' is, for instance, not a common term in Italy, but elements such as reparation are used as a restorative approach within probation. Even in a country as the UK, where 'restorative justice' is well known, it is more cautious to speak of 'elements of a restorative justice approach' that are 'featuring prominently' in a range of justice reforms and processes (Chapter 11). The term FGC is used in the Netherlands and Belgium, but one can wonder whether it should not rather be the generic term 'conferencing' and then to define in detail what exactly is meant.[5] 'Victim' and 'offender' refer to the specific setting of the criminal justice system, but multiple practices cannot clearly be distinguished from, or are intertwined with, criminal cases such as mediation in neighbourhood conflicts. Some countries do not limit restorative justice to VOM and conferencing, such as Belgium (community service and the 'written plan' are considered to be restorative measures for youth delinquents), the Netherlands (victim-offender conversations, damages settlement) and the UK (reparation orders, youth offender panels). The institutional context in which restorative justice practices are developing determines to a great extent the orientation to be adopted by new programmes and thus also influences attitudes and decisions on topics that should be given priority for evaluation or research (Aertsen, 2006).

---

5   For a discussion on the difference between New Zealand FGC and other conferencing models, see Vanfraechem (2004). For a discussion on similar terms covering different practices, see Miers (2007).

3   NEEDS WITH REGARD TO FUTURE RESEARCH ON RESTORATIVE JUSTICE

Looking at processes and output of empirical research on restorative justice in Europe, various needs for future research may be distilled.

First of all, both ongoing monitoring and thematic research are important to evaluate restorative justice programmes. On the one hand, an important need exists for most countries to develop and adopt uniform systems of ongoing data collection. This monitoring task is easier to realise in countries with only one model or organisation for restorative justice practices in place (which is the case in a minority of countries, notably in Austria and the Nordic countries). Monitoring can be taken care of by restorative justice services themselves (NGOs or umbrella organisations – e.g. Austria, Belgium – or central administrations within governments – e.g. Italy, Norway) or by research institutes closely linked to government (e.g. Finland). On the other hand, independent evaluative research requires a certain degree of autonomy in deciding what issues to evaluate and in which manner, but at the same time it needs funding as well, be it from the government or from other sources. This autonomy is not always sufficiently preserved, as we have seen for some countries. Researchers might feel under pressure and are, moreover, confronted with changing policies. Funding for ongoing monitoring and independent research should be an integral part of national budgets related to restorative justice programmes. In this respect, research is often not considered as an essential task, as for example training is. In COST Action A21, we had to conclude that several of the 21 participating countries did not comply with their obligation – as agreed on when joining the COST Action and signing the Memorandum of Understanding – to fund research on restorative justice on a national basis.

Secondly, the European perspective in restorative justice research could be further developed given its cultural, social and legal specificities: notions of 'community', 'citizen participation' and 'government responsibilities' are not the same all over the world, and even within Europe enormous differences between regions exist. In this context, it is not surprising that differences emerge between countries in choices between various restorative justice models (VOM or conferencing), between emphases in one model (direct or indirect mediation, or the diverging role of the police in conferencing) and between organisational options (voluntary sector or governmental bodies). Many European countries adhere to strong legalistic traditions within a context of centralised state structures, leaving much less room – at first sight – for local, flexible or pragmatic approaches that seem so important for restorative justice. In further consideration, however, this legalistic orientation may offer its own contribution to the public-private debate and to discussions on the function of legislation and jurisprudence in developing restorative justice practices and policies.
The supporting role of the Council of Europe and the European Union cannot be ignored in the domain of restorative justice (Willemsens, 2008). These European institutions are offering important tools with respect to cooperation not only

between practitioners and policymakers from different member states, but also between researchers. The aforementioned COST Action and the publication at hand are examples, as are the many (mainly practice oriented) research projects funded under the subsequent criminal justice programmes from the European Commission. In the COST Action Working Group on evaluative research, a design has been developed in order to collect in a comparative way restorative justice data from different European countries on a permanent basis. Unfortunately, no further funding for this project could be obtained. The European institutions, in order to enhance scientifically sound policies in Europe, should further support – in a structural way – such cooperation networks for enabling both comparative monitoring and cross-border research on restorative justice processes and their effects. Transnational and European cooperation should also be further developed in view of policy-making at the European level itself, including the follow-up of legislative initiatives such as the Recommendation No. R (99)19 concerning mediation in penal matters (Council of Europe) and the (planned review on the) Framework Decision on the standing of victims in criminal proceedings (European Union).

From a European perspective, special attention should also go to those countries where victim-offender mediation or other restorative justice practices are implemented more or less extensively, but where empirical research in this field has hardly been done. France and Spain may be examples of this unfortunate situation, while Central and Eastern European countries need support in this respect as well.

Thirdly, research topics need to be further developed (see also Bazemore and Elis, 2007). Satisfaction and recidivism – amongst other effects – have been largely covered as evaluative issues. However, it often remains unclear what the concept of satisfaction should entail precisely (see also Schiff, 2007). Measures of satisfaction (and other items) are susceptible to placebo effects or related bias. Not just the degree of satisfaction should be assessed, but mediating and influencing factors should be addressed as well. Other elements of the experience of those participating in restorative justice practices may be even more important, such as empathy and understanding, or feelings of fairness and justice (see also Harris et al., 2004). The internal dynamics of mediation and conferencing processes are not yet well known. The few studies done on moral emotions in restorative justice processes, for example through in-depth case studies and other forms of qualitative research, are very promising and relevant in the context of restorative justice. Recidivism research is – also in the countries dealt with in this volume – showing a series of methodological problems (see also Bonta et al., 2007; Shapland et al., 2008). Setting up research on an experimental basis is hard to realise; not all studies make use of a control group; a selection bias occurs when composing groups of participants; moderating variables such as demographic characteristics of victims and offenders, characteristics of the crime and the restorative justice programme are not considered; the concept of recidivism is not always adequately defined; different measures of recidivism are used; and follow-up periods are rather short or not comparable (Gielen, 2010). Moreover, recidivism studies related to restorative justice interventions mainly put the emphasis on only one possible type of crime prevention, namely offender-oriented prevention, while victim-oriented prevention and community-oriented prevention are left out of consideration (Crawford, 2010).

Another question that arises from the country reports in this book concerns the extent to which evaluation should include comparing restorative justice practices with processes within the criminal justice system. Such comparisons might be beneficial in light of enhancing restorative justice's credibility and its further implementation, but also entail the risk of putting too strong an emphasis on the relevance of criminal law principles and values. This research would therefore constitute a certain type of restorative justice reality 'in the shadow of criminal justice', using criminal law categories and concepts as a central reference framework. Further theoretical research may help to clarify the topic.

Part of the research in European countries is focusing on the applicability of restorative justice to specific issues such as domestic violence or restorative practices for immigrant communities. While the scope of restorative justice programmes should be further explored and enlarged – also in the field of less conventional types of crimes – we must be aware that new fields of application may demand other research methodologies and/or research questions (cf. Strang and Braithwaite, 2002; Duchateau et al., 2004; Vanfraechem, 2006).

Finally, almost all country chapters in this volume report about important developmental and implementation difficulties, when it comes to the wider organisation of restorative justice programmes. At the same time, most countries dispose of restorative justice legislation. Not much research is done on how legislation or other forms of national policy-making are implemented: much more attention should go to implementation theories and policies. Are restorative practices being implemented as they were set out, in order for restorative practices to remain true to a restorative justice philosophy and – for example – not fall into the trap of MacDonaldisation of practices (Umbreit, 1999) once they become standardised? As stated for Germany (Chapter 6): 'Organisation does matter' in determining the quality and nature of restorative justice practices. Therefore, research should also focus on underlying reasons why implementation is not always effective and why research findings are not always noticed by or translated into policies. Opinions, attitudes and forms of resistance in different institutional contexts should be studied much more. Due attention should go to partnerships and cooperation with criminal justice agencies. Selection and referral criteria, and referral procedures, must be investigated in a much more systematic way, as well as the follow-up of restorative justice files in further judicial decision-making processes. Communication with the public and creating awareness about restorative justice in different environments is lacking (theoretical and) empirical underpinning, as is cooperation with the media (Pali and Pelikan, 2010).

Restorative justice in Europe is standing at the crossroads. As a new approach to crime and insecurity, its potential is more and more recognised by national governments and European institutions. Several countries have included restorative justice in their policy frameworks. However, that political acceptance of restorative justice might at the same time form its weakness. Restorative justice can develop into all directions now: from cooption by the system and dissipation to a powerful replacement practice. Research can help making the difference. Researchers in criminology and related disciplines should not turn aside, but may assist in improving restorative justice practices by ongoing and thorough evaluation and critical reflection, while at the same time guarding their independence. Applied research must go hand in hand with theoretical studies. Research must also enjoy freedom to focus on topics which do *not* serve the political agenda or the immediate usefulness of restorative practices.

Over the last twenty years, restorative justice has been subject to a multitude of studies internationally and has, in this respect, benefited from scientific and public attention probably much more than most other fields of criminological intervention. While the present book shows that certain elements related to restorative justice in European countries are studied to a large extent, and that some countries have carried out extensive research starting from a coherent framework, it is necessary to both deepen the knowledge and broaden its scope. The creation of structural networks between researchers, practitioners and policy makers at both national and European level may further enhance restorative justice and its continuous development.

REFERENCES

Aertsen, I. (2006) 'The intermediate position of restorative justice: the case of Belgium', in Aertsen, I., Daems, T. and Robert, L. (eds.) *Institutionalizing Restorative Justice* (Cullompton: Willan Publishing), pp. 68-92.

Aertsen, I., Mackay, R., Pelikan, C., Willemsens, J. and Wright, M. (2004) *Rebuilding community connections – mediation and restorative justice in Europe* (Strasbourg: Council of Europe).

Bazemore, G. and Elis, L. (2007) 'Evaluation of restorative justice', in Johnstone, G. and Van Ness, D.W. (eds.) *Handbook of Restorative Justice* (Cullompton: Willan Publishing), pp. 397-425.

Bonta, J., Jesseman, R., Rugge, T. and Cornier, R. (2007) 'Restorative justice and recidivism: promises made, promises kept?', in Sullivan, D. and Tifft, L. (eds.) *Handbook of Restorative Justice. A Global Perspective* (London-New York: Routledge), pp. 108-120.

Crawford, A. (2010) 'Conceptual links and policy challenges', in Department of Juvenile Justice (ed.) *Restorative Justice and Crime Prevention. Presenting a theoretical exploration, an empirical analysis and the policy perspective* (Rome: Department of Juvenile Justice), pp. 1-22.

Duchateau, K., Van Poeck, B. and Hebberecht, P. (2004) *Het levensverhaal van jongeren van Turkse en Marokkaanse origine met een instellingsverleden* (Gent: Universiteit Gent).

European Commission for the Efficiency of Justice (CEPEJ) (2007)13 *Guidelines for a better implementation of the existing recommendation concerning mediation in penal matters* (Strasbourg: Council of Europe). Available at: http://www.coe.int/t/dghl/cooperation/cepej/mediation/default_en.asp.

European Forum for Victim-Offender Mediation and Restorative Justice (ed.) (2000) *Victim-offender Mediation in Europe. Making Restorative Justice Work* (Leuven: Leuven University Press).

Gielen, A. (2010) 'Methodological considerations and empirical findings', in Department of Juvenile Justice (ed.) *Restorative Justice and Crime Prevention. Presenting a theoretical exploration, an empirical analysis and the policy perspective* (Rome: Department of Juvenile Justice), pp. 23-81.

Harris, N., Walgrave, L. and Braithwaite, J. (2004) 'Emotional Dynamics in Restorative Conferences', *Theoretical Criminology*, 8(2), pp. 191-210.

Kurki, L. (2003) 'Evaluating Restorative Practices', in von Hirsch, A., Roberts, J., Bottoms, A., Roach, K. and Schiff, M. (eds.) *Restorative Justice and Criminal justice: Competing or Reconcilable Paradigms?* (Oxford: Hart Publishing), pp. 293-314.

Mestitz, A. and Ghetti, S. (eds.) (2005) *Victim-Offender Mediation with Youth Offenders in Europe* (Dordrecht: Springer).

Miers, D. (2001) *An International Review of Restorative Justice*, Crime Reduction Series Paper 10 (London: Home Office).

Miers, D. (2007), 'The international development of restorative justice', in Johnstone, G. and Van Ness, D.W. (eds.) *Handbook of Restorative Justice* (Cullompton: Willan Publishing), pp. 447-467.

Miers, D. and Willemsens, J. (eds.) (2004) *Mapping Restorative Justice. Developments in 25 European Countries* (Leuven: European Forum for Victim-Offender mediation and Restorative Justice v.z.w).

Pali, B. and Pelikan, C. (2010) *Building Social Support for Restorative Justice. Media, civil society and citizens* (Leuven: European Forum for Restorative Justice).

Raye, B.E. and Warner Roberts, A. (2007) 'Restorative processes', in Johnstone, G. and Van Ness, D.W. (eds.) *Handbook of Restorative Justice* (Cullompton: Willan Publishing, 2007), pp. 211-227.

Shapland, J. (2008) 'Hoe herstelrecht evalueren?', *Tijdschift voor herstelrecht*, 8(3), pp. 26-36.

Sherman, L.W. and Strang, H. (2007) *Restorative Justice: the Evidence* (London: The Smith Institute).

Schiff, M. (2007) 'Satisfying the needs and interests of stakeholders', in Johnstone, G. and Van Ness, D.W. (eds.) *Handbook of Restorative Justice* (Cullompton: Willan Publishing, 2007), pp. 228-246.

Strang, H. and Braithwaite, J. (eds.) (2002) *Restorative Justice and Family Violence* (Cambridge: Cambridge University Press).

Umbreit, M.S. (1999) 'Avoiding the Marginalization and "McDonaldization" of Victim-Offender Mediation: A Case Study in Moving Toward the Mainstream', in Bazemore, G. and Walgrave, L. (eds.) *Restorative Juvenile Justice – Repairing the Harm of Youth Crime* (Monsey: Willow Tree Press), pp. 213-234.

Van der Knaap, L.M., Leeuw, F.L., Bogaerts, S. and Nijssen, L.T.J. (2008) 'Combining Campbell Standards and the Realist Evaluation Approach. The Best of Two Worlds?', *American Journal of Evaluation*, 29(1), pp. 48 – 57.

Vanfraechem, I. (2004) 'Kritische reflecties over conferencing in Nederland en Vlaanderen', *Tijdschrift voor Herstelrecht*, 4(4), pp. 6-19.

Vanfraechem, I. (2006) 'Marokkaanse jongeren en herstelrecht: een verkenning', *Tijdschrift voor herstelrecht*, 6(4), pp. 34-40.

Walgrave, L. (ed.) (2003) *Repositioning restorative justice* (Cullompton: Willan Publishing).

Walgrave, L. (2006) 'Evaluatie in herstelrecht', *Tijdschrift voor herstelrecht*, 6(2), pp. 9-21.

Weitekamp, E. and Kerner, H.-J. (eds.) (2003) *Restorative Justice in Context: International Practice and Directions* (Cullompton: Willan Publishing).

Willemsens, J. (2008) *Restorative justice: an agenda for Europe. The role of the European Union in the further development of restorative justice* (Leuven: European Forum for Restorative Justice).

Willemsens, J. and Walgrave, L. (2007) 'Regional reviews. Section C. Europe', in Johnstone, G. and Van Ness, D.W. (eds.) *Handbook of Restorative Justice* (Cullompton: Willan Publishing), pp. 488-499.

Notes on contributors

Ivo Aertsen is a professor at the Catholic University of Leuven and holds degrees in psychology, law and criminology. His main fields of research and teaching are victimology, penology and restorative justice. Within the Leuven Institute of Criminology, he coordinates the Research Line on Restorative Justice. He started his professional career as psychologist in the prison system and in victim support. As a researcher, he wrote a manual on victim assistance for the Belgian police services and cooperated in the writing of a manual on implementing restorative justice in a prison context. Furthermore, he did research and published on the psychological needs of victims of crime, on victim assistance and on victim-offender mediation. His PhD thesis (2001) dealt with the relation of victim-offender mediation to criminal justice. Aertsen has been the chair of the European Forum for Restorative Justice (2000 to 2004) and has coordinated COST Action A21 on 'Restorative Justice Developments in Europe' (2002 to 2006). He is an editorial board member of several journals and is involved in various practice and policy oriented partnerships. He has acted as an expert for the UN, the Council of Europe, the Organisation for Security and Co-operation in Europe [OSCE] and the European Union. He is closely involved with the Secretariat of the European Forum for Restorative Justice in Leuven and is promoter of the various research projects run by the Forum.

John Blad is Associate Professor in the field of criminal law sciences at the Law Faculty of Erasmus University Rotterdam. His work is of a theoretical and integrative character, combining insights of the legal and the social sciences, especially sociology of law. His main focus has for a long time been on a) the problem of euthanasia in connection to the criminal law and b) the theoretical questions related to the idea of penal abolition. His main interest lies in the development of restorative justice in the context of the democratic state and under the rule of law. Courses he gives comprise theory of criminal law and punishment, criminal justice and crime and the meaning of criminal law in the democratic 'rechtsstaat'. In 2000 he founded both the Dutch 'Forum voor Herstelrecht' and the 'Tijdschrift voor Herstelrecht' (Forum and Journal for Restorative Justice). He is chief editor of the journal.

Beata Czarnecka-Dzialuk holds a PhD in law and is Associate Professor in the Institute of Law Studies of the Polish Academy of Sciences and in the Institute of Justice by the Ministry of Justice, dealing with juvenile law and justice, victim-offender mediation and restorative justice. She is a founding member of the committee for introducing mediation in Poland, co-author of the experimental programme of VOM in juvenile cases and of the research project on its evaluation.

James Dignan was Professor of Comparative Criminology and Criminal Justice at the University of Leeds (United Kingdom) until 2009, and was previously Professor of Criminology and Restorative Justice at the University of Sheffield. He has researched and written extensively on English and comparative penal policy and youth justice, and is an internationally recognised expert on restorative justice. His many publications include *Understanding Victims and Restorative Justice* (Maidenhead: Open University Press, 2005), the leading textbook on punishment *The Penal System: An Introduction* (with Michael Cavadino, 4th edition, London: Sage, 2007) and *Penal Systems: A Comparative Approach* (with Michael Cavadino and others, London: Sage, 2006).

Ida Hydle works as senior researcher at the Norwegian Institute of Social Research [NOVA] within youth research and as professor at the Centre for Peace Studies, University of Tromsø. She is a medical doctor and a social anthropologist and has a PhD in both fields. From 1992 to 1994 she was member of a specialist ministerial advisory committee for the legislation on the position of victims in the criminal justice system. From 2003 to 2006 she had a research grant from the Norwegian Research Council together with the linguist Ingrid Kristine Hasund on the project *Conflict regimes*. A textbook was launched in February 2007 on 'Face to face – on meetings between offenders and victims in cases of violence'. She is a mediator and facilitator in the Norwegian Mediation Service in Oslo. Her teaching- and research topics include restorative justice, legal anthropology, ethics, cultural awareness, violence and abuse prevention. She was a member of the Groupe Européen de Recherches sur les Normativités [GERN], Council of Europe, from 2003 to 2006 concerning Juvenile Justice in Europe and was the coordinator of Working Group 1 on Evaluative research in the COST Action A 21 'Restorative Justice Developments in Europe' (2002 to 2006). She has written and edited numerous books and articles on restorative justice.

Juhani Iivari is D. Soc.Sc., M. Theol., Research Director at STAKES (National Research and Development Centre for Welfare and Health) and docent (i.e. adjunct professor) at Helsinki University, teaching restorative justice in the Faculty of Law and in the Faculty of Social Sciences. His research and publications deal with social problems, youth delinquency, domestic violence and especially victim-offender mediation from practical and theoretical sights. He has written articles on restorative justice for many international publications and published 88 scientific articles on these topics. He has been a management committee member of COST Action A21 and board member of the European Forum for Restorative Justice, as well as member of numerous task forces on social and judicial issues by the Government of Finland. Since April 2008 he has been working on implementing the Law on Mediation in Finland.

Siri Kemény works as a senior adviser at the National Mediation Service in Norway [NMS]. She obtained her Master's degree in social pedagogics at the University of Oslo. Since 1990 she has been working with the development and implementation of victim-offender mediation and restorative justice. She was a restorative justice coordinator and mediator in Oslo, and an adviser in the Ministry of Justice in the field of restorative justice until she started working at the NMS when it was established in 2004. NMS is responsible for the nationwide governmental mediation service. She was the Chair of the European Forum for Restorative Justice from 2004 to 2008.

Hans-Jürgen Kerner is Director of the Institute of Criminology and full Professor at the Faculty of Law, University of Tübingen (Germany), with special responsibility for the fields of criminology, juvenile penal law, corrections (including prison law), and penal procedure. Apart from his work at the university, he holds positions in national and international associations, such as President, German Foundation for Crime Prevention and the Reintegration of Offenders, Bonn; Chair, German Association for Court Aid, Probation and Parole Assistance, and Care and Resettlement of Offenders, Berlin; member, Research Group on Victim-Offender-Reconciliation, Heidelberg, Germany; Honorary President, International Society for Criminology, Paris; life time member, American Society of Criminology, and Academy of Criminal Justice Sciences, USA. He is author, co-author, editor and co-editor of numerous books and articles, including some on victim-offender mediation and on restorative justice.

Katrien Lauwaert is a lecturer at the Department of Criminology of the University of Liège and affiliated member of the Leuven Institute for Criminology of the Catholic University of Leuven, in Belgium. She obtained a PhD from the University of Maastricht in 2008 on the topic of restorative justice and procedural safeguards. Her main fields of research are restorative justice, victimology and youth criminology. She is the chair of the Flemish organisation Suggnomè, which organises mediation for victims and offenders and acts as a forum on victim-offender mediation and restorative justice issues. Lauwaert is a former co-ordinator of the Newsletter of the European Forum for Restorative Justice and a current member of the editorial board of the Tijdschrift voor Herstelrecht. She was an active member of the Working Group on Policy Oriented Research of the COST Action A21 on 'Restorative Justice Developments in Europe' (2002 to 2006).

Anne Lemonne is research assistant at the National Institute for Criminalistics and Criminology and teaching assistant at the Free University of Brussels [ULB] in Belgium. Previously, she worked for several years as a researcher at the ULB and at the University of Copenhagen (Denmark) firstly, in the field of community policing and, secondly, in the field of restorative justice. Currently, she is performing an extensive evaluation research on the development of victim's policy in Belgium. She is a member of the European Forum for Restorative Justice and actively involved in the implementation of restorative justice programmes in Belgium.

Sönke Lenz was research assistant for the Institute of Criminology in Tübingen from 1998 until 2006. He holds a Master of Arts degree (Sociology/Comparative Religion). His research agenda centres on restorative justice, focusing on victim offender mediation [VOM] and victim-offender dynamics. Sönke Lenz is co-editor on *Täter-Opfer-Ausgleich in der Entwicklung. Auswertung der bundesweiten Täter-Opfer-Ausgleichs-Statistik für die Jahre 1993 bis 1999* (2003) and co-editor on *Täter-Opfer-Ausgleich in der Entwicklung. Auswertung der bundesweiten Täter-Opfer-Ausgleichs-Statistik für den Zehnjahreszeitraum 1993-2002* (2005).

Anna Mestitz is director of the Research Institute on Judicial Systems of the Italian National Research Council (IRSIG-CNR) in Bologna. She is a social psychologist engaged in research on judicial administration, more recently in the field of juvenile criminal justice and victim-offender mediation. Mestitz promoted and coordinated the Grotius project 'Victim-Offender Mediation: organization and practice in the juvenile justice systems', funded by EU. She was on the Management Committee of COST Action A21 'Restorative Justice Developments in Europe'. She has authored many articles and books, co-edited (with Simona Ghetti) the book *Victim-Offender Mediation with Youth Offenders in Europe. An overview and comparison of 15 countries* (Springer 2005). She co-authored 'Victim-Offender Mediation with juvenile offenders' in the *Encyclopedia of Psychology and Law* (edited by B. Cutler, Sage Publications 2007).

Christa Pelikan is a researcher at the Institute for the Sociology of Law and Criminology in Vienna. She has been working in the field of criminal law, especially juvenile justice, and in the field of family law. Starting in 1985, she has been doing accompanying research on the large Austrian pilot project on 'Victim-offender mediation in juvenile justice' and later on a pilot project 'Victim-offender mediation in general criminal law'. She has been chairing the 'Committee of experts on mediation in penal matters' within the European Committee on Crime Problems [CDPC] and has been a member of the Criminological Scientific Council to the CDPC of the Council of Europe. Recently she has been serving as one of the specialists working with the 'Group of Specialists on Assistance to Victims and Prevention of Victimisation' within the Council of Europe. She is a founding member of the European Forum for Restorative Justice and the chair of its 'Communication committee'. She has been participating in various EU funded research projects and in COST Action A21.

Denis Van Doosselaere has been working in the field of juvenile delinquency for more than twenty years. Since 1988, he has been the Director of Arpège, an organisation which pioneered the utilisation of community service, victim-offender mediation and conferencing in Wallonia, Belgium. He also worked as a mediator in the same organisation. As a psychologist and criminologist, he contributes to the School of Criminology at the University of Liège. His publications focus mainly on empirical aspects of alternative measures and restorative justice.

Inge Vanfraechem is a researcher at the National Institute of Criminal Sciences and Criminology (Belgium) and affiliated researcher at the Catholic University of Leuven (Belgium), Institute of Criminology, where she obtained her PhD on conferencing for serious youth delinquency (2006). Her main fields of research are victimology, restorative justice and youth criminology. Her research and publications include studies on victims of crime, victim assistance, victims and the criminal justice system, conferencing for youth delinquents and restorative justice. Vanfraechem has been the vice-chair of the European Forum for Restorative Justice since 2006, which she co-founded. She was a member of the steering committee of the European Vict Programme project 'Developing Standards for Victims of Terrorism' (2006 to 2008), an active member of the Working Group on Theoretical Research of the COST Action A21 on 'Restorative Justice Developments in Europe' (2002 to 2006) and is co-promoter of the European research projects on 'Restorative justice and prevention' and 'Conferencing as a way forward in Europe'. She is a member of the editorial board of the Dutch-Flemish Journal on Restorative Justice.

Elmar G.M. Weitekamp studied social work at the Fachhochschule Niederrhein in Mönchengladbach, Germany. After working for a short period of time as a Juvenile Court Aid in Mönchengladbach, he studied Criminology at the University of Pennsylvania in Philadelphia, USA where he received his Master's in Criminology in 1982 and his PhD in Criminology for the Graduate Group of Managerial Sciences and Applied Economics in 1989. He was a lecturer at the University of Pennsylvania before he started as a Senior Research Associate at the University of Tübingen, Germany. He was a visiting Professor at the University of Melbourne. He is a special guest Professor of Criminology, Victimology and Restorative Justice at the University of Leuven, Belgium; Distinguished Adjunct Professor of Sociology at the Central China Normal University in Wuhan, People's Republic of China; and Senior Research Associate at the Institute of Criminology at the University of Tübingen, Germany. He is responsible, together with Professor Gordon Bazemore (Florida Atlantic University), for the International Network for Research on Restorative Justice for Juveniles. He is the organiser and a co-director of the annual Post Graduate Course in Victimology, Victim Assistance and Criminal Justice in Dubrovnik, Croatia. His research interests include social and justice services for young people in transition; gangs; chronic and habitual offenders in longitudinal perspective, youth and criminal justice policy, victimology and mass victimisations of human rights, restorative and traditional justice mechanisms and victim-offender mediation issues.

Jolien Willemsens holds a degree in criminology and a Master in European criminology from the Catholic University Leuven in Belgium. She was the Executive Officer of the European Forum for Restorative Justice (2000 to 2008) and managed several European research projects in that capacity. She now works for an Executive Agency of the European Commission.

Information about COST

COST – the acronym for European **CO**operation in **S**cience and **T**echnology – is the oldest and widest European intergovernmental network for cooperation in research. Established by the Ministerial Conference in November 1971, COST is presently used by the scientific communities of 36 European countries to cooperate in common research projects supported by national funds.

The funds provided by COST – less than 1% of the total value of the projects – support the COST cooperation networks (COST Actions) through which, with EUR 30 million per year, more than 30 000 European scientists are involved in research having a total value which exceeds EUR 2 billion per year. This is the financial worth of the European added value which COST achieves.

A 'bottom up approach' (the initiative of launching a COST Action comes from the European scientists themselves), 'à la carte participation' (only countries interested in the Action participate), 'equality of access' (participation is open also to the scientific communities of countries not belonging to the European Union) and 'flexible structure' (easy implementation and light management of the research initiatives) are the main characteristics of COST.

As precursor of advanced multidisciplinary research COST has a very important role for the realisation of the European Research Area (ERA) anticipating and complementing the activities of the Framework Programmes, constituting a 'bridge' towards the scientific communities of emerging countries, increasing the mobility of researchers across Europe and fostering the establishment of 'Networks of Excellence' in many key scientific domains such as: Biomedicine and Molecular Biosciences; Food and Agriculture; Forests, their Products and Services; Materials, Physical and Nanosciences; Chemistry and Molecular Sciences and Technologies; Earth System Science and Environmental Management; Information and Communication Technologies; Transport and Urban Development; Individuals, Societies, Cultures and Health. It covers basic and more applied research and also addresses issues of pre-normative nature or of societal importance.

Web: www.cost.eu